SEMIOTEXT(E) ACTIVE AGENTS SERIES

Published by Semiotext(e)
PO BOX 629. South Pasadena, CA 91031
www.semiotexte.com

Special thanks to Georges Rivard and Jason Smith.

Cover Photograph: Peter Hujar, *Gary Indiana Veiled,* 1981
© 1987 The Peter Hujar Archive LLC
Courtesy Pace/MacGill Gallery, New York and Fraenkel Gallery, San Francisco

Design by Hedi El Kholti

ISBN: 978-1-63590-037-8
Distributed by The MIT Press, Cambridge, Mass. and London, England
Printed in the United States of America

10 9 8 7 6 5 4 3 2

GARY INDIANA

VILE DAYS

THE VILLAGE VOICE ART COLUMNS 1985–1988

EDITED BY BRUCE HAINLEY

\<e\>

CONTENTS

PRELUDE TO A PREFACE

The writings in this book first appeared a few years before the internet and cell phones and "social media" spread all over the planet, before print began its decline, and—mercifully—before anyone with access to a computer was empowered to comment on anything and everything published in a magazine or newspaper. In the mid-1980s, persons wishing to opine about something they'd read in an actual publication needed to write or type a letter, seal it in an envelope, address it, put a stamp on it, and mail it, a process requiring at least enough time and energy for intelligent people to reflect on what they were sending off, which might or might not appear in the letters section. The letters section was edited to screen out personally abusive, irrelevant, insane, or illiterate missives, and confined, by and large, to communications with a valid point to make about the actual subject of an article, a factual correction, or a respectful difference of opinion; the writer of the article had the option to reply.

I have never discovered a single worthwhile item in the comment threads attached to online stories. Even in pre-internet times, frankly, most letters to the editor were entirely nugatory, regardless of their parti pris. But the technological acceleration of our lives, especially in the way information travels, and the way published material is received, has had plenty of baleful, degenerative effects, foremost the monetisation and algorhythmisation of every human activity—in this context, the value of content, in many publications, is increasingly measured by the volume of audience reaction, which really is getting things arse-backwards. A claque of trolls isn't something to wish for. Neither, really, is a claque of admirers. Near the end of her life, my dear friend and collaborator Cookie Mueller said that she didn't especially mind dying, "because the future is going to all be computers anyway." As usual, she was right.

I didn't have to deal with the financial temperature of the paper, or the itchy keyboard fingers of its readers, when I wrote these columns for the *Village Voice*. I had an exceptionally gifted and protective editor, Jeff Weinstein, who offered me the job and then gave me remarkable freedom to write the way I wanted to, but also kept me from going over the edge, which, at times, I had a tendency to do. It was a pressured kind of writing, but the stress of it was very different than what writers today contend with. I never cared even slightly what the readers of the *Village Voice* thought about what I was doing, nor was I ever asked to.

Looking back, I think the ideal audience for the column consisted of people who made art, or liked art, but were also interested in the world and what was happening to it. These were Reagan years, quite terrible years (it's astonishing that Reagan has become embalmed in so many people's memories as a benevolent, exemplary president, when in fact he was doddering and, policy-wise, vicious). For me the most striking thing about reading the columns today is an eerie sense that they were describing the future as well as the then-present, a future that seemed for a while to have been avoided, but suddenly wasn't. This is not the kind of prescience anyone wants to have had, really, but there it is.

There was, in the '80s, a true state of emergency—the AIDS epidemic—that sparked an arduous, ultimately successful mobilization against the government's indifference and the murderously slow pace of medical research and drug approval; the plague was never far from anyone's mind, and carrying on with ordinary life, inside or outside the art world, required an almost schizoid degree of compartmentalization. 2018 feels a lot like the mid-'80s, only worse—more terrifying, more depressing, more apocalyptic, and even more urgently in need of concerted political resistance.

I was lucky to have a public voice in those faraway days. Of course, the primary task was to cover exhibitions, but much of the art being made in the '80s dealt with the world beyond four walls of a gallery, and it seemed perfectly natural to blend art criticism with commentary on the state of things. (Like everything else, the art world was becoming monetised to an unprecedented degree. Like the political situation, this would later appear almost innocent compared to what eventually followed.) Anyway, I took note—insistent note—of what was going on. I must have been aware that art criticism in that kind of weekly publication wasn't done in the way I was doing it, but what I actually cared about was the writing itself—how to connect the ostensible subject with the nature of the time we were living through, how to smuggle a few ideas into a context usually devoted to filigreed opinions, to convey what being alive in that moment was like. In that sense, I think, some of the least promising subjects in this book are also the most interesting, though that is, in fact, just my opinion.

This book would not exist without the determined efforts of its editor, Bruce Hainley, to retrieve its contents from archival limbo and decipher their smudgy passages, and the repeated urging of Hedi El Kholti at Semiotext(e), who tried to convince me for several years that it would be a worthwhile venture. I thank them both for their enthusiasm and hard work, and apologize for my ambivalence. My resistance had something to do with a strong distaste for the eighties nostalgia that has been an institutional mania during the past several years, and my initial sense, during the Obama administration, that those vile days were behind us, over and done. With the latest turn of the historical wheel, however, I now think this compendium may serve as a corrective to a lot of ill-informed notions of things past, and may also have some pointed relevance to things present.

—Gary Indiana, July 2018

December 6, 2004

ONE BRIEF, SCUZZY MOMENT

I lived in the East Village when it still had the narcoleptic desuetude of downtown Detroit, and was usually included with today's Loisaida under the less cozy moniker "the Lower East Side." (It had, of course, been called the East Village in the more interesting part of the sixties, but went back to LES in the grim seventies.) So, it's a little thorny for me to flip back a quarter-century to the three years I spent as an art critic at the *Village Voice* in the mid-eighties, or revisit the "East Village Art Scene" they loosely coincided with—a scene that, for one, brief, improbable moment, made the neighborhood the West Chelsea of its day, and forever banished the area's better Detroit-like qualities.

The Reagan-era scene itself ignored much of the far more interesting East Village art world that had come before it. Until hordes of trust-fund bohemians and storefront art salesmen invaded to give the nabe an entrepreneurial makeover—and lay the groundwork for an explosion in real-estate values that eventually wrecked its wealth of rent-stabilized apartments—the East Village was an ideal refuge for any artist born without a silver spoon. Contrary to its wild and crazy latecomers, they didn't make a rose garden from the Atacama Desert. There was plenty of life in the place before anyone thought to squeeze cash from it.

I was a bit anterior to the Wall-Hanging Art Boom spawned by Morning in America, though I found myself in the whirling center of it before it lapsed into remission. Since 1978, I had been a playwright and stage director who wrote little essays on film and other subjects, and published an occasional bad poem. I never much cared if I had any money. I lived so reclusively that I passed for deceased much of any given year. I was pathologically shy, but I forced myself to become a dervish of sociability whenever I embarked on another play. I believed that actors, like Germans of the thirties, were basically clueless children yearning for a headstrong, visionary father figure, even if he happened to be insufferably overbearing, zonked on speed half the time, and possibly insane.

When I moved into the neighborhood in the late seventies, I immediately assembled a theater troupe with the actor and painter Bill Rice, a slyboots sage revered in the authentic New York bohemia since Harry Truman. Our theater was a backyard garden—a jumble of bricks, concrete, and cinder blocks with little sprouts of vegetation here and there—behind Bill's floor-through studio at 13 East 3rd. Our company included inspired madcaps like Tina L'Hotsky, Queen of the Mudd Club. And Evan Lurie of the Lounge Lizards (formerly the Eels) composed all the music for our shows. He also appeared in our play *Curse of the Dog People*, as Fludd, an estate archivist hired by a family of werewolves.

We never agreed on a name for our company. I favored "Theater of the Obvious," but Bill preferred "Garbage After Dinner." His place was what used to be called "a beautiful mess." Large objects were constantly sliding from shelves. One storm-tossed night when our *bal musette* had moved indoors, Rene Ricard recited his electrifyingly caustic poetry from the garden doorway, his back to the audience, while he pissed a full bladder into the pitch-black downpour.

Bill Rice also hosted art shows, where I first saw Barbara Ess's pinhole-camera photos, Richard Morrison's haunting (and still uncelebrated) photographs, and a riveting, Brice Marden-ish monochrome painting that had taken months to execute, as its sole medium was the artist's semen. Other artists whose work appeared in Bill's studio—and who still exhibit at an East Village institution, La Galleria on 1st Street—include Mark Tambella, Francie Lyshak, and Rice himself. Tambella paints superlatively realist scenes of people working, talking, having sex, running. Lyshak makes figurative work of real uniqueness—fragments of landscapes hyperenlarged. Rice paints pictures of the guys from the men's shelter on 3rd Street; figures revealed by streetlight seeping through venetian blinds; traffic; everything you see and do in the dark. His work captures parts of the neighborhood that still haven't entirely gone away.

It seems impossible now, but at one time, circa 1979, everyone I saw on Second Avenue, day or night, was either someone I knew or someone I recognized: the vertiginously tall, incomparably fearless photographer Peter Hujar; the sublimely nose-thumbing sculptor Paul Thek; Nico (as in Velvet Underground Nico); Penny Arcade, wacko genius of one-woman stage anarchy; Herbert Huncke, the indomitable drug pusher who inspired much of William Burroughs's *Junky*; Larry Rivers; punk avatars Richard Hell and Tom Verlaine; filmmaker Nick Zedd; actress Black-Eyed Susan; Jean-Michel Basquiat (who went by his graffiti tag SAMO, then); filmmaker Amos Poe; Terri Toye (the most beautiful boy who ever became a girl); and sometimes Debbie Harry. Understand, these familiars didn't graze in packs—there were seldom more than twenty ambulatory individuals scattered between 14th Street and Houston at the same hour.

Before the galleries arrived in the mid-eighties and Avenue A became a beckoning, piquantly semi-dangerous place for kids from Dalton to ferret out a nickel bag of Mary Jane, the "old" East Village already had a full dance card of subterranean amusements. The Bar at Second Avenue and 4th doubled as a pickup joint and giddy living room/salon for a whole community of musicians, writers, actors, and painters, some already famous, like Robert Mapplethorpe and Edward Albee, many others famous later on. John Lurie played pool there in the afternoon.

One standout memory is a night when the legendary J. J. Mitchell, Frank O'Hara's lover years before, spilled an entire bottle of poppers up my nose.

A differently eclectic crowd of theater people converged most nights on Phebe's at Bowery and 4th, wired from performing at La MaMa or Theater for the New City. I met Cookie Mueller in Phebe's, and fell in love with her on the spot. Cookie had featured in John Waters's early films. She acted, designed clothes, and also wrote stories and a medical-advice column, "Ask Dr. Mueller."

In a strictly hedonistic way, Eileen's Reno Bar was integral to the East Village community. A narrow pocket of surrealism on Second Avenue between 11th and 12th, its ceiling surfaced in plastic jade plant—brown plastic jade plant—Eileen's had its flaccid nights of dead room tone. But most evenings brought a steady influx of pre-op transsexuals, clueless walk-ins, bisexual drug dealers, garrulous drunks with a schizophrenic flair, Ricardo Montalbán types from Europe lusting after chicks with dicks, and a few black-humored fags like myself, who much preferred the Reno Bar's nightly Halloween party to clocking the aging process in some drippy gay bar. Eileen's had the carnal whoop-de-do of a fetish convention. It was also full of crack whores working the track on 11th Street.

I once took a bar stool beside an enormous black woman I mistook for a drugstore cashier who'd rung up my toothpaste purchase that afternoon, which led to a dyslexic exchange of mis-understandings; I realized my mistake when she leaned close and declared in a tragic whisper: "You know something? My clitoris is as big as a penis. You know what I'm saying? My clitoris is the same size as a penis. I'm talking about a big penis. Can you understand what that makes me feel like?"

One Eileen's habitué named Joel wore a walrusy mustache and the woebegone, sagging face of the chronically defeated. His spot was the last bar stool in back, where a hideous painting, widely assumed to portray the Reno Bar's ancient founder, hovered behind Joel's thinning hair. (There was, and still is, an actual Eileen: I saw her a few weeks ago on the Third Avenue uptown bus. Older, but ever a star.)

My friend Louis Laurita and I felt sad for Joel. Laconic and melancholy as he bolted down five or six G&Ts, Joel would haul himself out to his pickup truck and we'd see it hopelessly circling around at five miles an hour, until Joel returned, slumped and abashed-looking, to drown his abjection in more gin. "Poor Joel," Louie habitually said. "Can't even get laid by a whore."

Around the time when the Barnes & Noble megastore opened on Astor Place, we learned Joel's last name was Rifkin. Over the years, he had strangled seventeen prostitutes in that truck. Here we'd been trying to cheer the guy up, and he'd actually been having the time of his life.

It may sound a stretch, but I date the transformation of the East Village from when Jack Henry Abbott, a murderer who'd just been paroled thanks to Norman Mailer's proclaiming him a literary genius, fatally stabbed Richard Adan, a waiter I knew who worked at the Binibon restaurant on Second Avenue, in 1981. It was the beginning of the end for that restaurant.

An obnoxiously trendy, moderately upscale restaurant named 103 opened near the vanished Binibon. It had stupidly angular tables and a snippy, impatient staff. It planted a proprietary yuppie flag in a low-income backwater where eccentricity was normal and having six bucks for a hamburger wasn't. It was only a restaurant, the food was okay. It wasn't Kmart. (We were spared that for another fifteen years.) But more upscale restaurants would soon sprout as the Art Mecca spread its vulpine wings. And already, with 103's arrival, longtime residents understood that one day, gentrification would shove them out of their rent-secure tenements into Hoboken isolation, or possibly a refrigerator crate on the Bowery.

But I'm getting ahead of myself. The globally hyped, short-lived phenomenon known as the East Village Art Scene originated in the basement of the building I live in. One day in 1981, through a doorway under the stoop, I noticed Patti Astor rolling paint over dingy walls, in a space I had long imagined the lair of elderly former concentration-camp guards—the only conceivable background of my landlord's maintenance hires.

Patti was opening a gallery. In Charlie Ahearn's movie *Wild Style*, she played a reporter whose car breaks down in the Bronx, where she befriends a charismatic group of graffiti artists. Patti's character inserts these artists into the downtown art world.

In my experience, life seldom imitates art and certainly never improves on it, but Patti and her partner, Bill Stelling, did smuggle Harlem and the South Bronx into a veritably albino art scene. The Fun Gallery, which later moved farther east, really was fun. Patti served Lava Lamp-colored cocktails. The openings carried the sexy charge of surplus beauty in the room. The place was totally free of pretension. And there were actual black people there. (The endemic racism of the art world speaks volumes about the people who run it.) Patti simply didn't care if she made any money: The point was to zap a little soul into the prevailing rigor mortis. Lady Pink, Futura 2000, Daze, and Lee Quiñones, among other graffiti artists, as well as Renaissance goofball-wit Arch Connelly, were all part of the Fun Gallery—long before the not-so-fun stuff happened.

That was, as the song goes, the start of something big. And the end of something small. Next, monkey see monkey do, more storefront art shops opened, a lot in 1982, and a full invasion by 1985. More, it quickly appeared, than enough worthwhile artists to fill them. I lack the memory cells to proper-name all the galleries whose press releases enhanced the horror of opening my mailbox. But I can recall what distinguishes a period of artistic excellence from a gas leak of mindlessly avid publicity. Consider what the otherwise sensible Dutch laid out for a tulip bulb a few hundred years ago.

The Fun Gallery spawned an embarrassment of epigones, mostly devoted to "Neo-Expressionism." The original Expressionism, of course, had been an effulgence of audaciously painted imagery, aggressively wrought in thick impasto, reflecting the harsh historical upheavals of its time. It dispensed with the delicacies and preciosities of Impressionism in the same way that Dostoyevsky dispensed with the sentimentalized aspects of Turgenev. In these instances, innovation wasn't primarily intended to negate the value of what preceded it, but to keep the recording of consciousness up to date.

But much of the new East Village "movement" amounted to "Self-Expressionism" of the kind that now flowers on television as 24/7 terminal self-revelation. Its crudity effectively captured nothing salient about the movement of history—except, perhaps, as an unconscious reflection of Ronald Reagan's ascendancy and the cultural glorification of greed. These new venues were filled with adolescent energy, prankishness, and their own brand of undifferentiated anger about everything wrong with the world. Unfortunately, few 20-year-olds even know what world they're living in, much less what's actually wrong with it.

Some who did know, and made very intriguing work from their perception, were Richard Hambleton, a creepy person whose shadow figures painted on all kinds of random surfaces really were disturbing and effective (even more so, strange to say, in broad daylight than at night); Kenny Scharf, who was far more personally engaging than his paintings were for a time, but eventually brought his work up to the same level as his personality; Kiki Smith, a born artist in every sense; and Marilyn Minter, whose paintings of movie-star faces and people wearing excessive makeup hold up much better today than many of the other "Neo-Ex" artists.

Rodney Alan Greenblat's playpen defacements of innocent blank canvas would have to be included in a truly comprehensive survey of the period. At the time, he was considered the cynical nadir of Neo-Ex, and a hilarious example of what arriviste orthodontists and jumped-up ambulance chasers in the legal profession were willing to waste money on as "art collectors" before the stock-market crash of 1987. I'm told that one collector couple known then as the "personal hygiene" practitioner and his wife are currently buying a porn channel in Florida. And they were among the better ones.

Many artists made no tangible objects but did things that really were art at the time, like Johnny Dynell and Chi Chi Valenti, who kept dull people out of the Mudd Club. (Ann Magnuson and a cohort of appealing freaks turned Club 57 into a breezy retort to the Mudd Club's manic-depressive door policy.) Those of us who always got in considered them the ne plus ultra of discerning crowd control and infallible fashion sense—Chi Chi's S.S. uniform made a statement so convolutedly funny and menacing it should've been bought by the Met years ago. Keith Haring used to have shows at the Mudd Club, before Tony Shafrazi gave him his first Soho exhibit. My memories of the place are mostly before midnight (if you can remember what happened at the Mudd Club after two in the morning, you were never there), but Johnny and Chi Chi are still making waves in the better precincts of nightland.

While much neo-east village art was tepid, a fair amount of the earlier East Village's more risk-taking chutzpah had started losing steam circa 1982. We should never forget that vast numbers of New York's best people—Peter Hujar, *Flaming Creatures* director Jack Smith, Cookie Mueller, Robert Mapplethorpe, painter Nicolas Moufarrege—died fast in the AIDS epidemic or a few years into it.

Another factor that took the neighborhood's flavor away: Too many esteemed local talents had acquired an insulating crust of uncritical coterie worship. The banal efforts of once-exciting artists received rote adulation from claques less concerned about quality than about sparing a friend's feelings. They no longer cared if what they presented in public sucked, as long as they presented something. You could blame the timidity of artists terrified of wider cultural arenas and their risks, or the small rewards of masochistic, self-induced failure. And, cruel as it sounds, you can also blame living in New York while cowering for decades in the same mousy sliver of it, as if you inhabited an unusually zany alpine village.

There was something necessary and painfully liberating about flushing away preciosity and giving nostalgia a kick in the ass. Even if the flush mechanism itself belonged in a toilet

All the same, avatars of the pre-Reagan-era East Village scene who didn't pale or die or lose their aesthetic savvy were rarely respected or even noticed by the people who took over—like Jeff Weiss, one of a handful of certifiable living legends who performed all through the eighties in a 10th Street basement apartment.

David Wojnarowicz, who'd lived in New York forever and had been a teenage hustler in Times Square, straddled the old and new scenes. He and I had a complicated relationship, and I'd like to settle some hash propagated by an art critic named Lucy Lippard in an *Aperture* publication devoted to David, in which she implied that I'd stalked him.

It happens that for about three months, David and I insistently sought each other's constant company, for differently confused reasons, and mostly in Paris. We said rotten things about each other in public, and in the course of our folie à deux, David wrote many deranged letters to me, and I to him. I disposed of his a year later. He, ever the pack rat, hung on to mine while assuring me he'd burned them. We later made up, but the crux of David's resentment is that I never valued his paintings as highly as his writing. We had basic disagreements about art. David believed that children are natural artists and their spontaneous expression is what an adult artist should approximate as closely as possible. I like children just fine, but that's horseshit. As David was probably the pick of the litter as far as Neo-Ex-slash-graffiti-art went, he also exemplified— not always in his work, but in his attitude—what I found lazy and self-absorbed about most of the artwork produced by the "movement."

After David's death from AIDS in 1992, a curator at the Grey Art Gallery asked my permission to display my deranged letters to David in a vitrine. I refused. I pointed out that I myself wasn't dead yet. I had a great fondness for David. I won't claim that I miss him the way I miss Cookie or my best, best friend, Dieter Schidor, Fassbinder's last producer, who suicided shortly after his HIV diagnosis. Among the dead, we all have our empathetic priorities. I am sorry David's gone.

Some of the gallerists in the new scene were arguably more interesting than the painters. Amid the places where Neo-Expressionism defined the style, Gracie Mansion and her partner, Sur Rodney Sur, stood out. Gracie's instincts and shrewd taste (Peter Hujar, Marilyn Minter, Stephen Lack) deserved, and got, her a lasting career in the biz. I've always respected her as a pioneer, ever since she launched her first "gallery" in her apartment bathroom. I wasn't always crazy about her early choices. At one of her shows, Gracie greeted me as I looked at something very disagreeable on the wall. "What do you think?" she brightly asked. "Oh, Gracie, I can't help it, I think it's a piece of shit." She whooped. "I don't think it's the worst piece of shit," she said. "You should see who I'm showing next, you wanna see shit. The pictures will get better, I hope, or they'll get really bad and he can make a fortune and blow it on heroin."

Pat Hearn also occupied a higher class of start-up art dealers. She had panache and daring, beauty and good breeding, but the rarest thing Pat had, in preternatural abundance, was grace. I adored her. I don't think Pat would mind my revealing that our cordial acquaintance ripened into friendship by accident, when we showed up at the same Debtors Anonymous meeting.

Colin de Land, who opened American Fine Arts, was the only matchingly brilliant figure Pat should have married, and she did, and now they're both dead, first her, then him, and nobody who knew them has ever gotten over it. Colin looked like an especially jaded, paling gigolo and cardsharp. I'm hardly the only person who ever offered him a blow job in his place of business. I may be the only person who never gave him one at one time or another, though once he married Pat, that was that.

Colin and Richard Prince invented an artist named John Dogg, and put up a well-received show of his work at Lisa Spellman's 303 Gallery. (A lot of people still believe that I was John Dogg. I wasn't. Colin and Richard came up with the ideas, and one or the other "made" the work—Goodyear tires and other store-bought objects. That was one show where presentation was, literally, everything.)

In 1985, the *Village Voice* offered me a job as senior art critic. This made my life easier and lousy at the same time. I now had to actually enter all those galleries instead of peeking in the windows. At times, the only tangible perk was having the chump for a fifth of vodka whenever twenty more phonies had flattered my ass off in the course of a working week.

The East Village was a small quadrant of what I had to "cover," and I was a bit slow to realize that a fresh constellation of galleries there (Nature Morte, Cash/Newhouse, International With Monument) were showing art much more to my liking than the inflatable children's toys of the waning Neo-Expressionist craze. This second wave favored conceptually crisp work by artists fluent in several media: Robert Gober, Gretchen Bender, Ashley Bickerton, Peter Halley, and Jeff Koons.

But year two at the *Voice* brought a distinct slackening of interest in the art world, art, artists, and, frankly, the sound of my own voice. It was also the year when all the galleries began fleeing the East Village. The rents kept soaring, driving some places out of business, while galleries that were making plenty wanted much larger spaces for their money, in one of the two real power centers of the art world, Soho and 57th Street. The East Village had already become a zoo, and NYU would go on to plant some ugly dormitories down and unleash thousands of rich kids whose idea of art was grazing the streets and poking into boutiques while asserting their pathologies by screaming into cell phones. But hey, shit happens.

And, as it happens, that's also the most succinct word to describe my third and final year as the senior art critic at the *Voice*. The job was powerful for one reason: Besides the *Times*, the *Voice* was one of the few places shows were reviewed when they were still up. You could move the merchandise while it was out on the rack. And I had become scramble-headed by the parasitic opportunism that too many artists, dealers, and collectors disguised as friendship, deep respect, or even sexual interest. In fairness to some who were my actual friends, my own bad behavior, triggered by the several drugs I took, got infinitely ickier thanks to having this job—which was basically to judge them in public. Of course, some of those lovely friends dropped me like a used paper towel right after I quit. Which, when I started publishing novels, they all learned to regret.

I still live in the East Village, but now I live in a luxury neighborhood, thanks mostly to an insignificant hiccup in the long burp of art history that created a seismic shift in the history of New York property values. (You knew it was all finished when the methadone clinic moved out.) While this has left the squalor of my apartment building completely intact, an architectural pentimento of former times, being able to get a deli delivery at four in the morning is among many happy improvements that hiccup left in its echoing wake.

I'm not prone to much sentimentality, but you should treasure your own history, however weird it is. William Burroughs once told me, "People like us are lucky because every shitty thing that happens to us is just more material." I want to remember the many people I love who are gone and remind myself how much I love the ones who are still here. And I'll let you in on a little secret: If you live long enough, you even get fond of people you thought you hated.

VILE DAYS

March 5, 1985

OLD ART, NO MONEY

When Gaston Porcile Vitrine walks into Il Cantinore on East 10th Street in Manhattan, the waiters subtly but unmistakably avert their eyes. A mild wave of embarrassed coughing ripples through the chicly conservative dining room. Before he became a failure, Vitrine was an ornament at one table of celebrities or another almost every night. He goes to the restaurant seldom now. One night recently, he sat alone at a table for four, growing visibly agitated as it became clear that the still-flourishing friends who had invited him had decided to stand him up. He picked listlessly at a small salad—clearly the only item on the menu he could pay for himself—and tried to ignore the incredulous and contemptuous stares that were trained upon him throughout his grim vigil by diners who had, not so long ago, felt honored to toot a few grams of coke with Vitrine in any toilet in town.

That was when the fashion happy art world of today had spread itself open to embrace Vitrine and the varicolored spermatozoa he had been spraying furtively on gallery doorways and the walls of nightclubs for six months. Dealers and patrons alike were discovering how little cash could be extracted from the "think art" of the '70s, when a younger, less cerebral breed of artists began painting the town with their comic-colored and often penetrating emblems of American consumer products, little creatures from outer space, television sets, and barking dogs. Suddenly, a fresh generation found itself in the fast lane—

partying with Andy Warhol and Stephen Sprouse, arriving at openings in fantastic hairdos and coke-filled, block-long limousines. Collectors all over the world began lapping up everything these once-impoverished artists produced, with Vitrine's sperms riding high on the list of necessary collectibles.

But then something went terribly, terribly wrong. Not all at once, but gradually, bit by imperceptible bit. Vitrine continued to paint as if nothing were happening, usually after a night of carousing while still dressed in the $2000 suits and braided gold-lamé wigs he affected. He had always wanted to be a star, and now, in fact, he was. But he was a star fixed in a notoriously fickle firmament whose contents are determined by the spectator, and by fashion. Vitrine had arrived at a look, a style, a manner, true—but looks, styles, and manners have a way of becoming tiresome. The public's taste for Vitrine's prolific Expressive Jismism became first jaded, then stale. The very people who had launched Vitrine now rumored among themselves that the artist had shot his wad, aesthetically speaking, and was churning out parodies of himself to keep his market saturated. Fellow artists began to shun Vitrine, failure being the equivalent of leprosy among the highest rollers in the art game, who measure their success in terms of physical girth and first-name acquaintance with the busboys at Indochine. As they fattened, Vitrine grew thin. His outbursts of petulance, his dreadful table manners, his lack of conversation—the things that had once endeared him to the gargoyles of West Broadway and 57th Street—now indicated a certain limitedness, an incapacity to measure up to one's publicity.

All this would have been bad enough for Vitrine, obviously. But an even worse fate, endemic in the entertainment world and perhaps in an art world too that is largely entertainment, befell him. On the way down, Vitrine encountered precisely the same people he had met on the way up. His habit of using people like Kleenex to enlarge the theater of his ambition had not gone unremarked or unremembered. Friendless, broke, and unsuited for manual labor, Vitrine had joined the ever-growing ranks of the once amusing, dependent on benevolence in a milieu where it is in short supply.

This is my first column for *The Village Voice*, and it is also an appeal: art is long, but public attention is often short. So I implore the reader, take pity on the Vitrines of our fair but unfair city. If you see Gaston Porcile Vitrine, or someone like him, marooned at an otherwise deserted table in some overpriced restaurant, tormented by the gay voices and hyena laughter of his former peers, won't you send him a *kir royale*?

* * *

In the last year and a half, the group show concept has taken on a weird and decidedly unaesthetic vitality, becoming an occasion either for gallerists to shove one or another set of brand names down the public's throat, or for enlarging the curatorial pretensions of numerous fishy-minded free-lancers. The more patently bogus recent curations have conflated "issues" culled from *Post* headlines and the titles of anthropology texts with aesthetic issues, and have presented as "tendencies" works that were whipped off on assigned themes.

"From Organism to Architecture," the group show currently on view at the New York Studio School (8 West 8th Street, through March 15), is like a breath of clean air after months of asphyxia. Organized by the estimable painter Ross Bleckner, this show is lucid, serious, and intelligently limited, where so many group shows have been sprawling, silly, and idiotically all-encompassing. Fourteen artists are represented by varying numbers of works; all the works are paintings, and none is egregiously large, spray-painted, or inspired by commercial illustration.

Max Beckmann's *Portrait of Wolfgang Frommel* (1949) presides over the double-room gallery with a gaze of brooding prescience, at a diagonal extreme from an untitled Cy Twombly oil on paper, an even gray gouged and scored with whizzing lines. Bleckner's own contribution to the show, *Fulcrum for Larry*, is one of the most impressive, an ensemble of immanent forms and ambiguous space invaded, but not at all demystified, by light. Pat Steir's *Flower* contains two versions of a sunflower, a dialectic between structural drawing in paint and chromatic definition of form.

Each of Kevin Larmon's three somewhat overvarnished pictures contains a small bowl of fruit revealed by a tiny incidence of light; the textures of this little bowl reach the eye in the grabby manner of small objects in dark Dutch still lifes. George Condo has two small, whimsical canvases in the show, one with words, the letters gleaming at their tips like television teeth, the other with a fish tail extruding from a striped something or other I won't speculate on, and there's a terrific Alexis Rockman—an esophagus-shaped funnel rising from one bowl pouring water into a smaller bowl whose stem coils around in the space just above, and slightly behind, the larger bowl. Peter Nadin's picture is an arrangement of pastel colors of almost equal value, which makes the Soutine-like landscape it contains ephemeral, an art-historical memory trace.

Four canvases by Iris Mitchell range clockwise from a chalky black and gray abstraction to a smartly inscribed cat standing in a gold and black surface. There are three works by Don McLaughlin that juggle linear spatial divisions and representational forms with dissolvent, drizzled colors. Victor Alzamora, who died in 1983, is represented by 10 paintings, each a fairly blunt, cogent solution of elementary, recurrent formal questions; as an ensemble, the Alzamora work articulates an idea of paint as a medium whose physical properties retain sufficient obstinacy and surprise for new things to be discovered in them. This is also the premise of "From Organism to Architecture" as a whole. For a while this show engages many interdigitating stratagems of picture-making—on a scale between linear and biomorphic abstraction to architectonic luminism—its key conceit is painterliness.

This emphasis ferrets out the problem of speed, and the problem of "depth," in relation to how pictures are looked at now. It underlines the difference between the art of painting and the less subtle, more widely practiced art of image-making. People have learned to look at pictures fast. In consequence, a huge number of artists have learned to make pictures that read fast. Something crucial, though, evaporates when painting comes to rely exclusively on "content," especially when the content is figurative, narrative, and plucked whole from an increasingly tedious, nihilistic mass culture: this is one of myriad places where Andy Warhol has led legions down the primrose path to aesthetic bankruptcy. "From Organism to Architecture" asserts a generally suppressed continuity of formal exploration that supports a dialogue between young painters like Rockman, Larmon, and Condo, older artists like Steir, Twombly, Gagnier, and Bleckner, and established masters like Beckmann, without sensationalism competing with careerism to deflate the dialogue of all significance.

FATAL VISION

[**Komar & Melamid**. Ronald Feldman Fine Arts, 31 Mercer Street, through March 23]

Komar and Melamid's mixed-media "New Paintings" exploit and desecrate the latest constructs of "the new" with the enthralling sarcasm and painterly imperiousness that's invariably ascribed to their work. However, as usual, a lot more than sarcasm and imperiousness is going on. In a contrary spirit not unlike that of consumer advocates, Komar and Melamid have made an exhaustive inventory of successful recent painting styles, shrunk the samples down to digestible dimensions (typically 13 ½ inches by 11 inches), put them to work on politically and sexually frontal material, and arranged them in deadpan formalist sequences. The studio-apartment scale of the work, the elastic range of its specific historical references, and the mediation of individual ego inherent in Komar and Melamid's collaboration deflate a mythology of art-making that has wobbled into deep senility: the artist as a volcano that erupts once or twice a year, its lava cooling into fantastic new forms for an awed and grateful public to decipher.

The most aggressive aesthetic implication of the 45 works on view is that the exact wording of postmodernism's bankruptcy statement can be as classical as yesterday, as arbitrary as today. The more subtle message emitting here is that it is always possible, even in extremity, to say a little more. The issue of context that has occasionally been wheeled out to differentiate what these émigré artists do from what "American" art is up to simply can't be applied here in good faith. Komar and Melamid's fused view of art and politics sees the U.S. and the USSR with equal clarity, whether or not our national vanity acknowledges it. Their work has been bulldozed in Russia and slashed in America; little wonder, then, that their new paintings tend to merge the two places into the same mental territory.

Since the author of these lines is featured in one of the works, I might as well begin there. In *Gary and Blok* (seven panels, mixed media), the American writer and the Russian one are separated by a swastika of plastic rats, a Balthusian study of numerous dildos, and a swastika-shaped game board on which numbered career moves are indicated for various professions (artists and intellectuals, etc.); Blok is flanked by a swastika floral arrangement.

But what does it *mean*, I heard myself asking one of the artists, stupidly. Surely you don't mean *that*.

However, K & M's new paintings mean what they look like they mean, constructing their meaning by turning the present moment's aesthetic and political tropes into earnestly secular motifs. A Constructivist version of the cross, featuring a Brisk 'n Bouncy Lowfat Milk container, serves as the root form linking Jackson Pollock being raised on Iwo Jima, the Soviet flag with golden dollar sign replacing the hammer and sickle, a photograph of Jasper Johns with gold nails driven through the eyes, and a Yalta-inspired variant on Johns's *Three Flags*.

The Yalta Conference is one of several iconographical anchors in the show, a symbol of East-West misalliances, of the seduction and betrayals composing modern life's song of expedience. The cackling wickedness of rulers and the infantilized credulity of the ruled are symbiotic themes that extend from politics to the culture industry, often embodied in *faux-naïf* methods of representation or objects redolent of childhood. In *Allies*, over the text of two solicitous letters between FDR and Stalin, we find a Venetian carnival mask; in *The Minotaur as a Participant in the Yalta Conference*, amid Jugendstil variants on the latest species of East Village bull, we find Lenin attempting to scare a little girl with a bovine headdress.

Appearance is the quintessence of deception throughout this elaborately varied production. In *Sounds*, a Soviet teen-party interior has an impeccably Conceptual-looking border of glass slides that deconstructs the image in a surprisingly rigorous way, since the slides are enlargements of herpes viruses. If you look carefully into the background of *Autumn in the Village*, which features the ultra-postmodernist insertion of a paint-smeared plastic bull, you will notice a male figure being lynched from an equally up-to-date motorized crane.

Images of castration, fucking, and execution, not to mention rape and torture, weave though this exhibition as subjects of formal study, as if assigned in some post-holocaust academy where the debris of art history provided an array of equally worthy techniques for rendering our century's favorite activities. While Komar and Melamid may appear to have flattened both subject matter and style into value-exempt monads, the moralism of this show is devastatingly thorough and unsparing.

The installation is a tour de force of arrangement, the pieces running evenly along the horizontal midsection of the gallery, with intermittent vertical branchings. The component panels, numbering in the hundreds, were produced separately in the studio before their eventual configurations had been decided. The number of panels in each work varies from one to eleven, the largest being *When I Was a Child Matzoh Reminded Me of a Braille Book* and *The Minotaur as a Participant in the Yalta Conference*. Except for the three single-panel pieces, each work is a montage sequence, optimally juxtaposing painting, photography, and sculpture; most of them read more coherently from left to right, or from bottom up, than otherwise. Before being spliced together in the gallery, the panels resembled bits of an immense rebus, satirically scaled for the new median-income art collector.

"New Paintings" echoes *Biography*, a 1973 work consisting of 197 square wooden miniatures (smuggled out of the Soviet Union while K & M still lived there, exhibited in New York in 1976). Like *Biography*, the new work is a polyglot inventory of the artists' lives, expanded to apply Soviet-bred skepticism about everything to the material of American culture. The show also casts a Proustian backward glance over Mother Russia; aside from the much-noted sarcasm, K. & M's paintings quite often convey a genuine ache of nostalgic longing.

They are also mercilessly, enduringly funny. It is a great pity that many seasoned gallery-goers, who after all are obliged to look at laughable things all the time, feel inhibited around deliberately humorous paintings. One is strangely moved by the sight of prestigious-looking individuals gazing with total sobriety at a picture of Franklin Roosevelt with a pickle on his head, Hitler clipping his toenails, or a condom dredged from a canal in Leningrad.

March 19, 1985

SEDUCTION AND PRODUCTION

"When you have a tan," asked a character in Renata Adler's *Speedboat*, "what have you got?" This is a useful question to apply when walking into art-related spaces, particularly now that so many range along city sidewalks that were once vivid with mixed ethnic life. Many an East Village gallery overcompensates for the missing bodega, the vanished bookshop, or the evicted antique store it has supplanted by stuffing itself chockfull with fun-colored knickknacks and smile-covered gewgaws that make cute noises and wiggle back and forth and make you think Gee! What a happy planet the little asshole who made this stuff lives on!

That happy planet is no stranger to our world. It owns our world, in a technical, legal sense, and was identified years ago as the Mysterious Planet Debby. The *horror vacui* concept of the stuffed gallery originated on the Planet Debby and was brought here by certain accessory designers who were not really humans, but Debbies—creatures from an alien world of debutantes whose efforts to ape our authentic Woolworth tchotchkes and declining humorists only betray their ineptitude and planetary origins. When on earth will the Debbies go back where they came from?

Well, now for the truly bad news: the Debbies can't go home any more. The atmosphere of the Planet Debby is too thin for creatures who have learned to breathe our polluted air, since its composition is exactly that of a Connecticut suburb. Once here, the Debbies are doomed to a life of compulsive imitation and moneygrubbing, it is all they know, and according to those who have studied them closely, it is all they can learn. We are more fortunate: we can learn from the Debbies.

For instance, **Allan McCollum** just had a brilliantly witty show at Cash/Newhouse (170 Avenue B, closed) that commented on the Debbitic *horror vacui* installation effect as well as the ravening and unreflective visual appetites the invading Debbies have stirred up among Yuppies and Guppies who were once perfectly content to hang a tasteful LeRoy Neiman reproduction in their homes, or perhaps a Lowell Nesbitt flower picture. Or an Andy Warhol.

McCollum is a serious artist addressing serious questions, not all of them Debbie-inspired. There were hundreds of paintings in this show. Each of them was different and all of them were the same. None of them was a painting. McCollum's recent works are solid-state plaster simulacra of paintings, some square, some rectangular, shaped to conform to the frame/matte/painting configuration that says "picture" to us. These objects are painted to further the illusion of joined elements. The middle, image part, the one we associate with "payoff," is black. Incidentally, this black is a rich, thought-out black, a painterly black. Still, there is really nothing there at all, except some evidence of the hand, a few tiny quirks of light. What does this tell us?

One thing it *might* tell us is that we don't see much more than some evidence of the hand and a few tiny quirks of light in many paintings that are shown now. So why bother paying epic prices when you can have the same thing, or an ensemble of the same things, at a reasonable sum, without indulging the often dubious adventure offered by the artist's personal "imagery"? McCollum's work can be hung anywhere where a picture is appropriate and, indeed, these works achieve the functional scope that most pictures have after acquisition. The destiny of all visual art is a quizzical kind of death.

Another thing McCollum's work might tell us is that the desire we manufacture to collide with images is about something happening inside our heads that can't be authentically gratified by passively looking at a picture, completed by standing in a gallery, or betrayed by an image's refusal of complicity. We all want to participate in the construction of reality instead of being raped by someone's mastery or lobotomized by someone's horseshit; there are many powerful things in our popular and intellectual culture that operate against this feeling, including certain kinds of art. McCollum's work invites us to examine the culture of hypnosis and hallucination by withholding the means for accomplishing either.

So does **Joseph Kosuth**'s. "Fort! Da!", at Leo Castelli Gallery (420 West Broadway, through March 23), is an incendiary effort of patience: for years, Kosuth has been showing people what is "there," in the gently coercive manner of a grown-up who knows your problem and wants to get you to see Square One so he can go home and get a little rest. The context of Castelli Gallery is certainly charged in a different way than Cash/Newhouse. The enveloping but uncoercive physicality of the McCollum show worked smartly in an East Village gallery, and the Kosuth show works smartly here, right down to the fact that the Kosuth work cost much more to execute.

The Duratrans photo process Kosuth has used to make the six gigantic (six foot by ten foot) images displayed is ordinarily used only by McDonald's and others who present America to you in the form of gigantic images of broiled meat and sesame rolls. In this application, what you see in the gallery is the gallery, photographically duplicated on plastic and hung opposite whichever wall it represents. Each image is spiked with colored Xs, a Piranesian annotation of illusory space, and each carries a motto printed in the kind of corporate typeface that usually tells us what to buy, what to eat, and what to think. Here, the messages undermine the hermetic self-sufficiency of the received image and, along with the Xs, refer our attention back to the physical reality we're standing in. The viewer participates in making the work and is free to unmake it at will. It doesn't ask us to gasp at the awesome spectacle of the artist's subjectivity, but rather to relate our perceptions to his, and to clarify what they are.

Kosuth's "Fort! Da!" pieces are beautiful objects, hanging in a gallery on sale. The fact that their meaning will change drastically as soon as they are removed from the location they depict incorporates the fate of "beautiful objects" into the discourse between the work, the gallery, and the viewer. McCollum's painting-surrogates in the Cash/Newhouse installation similarly anticipated the disappearance of their ideal situation, their dispersion through the flow of individual sales into far-flung environments.

"Fort! Da!" is an expression Freud cites in *Beyond the Pleasure Principle*, a child's expression: here and gone. We know what lies beyond the pleasure principle, and that it participates heavily in the cycle of limitless seduction by limitless production. "There are readers blinded by pictures they can't see," as one of Kosuth's texts reads. Another says, "There is this, which was here, and there is this which is here, there is a missing location and the presence of that." The world is everything that is the case, says Wittgenstein. (*And in the second place, because* Renata Adler.) We walk into this place with our expectations, and surprise, we're the only people in here. The frisson that makes whatever happens happen is what you've got when you've got a tan.

March 19, 1985

PEEPING TOM

[**Eric Fischl**. Whitney Museum of American Art, 945 Madison Avenue, through May 11. Mary Boone Gallery, 417 West Broadway, through March 29.]

Eric Fischl's current retrospective at the Whitney Museum, supplemented by a show of four large paintings at Mary Boone Gallery, anthologizes a body of work that has loomed into critical prominence over the past five years with particular urgency. Fischl, it is claimed, like almost no other artist in America, depicts uncomfortable truths about American life and culture, the wreckage of the American dream, and the oily, icky libidinal impulses of American middle class. Incest, masturbation, interracial sex, lesbianism, bestiality, and child abuse are but a few themes adumbrated in Fischl's paintings. Under these lurks a profound desolation, an inner void that is never really filled by the vagrant carnal romping and TV viewing with which Fischl's characters pass the time.

Fischl's method is literary and anecdotal. The situations he depicts have an implicit narrative momentum, rather like film stills. The privileged viewpoint of the spectator is intended as one of complicity. Something is about to happen, usually, which the viewer can easily imagine. The figures in Fischl's paintings are often naked, a circumstance that effectively strips off a whole layer of self-defensiveness. They are generally on vacation, or engaged in leisure activities around the family pool, recumbent on chaises longues, playing with dogs, swimming, and drying themselves off.

Fischl's characters are, invariably, members of middle-class nuclear families, whether viewed *en famille* or in isolation. We know this because of the quotidian vulgarity of their bedrooms and lawn furniture, their occasional clothing, the canned quality of their expressions—Dad's approving smile over the charcoal grill in *Barbeque*, Junior's brooding self-absorption while beating off in *Sleepwalker*. For all their atmosphere of imminent transgression, with people peeling off their clothes or hugging their little daughters with suspicious energy, Fischl's paintings mainly convey a desperate limitation. His people are trapped in a continuum of tacky forms, a shared reality of emotional and intellectual impoverishment.

One could probably develop the idea that Fischl's pictures offer unflattering views of the class just below the class of people who buy them. Their appeal, in some quarters, is no different than that of a John Updike story in *The New Yorker*, full of masterful bourgeois self-criticism and lapidary illustrational style, an ambitious expenditure of artistry on a subject of quite limited interest. The explicitness of Fischl's representations leaves little to the imagination, and what it does leave is an invitation that many people have no trouble declining. The chief audience for Fischl's work, like the audience for *The New Yorker*, equates its metaphysical existence with its ability to accept its darkest urges when these are reflected in art—particularly when they can be readily projected on other people. But unless one is white, middle-class, and heterosexual, one is likely to find an alien pathos where others discover the shock of recognition.

Discarding the snob appeal of Fischl's work as well as its presumed allure of bourgeois dirty-mindedness, however, we are still confronted with a heavy chunk of waking-dream familiarity. To some extent, the middle-class world belongs to everyone through the miracle of television, and perhaps the repressed pathology of that world has floated into universal consciousness as well. It is Fischl's peculiar achievement to delineate this pathology *as if it were nothing else*. Looked at in this way, Fischl's pictures become unrelieved symptoms, eternal reruns of a sinister, debilitating sitcom.

The lineaments of this sitcom seem borrowed from various sources—David Hockney, *Ozzie and Harriet*, beaver periodicals, and, less obviously, from those now-ubiquitous magazine views of affluent artists's "lifestyles." The true horror of Fischl's world lies not in its eruptions of Oedipal and other forbidden desires, but in its unmitigated ordinariness, the uninflected quality of its adolescent boners and backyard exhibitionists. In this Fischl is not all that different from Norman Rockwell: both artists offer reductive, generic versions of a class, a milieu, and "feelings." True, Fischl is more sophisticated, more skeptical, more humorous than Rockwell. His characters are motivated by lust and emptiness. The child figures Fischl paints are doomed to repeat the sterile patterns of their parents. Fischl gives a literal form to the secret terrors of kitsch; he gives kitsch a human face, a human setting. Rockwell *is* kitsch, whereas Fischl is a realist in a period of kitsch triumphant.

The downtime atmospheres of Fischl's paintings are essential to his strategy. Liberated from routine, Fischl's vacationers and partygoers enact their interiority in terms of play. Fischl typically shows them "occupying time" in a reality that threatens to reveal the void at any moment. They obey the kitsch mentality in their modes of escape: cruising, talking on the phone, staring into the TV. As Fischl demonstrates in *Inside Out* (not featured in these shows), where a woman straddled by a naked man reaches up to change the television channel, gratification is less compelling than desire in a kitsch world. Distraction is the kitsch version of living, encompassing sexuality and sleep, and most effectively expressed as a multiplication of mindless activities, or a proliferation of identical objects. Some of Fischl's most effective paintings are turbulent with overcrowding, like the nude fishing expedition of *The Old Man's Boat and the Old Man's Dog*: everyone, including the dog, pursues distraction with a fixity bordering on violence. In *Saigon, Minnesota*, the carnivalesque animation of a suburban backyard softens the individual grotesqueness of its character; the whole distracts us, and probably them, from the sum of its parts.

What is most remarkable about Fischl's characters is their evident lack of self-consciousness, even in moments of extreme vulnerability. In this they are, in fact, dissimilar from people in *The New Yorker*'s fiction pages. However mutually involved, Fischl's creatures are deeply indifferent to one another, disconnected—or, like the mother observing her daughter's ballet practice in *Bayonne*, simmering with bored resentment, or caught awkwardly off-guard, or lapsing into autistic coma. Fischl continues to enrich these people with complex morphologies of "behavior," enlarging a sequence of counter-stereotypes in the manner of a sociological report. By uncovering the Freudian underbelly of this affluent, consuming class, Fischl has penetrated a resilient surface to reveal another surface, the outside of the underneath.

LIVING WITH CONTRADICTIONS

[**Gerhard Richter**. Marian Goodman, 24 West 57th Street, through March 30; Sperone Westwater, 142 Greene Street, through March 26]

Like many exponents of paradox in contemporary art, Gerhard Richter seems disingenuous toward the seminal ironies suggested by his work. In his interviews Richter sounds, like Warhol, placid about the condition of things, and prepared to dilate blandly on the unseemly excessiveness of interpretation. "Today, I…no longer attach any special importance to whether I am objective, because everyone is objective."

Borges once advised writers never to strive for modernity, because one is modern whether or not one wishes to be. *Don Quixote* as written by Pierre Menard is not, cannot be, the *Don Quixote* of Cervantes, though every word of the two works is identical. Similarly, the slathery, splattery, streaked and squeegeed Abstract Expressionist paintings Richter is showing at Marian Goodman and Sperone Westwater aren't, and can't be, Abstract Expressionist paintings in the sense that a Jackson Pollock or a Hans Hofmann is. Like money, time changes everything. Richter's new works are astute, vivacious; they carry no whiff of the academic. Had Richter, or someone else, produced these paintings in the 1950s, they would undoubtedly be parked today in some mausoleum like the Rothko Chapel. Things being what they are, we have hardly a current clue about how to deal with them. It is probably imprudent to do so, but I'm going to try anyway.

Not long ago I was introduced to someone who told me about a great, unknown Abstract Expressionist, a painter who had shown his work in the '50s and then willfully dropped from view. He was, evidently, preparing to show his work—in England—for the first time in 30 years. I was given the painter's New York address. For weeks it occupied a reproachful, conspicuous area of my desk. In the end, I'm afraid, the prospect of participating in another ironic art resurrection eventually suggested the ceremonial tedium such events bring in their wake, and with a scarcely troubled *why bother* I at last threw the address away. But of course the oddity of the idea, the concept of an important *unknown* Abstract Expressionist, coated as it is with so many of the modernist dilemma's hardy germs, can't be thrown away so easily, with quite so much bravura. Or can it?

The problem, if it is one, is enhanced in Richter's case by the banal, luscious, smudgy-smooth pastoral landscapes included in the uptown portion of his show (leaving aside the immense body of work Richter has made in the past, articulated with an embarrassment of stylistic diversity). Richter often handles paint like a master violinist playing third-rate chamber music at formal tea. He hits all the proper notes with ghastly precision and expressiveness. One is made to realize how dated the tune, how thoroughly a product of its time it really is.

A sense of history is often gruelingly oppressive to artists; a time in which the historical sense is generally anathema will naturally have all kinds of unqualified people flocking into the profession. Aside from the occasional infant prodigy, however, artists have usually known where their material came from, and worked toward some increment of originality by working through their "influences." Richter's originality is distressingly contemporary. His work circumvents most of the critical paradigms that genuflect before "the new" (a phrase that could usefully be shrunk to "the nuance"). Richter's pictures seem to insist, really, on "the same, but slightly different."

Throughout most of his career, Richter has painted from photographs, but in a decidedly different spirit than the Photo-realists. For Richter, clearly, copying a blurred, clumsily framed black-and-white photograph is just as meaningful as copying a perfectly focused, artfully contrived colorama. For one thing, the labor involved is the same in either scenario. It's probably just as hard to write a Harold Robbins novel as it is to write *The Idiot*—maybe a lot harder if you happen to be Dostoyevsky.

This isn't to suggest that Richter's new, non-photo-derived paintings, which capitalize on an unequivocally Ab Ex, splashy pink and yellow acidity, are painstakingly vulgar or inferior pic-torially. They're glorious and out-of-date, an entirely different can of worms. Their appearance at this time crawls with impli-cations. The heaviest of these is their allusion to the 1950s, and to the heroizing of subjectivity and emotion that Abstract Expressionism served all too readily. The loathing of the demon intellect that made growing up in the '50s feel so much like cringing in a bomb shelter found its spiritual alibi in the tran-scendent effusions that put Jackson Pollock in *Life* magazine. Significantly, antisex hysteria was rampant then, as it is now, and the canvas seemed the perfect place for it to explode harmlessly and meet the kiss of a thousand pocketbooks.

Of course this is not all. No description can or should be all. As the moment of Abstract Expressionism recedes further in time, the formal aspects of Ab Ex paintings become ever more appreciable to the general audience. One can argue, though, that the mythos, and the bombast, have simply been leached out of Abstract Expres-sionism and poured into neo-Expressionism. We are constantly being urged to view the merest splotch of muck on a shattered teacup as an indispensable rune of contemporary angst—by the same critical machinery that regularly encourages us to look back at Abstract Expressionism with a slightly jaundiced eye.

Given the prevailing atmosphere of turgid, universal valorization of all things painted and displayed, Richter's work makes a startlingly direct interrogation of the notion of sincerity in the work of art. By reviving a grandiose, obsolescent style of work when an equally grandiose, formally different one has climbed to its apogee, Richter makes it easier to ask—as hardly anyone has, in public, for a long time—whether a work of art is honest. Not sincere, but honest. The concept of artist as oracular child who can see into the near future becomes redundant, and boorish, when almost anyone can see into the near future, and the present, without assistance.

To put it differently, Richter's recent paintings roll the cherished assumptions regarding the past 30 years of art history into clear, properly distanced view. This may not have been what they were primarily intended to do, even if the artist fully realized that they could be received in this way. Richter would probably say he wanted to make paintings that were different from the ones he made before, and this would be as accurate, if not more so, as what I have just written.

April 2, 1985

POSTAPPROPRIATION

Images are portable. They can travel anywhere without translation, although they mean different things in different places. The supreme art of the 20th century would have been the silent film, if the mechanical reproduction of sound hadn't offered the means for reducing a potentially universal art to a morphology of local speech patterns.

Total accessibility has its drawbacks. As you read this, you are decoding a complicatedly wrapped message, using culturally specific skills that did not fall from the skies. For many centuries, language led its own peculiarly deviant life, while images followed certain parochial ideals. Literature seldom has been as lavishly loyal to prevailing religious and political pieties as art has. Historically, "nondecorative" visual art has placed itself at the disposal of ruling elites. In former times, these consisted of priests and politicians. In our time, art itself has become a tyrannical religion, replete with its own Greater and Lesser Mysteries, its own hermetic vocabulary, its own saints and miracles.

Since this is the case, the viewer may be misled into assuming that the **Cockrill/Judge Hughes** and **Mike Bidlo** combination show currently at Semaphore Gallery (462 West Broadway, through April 13) raises different questions than it does. Cockrill/Judge Hughes are showing nine pictures featuring an array of media caricature: Jackie Kennedy and Ronald Reagan, Brooke Shields, and other overobvious material intended to convey the artists' burningly urgent political message. These aggressively stupid images exploit the vogue for lousy painting that conflates adolescent nihilism with political consciousness, and—more to the point—also exploit the artists' brief notoriety as plaintiffs in a plagiarism suit against David Salle.

These are hardly paintings. They are posters. *Suck*, a crypto-medical diagram of a large penis entering a woman's mouth, says it all: you suck, art sucks, the whole world sucks. Mike Bidlo's work, in the next room, doesn't exactly refute this message. Bidlo's 96 replicas of a Brancusi sculpture, *Mademoiselle Pogany* (1912), don't masquerade as a political act. They simply make grandiose and cynical-looking use of image-appropriation, a practice initially intended to deflate the bullish stance of artists like...Mike Bidlo.

Bidlo's duplication of other people's art has the cachet of a Conceptual art activity. After all, Sherrie Levine's photographs of other photographs and her paintings of other paintings compel questions about originality, sure, historicity, and patriarchy. However, Levine has been fastidious in her choice of targets, intelligent in her varied methods of examining specific images. Within the margins of her self-circumscribed field of inquiry, Levine has also managed to maintain, and convey, a sense of the pleasure of art-making. Bidlo's work, by contrast, operates like a virus colonizing healthy cells and defective ones alike, bleaching the interest out of paintings, sculptures, entire rock bands, and God knows what else. For Bidlo the pleasure factor exudes from publicity rather than from mere art. The company his present work keeps would seem to confirm this. Bidlo's litigious companions in Semaphore apparently feel it is wrong for an artist like David Salle to incorporate other artists' images into his work. Bidlo, on the other hand, has fashioned a career by presenting exact copies of other artists' work. This is the kind of irony that makes straightforward sleaze look enticing. Just because any idea can be appropriated and transformed into gunk doesn't mean that gunk is precious. Gunk is gunk, even when it looks like Jackson Pollock and issues interesting press releases.

A more piquant eschewal of originality than the above is on display at Christminster Gallery (336 East 5th Street, through April 7). **"Paint-by-Numbers: Paintings from the Peter Deatt Collection"** contains 87 works, in most cases anonymously wrought, spanning three decades of industrially assisted image-making.

Paint-by-numbers paintings are by their very nature kitsch, and none of the painters whose handiwork appears in this show had any qualms about it. The right color was invariably used to fill in the indicated area. Even so, individual differences manifest themselves in pictures of identical origin. One *Last Supper* may be flatly painted, but another will feature a thick impasto of surprisingly well-modulated color. Some painters-by-number evidently stirred their little cups of oil paint more thoroughly than others.

Thematic material here provides a plangent insight into kitsch and its persistent appeal. Shipwrecks and their gloom are a favorite, derived from the melancholy world of Caspar David Friedrich. Fishbowl kitties and waltzing Pierrots and Pierrettes are eerily familiar, as are the saucer-eyed cuddly poodles, the landscapes of autumn foliage, and the unexpectedly single *Toreador*. Urban motifs are predictably spare. Kitsch is essentially bucolic in sensibility: no Eiffel Tower without a can-can dancer prancing in front of it, no city street without a Hopperish atmosphere of emptiness beckoning one to the humble joys of the countryside. The most contemporary artifact on view in this show is an unpainted one, a paint-by-numbers E.T. What else?

The quintessence of kitsch reveals itself most naturally in the translations of fine art masterpieces, Gainsborough's *Blue Boy* and the already mentioned da Vinci *Last Supper*. The simplification of line and color effected therein—the mutation of aura into homily—is what kitsch is and always has been all about: a blurred reflection in which it is possible to see a safe and never-changing world, where men are boys, and girls swoon and frolic when the guys serenade them with their sweet guitars. Paint-by-numbers has its heart in the corn of subdued Romanticism, where life is sad but never tragic, happy but never complicated. There is no darkness in a paint-by-numbers world.

There is also very little light, which is strange. Most of these icons have a buffed, subdued appearance, a lackluster feeling. This is partly owing to age, partly to the pedagogical intention of the craft itself, i.e., to teach the hobbyist how to shade and blend colors. Few of the results are visually appalling, as true kitsch tends to be. Not to worry a point unduly, but the reason for this is that a lot of paintings similar to these circulate today as serious art, as do a lot of paintings that look considerably worse. Paint-by-numbers paintings are the purest examples of the Disney version of art. But they are hardly the only examples one can think of; just pop into Semaphore Gallery this month if you want to see others.

A final word—of praise—for **Peter Campus**. His current show of silverprint photographs at Paula Cooper Gallery (155 Wooster Street, through March 30) is one of the welcome surprises to turn up lately: large landscape photographs that avoid making any loud point about objects in the visual field, more like graciously unobtrusive cinematography à la Renoir than that dreaded ubiquity, art photography. Campus's framing, in all but a few instances, dispenses with the *punctum*. This absence is so effective that the pictures that don't observe it—landscapes organized into flashy geometries—tend to distract and irritate. The rest are free to mean nothing but themselves.

April 9, 1985

IMITATION AND ITS DOUBLE

[**Vera Lehndorff & Holger Trülzsch:** "Oxydationen." Bette Stoler, 13 White Street, through April 20.]

In the 1963 guidebook of Madame Tussaud's, the waxwork simulacrum of this institution's founder is indexed with a surprising paragraph: "With the commencement of the Reign of Terror she was in very real danger of falling a victim to the guillotine. The authorities, however, were alive to the need of a propagandist to show...how ruthlessly they were prosecuting their task of exterminating the aristocracy. David, the official artist to the Revolutionary Tribunal, suggested that the young Swiss modeler should be put to productive work. Madame Tussaud was, as the result of his intervention, forced to take death masks from the freshly severed heads." Mimesis and death often have this kind of intimate relationship. The sociopathy of the junkie and the serial murderer mimics the surrounding styles of social exchange, the verbal and physiognomic forms of reciprocal meaning. In *Zelig*, Woody Allen compulsively becomes whoever he beholds, trapped in a kind of hyperkinetic catalepsy.

Mimesis is generally thought to be protective imitation. An organism blends into the environment, becoming inconspicuous and therefore safe. In "Mimicry and Legendary Psychasthenia," however, Roger Caillois cites forms of insect mimesis that do not protect the insect. Some even render the creature more vulnerable ("geometer-moth caterpillars simulate shoots of shrubbery so well that gardeners cut them with their pruning shears.") Caillois regards this type of organic camouflage as a luxury, even an incitement to cannibalism. Some mimetic creatures fool their own kind well enough to eat each other. Caillois also develops the idea of morphological mimicry as "an actual photography," or "sculpture photography": *teleplasty*. If we apply Caillois's idea to the work of Holger Trülzsch and Vera Lehndorff, it could then be said that the 33 photographic objects now on view at Bette Stoler Gallery are examples of double photography, or teleplastic photography. In elaborate preparation for each camera exposure, the artists paint Lehndorff's body to exactly mimic part of the space to be photographed. She enters the space and displaces the area she's been painted to imitate. In certain images she disappears almost completely. She would become invisible in many of them if they were hung upside-down.

Robert Hughes mentions Piranesi in his catalogue essay for this show. Like his *Carceri* engravings, the "Oxydationen" photographs are exemplary melancholy objects, views of fragmentary structures in states of advanced decay. Piranesi's *Carceri* features an idealized, labyrinthine prison from which all hope of escape has long settled down into a listless wish. In "Oxydationen," the world is a prison of slowly rotting architectures, the human body being one of them, as well as its own prison within the surrounding penitentiary.

As in Piranesi, there are abundant visual blandishments in this jail of a world, and surprises—a scumble, in fact, of nuances. But the bracketing conceit is death, and one is likely to think not only of Piranesi but of those human outlines imprinted on the walls of Hiroshima, or of neurologist and author Oliver Sacks's descriptions of encephalitis lethargica victims who move through life in slow-motion; of mortuary sculpture; of the fetid, vegetal anamorphoses of Arcimboldo.

These pictures recommend a way of being in the world that is appreciably at odds with the dominant model of art-making, and of being an artist. That the architectural backgrounds inspiring these images were never interfered with tells us something of the artists' attitude toward the work of art and its appearance in the flow of things. The addition of another image to the vast inventory of existing ones is already an audacity, an excess of will. The method of Trülzsch and Lehndorff restricts their assertion from physically altering what already exists in the environment. This is an art of reflection rather than intervention.

Restraint of this methodical sort is one polarity of the modernist enterprise—a diligent "underwhelming" of the viewer's sensorium. At the opposite pole we find the heroic explosions of expressionism, where the desire to be seen presumes an a priori understanding between the artist and the cosmos, exempt from social reality. One can trace a jumpy line from the Enlightenment, when art was keenly interested in knowledge, in how things worked, in the archaeological recovery of the past— Piranesi, again—to the subsequent fear of advancing industrialism and social fragmentation, the concomitant desire for submission to an irrational wholeness, and the embrace of "instinctual" creativity. Here we can locate the argument in art between "heart" and "head" that's been running ever since.

This is an unfavorable period for, let's say, an art of distance. I don't mean just Conceptual art, but any art that is mediated by self-critical intention and an acknowledgment of context. Current taste is pitched toward the art of "self-expression"—organic, explosive, repetitive, obsessive—rather than art that exhibits a perspective on its own materials, containing a certain calm, a certain measure, a focused address. We might compare Wagner and Ibsen, as Shaw did: Wagner is much louder and irresistibly moving; but Ibsen is truer, more civil, and engages our autonomy instead of our receptivity to manipulation. Both kinds of art are valuable, and in either, the creative act drags the swamp of the unconscious.

The "Oxydationen" pictures add to an internal argument in contemporary art between "value" as determined by what a work of art does and "value" as fixed by what a work of art technically is. Much of the genuinely pertinent art being done right now is being done in photographic media. But the most celebrated art is that which better fulfills the condition of the commodity fetish: bigger and bigger paintings and larger and larger sculptures. One doesn't have to talk about money to deplore this situation, because the cash-effectiveness of these monstrosities is their least harmful long-term effect. What most of the giantism that appears now says in itself, and emits into modern consciousness, corrupts the mind in ways that Wagner would have shrunk from in a neurasthenic swoon.

Artists like Barbara Kruger, Jenny Holzer, and Cindy Sherman use photographic work to examine the structures (critical, psychological) that support art's commodification and its merger with modern advertising. Relatedly, Lehndorff and Trülzsch's pictures recontextualize painting in its present condition of stasis, producing images of what we would have to call temporary paintings, fixed by a photographic process and consequently distanced, metaphysically and economically, from the exacerbated realm of the commodity fetish. With respect to the ego model involved, it's clear that there are two artists, one invisible behind the camera and the other trying to be as invisible as possible in front of it. The moment of coincidence between the body and the structure enclosing it is the moment of absorption and disappearance, the moment when the eyes close (since the eyes are the only parts of the body that can't be painted over). The body becomes a painting and the painting merges with the wall and disappears. Surely this is one of the most discreet and prescient actions contemporary painting could accomplish. That we can witness it at all is a victory for intelligent photography.

April 16, 1985

DEBBY WITH MONUMENT

A package has arrived from the law offices of someone named Gustave Harrow. The enclosures relate to the proposed removal of a large piece of Cor-Ten steel from the plaza of a downtown office building. Testimony on behalf of this piece of steel has been extracted from nearly every bureaucratic luminary and bright star in the art cosmos.

These expert witnesses are unanimous on several points. The work was commissioned under contract by the General Services Administration's Art-in-Architecture Program. The artist states that removal of the work equals its destruction, as its aesthetic impact is site-specific. The public is slow to understand new art and therefore is unqualified to pass judgment on it. Removal of the work would set a dangerous precedent. The hue and cry against the work suggests "certain events, practiced in Germany's history between 1933 and 1945, which were addressed against modern art and literature." In case the public has any question about what exact dish it's been served by the GSA, European museum director Rudi Fuchs has this avuncular wisdom to offer: "… would the City of Rome ever consider to remove Bernini's fountain from Piazza Navona because it takes away a bit of sunlight? Of course not. But Richard Serra might be your Bernini." And I, to paraphrase Dottie Parker, might be Marie of Romania.

The question that seems most directly relevant to these proceedings could not very well crop up in them, but it's more or less the same one that bubbled to mind when the DIA Art Foundation began closing up its "permanent" art installations and receiving lawsuits from its "permanent" artists. Who on earth did these people think they were dealing with in the first place? Granted, everyone in public life is somehow involved with power. But if you are so enamored of it that you regularly ornament its dinner tables, ride cackling through the night in its limousines, and sign worthless contracts with it, it is no problem of mine or anyone else's if power decides, one bored afternoon, to add you to the menu instead of inviting you to eat.

Artists lavishly favored by the status quo often acquire the mentality of naturalized debutantes, complete with the delusion that favor and *arriviste* Debbyhood will last forever. "Forever" is a word with all kinds of funny meanings on the Planet Debby, but none of them is remotely synonymous with "permanent." On the Planet Debby, "permanent" is strictly a noun meaning hairdo.

The excerpted testimony supporting *Tilted Arc* reads like Flaubert's *Dictionary of Received Ideas*. Every conceivable cliché about art's relation to society has been put to work for Richard Serra by a chorus of well-off, well-meaning art specialists, who naturally see the fate of the Republic riding on the GSA's decision. Some of the clichés are true, but in this matter they are largely irrelevant. The General Services Administration is not God. Neither is Richard Serra. Either entity is capable of making a mistake, and in this case they both have. It would indeed be a dangerous precedent for the GSA, which failed to consult the public in the first place, to blithely expunge the detested object without Richard Serra's agreement. Acting by fiat, the GSA neglected its duty—obvious in this case, since many of Serra's sculptures have encountered a hostile public—to protect its funding from the kind of right-wing attack that initiated this controversy. But it is ridiculous to suppose that Richard Serra's pugnacious resistance to reasoned argument is a thing to be supported or blown into a political cause.

The only legible aesthetic argument favoring Serra's *Tilted Arc* as a site-specific work would logically demand its eventual removal, and that of everything around it: not a bad idea, depending on the methods used. The piece heightens the alienation effect of a hideous modern office building and further orchestrates the processional regimentation of the office worker en route to and from work. It is a physically abrasive, hateful piece of art. If its intention is to raise public consciousness of the surrounding architecture's inhumanity, a future public intent on overcoming its oppression would start by removing *Tilted Arc*. This enlightened public would then proceed to demolish the Jacob K. Javits Federal Building, the disgusting turquoise fountain in the plaza, and stop going to work.

This is not going to happen, and neither will *Tilted Arc* be removed, unless the powers that be perceive some unlikely, real threat to their own authoritarianism being generated by the sculpture. This public art piece does constitute an act of aggression by an individual in public space, similar to those permitted and encouraged in architectural construction by the government and various corporations. In this sense it could be interpreted as an individual's assertion of superior importance to the government and the corporations, and therefore admirable.

But this particular individual is not proposing anything terribly distinct from the aims of corporate and governmental hegemony in the public realm. He is, like them, assuming noblesse oblige over large numbers of citizens, who—hypothetically, anyway—own the space that this work occupies. Serra's unbudging insistence on the site-specific immobility of this work refuses all accommodation with the public he designed it for, and thus it becomes a fixed component in an ensemble of oppressive architecture. Moving the piece by even 20 degrees would afford better access to the plaza and the building, but Serra has obviously read *The Fountainhead* and thinks this would be deadly compromise with squat-minded office sheep. *Tilted Arc* is a prototype of what the government and the corporations would gladly do if they could get away with it in such a blatant manner, the dream-fulfillment of a macho universe of bigger and bigger ugly obstructions to freedom of movement.

Serra has nothing to fear: his dream will undoubtedly be realized throughout Manhattan, if not the world, even if the realization does not have his name stamped all over it. If he is a true idealist, as he seems to be, this absence shouldn't bother him. But since he is also an artist, it does. In his public utterances on this matter, Serra has come increasingly to sound like Albert Speer, though he probably imagines himself Thomas Mann, Bertolt Brecht, and Walter Benjamin all rolled into one. Perhaps the answer is to sell him the entire building complex for a dollar and let Serra pay the taxes on it.

Let me draw your attention for a moment to the notion of public sculpture. If public sculpture consists of aesthetic objects placed in public space by the state and by corporate boards, it is the duty of every citizen to pay attention to the myriad examples of public sculpture which the state and corporate boards have placed on the sidewalks of the Lower East Side and other New York neighborhoods, without fanfare, since the election of Ronald Reagan.

I am referring to that genre of public sculpture known popularly as "the Homeless." These lifelike sculptures are positioned on every street, and typically solicit money "to get something to eat," "to buy a drink," and for other less intelligible purposes. Anyone who has observed the proliferation of these objets d'art and listened carefully to the messages they emit will have noticed certain refinements in the genre over the last five years.

In the late 1970s, most of these sculptures were decrepit, caked with grime, and seemed to display the latter stages of terminal alcoholism. Since the election of our current leader, however, fewer and fewer of them have been hopelessly incoherent. This is because there are thousands more of them, recently dispossessed. But the people who occupy their former homes know enough to regard them as nonhuman entities, to confront them as aesthetic objects—untouchable vehicles of "aura," worthy of investment on the basis of their degree of cleanliness and lucidity. A sculpture that pukes its guts out in a gutter cannot be compared in aesthetic value with one that dresses with a certain flair and has an engaging rap programmed into its circuitry.

These public works wear down, exposed as they are to the elements and to the indifference of the human swarm that passes by them: they die, in public hospitals or on the street— uncollected by avatars of aesthetic sensibility like the Thyssen-Bornemiszas who financed Hitler as well as Andrew Crispo; unremembered by the Gracie Mansions and Bianca Jaggers who have given so much, so unstintingly, to the society in which we are forced to live by the sheer accident of birth.

Yet they define the space of public sculpture in a sense that a hunk of steel emanating from a drawing board in Richard Serra's office never could. They occupy real space, as distinct from the space of idealistic projections, utopian fantasies, and masturbatory empires. They are the brothers and sisters of the people huddled in the halls of the Jacob K. Javits Federal Building waiting to be photographed for immigration documents. They couldn't care less if Richard Serra's contract with the GSA is abrogated. Their contract with anything has been severed at the nerve by the government Richard Serra expects to do the proper democratic thing. That government has demonstrated, for the past five years, that it is capable of any deception, any illegality, capable indeed of anything. Compared to what it does every day to those ordinary people who can't understand modern art, knocking over some egomaniac's prefab sculpture is a hilarious canard. In case Richard Serra never heard this from anybody else, I'd like him to hear it from me: lie down with dogs, get up with fleas.

April 23, 1985

THE WINDEX OF VULNERABILITY

[Gretchen Bender. Nature Morte, 204 East 10th Street, through April 28]

On the wall opposite the front window of Nature Morte, there is an eight-foot-high, four-foot-wide, two-piece Plexiglas construction, lit by a square fluorescent fixture behind the upper panel. The top section is a Duratrans version of a Jack Goldstein painting: something like an eyeball with a deep red-violet pupil and an iris a lighter shade of the same color, with a blue-violet ring around it, a sky-blue halation around that, all floating in a shock-white which also crackles up from the perimeter of the pupil. The outer circumference shades off from light to deep blue into ink black. The lower panel is a black-on-clear-Plexi photo silkscreen that casts a grainy shadow on the wall behind the see-through areas. It shows an upheld human hand, clutching a human heart.

The horrific allure of this high-tech splice by Gretchen Bender equals the amorphous quantity that binds media image to media spectator like a hypnotic jelly. The atavistic offering to the eye is the spectator's own heart, just as the eye is the spectator's own eye. In the universe of media spectacle, what we're shown is what we create the desire to see—with a lot of help from our invisible friends "out there," in Corporationville, who bring good things to life. They anticipate our image needs, expanding our capacity for symbolism as an alternative mode of life. They are guiding us, ever so gently, into the fourth dimension, where we are destined to become media-perfect symbols of our former selves. And, of course, they are us, too, especially now that "we are the world."

Bender's work folds in plenty of material from static visual media like painting and photography, but its current emphasis is on movies and television. In the Nature Morte show, four light boxes in black Plexi have slide strips running across them. These carry teeny white titles of future film releases, gleaned from *Variety*. Up close, they sparkle. Needles of chill blue and glacier white twinkle at their serifs. They have been through the star filter.

REVOLUTION

LIFE FORCE

MADE IN HEAVEN

SWEET DREAMS

A profusion of image-bearing paper strips shoots down from the ceiling along the opposite wall. The pictures are whole and partial television frames, captured hot off the cathode by a Mitsubishi Electric video printer. Now we can have what *we* want us to see, and keep it, too. The pictures are 3 ¼" x 4" except when sliced into synecdoche. (Bender has had fun with the top of Johnny Carson's head, among other things, making it look like a phase illustration of the moon.) These muddy, purplish sepia extracts of corporate video freeze an incessant torrent. Their extreme weirdness becomes even weirder when we consider that this stuff represents what many people look at during most of their free time: creamy cake frosting, Willy Nelson, wave patterns, explosions, *ABC News*, Sally Fields accepting an Oscar, Calvin Klein's *Obsession*, a box of napkins flying through the desert, horizontal wobble, vertical roll, screaming victims, unpleasant-looking alien life forms, situation comedies, situation docudramas, situationist MTV, metallic ball forms spraying off bits of glittery magma, clips from *Amadeus*, Prince, Japanese variety shows, corporate logos spinning in hyperspace—all simmering at equal temperature, everything melting into everything else.

Bender is trying to vivisect the libidinal suckers that project from the media worm. If the results often seem as confusing as the stuff on the operating table, it's because the creature in question is notoriously adept at mutation. "The media," like Dr. Fu Manchu, wear a million masks and are everywhere and nowhere all at once. Unlike Fu Manchu, mass media do not seem to know with any precision what they want to do, except to perpetuate themselves, sell products, and attempt to maintain the population in a state of dippy-sexy idiocy that lends itself to manipulation.

This is already a great deal, of course. The scientific precision with which demographics are translated into huge economic events certainly works as the white bread equivalent, in real life, of Sax Rohmer's Yellow Peril. However, as H. M. Enzensberger pointed out many years ago, the consciousness industry cannot create by itself. To function effectively, it must offer its trance subjects the continual impression of originality, nuance, innovation; it must, therefore, remain permeable by things that are alien to it, things it may regard as insignificant that carry seeds of large, incalculable changes. Like artists and intellectuals. This is obviously a window of vulnerability that some of *we* who are the world would like to close: Jesse Helms, to name one, and the Reverend Falwell, to name two. All the more reason to pay attention to the mechanism. We might just figure out which of all of *we* is really *whom*. We can't always be sure what we are trying to tell ourselves, world though we are. Some of we have more to say about it than others, and not all of we want the same things.

BIG TROUBLE
RETURN OF THE LIVING DEAD
BETTER OFF DEAD
TARGET

Gretchen Bender thinks that a static breakdown of image gush is useful, but inadequate to the moment. The works in her show are sketches and research products related to her video performance, *Dumping Core*. *Dumping Core* was shown at Millennium on the night Bender's show opened. Its present edit runs 15 minutes, a dark symphony of computer graphics, corporate symbols, specks of light, snippets of TV narratives, news images, commercials. Stuart Arbright and a music group called Death Comics provided the raw material for the sound track: special effect movie music, computer drumbeats, available noise.

Dumping Core was shown on several monitors. As someone allergic to video art I expected the worst and was surprised enough to stay for another screening. These kinds of video presentations were epidemic in the '70s, and to see them twice was usually to glean even less from them the second time. *Dumping Core* was, is, different—not so much "video art," which tends to be as beautiful as Xerox, but television deconstruction with at least as much control as television.

Image-sequences were pulsed across the monitors in syncopation with scanning patterns created by earlier parts of the work, then withdrawn, dumped, replaced by others. All the material came from the currently familiar repertoire of mass media. In this context, worked through various kinds of repetition and set to appropriate bursts of military noise, this stuff performed a bizarre dance of seduction and self-betrayal. Corporate symbol, bathed in its luxurious special effects, accompanied the sounds of corporate reality—in the little window of the world we never were.

April 30, 1985

THE REST OF EVERYTHING

There is every excuse to impose a decorative order on existence. Life could be a Byzantine fraud, and it's all we have. A sense of order is, in the end, nothing more than the chill we get from reading Gaston Leroux's description of "a drawing room at the bottom of a lake" in *The Phantom of the Opera*. Form is oppressive; formlessness is terrifying. Embellishment is a domestication of this paranoia: consider the intricacies of Islamic carpeting, fraught with centuries of faith and phobia. *It is there*, the visual hum of being.

Part of the decorative scheme is a horror of the void. The other part is categories. If we didn't know what this newspaper space was designed to contain, I would be telling you about E. K. and Click Playgroup, *The Purple Rose of Cairo*, and the delightful reemergence of E. M. Cioran in the pages of the *Atlantic*. These were all things that decorated a fairly anemic week in the art world. They all agree comfortably with my personal idea of what "art" includes. In the context of newspapers and magazines, however, everything cited above divides into rigid categories. Music, literature, cinema, art: one can relate things inhabiting different slots in the grid, but the grid itself is a semantic geometry imposed on perception.

It wouldn't be useful to weave a pattern around the things that blipped across the screen this week. A different choice of works to look at might have yielded a unified conspiracy concept, or a speculative essay on the renewed significance of Nancy Grossman's sculpture. The Clemente shows seemed a refinement of the idea that too much of a good thing is beyond the scope of any contemporary artist. The show Tricia Collins and Richard Milazzo organized at Cash/Newhouse, "Final Love," will be down before you read this, so I can only urge you to view their next curatorial effort: they invest so much excited thought and sly wit in what they do that whether one agrees with them or not feels perfectly irrelevant. Daisy Youngblood's sculptures at Barbara Gladstone are pellucid, morbid objects, but they fall outside the scope of this week's subject.

This is further to saying that in a given week, even in a given month, there may be too much going on for a coherent pattern in a given field to emerge. Or too little happening for the objects of attention to mean much without excessive help. Of course, too much or too little for one person may be quite enough for another, depending on the moment of encounter. The same person for whom something does nothing on Day X may find the same something looming large in his or her sensorium on Day Y, weeks, months, or years later. The autonomy of an artwork assumes the work's enrichment as it persists through time, although public encounters with a work may be limited, in a given era, by the vicissitudes of private ownership. Presumably, collectors experience the fullest range of a work's potential affect, encountering it often under diverse conditions.

The interest of an artist like **Joyce Kozloff** relates to this kind of ideal multiplicity of affect. It engages a sizable chunk of psychological space between the rarefied art object and "the public." Kozloff's principal current work consists of ceramic architectural decoration. Some of it occupies much-traveled areas like the Harvard Square subway station in Cambridge, eliciting attention in a differently distracted way than work in a gallery. It is art meant to be seen repeatedly by the same audience and strives for an ambient quality while providing long-term visual interest.

Technically, Kozloff's work is decorative art, ornamentation of space. Writers like E. H. Gombrich have stressed that such art normally doesn't grab our attention but rather serves as visual background. The Kozloff projects on paper being shown at Barbara Gladstone Gallery (152 Wooster Street, through May 4) belie this limited idea. They are watercolor architectural caprices, projecting the stolid calm of Viollet-le-Duc's studies from Italy. Moreover, they are charming fantasies which presume a certain order in things, and at the same time recommend ways that existing objects could be shifted and used to produce pleasure. For instance, see *Otto Wagner on Union Square*, which transports the Vienna Stadtbahn entrance idea to 14th Street.

Kozloff brings visual patterns from Islamic and other sources into designs for spaces where their cultural specificity dissolves, in a certain sense. Ornament exudes from particular models of consciousness. Thrusting different kinds of ornament into proximity relieves them of overdetermined meanings and affords traditional ornament a second breath. Kozloff has reinvented the Palazzo Ducale in Urbino as a subway station, the Jardin des Plantes as an elevated Metro, and a Chinese vase design as the plan for a public swimming pool, in lapidary colors, with the linear complexity of Persian rugs and mosque façades. Looking at Kozloff's watercolors, one wishes these caprices were realized on a grand scale, in New York City—they would enrich our environment sensually, rather than brutalize it further.

Peter Halley's current show at International With Monument (111 East 7th Street, through April 28) addresses our ravaged psychological environment in terms of the spatial and cellular configurations we're trapped in. Halley's big, rebarbative paintings feature Day-Glo and geometric areas encrusted with stucco; they are sectioned to suggest units of energy squeezed into tightly sealed containers. The abstract squares and rectangles shown in these works represent systems of imprisonment (factories, jails). The arithmetic exactitude Halley uses to isolate surface areas looks like it's at war with the oppressive heaviness of the stucco and the mind-numbing garishness of the Day-Glo— as if the inchoate energies of life, as well as the physical muck life moves around in, were sharply intersected by impermeable lines of force. These pictures combine extreme ugliness with formal elegance. Some of them even evoke the idea that perfect elegance can be read as perfect ugliness. Unlike the now-generic "bad" painting that first added magenta and chartreuse to its aerosol palette, Halley's work displays an artisanal rigor appropriate to its thematic content.

Halley's pictures simulate uniformity, regimentation, coercion. They deal with the physical organization of space, but also with the spatial organization of consciousness. Form is projected onto formlessness by architecture, transport systems, lines of communication, speech patterns, art. Kozloff's work proposes the reform and refinement of the extant, thickly evolved "spatialization" of our surroundings. Halley's work raises awareness of this spatialization's rigidity, its repressive layering, its repetitiveness. Halley's method opens space for this work by condensing several metaphors of closure; Kozloff slices into the web of received forms and moves pieces of it to new locations.

May 7, 1985

FRAMING CREATURES

Hunt Slonem's current show at Barbara Braathen Gallery (76 Duane Street, through June 1) is called "All About Eden." The 18 or so oil paintings on exhibit show a fruity-colored jungle paradise of palm fronds and lily pads, amicably co-inhabited by tigers and toucans, monkeys and ducks, rabbits and turtles. The paintings are largish—mainly 84 inches by 72 inches— and densely textured. If "vibrant" weren't a dead word to describe color, one could say that Slonem's paintings vibrate all over the place.

Slonem uses raw and mixed colors with equal facility, juggling them within figurative boundaries to produce a sensuously overripe, overpacked pictorial effect. *The Shimmering Pulse of Expectation,* a juicily crowded daydream of tropical vegetation, looks like an effusion of brushstrokes that sprays outward from deep inside the picture itself and settles fortuitously into clear composure. The impasto in this work recalls the patterning in certain Klimt paintings of trees and parks. The acidic orange and blue squiggles and blobs, however, have more in common with Georgia Marsh's recent abstract gouaches on Chinese vellum.

The almost illustrational drawing style Slonem employs, combined with the disarming innocence of his equatorial fantasies, places him outside the ken of "engaged" or polemical art. More interesting still, Slonem has no especially salient ties to the limp and lavish "painterly" self-expressionism that so often masquerades, lately, as an art of social protest. There is a tendency within the *nouveau Fauviste* crowd to view Slonem as a naïve child in a room full of crafty grown-ups, a latter-day Henri Rousseau; that is exactly wrong, but a predictable critical stratagem for infantilizing a really good artist.

Slonem's work isn't naïve at all: it is reproachful, in a sense, even inconsolable, despite its sweetness, its ostensive lack of argument, its visual generosity. In a picture like *The Great Antediluvian Passion*, which has a variety of wildlife ranged in an ascending S-form, the narrative detail near the base of the canvas—an ocelot raising its paw as if to make friends with a white-faced teal—diverts attention from a less homiletic but finally more moving circumstance. The toucans, monkeys, parrots, and lemurs perched in the picture, and possibly even the three large turtles ambulating across the bottom, are *looking at us*, appraisingly, with wary curiosity. They peer from an artificial, tropical fantasia, grouped most unnaturally, perhaps huddled together for protection from us.

Slonem's pictures articulate a fabric designer's fantasy about what remains of nature. But their very ebullience and baroque elaborations deliberately refract our gaze from felicitous Eden to the inorganic world, where Slonem's souvenirs of vanishing flora and fauna can exist only as nostalgic decoration. There are places in the world where Slonem's dream creatures still populate the trees and puncture the night with their voices. But they won't be there for long. A world of uninhibited commerce has them marked for destruction, along with their natural habitat.

At the outset of industrialism, an effulgence of feeling for our fellow creatures manifested itself in art and literature, passionately. The writings of Darwin, connecting man biologically with the rest of the animal world, refuted the Cartesian, mechanistic view of nature, as well as the Catholic myths of species superiority founded in the Biblical fairy tale of Creation. In non-Catholic countries like England, particularly, Darwin's enlightening research brought wide respectability to a body of humane thinking fostered by the Romantic poets and by the growth of pet-keeping among the middle and lower classes. (The rich always had their animals.) Then, too, a fascination with nature may automatically have accompanied the perception that it was on the verge of disappearance.

The response in art was the pictorial exploitation of things that had always been around—sunsets, rainbows, meadows, wild beasts, barnyard animals—as these became distant form urban perception. Painters of animals enjoyed a great vogue throughout most of the 19th century. *Les Animaliers,* the recent show (now closed) at the School of Visual Art's museum, contained choice examples of the genre in France, ranging from the near-sublime Gérôme's *Camels at the Watering Place* to several near-execrable offerings by the fascinating Rosa Bonheur. This show worked as a poignant reminder that our relationship to nature has drastically changed since the last century, when artists scrambled to the countryside for inspiration.

Our continuing alienation from nature has become effectively invisible. Nature registers as beautiful, irrelevant, yearly glimpsed scenery. Most of us never witness what human beings do to the natural world and its creatures. But we suffer for it morally. For instance, whenever those Satan worshippers over at Procter & Gamble dream up a new detergent, they rub it into the eyes of hundreds of rabbits immobilized in laboratory harnesses. And whenever we lift a morsel of white veal to our mouths, we can rest assured that the calf it was ripped from was deprived of iron and roughage throughout its brief passage from birth to slaughter—in a pen it couldn't turn around in. Those guys in the boardroom who bring good things to life bringeth and taketh away at a distant remove from our attention.

David True's paintings and etchings at Edward Thorp Gallery (103 Prince Street, through May 11) and **Daisy Youngblood**'s sculptures at Barbara Gladstone (152 Wooster Street, through

May 4) reflect the dire condition of the organic in different ways. While Slonem's paintings are utopian, True's seem distilled from the negative utopianism of the apocalyptic. In some works, True's striking use of two and three panels of unequal width, slightly spaced apart, extends the elusive, ravaged physicality of his animal and human images into narrative spaces. The figures themselves are sometimes partly drawn, partly painted, sliced up by the compositional velocities. True extends from one panel into another.

True's dogs and deer graze between verisimilitude and artifice; one antlered animal is basically a sawhorse draped with strips of hide, another is a horse wearing an antler-barrette. Humans often appear as cryptic, vaguely moronic presences, faces of the "draw me" variety in large scale, staring down or up at leaping and arcing animals. True evokes the tangled reciprocity between marginalized nature and marginalized people and their artifacts in *Near Dark Light* (84" x 108"): a deer is attached to the roof of a car, the car trapped in the topmost branches of a tree, while the presumed driver is buried nearby, reduced to a shirt, necktie, and a pair of legs.

Youngblood's eight new sculptures in low-fire pigmented clay are modest in scale, modeled with a nervous elegance that balances fragility and hollowness with an intense projection of sympathetic form. Their colors range from the mottled bluish bronze to an almost powdery light blue-gray and ocher; the emphatic deathliness of Youngblood's subjects—an upright steer with a skeletal head, a prostrate, slit-open antelope—is unexcited, melancholic rather than apocalyptic. Youngblood's works look like archaeological discoveries, miraculous little treasures preserved by a volcanic eruption. In this show, the human presence is confined to an immutably silent mask and a torso attached to a head whose face has forgotten how to scream.

May 14, 1985

MAPPLETHORPE

[**Robert Mapplethorpe.** Robert Miller, 724 Fifth Avenue, through May 15.]

Robert Mapplethorpe's photography demands the kind of diplomatic immunity that only the most persuasively self-abandoning artistic venture deserves. Like the late novels of Céline, many Mapplethorpe pictures mirror experiences that would normally compel other responses than aesthetic ones. The strength of Mapplethorpe's art is that it defines strong experience more intensely than an uninvolved, moralizing observer could, while registering the peculiarity of its own enterprise. In Céline's work, the freighted material is daily life among the middle echelons of Nazi society, while in Mapplethorpe's it has often been the dehumanized extremities of homosexual lust.

Scarcely a photographer alive could cover the terrain Mapplethorpe has without plunging deep into witless vulgarity or blatant exploitation. Mapplethorpe's influence on other photographers has been unsalutary, for the same reason that William Burroughs's influence on other writers has been entirely deleterious. An obsessive artist spawns epigones galore, but his/her self-imitations are as close as anyone gets to the real thing. Mapplethorpe combines a preternatural refinement with an insatiable appetite: he can traffic in banalities and make them fresh, or tunnel into forbidden zones of scopophilia without losing grace. His signature is so distinct that he can easily plunder other photographers' cherished turf and claim it, while no one seems capable of "doing a Mapplethorpe"—attempts range from tacky shock tactics (Joel-Peter Witkin) to the eroticization of contempt (Bruce Weber).

Mapplethorpe's career has been one of escalating risk. After minting his horrific S&M images in the '70s, he proceeded to photograph, among other things, naked black men, blacks holding guns and knives, blacks with enormous baskets, and blacks with huge cocks snaking out of their trousers. He filled an entire book with pictures of bodybuilder and curator Lisa Lyons that outraged feminist antipornographers. What is even more damning to many people, is the fact that Mapplethorpe continually accepts portrait commissions from the high and mighty, and will photograph almost anything for sufficient remuneration. The qualms various people express about Mapplethorpe's work are certainly justified, when they aren't inflated into censorious hyperbole. There are at least two ways of viewing every Mapplethorpe photograph; for viewing Mapplethorpe's production as a whole, there are many.

Mapplethorpe's current show of platinum and large color transparencies offers a respite from some of the "issues" that attach, barnaclelike, to Mapplethorpe's *content*. As far as I know, only the works in color, mounted on light boxes, have not been shown previously in silver print versions. These pieces feature models in high punk fashion lit by varicolored lights, some encircled, Deco-style, in colored backlighting. In these works Mapplethorpe achieves a strong sculptural effect of volume with colored gels. Mapplethorpe has manipulated the gels to draw precise lines and areas of color on the model, where fashion photographers would "bathe" the subject in an undifferentiated field. One female nude, cropped midthigh and above the breasts, absorbs Mapplethorpe's lighting as if it were body paint. Some of the models are black, one who isn't is holding a knife, and all of them exude the minatory eroticism that is one of Mapplethorpe's difficult qualities.

The platinum prints are arranged in red, black, gossamer, and white frames. The free range of subject matter indicates that Mapplethorpe has edited this show according to what would translate into platinum beautifully, and it all does. And the promiscuous mixture—leg in fishnet stocking, marble cross, art collector Doris Saatchi—achieves the opposite effect from Irving Penn's recent retrospective at MOMA. Penn's work looked consistently commercial. Mapplethorpe's looks consistently like art, however slick and fashionable Mapplethorpe tries to be. Penn's "art" photos served as ineffective apologies for a career in *Vogue*; Mapplethorpe's forays into *Vogue* territory test the edges of fashion.

Mapplethorpe's show isn't pointed anywhere, ideologically. But the reification of certain images from glossy plastic laminate into the richly willed preciosity of platinum carries its own current of audacity. His selection is shamelessly "incorrect." *Francesco Clemente* and *Doris Saatchi*, for instances, might be the obligatory obsequies in any number of photography shows. Yet Mapplethorpe's portraits forcefully undermine the bloated self-importance of these subjects by etherealizing them beyond the call of duty. Clemente stands in an awkward, self-pitying pose in front of one of his larger masterpieces, trying for a look of unwilled magnetism—the sort of look Giacometti came by naturally. Saatchi wears the fraudulently pensive, angelic countenance of some Knightsbridge socialite searching her memory for what intense concentration might look like. At the same time, the flesh wears off these people as if time were melting them down. So does the force of their assumed pretentions. They look marooned in their chosen attitudes.

Mapplethorpe's portrait subjects never appear as if they've been manipulated against their better judgment. They invariably read as people in collusion with the demonic vision they believe they're encountering. For me, Mapplethorpe's brilliance resides in the space he allows his subjects, whether or not they perceive this space in a useful way. He wants a beautiful picture, and won't print anything less. But it has to be a truthful picture, one that the subject would, on some level "agree with." On this point, the racism attributed to Mapplethorpe's studies of blacks seems a callow charge. It presumes a white proprietary interest in the behavior of black people who have chosen to appear in front of Mapplethorpe's camera.

There are few of the stormier porn images in this show, though one, a white man's fist clutching his enormous, stiff, bent dick, has the same harsh elegance as the numerous voluptuous studies of flowers (which are, lest we forget, sexual organs). One of the most startling pictures shows a dead pheasant dangling from a string, like something in a Harnett painting, its tail, feet, and body breaking the image area into peculiarly balanced pieces. Another is *The Coral Sea*, a study of an American aircraft carrier in Naples Harbor. The photograph is 19 ¼ inches across and 22 ¼ inches high (most of the pictures in this are 19 ¼ inches square); the carrier itself, which is almost flush with the picture's bottom edge, runs 10 inches across at its widest points and two inches high from the top of the mast to the water line. In other words, the ship is almost invisible at first glance. It's surrounded by an almost uninflected field of gray. The line between the water and the sky has been obliterated by 4 a.m. mist. This picture needs a close, careful look to reveal the war planes parked across the carrier's deck, the curved strings of light running down from either side of the mast. The splendid isolation of the ship, its subtle presence in a neutral-colored fog, its quiet threat to the surrounding calm: *The Coral Sea* is a perfect metaphor for Robert Mapplethorpe.

May 21, 1985

ART OBJECTS

[**Hans Haacke.** John Weber, 142 Greene Street, through May 25]

Since 1971, when his work documenting Manhattan's real estate network was banned by the Guggenheim Museum, Hans Haacke has become—despite growing competition—one of the most often censured and censored artists in the free world. A recent Haacke piece, *U.S. Isolation Box, Grenada 1983*, rattled the ordinarily dreary Savonarola of Suburbia, Hilton Kramer, into delirious imitation of Joseph Goebbels. Curiously, the wooden sculpture that promoted such mouth-foaming editorial asperity in *The New Criterion* itself asserted no polemical pushiness, beyond the plain labeling of what it duplicated, i.e., a torture device used by the U.S. military in a prison camp.

Many of Haacke's elegant-looking art objects transport widely available cultural data (photographs, texts, statistics) to the rarefied precinct of art, recasting them in standard materials and familiar Conceptual schemes. Because of their content, the shift in context plays havoc with the communal fiction that art knows nothing about the social, economic, and ideological forces that permeate it. *On Social Grease*, a 1975 exhibition of six engraved aluminum plaques, immortalized PR fatuities (from Nelson Rockefeller, Frank Stanton, Richard Nixon, and others) about the corporate sector's tarty embrace of the arts. Embalmed as art, these tossed-off bits of speechwriter's verbiage emit more sincerity, and hence more menace, than they were intended to. In plaque form the message is: art is a religion of unknowing that can make big business look like God. Haacke's work is sacrilegious, destructive of an entire belief-structure. By contrast, much contemporary modern art is merely blasphemous, aimed at shattering (or, more typically, tweaking) aesthetic norms. It ultimately reaffirms the status quo by joining it, despite its own intentions.

In Haacke's new show, certain prominent cultural show-persons are pinned to their less advertised political and business operations. *Voici Alcan* (1983) consists of three photo-enclosing, 86 ½ inches by 41 inches aluminum-edged display windows suspended from cut-plastic symbols of Alcan Aluminum, Ltd., a Canadian-based multinational. The left panel, a sepia ad for an Alcan-sponsored presentation of *Lucia di Lammermoor*, runs the company's ad copy at the bottom, augmented by the information that "from a nonwhite work force of 2300, the company has trained eight skilled workers." The central panel contains a post-autopsy color photograph of Stephen Biko, the South African black leader murdered by police interrogators. Its text says that "Alcan's South African affiliate sells to the South African government semifinished products…used in police and military equipment." The right panel, sepia again, features a related text under an ad for the Montreal Opera Company's Alcan-produced *Norma*.

Voici Alcan duplicates the technical hermeticism of corporate advertising, the appearance of egregious expense, persuasive type-face, arresting scale, and perfect printing. It also possesses the awful gravity of art. Biko's tortured, sewn-together body ridicules the flanking pictures of costumed "emoting" opera stars. The panels' uniform, banal streamlining purveys a pathetic reality, reality "sponsored," "presented," by faceless entities for whom an opera extravaganza and a convenient political killing are all in the day's work. In this piece and many others, Haacke sticks the logo on both displays of economic power.

Taking Stock, Haacke's 1983–84 oil portrait of Margaret Thatcher, is regally scaled (95 inches by 81 inches by 7 inches) and wrought in a naturalistic style of bright-lit court flattery. Thatcher, in a blue gown, head defiantly up-tilted, sits in front of a red curtain, near a table adorned with a classical sculpture. A column runs aside the curtain. Part of a bookcase is visible in the far background. On its top shelf are two cracked plates; one bears the portrait of Maurice Saatchi, the other that of his brother, Charles.

The books are titled with names of various businesses, municipal organizations, and political parties with which the advertising empire of Saatchi & Saatchi has accounts, including Black & Decker, British Arts Council, Campbell Soup, Conservative British Elections, Daily Mail, IBM, Johnson and Johnson, South Africa Nationalist Party, Serpentine Gallery, Walt Disney, Wrangler. Inscribed at the base of the column: ES SAATCHI TRUST/ITECHAPEL GAL/TRONS OF NEW/ART COMMITTEE/HE TATE/GALLER.

The Thatcher portrait is a pomp-heavy icon of a modern monster, who not long ago was transformed from lowering dowdiness into royal rigor mortis by the image-brilliant Saatchi firm. It ran her election campaigns of 1979 and 1983, softened the shrillness of her voice, crowned her with a less terrifying hairdo, and taught her to carry herself like a queen—rather, like *the* queen. The Saatchis also worked alterations on the opposition. To quote from Haacke's text, "One of the ads suggested that the Labor Party platform was identical with that of the British Communist Party...after the Tory victory of 1979 Mrs. Thatcher handed the $25 million British Airways account over to the Saatchi's...."

Haacke's portrait is rich in dreadful allusion. On the table edge, a drooping sheet of paper reads: "In the year 1978 Brogan Developers Ltd. (Saatchi Investment Ltd.) sold artworks valued at £380,319." Doris and Charles Saatchi are insatiable collectors of contemporary art. Charles, while an active member of the Tate Gallery's Patrons of New Art Committee and the Whitechapel Gallery's board of trustees, gobbled up a mother lode of then-cheap pictures by Julian Schnabel (ergo the cracked plates) and other not-quite-legends. Surprise, major shows of these artists were already being planned at either the Tate or the Whitechapel. The Saatchis acted as major lenders therein, and their collection's value was immeasurably boosted thereby.

MetroMobilitan, devised specially for the Weber Gallery show, is a scaled-down fiberglass model of the entablature above the Metropolitan Museum's entrance. It features a center plaque with a legend from a pamphlet, "The Business Behind Art knows the Art of Good Business—Your Company and the Metropolitan Museum of Art." Three wide, Met-style banners flutter from the architrave. The middle one advertises "TREASURES OF ANCIENT NIGERIA," a 1980 Met exhibition funded by Mobil Oil. Left and right banners carry quotes from Mobil's letter of refusal, in response to shareholders' requests, to curb its dealings with South Africa's police and military: "Total denial of supplies to the police and military forces…is hardly consistent with an image of responsible citizenship." Recessed behind the banners, an immense black-and-white photomural shows a Cape Town funeral march for blacks murdered by police.

Like the other works in this show, *MetroMobilitan* has a strong artisanal poise, a precise economy. It's didactic enough to fire restless thoughts, and displays a brazen, courageous wit. Haacke's art is generous, though never at all slavish, to the sensual needs of the spectator. It supplies what Haacke, citing Brecht, often calls the "culinary" element. Indeed, Haacke's work would not be effective as plain printed documentation, though it could be synopsized that way. It relies on the aura of art for its power, and things being what they are, probably needs it for protection.

May 28, 1985

GOODBYE, JACKIE

When I saw Jackie Curtis a few days before his death last Wednesday, he looked healthier than he had in years and said he was taking acting classes under an assumed name. "I want to expand my range," he said, "so I can do male parts…I don't think I'll act as a woman for a long time." Jackie had already done beautifully realized parts "as a man," as Eric Mitchell's depressive roommate in the film *Underground U.S.A.* and as a male hustler who robs my luxury apartment in Michel Auder's video *A Coupla White Faggots Sitting Around Talking*. Despite Jackie's indubitable status as a glamorous movie star, he was always a bit insecure of his craft, and looking to sharpen it. He spoke that last time of starting a whole new life.

Jackie's range encompassed more than gender. Five minutes of conversation with Curtis could plant you deep in a fantasy that transformed the effervescent clutter of his apartment into Carole Lombard's dressing room. He was one of those rare people whose sense of unreality would never take no for an answer: Jackie wouldn't permit you to get depressed in his presence, never had a bad word for anyone unless it was screechingly funny, and even then he couldn't be really mean if he tried. Well, perhaps on one or two odd occasions.

He was born 38 years ago. His real name was John Holder. Jackie Curtis was an ingenious writer whose poems and plays reflect his daffy wit and frazzled elegance. Many of the plays were produced at LaMama Theater: *Glamour, Glory and Gold, Heaven*

Grand in Amber Orbit (directed by John Vaccaro in 1969), *Vain Victory*. Among many other roles, Jackie played the female leads in *Tyrone X, I Died Yesterday*, and most recently *Champagne*; he had large parts in several Warhol movies—most conspicuously in *Women in Revolt*—and in Dušan Makavejev's *WR: Mysteries of the Organism*.

Jackie's theater extended into the street. But he stopped going out in drag (except on festive occasions) several years ago, saying that "life is too hard for women these days." But even without makeup and thrift-store glitz, Jackie had the charm and serendipity of an elegant child dreamer, drifting bewildered and bemused through a world of silly adults and absurd happenings. No irony was too horrid for Jackie Curtis to wrap it up in a daydream of spaghetti heels and studio lighting.

Jackie saw straight through his own Hollywood rewiring of Lewis Carroll. His life was not happy nor particularly well favored, and it was ended with grotesque abruptness. But Jackie gave a special sense of flamboyance, of sophisticated outra-geousness, and of camp-without-cruelty to his friends, and to the world, that no one who ever encountered it will fail to remember with affectionate delight, and with a profound sense of loss.

May 28, 1985

STATION TO STATION

[**Arts on the Line**, Massachusetts Bay Transportation Authority, Red Line Northwest Extension, Cambridge and Somerville.]

Because of the recent flush of interest in public art, I visited Cambridge, Massachusetts, for a look at the three new subway stations that branch westward along the Red Line from Harvard Square. Twenty works of public art, tightly integrated with the architectural planning, ornament Porter, Davis, and Alewife stations, as well as the renovated and expanded station at Harvard Square. Surely some insight regarding public art could be promoted by examining these freshly unveiled examples?

Some such thought, anyway, must have crouched behind the gentle but, looking back on it, rather firm suggestion that I punctuate my month's agenda of sexually bald and politically frontal exhibition art with a week's dose of forward-looking, civic-oriented stuff. I am nothing if not obliging, so here it is. But let's contextualize this northward junket just a wee bit in advance.

Public art, if defined as art in public places, is not a new thing. One sort of public art is commemorative, incantatory, or placatory: this kind of carbon-dates as far back as cave painting. Statues of gods in ancient Greece, statues of emperors in ancient Rome, Mount Rushmore, and the Statue of Liberty all snuggle into this category. Another species of public art is ornamental:

bridge and aqueduct design, architectural embellishment, and various other decorative elements of practical construction. In the former case, public art enshrines a metaphysical or civic ideal, glorifies a leader, commemorates the dead. In the latter, it makes the built environment more tolerable to behold.

In a sense, both types of public art are utilitarian. The subway decoration makes you feel slightly better about going to work by train, while the Statue of Liberty reinforces the ideal of "freedom" that accounts for your having to do so. Monuments make a society's or ruler's goals stolid, imperious, and seemingly immortal: no afterthought, then, that revolutions and new dictatorships require extensive statue bashing and demolition work, followed by profuse monument building and official portraiture. One plausible solution to the *Tilted Arc* dilemma would be to move the thing to Bitburg as a memorial to World War II's SS victims. I suppose it could also be dropped on Managua, but then it would cease to function as a monument.

At any rate, the public art on the Red Line Northwest Extension performs the more prosaic chore of livening up the commuter's visual environment. At Harvard Station, Joyce Kozloff's beautiful ceramic tile mural, a jigsaw of New England visual motifs (from quilt patterns to mortuary engraving) runs along the wall above a curved, descending pedestrian ramp. Nearby, György Kepes has devised a vari-shaded blue stained-glass wall with a segmented red-orange line streaking across it. The elegantly refurbished zones of Harvard Station were designed by Skidmore, Owings, and Merrill, the very firm that has caused so much of Manhattan to resemble East Berlin. Evidently, this organization's aesthetic is infinitely pliable.

In Porter Square, Mags Harries's bronze gloves rest along the metal divider between rubber escalator handrails. These gloves are wadded and twisted to resemble accidental discards. If you open André Breton's *Nadja*, you will see that precisely such a glove was considered, in the 1920s, the surrealist object par excellence.

Today's commuters scarcely register them (I watched), proving that surrealism has not only triumphed throughout American culture, but has also been superseded by TV-induced somnambulism. Also remarkable, at least for the wide-awake, is Susumu Shingu's red windmill sculpture in the Porter Square entrance plaza, with its gliderlike metal scoops digitating lazily in the wind, auditioning for several minutes in an Antonioni film; William Wainwright's aluminum and rainbow-refracting Mylar mobile in the mezzanine; and several cryptic boulders, bisected by thick slabs of greenish mottled bronze, fashioned by David Phillips.

At Davis Square, there's a painted sculpture of shaped aluminum sections projecting from the wall above the outbound train platform, this by Sam Gilliam. It catches ambient light from an overhead grid of rectangular skylighting, and faces a brick wall with sequences of inset ceramic decorated with neighborhood children's designs. Upstairs, masonry statues by James Tyler depict typical patrons of the subway and its plaza, a bit too generically for my taste; there are, for instance, two middle-class pedestrians gaping at a mime, and a flower salesman whose T-shirt reads I AM NOT A MOONIE. Would that he were.

Alewife Station: this looks the most lavish new Red line station, with a site work of inventively balanced slabs by Richard Fleischner and sinuously shaped maple love seats by William Keyser Jr. above ground; an appealing geometric arrangement of suspended neon rods by Alejandro and Moira Sina and abstract porcelain murals by David Davison below; a mural of inquisitive bovines by Joel Janowitz comprising a false exit at the mezzanine, and Nancy Webb's bronze floor tiles. Alewife is the furtherest-flung new station, surmounted by a multistory chromium-and-glass car park. Its surroundings are also the most barren. So here you have this triumph of underground design poking up in the middle of nowhere. Of course this isn't really nowhere but somewhere along the route chosen by Paul Revere to spread the British invasion news through every Middlesex village and town. A veritable Navel of the Republic.

The Red Line Northwest Extension is an impressive achievement, everything considered. The subway branch line won out over proposals to deface the area with more highway construction. It took seven years of direct planning and construction, and had actually been in the works, in one or another plan, for over 50 years. What lessons can New York extract from Cambridge's example? (And, is this the sort of reflection I was supposed to spin from a day on the train?)

None, really. Cambridge is a quiet academic town where the divisive realities of urban life melt away in the general uneventfulness. The Boston-Cambridge area's legendary racism is so firmly institutionalized that psychopaths like Bernie Goetz can amble through all but a few neighborhoods without paranoia. Its desperation is a quiet, candlelit sort, plangent at faculty dinners and young professional brunches in spacious, plant-festooned wooden frame houses. Each neighborhood has its entrenched, intractable character, and there is, somewhere or other, a neighborhood for anybody. It may be periodically terrorized by chinless, drunken townies in fag-and-nigger-hating frenzies, but it isn't likely to disappear in a hurry. Things move slowly, and one's personal ghetto isn't grossly vulnerable to overnight rape by a Donald Trump or a Harry Helmsley.

Urban improvement works well for Cambridge. New York needs an urban revolt.

June 4, 1985

THE DARK SIDE OF GILBERT AND GEORGE

An extensive view of Gilbert and George's 18 year collaboration is currently available in a traveling retrospective now at the Guggenheim Museum (1071 Fifth Avenue, through June 16) and at Sonnabend Gallery (420 West Broadway, through June 1) in a show of recent works. The artists commenced their mutual career in art school, first exhibiting themselves as "living sculptures" identically dressed in worsted suits, their exposed flesh areas and hair painted to resemble bronze or colored polystyrene. Apparently, Gilbert and George have sustained this dandyish presentation of themselves, publicly and privately, right up to the present day. According to their retrospective's catalogue essay (by Brenda Richardson), Gilbert and George "... move through life in the same uniforms which have become so familiar from the self portraits that recur in the photopieces, and they project into the world an impression of theatricality which can be frightening in its consistency."

Besides appearing in museums as objets d'art, Gilbert and George initially showed large display pieces fashioned from post-cards. These often contain serially repeated images arranged in symmetrical cross patterns. Other early works feature individually framed photographs linked by an overall design scheme. Though Gilbert and George refer to these collages as "sculptures," there is actually nothing in their entire output that strictly qualifies as such. But the artists' insistence on this term to describe two-dimensional objects is significant, and I'll return to it.

Gilbert and George's present exhibitions offer dozens of large photo-pieces in their current manner, the lion's share of which are, or contain, self-portraits. George is a tall, bespectacled, balding man whose physiognomy might be that of an embittered bank clerk, while Gilbert is stubbier, mildly handsome, and slightly less portentous-looking. Their recent works consist of photographically derived, square images, assembled in imposing square and rectangular grids that form large, cohesive pictures. The formal complexity of the work is formidable, even in a relatively simple piece like *Coloured Black*, in which a crude stencil drawing of an African mask is translated into a four-panel (red, blue, green and yellow) image. Larger works evidence a staggering sophistication of technique, a blaring audacity of visual language that mixes black and white with voluptuous color, tinted photographs with photographed drawings and designs, and the rigidity of the regular grid with expressionistic internal material.

This said, I should affirm that the content of Gilbert and George's work is no less striking than its spectacular formal quality. Their early efforts in black and white with the later addition of red, then yellow, playfully treat subjects such as intoxication, loneliness, fear, race relations, and urban desuetude. However, since 1980 the artists have narrowed their focus, in increasingly splashy colors, to a limited range of material: themselves, crosses as religious symbols, adolescent working-class men, flowers, monumental sculpture, and urban architecture. Or, more descriptively, adolescent working-class men depicted as sex objects, Gilbert and George leering at adolescent working-class men from various elevations, Gilbert and George mooning up at adolescent working-class men from supine positions, Gilbert and George bowered in flowers and gazing at flower-festooned adolescent working-class men, the compositions sometimes decorated with religiously symbolic crosses, sometimes not, Gilbert and George looking at each other, Gilbert and George praying, an occasional chunk of photographed sculpture or modern building thrown in for heightened suggestiveness, and so on.

Perhaps the smell of dank tenement hallways and boiled cabbage that pervades these works would be less acute if Gilbert and George were themselves comelier as objects. Perhaps not. Their gelidly pederastic interest in the extremely junior youths in their pictures might then appear less masochistic, and at the same time less exploitative, than it obviously is. Leaving aside the strong impression that the formal elaborateness of their art-making must somehow mimic whatever intricate, predatory formalities are involved in luring these teenage Adonises with rotten teeth home to the studio, the lurid obeisance to formal religion displayed throughout G & G's recent work is consistent with a long tradition of dandyism, traceable to Oscar Wilde and the more turgid, cloying passages of *De Profundis*. This, in turn, echoes the normative hypocrisy of a conservative yet sexually liberated age, in which any desire is permissible if the desired performs as an economic object rather than a human being, and the desire is gratified by exploitation rather than parity—hence providing a source of sadomasochistic guilt, and therefore available as a religious experience.

While Gilbert and George have been widely praised for their boldness of subject matter, the sensibility infusing its treatment is the most self-abnegating and destructive mode of homosexual dandyism, infatuated with religious ceremony as the spiritual equivalent of furtive seduction. Beautification is the necessary first step toward guilty orgasm. One can't simply be a person, one has to be a "living sculpture." All those icky urges must be filtered through the damp handkerchief of Art, ritualized into a pattern of deadly sameness. Image must be conflated with substance—ergo, the labeling of postcard collages as "sculptures." The diminishing lack of vitality in Gilbert and George's work is partially concealed by a desperate burgeoning of technical novelty. As the iconographic routine becomes deadlier, the colors become abrasively active, vivid, autonomous, like an accelerated putrescence. Quantity overwhelms fastidious articulation. Where formerly a single boy, or two, lent mystery and magic to the shorted narcissism of yet another regressive self-portrait, now 10 or even 20 bare-assed or besneakered youths fail to convey anything besides anonymous victimization. *Life Without End,* the central work at the Guggenheim, represents the giantism typical of contemporary artists whose content has become repetitive. If you can't make it different, blow it up. Here we get a stiffening dose of everything: droopy flowers; a lineup of pedo-objects in windbreakers; spooky Gilbert and porcine George glowering amid the overhanging vegetation, elsewhere praying and posing; a Nude Youth, hands clasped across his kissy-smooth fanny, agape at the portal of what is surely the Chapel of Love; an impassive, standing youth in T-shirt and jeans projecting the vague belligerence of rough trade; another one squatting on his haunches; yet another who looks like Roger Daltrey as a child; a few other faces, some sparse streaming tendrils of plant life, scattered branches of winter trees, budding phallic vegetables strewn about like tumescent garni.

This theatricality is indeed frightening in its consistency, of a piece with reactionary modernism in its late, post-Warhol phase. It appeals to the period's unhealthiest obsessions, i.e., moronic religious piety and lust without content. Its frank avowal of dandyism—the stylization of the self and others into aesthetically consistent objects—has always been read, and exonerated, as ironic, just like Andy Warhol's obsequious portraits of fascist politicians and the superrich. These seemed ironic in a critical sense when they first appeared, because of the kind of artist Warhol was widely taken to be, and perhaps at one time was: a sexual and economic outsider equipped with class-instilled liberal sympathies, suddenly operative, via art stardom, as a subversive parvenu in the world of power. Warhol's was the mingy irony of mere reflectiveness, eager to become whatever it beheld, whether it was Candy Darling or the Shah of Iran.

In a rather more committed way than Warhol's, Gilbert and George's early work deploys the outsider's ironic relation to official art culture, investing obscene graffiti, urban detritus, and proletarian boys with beauty and dignity. This work was rapidly embraced as high art. The artists became rich, a circumstance that has clearly altered their relationship to their own working-class backgrounds. They retain an ironic tone, which now conveys the sarcasm of the vampire towards his victim. Irony without criticality is a sacred tusk of reactionary modernism, the ne plus ultra of the modern dandy. It's the nature of dandyism to shrink into fetishistic preciosity or to swell into authoritarian loutishness, if it goes anywhere at all. Gilbert and George, and Warhol, have done both without ever budging very far. I didn't go to the Gilbert and George shows expecting to find any of this in their work. I'd always thought I "liked" Gilbert and George, and in a radically qualified sense I still do. The power of their art seems indisputable: it has the kind of overpowering beauty that coats its liminal messages with anaesthetic as they travel into your brain. But beauty isn't enough, and it certainly isn't everything.

At a different time these works might meet us in a different way. Today, when the male body has replaced the female as the primary fetish object of the culture industry, Gilbert and George's work resonates with the empty sensualism of mass advertising, emitting "desire" in the form of sexy asses, firm pectorals, and big dicks. It reflects a century-old canon of "the beautiful" that needs to be overthrown, to be defeated by a more knowing, more subtle appreciation of what human beings are. What this art celebrates is a class system in which the victims are redeemed by artistic ministration, rescued from the obscure squalor of their lives for a few glamorous moments, their bodies pictorially captured and consumed by the class that keeps them down. One can admire Gilbert and George for the artlessness of their art. Technically superb, it shows what artists can do without any urgent insights and how much they can tell us without intending to.

June 11, 1985

PARADIGMS OF DYSFUNCTION

The notion of periodic upheaval as cultural tonic persists as
modernism's claim to vitality. Any assertion of difference—even
a regressive one like Neo-Expressionism—functions as a sign of
"the new" within the culture industry. Though a considered
experience of technological society demonstrates that "the new"
is seldom progressive in any life-enhancing way, "progress" in art
is viewed as autonomous from other, more concrete, cause-and-
effect kinds of innovation.

Progress in art supposedly expands a metaphysical hyperspace inhabited by allegedly desirable things like "our cultural
heritage," "our sense of ourselves," "the human spirit," and other
concepts suitable for framing. But there is another sense in
which *every* cultural phenomenon, including the "new" work of
art, brutally layers over others, leaving only the spoors of a van-
quished plenitude. Perhaps the active ingredients in modern
culture are akin to plutonium, generationally transmissible
though in ever-decaying condition.

Jeff Koons's recent show at International With Monument
(111 East 7th Street, closed) contained three kinds of work.
There were eight soberly framed ads for Nike sports sneakers,
depicting tall, (mainly) black men with basketballs, costumed or
posed in allegorical or anecdotal situations. (These are unre-
touched, from-the-company ads, used with permission, rather
than appropriated images.) Five aquarium tanks contained water

and basketballs. The balls were mysteriously suspended midtank, some half-in, half-out of water, others completely immersed. (This effect is achieved by weighting the balls with injections of water or mercury and saturating the bottom half of the tank water with sodium chloride, or so the artist said, making the ball too heavy to float and the water too heavy for the ball to sink.) Koons also showed seven meticulous bronze casts of inflatable objects, including a soccer ball, a snorkeling vest, a buoyancy jacket, and a small lifeboat.

Along with the obvious, surreal paradox of the bronzes, where objects designed to bounce or float assume a massive weight, the bizarre stability of the aquarium basketballs depicts an ideal, unrealizable state of things, an impossible harmony between discordant physical properties. Considered in relation to the Nike ads, the inversion of gravity accomplished in the other works acquires social implications. The black men in the ads appear as dualistic signs. While draped or captioned to suggest typically white modes of authority (*Moses, Dr. Dunkenstein, The Dynasty on 34th Street*), they are shod and usually dressed in professional sportswear. This pictorial equation of "establishment" power with the circumscribed power of sports eminence prescribes the latter to black men as a vivid, accessible substitute for the former: "equality" within difference, basketball as salvation.

One can easily extend this conceit into a metaphor of art-making in the race-and class-stratified society we live in. Art-making has become a salvational sport, the basketball of disaffected, middle-class white kids. It promises rescue from marginality through stardom—the aqualung of the very special. However, personal aggrandizement does nothing to affect the social system's unnaturally sustained balance, and one's private escape vehicle can sink in the time it takes to launch it. Koons's marvelously skeptical show was a cogent reminder that we are really all in the same boat, even though the steerage passengers are likely to drown first.

Lothar Baumgarten's current show at Marian Goodman (24 West 57th Street, through June 15) operates as a taxonomic systems-model somewhat more explicitly than Koons's. Baumgarten has installed numerous photographs showing the mesa-landscapes of the Guyana Plate, the region where present-day Brazil, Venezuela, and Guyana meet. In the wall spaces between photos, Baumgarten has painted double rectangles; the lower ones bear the names of the region's exploited minerals, the upper ones feature upside-down names of animals that've become extinct in the area because of deforestation and mining operations.

"These incarnate devils laid waste and spoiled above 400 miles of most fertile Land," a priest named Las Casas wrote in 1656, "and an infinite number of Villages abounding with Gold and Silver." Las Casas's passionate indictment of the Spanish conquistadors, *The Tears of the Indians*, provided the conquistadors' barbaric successors, the British under Walter Raleigh, with the moral alibi for their own rape of Venezuela. The depletion of the area continues today, under the auspices of American mining and timber companies. Baumgarten lived among the scarce remaining Indians for over a year, adopting their way of life, coming down with their diseases. After a long period of assimilation, he permitted himself to take photographs.

Some pictures in the present show are decorated with phonetically spelled words in the Indians' language, naming indigenous fruits, trees, and fish. The pictures are beautiful objects, but Baumgarten's intention is not to exhibit "photography." The artist means to insert the flavor, the smell, of the Guyana Plate region into a specific gallery situation, to summon its spirits to 57th Street. In the rectangular wall paintings, the industrial elegance of the typefaces matches those used on shops and galleries. Baumgarten's show is an attempt to merge two atmospheres, two cultures, two temporal environments.

Baumgarten's photographs give the topography of the erstwhile El Dorado, a real place on which the Spanish projected a fictive utopia of riches. The riches were there, in fact, but the region has been destroyed in the process of getting at them. The overlay of names in certain pieces prompts the thought that "riches," in the sense cherished by the Spanish and English invaders, are symbols that purchase actual things; the names of things are the residue of the real, the trace-sounds that persist when the signified objects—animals, trees, huts, tribes—have been obliterated.

Baumgarten, like Koons, constructs a large part of his art with a view to leaving certain things alone, letting them speak for themselves. Koons, in some shows, has exhibited isolated but unmolested industrial artifacts such as vacuum cleaners and rug shampooers. Baumgarten transposes visual and linguistic information, as directly as possible from its place of origin, to the site of his work. Inasmuch as Koons and Baumgarten maintain a close ethical fidelity to objects and facts already in the world before their artistic intervention, both are engaged in a poeticized anthropology. Baumgarten finds nature murmuring under the floorboards of culture, the repressed returning as the vestiges of the primitive. For Koons, culture has succumbed to the mechanistic, the futile, the repetitive stasis of technological novelty. Culture has devastated nature, eliminating its own impetus and thus trapping human society in spiritual embalming fluid. In this paradigm of dysfunction, the brain has become an extremely useless basketball.

HONEY, POLLEN, AND GARNETT PUETT

At the opening of Grace Borgenicht Gallery's invitational exhibition, someone took a bite out of a Garnett Puett sculpture.

A novel could begin that way with little disgrace.

A swarm of bees still working on another sculpture was removed the following day, out of deference to a gallery employee traumatized in childhood by a wasp sting. As Garnett Puett was later anxious to explain, honeybees are not avid stingers. The bees Puett works with are so intoxicated by the presence of "queen substance" that, even if you threw a hive on the floor, they would gravitate pacifically to the debris without stinging you. "They're like junkies," Puett observed.

Garnett Puett is a fresh-faced, well-spoken 26-year-old sculptor from Georgia whose family has been in the bee business for four generations. He kept bees before deciding to become an artist, and continued beekeeping to support himself through art school. When he made conventional abstract and figurative sculpture, he didn't like to finish them. His works always seemed to need something. Puett moved to New York in 1983 for graduate study at Pratt, already mulling the idea of merging his two professions. In fact, once he got here he decided making bee art would be more fun than going to Pratt. Early results were vandalized by kids in Puett's Loisaida backyard, who "got off on watching the bees getting wasted!" Now Puett works indoors.

The artist sculpts plaster forms, then paints their interiors with melted beeswax, removing the plaster when the wax dries. Puett then coats the pre-sculpture with honey and installs a small cage containing a queen bee somewhere on the surface. The queen cage and its occupant are shipped from the bee farm in a wooden box, accompanied by a substantial bee swarm. The swarm nourishes the queen en route, and would gladly perish to keep her alive.

The sculpture-in-progress, then, is placed in a protective container. Glass walls of the container are usually covered with removable light baffles—bees, like birds, become confused by light coming through glass. The honey coating on Puett's sculpture persuades the swarm that the template is a suitable location for hive-building. The bees then set about liberating the queen, whose cage is sealed by a little block of candy. Worker bees commence fabricating comb structures in the queen's vicinity, molding the wax manufactured in their bodies by chewing it with their powerful mandibles and patting it into shape with their thread-thin legs.

After the queen buzzes forth, she flies about the construction site, soon mating, for the first and last time, with one of myriad "huge, fat, ugly" drones. She stores up a lifetime supply of sperm from this single encounter, releasing tiny amounts of it when fertilized eggs are needed to produce female worker bees, withholding it when the hive requires more drones. The queen regulates the population of the hive according to the availability of food: pollen for the baby bees, honey for the adults. The bees glean both substances from flowers. They collect pollen on their hind legs and roll it into balls, winging huge amounts of it back to the hive. They extract nectar from flowers with sinuous sucking tongues, store it in their stomachs and regurgitate it as honey.

While Puett supplies honey to promote hive expansion around the works-in-progress, the bees have access to the outer world through openings in the box. They forage freely throughout the city. The bees travel up to 10 miles to gather food from window boxes and scraggily tenement gardens, fructifying trees and flowers, returning from as far as New Jersey at the end of the day. They navigate by sunlight, undaunted by traffic, skyscrapers, and industrial pollution. (Our environment must be less toxic than we imagine, since Puett says that his bees would all drop like flies if the air were heavily poisoned.)

The construction and maintenance of a hive require an incredible degree of sophisticated interbee communication. In the backyard of Art Mart, an East Village gallery where two of his pieces were recently shown, Puett showed me a hive developing along the surface of a human head-and-body cast containing "at least 80,000" bees. Countless little amber bodies hovered around the combs, waggling their feelers and legs in an apparent frenzy. The bees were, in fact, dancing. The vibrations produced by every movement of the bee dance communicate the precise distance of a food source, its quantity and quality, and the amount needed for a specific purpose. Information about the environment is passed among thousands of bees incessantly. They also talk by rubbing each others' feelers. The bees put in a very full day, stocking and maintaining the hive, cleaning it, removing the dead. If a foreign object is introduced into the hive, the bees quickly quarantine it with a thick seal of wax.

Puett has allowed the bees to obliterate some of his figurative sculptures, but he's learning how to manipulate their comb-building patterns for particular effects. When a work seems finished, he stops feeding the bees. The hive population drops and the survivors use up stored food, thereby cleaning the work and removing material that would decay unpleasantly in a gallery situation. Since the bees spread the comb along the walls of the containment box, Puett heats the surface before pulling off the glass. This prevents the wax from shattering. The bees will quickly repair the resulting deformities in the stretched wax, creating a uniform cellular surface. This done, the bees can be coaxed away from the completed work of art by moving the queen to a fresh sculpture base.

Puett's collaboration with the bees has produced several eerily beautiful sculptures, five of which can be viewed at an invitational exhibition at Grace Borgenicht (724 Fifth Avenue, through June 21). They are artifacts partially overtaken by nature, manmade forms articulated or completed by natural processes, the fleshy residues of thriving ecosystems. Their tactility has a certain repulsiveness, similar to the feeling of uncooked tripe on the tongue, as well as a powerful sensuality. They resonate with the presence of life and also exude an aura of death and abandonment, like a shed snakeskin or an empty tortoise shell.

One highly appealing aspect of Puett's work is its lack of brutality: in recent years, people calling themselves artists have sometimes inflicted hideous suffering on animals used in films, performances, and art works, supposedly to draw attention to the violence we've come to accept in human society: "How can you care about a dog if you don't care about other people?" A work like Tom Otterness's *Shot Dog Film*, in which the filmmaker kills his own pet, answers its own question: anyone would rather see the dog shoot Tom Otterness. Puett manipulates the populations of his beehives, but maintains the integrity of their organic environment and the natural progression of the bees' lives. His work involves nature as a friend and collaborator rather than as an antagonist, animal husbandry instead of animal exploitation.

JUST AN OPINION

And then. And then there was a week at the end of the season when everything ran in flashes. Everyone seemed to be talking at once about air conditioners and Greek Islands, rent versus ownership, shifting power configurations, foiled alliances, cats and dogs who ran away and miraculously returned, death and loss, stunning discotheques. I received a lot of disturbing mail. Publicists put my address on their A-minus list for theme parties, parlor-liberal benefit brunches, and birthday galas for obscure celebrities. Instead of throwing them away, I began giving my unsolicited invitations to a friend, who sold them to people standing outside the indicated nightclubs.

A deranged person figured out which three hours I spend every week at the newspaper office and started calling, barking congratulations for "really giving it to them." This person's voice crackled at the far register of some irreversible madness. "You really let them have it this time," the stranger would screech. "You really gave it to them." I would stare at the melting letters on the display terminal, hypnotized by the patter of her mania against my eardrum. "You'd know me," she threatened one day, "if you ran into me on Second Avenue!" Quite unconsciously, I started to avoid Second Avenue whenever I could.

By the way. "By the way, you should probably know that Varnish has written an attack on you that we're considering publishing."

"Varnish?"

"No, not Varnish, *Varnadu*. Like Xanadu. He won the Joseph McCarthy I am a Genius Award. Also, I ran into Schmitz-Craves, the photographer, at a dinner for Diane Thrilled, and he said your essay on Prim was an insult to all creative people everywhere."

"He knows them all, I suppose."

"I defended you, naturally. As best I could."

But is Varnyard really a big genius? How much do they get with those awards? Who is he, I've never even heard of him?"

"Well, according to most people he's a careerist wastebasket, but that takes a certain knack, no? And to get the McCarthy I am a Genius Award and all that money on top of it ... *genius*, wouldn't you say?"

It was. It was going to be a column on group shows, but then this happened: you *left my place at around 12:30*. I agreed to be on this radio program with Patterson Sims to discuss the Whitney Biennial *said you were walking as far as 6th Street to check out the sidewalk sales* and was asked why I hadn't written about it. Patterson Sims said, If you had, it would've forced you to clarify your ideas about the show, *then catch a cab home and phone me. As soon 1:30, which is, of course, perfectly true. And I'm very worried, because you always call.* And this led me to wonder why, after all, I should cover group shows in June *even if you run into an old friend* when almost every gallery puts one up in June. *Anything can happen in 15 blocks. Despite or because of gentrification.*

The idea. The idea of writing a column on group shows proved more alluring than actually writing one. The June or July group show is a sort of variety package for the nonbuying art public. Galleries can insert tentative additions to their stables without creating a big and possibly fizzled fuss about them. Theme shows in the summer months have an unseasonably forced look about them, while the plain showroom medley looks patently mercantile.

There was a group show of **"Funny Art"** at Concord Gallery (451 Broome Street, through July 12), some which wasn't. In the **"Peter Blum Edition"** show at Lorence-Monk Gallery (588 Broadway, through June 29), the only prints that really jump off the walls are Barbara Kruger's cinematic freeze-frames that spell out WE WILL NO LONGER BE SEEN AND NOT HEARD. But the tonal diminuendo of the other editions has to be an effect of placement, since I remember admiring Eric Fischl's pieces months ago at publisher Peter Blum's studio. In the **"Logosimuli"** show at Daniel Newburg Gallery (44 White Street, through June 30), a few things seem absurdly out of place—stuff you'd include to please friends or to round out a shaky schematic—while others, particularly Colette's crumpled-silk colonization of a corner area and a mirrored piece by Suzanne Etkin festooned with silver-paint body imprints in back, are rigorously apt in location and upsettingly direct in effect.

In some cases. In some cases we went in and looked and stayed with what registered instantly without a backward glance. So we went to the **B.A.M. Benefit** show at Mary Boone (417 Broadway, through June 29). A shaggy dog painting by Alex Katz, just the dog's head with its tongue sticking out. One of Artschwager's familiar relief paintings with ink drizzled over the surface, containing some hard flat swatches of, I think, grayish white. A Bleckner with something like a chandelier of square cylinders looming in the deep nighttime space only Bleckner knows how to paint, a space that's neither indoors nor outdoors but *other*. In the foreground a crystal goblet. A very large David Salle, not my favorite one, but with this coy Italian-looking laundry slapped over a balustrade near the top. A tiny wood sculpture by Joel Shapiro near the gallery entrance baffles, so teeny-tiny that it becomes bigger than all the huge paintings nearby, expands like an atomic bomb, its charm turning sour. I don't recall the rest of the show, except for the Warhol *Mao*, which reminded me of a gold American Express card being brandished at Zabar's to pay for three bagels.

You could. You could consider any collection of things a group show. There was a group show in journal form that went beyond anything hanging on a wall: this was *Wedge*, Numbers 7/8, Winter/Spring 1985 THE IMPERIALISM OF REPRESENTATION/THE REPRESENTATION OF IMPERIALISM ($11 to 41 Perry Street, New York, N.Y. 10014). *Wedge* is one of the very few "alternative" periodicals besides *20*, that makes strongly convincing, concrete connections between art, the art world, and the big world of money, media, death, and power. This issue is brilliantly designed by Louise Lawler and Mark Magill, edited by Phil Mariani and Brian Wallis, and has contributions by Silvia Kolbowski, Allan McCollum, Laurie Simmons, Barbara Kruger, Gayatri Chakravorty Spivak, Edward Said, John Strauss, Jürgen Habermas, Suzanne Jackson, and Gary Indiana.

Connect the critical space. Connect the critical space of *Wedge* with the group show at Nature Morte. Aside from artists already mentioned, this includes Steven Parrino's distressed or, if you like, gnawed black-and-white paintings, the maximum black on the minimum white to block out a work, but mauled, chewed up in places, *damaged*. David Robbins has a segmented Cibachrome piece: pictures of perforated Kennedy half-dollars at the ends (hole-through-head effect), images of hypno-patterned plaid or plastic (cf. Sarah Charlesworth's photographs of Tartan designs), and photographed arrangements of pin-on buttons with messages like WHAT THE FUCK ARE YOU LOOKING AT? A good question in almost any circumstances. Jeffrey Pittu has two small-scale, silver-blue Cibachrome montages of young male beauties scrutinized by older male authority figures, evoking *Mädchen in Uniform*-vintage German movies and indicating a deconstructive approach to commodified homoeroticism. Meyer Vaisman's entry is a superbly unexplicit laminated painting, the sides surfaced in what looks like pinstripe trouser material.

With other work. With other work like Tim Rollins's collaboration with his students in the **Barbara Gladstone** group show (152 Wooster Street, though July 26): coppery-gold horn forms painted on pages of Kafka's *Amerika*. Gladstone also features a light-emitting diode message machine by Jenny Holzer that you can stand and watch for at least a half-hour without getting tired. Or Philip Taaffe's beautifully worked pastiche painting surfaces in **Pat Hearn**'s group show (94 Avenue B, through the summer).

You would. You would have a column with no conclusion, God forbid, so I'll appropriate some words about patriarchal aesthetics from a work by Allan McCollum: "It should be with a polite and parental indulgence, however, that we allow the modern artist his illusions concerning the apolitical nature of his craft, or his pretenses to pacificism—for it is he, after all, whom we have elected to maintain the posture of the one who reflects, in order that the rest of us may perform without reflection; and apart from his envy, and a certain impotent rage, his artwork exists to express very little, really, except perhaps that peculiar and poignant way he has of imagining himself to be...."

July 2, 1985

DEEP FAT

As a conceptual art event devised by such punctilious collaborators as Lily Auchincloss, Oscar de la Renta, Skitch Henderson, and Chita Rivera (all members of the U.S. Grand Sumo Tournament Committee), the festival of kinetic obesity held recently at Madison Square Garden (on June 14, 15, and 16) achieved a surreal multiplicity of effects. The Grand Sumo Tournament had previously visited the Soviet Union in 1965, the People's Republic of China in 1973, and Mexico in 1981, but our happy land had never before witnessed the epic crashing of steel-bellied warriors that is sumo. Exoticism, pedagogy, theater, and politics twinkled like quasars during opening night. The overture included a recital from the formal correspondence of Ronald Reagan, a stand-up-and-be-counted-if-you-don't-want-your-face-bashed-in rendition of the national anthem, and a rousingly hissed cameo visit by Mayor Koch. These brief yet pungent episodes of patriotism did not seem out of place at a sporting gala wherein the main draw was the grotesque physical volume of the athletes.

The ceremonial mise-en-scène—ornate costumes, a raised proscenium with a ring of straw bales and imported sand, a Shinto rooftop looming above the wrestling—inscribed the solemnity of ritual inside the décor of sport. Spectators were appropriately subdued, except when the Hawaiian-born wrestler "Sale" Konishiki appeared. At which time they behaved like drunken Yahoos on amphetamines. Dick Cavett's sleeve and Eddie Murphy's hair were visible from the $100 seats in Section 40. John Wheeler, author of the remarkable sumo book *Tahamiyama*, provided English commentary over the sound system without a flaw.

After six or seven matches, one adjusted to the routine: first the wrestler's entrance into the ring, the solemn clapping to attract the gods, the raising and stomping of the feet to drive away demons, the nose-blowing, the ingestion of water proffered by the antecedent combatant, the spitting out of the water, the wiping of the mouth with paper, the spraying of salt through the fists to purify the ring, the squatting-down face-off between opponents who glare at each other ominously, rise, walk off, and repeat the whole business for as long as four minutes and ultimately collide, grapple, clutch, slap, squirm, heave, lift, and push until one or the other hits the sand with something besides his foot or goes flying outside the straw circle.

These sumo wrestlers emanate a fearsome dignity. Their fat is all muscle. In the draining demonstration preceding the wrestling, these behemoths (who sometimes weigh over 400 pounds) graced through the kinds of strenuous exercises that would make well-toned, conventionally proportioned people cower. The *sumōtori*'s art is a demonstration of physical power harnessed by codes of obedience, discipline, civility, and concentration. If sumo today is a bizarre residue of imperial display, we can still perceive its raison d'être as the shackling of a human organism to a higher power. In several of its early contexts, sumo glory entailed a submission akin to a Christian saint's, or to the heroine's in *Story of O*.

Like the castrati who gave their all for the popes, the wrestlers who smashed together in the *dohyō* had altered their very form for the glory of the emperor. Today's sumo is a spiritual discipline set to a secular purpose, a self-creation of identity that involves one's physicality. Whether or not it's grotesque is a matter of opinion and cultural perspective. If we ignore the culture-specific signs of glamour and repulsion that make the *sumōtori* seem physically distorted, their affinity with John Travolta, Sylvester Stallone, and Jamie Lee Curtis becomes obvious.

There is a physical detail in sumo that I found unexplained in the literature. The wrestlers wear silk belts that wrap around the waist and groin, the *mawashi*. But there is also a frill attached to it, a length of strung-together, tensile ropes of fabric that sticks out. The wrestler gathers this up when he hunkers down to glower, tucking its tendrils up along his inner thighs away from his groin. The tucking motion is extremely graceful and automatic-looking, like a peacock furling its feathers. At some juncture in almost every match, this superfluous fringe falls off one or both of the wrestlers. It would then be scooped up by the referee, a man in priestly Shinto garb whose physical slightness and delicate movements in the ring exaggerated the wrestlers' hugeness.

The silk fringe, I think, must once have contained rice seed, since sumo originated as an agricultural ritual. While the sumo tournament supplied a sensation of "tradition" and human diversity—the survival of a prehistoric art form into the age of laser discs—what interested me was the jettisoned fringe and its remoteness from any anticipated harvest, the mannerist applica tion of ritual.

Except for a distinct architectural style, sumo wrestling is the only indigenous Shinto art form. In turn, Shinto is the only indigenous Japanese religion. It didn't have a name, and wasn't even thought about as a religion, until the 6th century, when Buddhism and Confucianism spread through Japan from China. Shinto was, is, a shamanistic faith, its many gods inhabiting the winds, the mountains, the trees. Shinto possessed no scripture, no iconography, no moral code. Sumo wrestling matches first transpired among rice planters of the Yayoi and Kofun times (100 B.C. to 562 A.D.) "to discover the will of heaven."

Throughout Japanese history, in spite of foreign religious influences, Shinto has remained the national faith. People who are Buddhists or Christians are also, in some mysterious way, Shinto. The emperor is Shinto by direct descent from one of the gods—or was, until the Americans forced him to repudiate the lineage following World War II. Imperial patronage is partly responsible for sumo wrestling's longevity.

The first recorded match occurred between wrestlers named Kehaya and Sukune in 23 B.C., during the reign of Emperor Suinin. Under the Emperor Shōmu (724–749 A.D.), sumo tournament schedules became formalized. Sumo was incorporated into the court ceremonies of the Heian period (794–1185), along with equestrian archery, to promote an ideal of militarism. Sumo's practitioners were still farmers, and the agrarian-mystical nature of sumo only required that the wrestler knock his opponent over. In the 12th century, when power shifted from the court to the army, *sechie-sumō* became *buke-sumō*, warrior sumo. The wrestler now had to pin his adversary to the ground.

From 1185 to 1582, sumo functioned as an aristocratic entertainment. Nonprofessional sumo became popular in the countryside; *kanjin-sumō* was offered publicly to raise shrine-building and charity money. This practice fell off in the Tokugawa period. Sumo was intermittently banned between 1648 and 1720, because samurai fighting usually broke out at matches. Sumo became a clandestine sport for a time.

Around 1684, the professional organization of sumo caught up with its wide popularity. The 18-foot ring created a new morphology of combat gestures. The sport got faster, more ritualized, and more recognizably a "sport" in a Western sense. It became the spectacle of choice among the rising Japanese middle class, part of "the floating world" of hedonistic urban pleasures (Kabuki, Bunraku, the courtesan culture) that existed between the 16th and 18th centuries.

As an adjunct of Shinto and therefore a symbol of the emperor, sumo continued after the Tokugawa period with nominal modifications, despite later vicissitudes of fashion. Like the queen of England, sumo provides anachronism with the power of perfected charm, operating as a symbol of cultural rootedness, history, legitimacy. It serves the pedigree requirements of prevailing authority, preserves the enchanting manners of a fully expired past. As the wrestlers in Madison Square Garden mimicked thunder with their clapping, the spectator's eye could wander above the Shinto ministure to glimpse the deities hovering above. BURGER KING, ITT, COCA-COLA, TEXACO, YAMNOUCHI, PHARMACEUTICAL CO., LTD., ZACT SMOKERS' TOOTHPASTE, SUNTORY, WATANI, SEIKO, MINOLTA, HERTZ, BUDWEISER, PLANTERS, DATA GENERAL, KODAK.

July 2, 1985

THE COLLINS-MILAZZO EFFECT

What are they saying?

"What may today facetiously appear to be a gratuitous distribution of polysensate or psychobiotic objects and creatures…"

Come again?

"…within a trans-subliminal environment determined, ultimately, by an alien phenomenology…"

Trans-subliminal? Say what? Tricia Collins and Richard Milazzo (sometimes referred to privately as "the Milazzi") curate art shows and publish a magazine called *Effects*. Every so often, they emit art criticism in the form of dialogues and thickly worded press releases. Their shows, this year and last, have been remarkable for their conceptual subtlety and palatable size. They've presented new art in terms of contiguous ideas rather than similar subject matter—"Paravision," say, as opposed to "The Animal Within" or "Sex."

Their last show explored "the psychedelic option," pulling in seemingly incongruous wallmates: Jane Bauman paintings of maps and empty Polaroid frames on phonograph records, a monochrome painting by Olivier Mosset, hybrid works using sculpture and photography by Gretchen Bender and Alan Belcher, deceptively "straight" paintings by Gary Stephan and Ross Bleckner, and technically odd, disparate woks in disparate media by David Robbins, Richard Milani, Jeff Koons and Ricardo Regazzoni, among others. If these works had been jumbled into proximity along with a few gratuitous selections, the show would undoubtedly have flopped on an important level: the subtle, strong thread running between art in different media and styles needed the particular effect of installation achieved to make it visible.

Collins and Milazzo's magazine, *Effects*, is strikingly designed (like *Real Life*, black-and-white offset on thick paper), thematically ambitious, impressively stocked with texts and pictures by seminal contemporary artists. The couple's own writings give many an admirer pause. In truth, the work tends to become a sticking point when the subject of the Milazzi arises in conversation. There was the serpentine text about Robert Longo in *Flash Art*. The gnarled metaphysical telegraphy attached to the "Final Love" show at Cash/Newhouse and "The New Capital" at White Columns. And "The Look of Critique: Anomaly and Instrumentality in the Meta-Spectacle" in the *New Observations* issue they guest-edited. The allusions to "mortal geometry" and "the novocaine of the pedestal." The ingenuous discoveries of the New Distance, the New Concept, the New Spectacle. The press release for one of their first shows, "Civilization and the Landscape of Discontent," even espies a New Moral Order.

The Spotting of the New around every bend can easily suggest an overindulged subjectivity. Collins-Milazzo's authorial recourse to Socratic form isn't exactly reassuring on this score, and the baroque vocabulary often defies translation. Not since *Anti-Oedipus* beguiled a generation of autodidacts have quite so many polysensate, psychobiotic objects and creatures mushed their way through that flaccid body we know as Art Writing. "Don't even *try* reading this," one gallerist cautioned, handing me a Collins-Milazzo manifesto. "I don't think it's supposed to be serious, but I'm not sure."

It's only fair to add that Collins-Milazzo regularly warn people off their own prose, which Collins sees as "problematic for a lot of reasons…it doesn't perform a service, in terms of other people wanting to publish it." In other words, they aren't keen on pitching names, even though certain artists recur in their polemics and group shows (Robert Longo, Peter Nagy, Ross Bleckner). The artists simply fuel the quest to make connections. The breathlessness of the pursuit conceivably produces the intermittent otherworldliness of the writing, the talk. The texts can be obscure, but their enthusiasm is exemplary. And their insights are often marvels of convoluted accuracy.

"I want to be a professional spectator," they jointly proclaim in "Sentimental Pressure," the catalogue text of a Longo-curated show at Artists Space. "We have perfect athletes. Why not perfect spectators?" In person, Collins and Milazzo complete each other's sentences when they aren't interrupting each other; between themselves, they incessantly hone the blade of mutual perception. They've been called the Sartre and de Beauvoir of the East Village, with something of Burns and Allen, Nichols and May bubbling up when their aesthetic speculations reach an especially high pitch.

"East Village" is the section of the compliment which they'd just as comfortably dispose of. Though most of their shows have occupied East Village galleries, the mix of artists they've shown on each occasion has more or less obliterated the geography. The finesse of Collins-Milazzo's presentations has helped knock down the wall that until recently excluded (and protected) ostensibly "East Village" art from mainstream critical attention. (It's gotten gallons of press, and about a thimbleful of legitimate criticism.) The conceptual audacity of Collins-Milazzo's shows has drawn helpful attention to new artists—not simply from collectors, but from established artists and critics who aren't normally frantic to see "East Village Art." People who can't fathom Collins-Milazzo's ideas have found the shows visually spectacular and *serious*. (This year, serious is the New Fabulous.) In refusing to group art according to media, Collins-Milazzo cut across several inhibiting, arbitrary, market-dictated distinctions (between painting and photography, for instance) to locate deep structures of general artistic practice. By the same token, their shows have a diverse visual appeal not generally associated with conceptual art.

Then too, Collins and Milazzo haven't trained their attention on artists hitched to the East Village hay wagon. Invited to curate a show at the Fine Arts Gallery at Florida State, they were deeply bothered when the local staff, after urging them in vain to incorporate "East Village" in the show's title, supplied visitors with copies of a notoriously hyperbolic East Village article as a guarantee of authenticity. "There's nothing expressionistic about the work we show," Milazzo asseverates, "though there is something expressive about it—"

"—expressionistic is too personal," Collins finished disdainfully, "angst and all that." Since most collectors fidget in the absence of a label, the art Collins-Milazzo have shown and written about is perhaps likely to get tagged, eventually, as "neo-Conceptualist." Much of it's drawn from, or related to, Metro Pictures' original stable of artists who investigate photographic media and imagery—ergo Robert Longo, with whose work Collins-Milazzo felt a strong, immediate tie. And hence their involvement with Metro-influenced Nature Morte, one of a handful of galleries *in*, but distinctly not *of*, the East Village.

Collins and Milazzo simply happened to gravitate, separately, to the East Village. For them it's a neighborhood rather than an ambition. Tricia Collins was born in Coral Gables, Florida; she retains the lilting, cautious locution of a Southern backwater escapee. She took art courses at Florida State and formed a small collection of local art. She moved to New York in 1979. "And the first thing I did was rent this little gallery space on East 11th Street, during the summer. This photo gallery that was closed let me have the space for $100 a month." She put up two one-person shows of Florida artists. Collins loved the East Village's ethnic mix and apparent lack of encroaching gentry. "I'd been living on Bedford Street and Grove, and I walked over here and thought I'd found paradise."

She met Richard Milazzo "over a Budweiser" in the Grass Roots Tavern on St. Marks Place early in 1982. A native of Astoria, Queens, Milazzo had a City College degree in literature and, as a terribly reclusive publishing partner for Out of London Press, a Lamont Cranston-like connection with the art world. "The thing about meeting Tricia was, she represented talking to people directly, being social. I was never—I was frightened of people, never answered the mail or anything like that." ("Not that I wasn't frightened of people," Collins interjects. "But I was more frightened by the telephone.")

They started *Effects* magazine in response to an Out of London censorship incident involving a David Salle text. They also got married and moved into a tiny Second Avenue apartment. Collins's sociability led to dinner parties. They invited artists, dealers, made contacts in the murky art scene developing on the lettered avenues. A salon evolved. Curating a show occurred to them more as a way to formalize their living room than as a career decision. They had made friends with Peter Nagy of Nature Morte, and there happened to be a space in the gallery's schedule for the following year. Later the idea to do a show at International With Monument came up in conversation with artist-gallerist Meyer Vaisman. It was all very informal. "It didn't seem that public at the time," Collins says. "Nature Morte wasn't that well known, and International was only a few months old at the time. So it was really off the beaten track." As it happened, though, the galleries scheduled the two shows for the same month, so the Collins-Milazzo curatorial debut made a certain impact. And this led to another show, and another, leading to a public identity as freelance curators and advocates for thoughtful art.

July 9, 1985

DADA BLACK SHEEP

Dada was concocted by Hugo Ball in 1916, partly as an intellectual emetic. Dada attacked the senile values that had led to the World War. Dada intended, among other things, to flush away the spiritualized fatuities of the Expressionist movement. We've already experienced Expressionism's fatuous return. With Ronald Reagan doddering high in the saddle, the World War cannot be far off. Dada's comeback seems inevitable. If the Viconian principle of eternal recurrence holds true in art, the Museum of Modern Art's current show of collages, prints, assemblages, and diverse other *Merz* artifacts by Kurt Schwitters may bode a rebirth of Dadaism in an art culture famished for novelty and addicted to sudden revivals.

In popular memory, Schwitters figures as a Dadaist of the obscure Hannover branch. He was actually a latecomer to Dada, which had achieved its most concentrated state as antiart in Zurich during the war. By 1916, when Schwitters turned up in Berlin and asked to join the Club Dada, the movement had spread as far as New York, mutating as it traveled. The Berlin version of Dada was avidly political, containing provocateurs such as John Heartfield, George Grosz, Hannah Höch, Raoul Hausmann, and Richard Huelsenbeck.

Berlin Dada was perhaps the most markedly anti-Expressionist Dada group. In *Dada Forward* Huelsenbeck wrote, "Under the pretext of turning inward, the expressionists in literature and painting have banded together into a generation which is already looking forward to honorable mention in the histories of literature and art and aspiring to the most respectable civic distinctions." Partly because of his association with the Expressionist group Sturm, Schwitters was rejected by the Club Dada. In retaliation, Schwitters invented *Merz*, the umbrella-name for his own artistic production.

Under the auspices of *Merz*, Schwitters aligned himself with Dada but remained slightly distinct form it. The hard core of the Dada movement regarded Schwitters with skepticism, as a Dada fellow-traveler. Schwitters "looked like a bourgeois." Like Picabia, Schwitters came from a comfortable background; family money supported his art career. But Picabia's penchant for self-destructive escapades and squandering largesse was less suspect than Schwitter's unadventurous lifestyle. Though none of Dada's memoirists explicitly say so, Schwitters's easy shifts of aesthetic allegiance were probably read—especially by didacts like Huelsenbeck—as avant-garde opportunism.

Before Dada, Schwitters's art-making had passed through a spectrum of stylistic modes: Impressionism, Expressionism, Cubism. After Dada, Schwitters incorporated formal elements from Constructivism and De Stijl; in the '20s he declared Dada's "epoch of destruction" over. But in Dada, undoubtedly, Schwitters's whimsy found its spiritual home. Dada was a liberation from the kinds of content prescribed by art history. Cubism had made ordinary paper objects, fragments and shards permissible as pictorial and sculptural elements; however, Cubism extended the line of formal adventurism that celebrates new ways of looking at the same things. Like Futurism of the prewar period, Cubism introduced time as a plastic element in works of art, depicting static objects from diverse points of view simultaneously or successive views of moving objects.

These were revolutionary advances, as were Marinetti's jubilant anticipations of World War I as "the world's only hygiene."

But the war itself went much further than the avant-garde in altering perception. Dada, born in the cabarets of neutral Switzerland, digested the surrounding collapse of all values and spat up reconfigured ruins. Schwitters's work represents the "positive" polarity of Dada in its rescue of an exploded world's passing debris: buttons, scraps of wood, train tickets, feathers, shreds of newspaper, and product decoration. But this aleatory use of found material and iconography in cryptic charts of consciousness reflects "negative" Dada's view of the world as a graveyard of meaningless forms.

Schwitters's reliefs and collages are ruminative objects that fix little segments of passing time: the time of Schwitters's interior life and the "objective," verifiable vintage of their components. In works like *Merzpicture Thirty-One*, from 1920, Schwitters deflects interest from discrete collage elements, blending their contours into dynamic pointed shapes; pictures such as *Colored Squares* (1921) contain no found imagery or typography and thus avoid the initial appearance of collage. Even when their surfaces are festooned with distractions, Schwitters's works exhibit an unfaltering, daredevil agility of composition—as in the collage *Blue Bird* (1922), where quadrants of varisized typefaces, endpaper designs, and printed numbers compete with a magenta arrow, jagged swatches of colored paper, and a black-and-white rotogravure drawing of a masquerade ball for attention. Or the more complex (*Difficult*) (c. 1942–43), which has the overall effect of thin strips shooting up and splaying out from a narrow base though it has numerous, squat horizontal passages of magazine illustration and printing interrupting its diagonals.

Schwitters smuggled a medley of personal atmospheres into each of his "periods." A melancholic desuetude in his multilayered, pre-Dada assemblages also haunts certain bulky, paint-crusted reliefs of the 1940s. The succession of "influences" and aesthetic affiliations caused variations in Schwitters's surface textures and design schemes; private obsessions carried through. A print work dating from Schwitters's Constructivist period has the rigorous arrangement of jazzily balanced, sharply defined lines, the machine-age imagery and streamlined cleanliness of avant-garde Soviet posters. Hilariously, it also features two cuddly kittens, relatives of the ones in *The Cherry Picture* of 1921. Richard Huelsenbeck called Schwitters the Caspar David Friedrich of the Dadaist Revolution, and not without cause. Many Dadaists used postcard and magazine kitsch as ironic pictorial material, but in Schwitters's work the irony has gentle edges.

Schwitters was, in fact, a Romantic, complete with a dark side. His *Merz* eccentricity was sufficiently bombastic that Schwitters longed for a *Merz Gesamtkunstwerk*, a total work of art that would also be a world. He laid plans for a public version of this work, the *Merzbuhne* or Merz Theater, envisioning a grandiose structure full of kinetic design elements. This was never realized, though Schwitters conceived and performed numerous theater pieces. Privately, throughout the '20s, Schwitters labored at his *Merzbau*, an amorphous structure of grotto-punctured columns that were gradually connected. The *Merzbau* started in Schwitters's apartment, in the house he owned in Hannover. It expanded into the apartment upstairs, displacing Schwitters's tenants. The *Merzbau* was an uninhibited display—or so we might assume—of the psychosexual cesspool from which Schwitters refined his art, the raw product undisguised by the rhetoric of form.

In the *Merzbau* grottos, various concavities contained relics of Schwitters's friends: nail clippings, locks of hair, dolls, assemblages, cigarette butts. Numerous caves and corners were devoted to mythological subjects, culture heroes, and erotica. One area of the *Merzbau* was called *Kathedrale des erotischen Elends* (Cathedral of Erotic Misery) and featured the Love Grotto and the Sex Crime Cavern. Elderfield quotes Schwitters's description of the *KdeE* and comments on its "obsessional fixation with human subject-parts and with the themes of sexual violence, death, and desecration." (Elderfield also speculates that "*KdeE*" is almost the acronym of a large Berlin department store, the *KaDeWe*. I'm not sure what the *KaDeWe* was offering in the '20s, but one of its present-day blandishments is an entire floor of meat products, guaranteed to nauseate with its aura of death and desecration.) Curiously, Schwitters buried these fetish-troves inside fresh construction as he went along. In photographs, the late stages of the *Merzbau* look like Expressionist architecture, or sets for *The Cabinet of Dr. Caligari*.

In effect, Schwitters's *Merzbau* achieved both art and antiart, preserving artifacts of his innermost sentiments and urges within a structure concealing them from public view. He and a few friends would know they were there. Lacquered decoupage boxes that Schwitters designed in the '20s served a similar purpose, as repositories for found objects. Aesthetic domestication, as the Surrealists tirelessly demonstrated, infects even objects of horror or ugliness with an incongruous charm. For Schwitters, all the world existed to end up in a *Merz* picture—mateless gloves and sex murders, Renaissance Virgins and underwear ads, Anna Blume and Adolf Hitler. A cultural revolution that packs easily into a suitcase and looks well on a museum wall is the bourgeois dream most Dadaists struggled against; Schwitters was half-enchanted with it. He created incessantly, and so his art is aesthetically superior to most of the art produced by Dada. For the same reason, Schwitters cannot be considered an important artist, the way an artist like Marcel Duchamp (whose actual art production is decidedly minor) can be.

Schwitters had to abandon the first *Merzbau* in 1937. It was destroyed by Allied bombing in 1943. A second *Merzbau*, built during the artist's exile in Norway, burned down in 1951. He started a third in the English countryside, completing one wall before his death in 1948. Apparently the *Merzbau*, containing Schwitters's most cherished, self-revelatory work, was fated to disappear, leaving only photographic residue—the kind he often rescued from oblivion.

July 16, 1985

THE WAGES OF ANGST

"Some of the hostages seem to exhibit the Stockholm syndrome, a paradoxical sympathy with the outlook of their captors."
        —*Daily News*, Monday, July 1, 1985

"…related to that theme, there was the constant undermining of testimonials, statements, or declarations broadcast, printed, diffused, or portrayed by the media, either that so-and-so is brainwashed when he speaks, or that X and Y Iranians are propagandized or fanatical enemies."
        —Edward W. Said, *Covering Islam*, Vintage, 1981

"President Reagan, waiting to address the nation in the Oval Office yesterday following the release of the 39 American hostages, joked that 'after seeing *Rambo* last night, I know what to do the next time this happens.'"
        —*New York Post*, Monday, July 1, 1985

"On pretext of carrying on propaganda for the soul, they have…found their way back to the abstract, pathetic gestures which presuppose a comfortable life free from content or strife. The stages are filling up with kings, poets, and Faustian characters of all sorts; the theory of a melioristic philosophy, the naivety of which is highly significant for a critical understanding of expressionism, runs ghostlike through the minds of men who never act."

> —Richard Huelsenbeck, "Dada Forward," 1920. Reprinted in *Dada on Art*, 1971 (ed. Lucy R. Lippard)

"In a featureless former printing plant on a bleak Manhattan street, paint has transformed a warren of dark, ungainly spaces into a family home filled with Mediterranean sunshine and peopled with gods, kings, saints and apparently unrecalcitrant sinners."

> —Doris Saatchi, "An Artist's Life, 1985: The Art-Encrusted Loft of Julian and Jacqueline Schnabel," in *House and Garden*, July 1985

"Before I became a journalist and was a lowly fiction writer, I used to believe everything I read in a newspaper, too…. Well, let me be the first journalist to admit that everything you're going to read here might not be true. Empathy makes for tact, seldom honesty."

> —Cookie Mueller, "Art and About," in *Details*, June 1985

"In the Schnabel household, it is art that counts above all else and art is everywhere. …Mostly there is art by Schnabel, massive constructions of animal, vegetable, and mineral matter that seem to hold up the walls like ramparts against the encroaching outside world."

> —Doris Saatchi, op. cit.

"When the Tate staged a Julian Schnabel show in 1982, nine of the eleven pieces exhibited were on loan from the Saatchi collection…"

> —Kenneth Baker, "The Saatchi Museum Opens," in *Art in America*, July 1985

"The South African subsidiary of Saatchi & Saatchi was hired by the governing Nationalist Party to promote the adoption of a change of the South African constitution. Foes of apartheid say

that in effect it cements the racist system which reserves political power exclusively for the white minority (16 percent of the
population)."

> —text by Hans Haacke for the exhibit of *Taking Stock* in
> the show "4 Works: 1983–1985" at John Weber Gallery,
> May 1985

"Just as Christ's mortal suffering was relieved by His divinity so
does the man…who sits on the end of his cot in the men's shelter,
although bereft of everything else, still have his magnificent
penis-hanging proof of his superiority over the white man."

> —Rene Ricard, "An Art of Regret," in *Artforum*, Sum-
> mer, 1985

"I try very hard to teach people about contemporary art, but
the bottom line is that this has financial value, and you really
have to understand that you have a responsibility to the financial community."

> —Holly Solomon, transcript of GSA Hearings on
> Richard Serra's *Tilted Arc*, quoted in *Harper's*, July 1985

"A catalogue of the Saatchi collections with contributions from
well-known art critics and historians has been prepared by Doris
Saatchi, who also writes for *The World of Interiors, Artscribe,
Architectural Review*, and is the London editor of *House and
Garden*. Questions have been raised about art works owned by
the company exhibited with labels attributing them to the collection of Doris and Charles Saatchi."

> —Hans Haacke, op. cit.

"Several of the essays actually transcend the put-up job character
of the whole affair. Peter Schjeldahl, for example, has produced
the best statement on Philip Guston's late work I've read yet…
Hilton Kramer is about as convincing and wholehearted as it is

possible to be in defense of Julian Schnabel, which is to say he is tellingly reserved."

—Kenneth Baker, op. cit.

"Hughes sees Schnabel's exaggerated, Neo-Expressionist style as a cover-up for simple ineptitude. Ask around the art world and you'll find that this low opinion is widely shared....But the collectors love him. Since 1979, his shows have been sold out even before they opened, and there is a waiting list of buyers eager for whatever he produces next."

—Pepe Karmel, "Art and Exhibitionism," in *Vanity Fair*, July 1985

"One of the odder aspects of the late Shah's regime was its wish to buy modern Western art, so as to seem 'liberal' and 'advanced'...The main beneficiary of this was Warhol, who became the semi-official portraitist to the Peacock Throne. When the *Interview* crowd were not at the tub of caviar in the consulate like pigeons around a birdbath, they were on an Air Iran jet somewhere between Kennedy Airport and Tehran."

—Robert Hughes, "The Rise of Andy Warhol," *New York Review of Books*, February 18, 1982

"When it comes to buy, the first impulse is to reach for the most talked-about artists—a name often dropped in the art magazines, but which hasn't been around long enough to be old, Keith Haring, for example, is old; so is Jean-Michel Basquiat...whose simplistic renderings of primitive figures now get snapped up for $20,000 or more.... neo-expressionism recalls expressionism—or at least tries to by energetically expressing emotions in a fast way. Jeanette Iannucci of Limbo Gallery describes it as the 'let's deal with angst' school of painting."

—Deborah Michel, "ART CHIC, The ABCDs of Buying Future Basquiats," in *On the Avenue*, May 1985

"What makes Julian run? To hear Schnabel tell it, it's his angst. In a 1984 issue of *Artforum* he wrote: 'One need not talk of agony but it is the reason why I began to work. It is the reason why I continue to work...'"
　　—Pepe Karmel, op. cit.

"The manuscript has been lost ... but it did contain what would become my criteria of discernment... My approach was occult, trusting my intuition by keeping myself in an almost trancelike state before the subject."
　　—Rene Ricard, op. cit.

"And not only is Ricard Schnabel's court critic, he's also court couturier, helping Schnabel's wife design what *Vogue* describes as 'her own waist-cinching, Ava Gardner-style short evening dresses.'"
　　—Pepe Karmel, op. cit.

"With the noteworthy exceptions of Andrew Young, no high public figure in the United States had anything to say in 1979 about what...the previous regime meant to the Iranians as they took action against the United States. And collaborating in this silence, the press treated the ex-shah exclusively as a charity case for at least twenty days after he was admitted to the United States."
　　—Edward W. Said, op. cit.

"And now that they are free, some hostages will suffer post-traumatic stress syndrome, a set of terrifying symptoms centering on their captivity. The symptoms include flashbacks, nightmares, insomnia and depression."
　　—*Daily News*, July 1, 1985

Angst: a feeling of anxiety, apprehension, or insecurity.
　　—*Webster's Ninth New Collegiate Dictionary*

July 23, 1985

DEAR DECADE

[James Nares. Patrick Fox, 56 Bleecker Street, through July 27.]

This isn't entirely to do with the recent paintings of James Nares but with an array of things suggested by them. If I hesitate to deal with the paintings directly it's because their relation to his films has never been entirely clear. The best I can do here is speculate freely and hope for the best.

Nares did a lot of performance work in the '70s. He was a member of an artists' collective called Colab, and one of the collaborators on *X Magazine*. He played guitar in the Contortions and did the camerawork on numerous Super 8 films, including John Lurie's *Men in Orbit*. With Eric Mitchell and Becky Johnston he founded the New Cinema on St. Marks Place He made a Super 8 film, *Rome '78*, in 1979. In 1980 he made an hour-long videotape, *No Japs at My Funeral*, and shot Johnston's *Sleepless Nights*. In 1981 he made a 10-minute Super 8 film called *Waiting for the Wind*. In the same year he played percussion with the Del Byzantines. Since then Nares has mainly been painting.

This is a dense compression. Things don't really move according to decades, but the change from the '70s to the '80s was in fact dramatic and rather nauseating. In the '70s one suspected the future was going to be unpleasant but entertained some hope it would not be utterly predictable. At the end of the

'70s certain shifts became palpable. A kind of negative idealism segued into a species of affectedly brainless optimism. The difference between the Mudd Club and Club 57 reflects this clearly. The Mudd Club was about exhibiting the dark underside of high culture; Club 57 was about wanting to be on television.

Downtown culture—if we need to rope it off that way—exuded a politically informed, enlightened absurdism in the '70s. In the early '80s the culture began to project an earnest, uncritical embrace of absurdities. Many artists working in several media "went back" to painting with disconcerting abruptness. Nares was one, or so it seemed. He had in fact been making paintings all along, but not showing them.

Nares's paintings are astute, intelligent works, inexpedient, and if I am puzzled by them it's probably because I experience them as *displacements*. Nares's vision of the world has been quite clear. In *Men in Orbit* two ridiculous astronauts knock around in a space capsule, their disorientation simulated by a fast-rotating camera. These media heroes are depicted as beer-guzzling slobs who have lost the power of coherent speech. In *Rome '78*, Nares recasts a platoon of then-underground celebrities as power-hungry contestants in Imperial Rome, clanking around in armor and adoring themselves uninhibitedly.

No Japs at My Funeral is an interview with an IRA "terrorist" intercut with British television footage of the war in Northern Ireland. In the course of an hour we are forced to understand that the interview subject is a likable young man cornered by historical chance into doing what he must do: a person who eats and sleeps and makes love like anyone else and does not have the moral option of living quietly. *Waiting for the Wind* has the camera knocking wildly back and forth as it speeds up endless, overlit stairways. It cuts to a stationary shot of a man lying in bed who wakes up repeatedly in a fit of terror, throwing off the sheet and flailing around helplessly on the mattress. Next, the furniture and fixtures in a stark loft space are whipped up by a violent, invisible force, smashing into ceiling and walls. The destruction is relentless, hypnotic, beautiful. Finally, the camera zooms again and again from a long-to-close shot of the moon.

From the above, it's easy to assume that Nares sees the human being trapped by structures larger than him/herself, inadequate to history, torn apart by received circumstances. There is a painted plaster head in Nares's current show that's sliced up like a loaf of bread. A painting called *Rope-A-Dope* shows a vaguely human figure with the coil of a heart-shaped "rope" encircling its long neck. *Headspin* features a disembodied face gripped by the forehead and chin by two hands preparing to wrench it around. In *Nemosapiens*, three demonic presences perch on a thick bough from which two humanoid shapes have been hanged.

In Nares's paintings, there are numerous allusions to implacable forces at work. Drawings and small paintings Nares did after a trip to Egypt carry a heavy presence of death—these are simply wrought things, blunt pyramids and palms in sienna—and a gravity peculiar to Nares's work since *Waiting for the Wind*. In the latter, the reiterated zoom-to-the-moon was startling because it seemed to link the distressed figure on the bed and the cyclone in the empty loft, not to traumatic history or weather conditions, but to occult, inescapable powers. Relatedly, the painting *Spirit of St. Louis* has a propeller form painted against a light background in the upper third of the canvas: whirring pointlessly because it's detached from any aircraft, a picture of gratuitous propulsion. But lower down, where the background color becomes dark, what looks like raised forms hover just behind the painting's surface. They strongly suggest Mayan or Aztec symbols carved in the face of some temple of sacrifice.

Many of Nares's recent paintings are done on skin-thin layers of silk stretched over metal panels. The way the silk absorbs paint, superimposed on whatever paint finds its way onto the metal, creates an illusion of build-up. The ground texture gives a smearing and streaking quality to huge brushstrokes of thin paint, making a subnetwork of realistic volumes by shading in discrete parts of each stroke. Nares's work has an internal dynamism, often an exploded quality, typical of thickly worked oil painting. This tension between apparent and real volume echoes another: Nares's figures sometimes suggest an almost monumentalized pain, as in the massive, twisting shape astride some uncontrollable machine in *The Passenger*. Yet these figures are generic, undifferentiated Everypersons and therefore allegorical.

The haplessness of Nares's creatures isn't uninformed by whimsy. But this is the painter's humor, not the subject's self-conscious irony. The subject is mute, possibly no longer conscious. The egocentric birdbrains and gibbering poseurs in *Rome '78* may have been tools and plumbers of imperialism, but they also had vivid lives and smart mouths. The presences in Nares's paintings are thrown to an unchosen, ravening destiny like lumps of bewildered meat. With a perfected artistry that looks like poise and is actually sardonic wit, Nares elucidates the difference between the 1970s and the 1980s.

August 6, 1985

BANKS OF AMERICA

The horrors of urban life without a bank account are sufficiently grave to impel any urbanite to open one. Strange to say, this is not an easy thing to do, and the time between a bank's embrace and the honeymoon's conclusion is briefer than the coital syndrome of the hummingbird. Although banks themselves have seen to it that almost any penny earned spends at least a few moments cloning itself for the banks, the expense of processing penny-ante transactions has borne home the perils of unlimited hoggishness to most financial institutions. The cash machine and corresponding cash card only partly alleviate the trouble caused by pesky small depositors. Alas, there are ever new clients awaiting the issuance of their secret code numbers, proles with tiresome special needs, and countless others "on probation" for careless automatic withdrawals.

In an effort to persuade low-income and erratic types to take their unproductive money elsewhere, the larger Manhattan banks have introduced a revolutionary new idea: the hour-long bank line. My "personal" branch of ChemBank at 8th Street and Broadway can be counted among the avant-garde. For several years now, hours of peak customer traffic have unfailingly coincided with teller lunch hours: a simple yet effective piece of human engineering, annually driving off a percentage of those whose earnings have negligible interest for the bank. Among larger more welcome depositors, the concept of a lunch *hour* becomes increasingly alien as one shinnies up the economic scale; so does the concept of physically visiting the bank.

Like the modern hospital, the modern bank is less concerned with human individuals than with numbers. The hospital extracts huge amounts from even the least promising mark's insurance company, but the bank can only skim a wee secretion from the money you actually have, so unless you happen to be Malcolm Forbes, the bank doesn't need your particular money. (And if you are Malcolm Forbes, you probably own the bank.)

Most institutions that make themselves indispensable to the ordinary conduct of life eventually perceive an advantage in striking the human note, however extraneous to the business at hand. The human note is popularly known in corporate hallways as "throwing peanuts to the monkeys." The stray peanut here and there distracts the ever-hungry chimp from its cage's structural inadequacies. For example, a much-needed waiting lounge and rubber tree have been removed from my ChemBank, but video displays have been added.

The human note, in this case, takes the form of canned entertainment, though of an ill-calculatedly pedagogical cast. A Valium-calm voice murmurs pleasing triteness about mortgage rates and loans, while the things borrowed money can buy pass before one's eyes: Johnny's graduation, Janey's dental installation, that new family car on its first gleeful outing. (The generic style could easily handle Grandma's funeral or Little Bobby's chemotherapy, but "sad" events like these receive merely allusive audio coverage.) Also, families who have undergone group lobotomy appear, beaming irrepressibly, to gibber about the soothing effects of home computer banking. Youthful dad puffs his briar and marvels at the ease with which busy but pertly coiffed mom has figured out the home terminal, while adorable school-age Billy, cute as he is, already lives in a computer-fluent world of electronic transfers and memory dumps. This demonstrates once again that technical aplomb and brainlessness do not exclude but embrace each other. Even senile Gramps chuckles that he, too, manages his assets automatically.

It is often amusing to watch professional actors impersonating imbeciles, but most people who bank also own television sets and can do this at home. Commercials for yet another technological invasion of one's living space do little to prevent the average customer from getting *pissed off* whilst blowing his or her entire lunch hour in drab, irritating surroundings. Contemporary institutions like banks and hospitals devoted to the financial exploitation of human needs function on the premise that people will not, in any appreciable numbers, get pissed off collectively. The problem, then, is to effect the maximum exploitation while stopping short of the *general piss-off point*. But the maximum exploitation can only be achieved by pushing things way beyond this point, by continually extending what I shall call the *margin of piss-off* by artificial means. In the case noted above, livelier video material, better placement of display monitors, and perhaps the return of the waiting-lounge and rubber tree might allay the inevitable *general piss-off* in the short run. Removal of five or six perpetually inoperative teller windows might further allay the *risk of piss-off factor*. Actual failure of the bank, of course, would highlight the limitations of environmental design vis-à-vis a major crisis.

Another banking tactic for banging the gong of business humanism is the installation of art-in-the-bank, and/or the exhibition of art-of-the-bank. At ChemHeadquaters on Park and 48th, a severely postmoderne niche off the bank's immense lobby serves as the Chemical Gallery. While no larger than your average Chanel display in your average Hilton Hotel, the Chemical Gallery presently contains 13 rather choice works from the Studio Museum in Harlem: an Ibo totem from Nigeria, a funky Betye Saar combine sculpture/altar, a carnally evocative Romare Bearden collage, and a Richard Hunt bronze that retains its elegant force even in this etiolated setting. The other works are also of extremely high quality. It's no fault of the art that this gallery makes it look like part of a Chanel display. No fault of the curators, really, either, since they've done the best they could with the space.

The fact that Chemical Gallery is more alcove than gallery isn't really the problem: fantastic things have happened in less space. But what we have here is a space shaped and lighted to suggest a mausoleum-turned-boutique at the bottom, the drainage system of a public bath at the top. It's a chillingly dead area, a suite of vitrines just off the central sepulcher. The hyper-tech style of the building guarantees that anything in the gallery will take on the necrophile glow of a trophy. Since this is, after all, Chemical Bank—with its thousands of entry-level black employees (making the effects of Reaganomics less obvious) and its primarily white management's lavish support of the South Africa government—the display of black art might be thought responsive to the tastes of Chemical's workers. But an employee told me hardly anyone ventures into this gallery; the space sucks the life out of anything that enters it.

An immense foliage-filled atrium constructed on the Park Avenue side of the building, though somewhat enlivened by a temporary planting of spices and medicinal herbs, has a similarly arid quality. It's an environment in which every transplanted sign of nature merely heightens the absence of naturalness required for anyone or anything to function *in* the building. The only really suitable exhibition for the Chemical Gallery would consist of bales of currency and stacks of Krugerrands, since works of art can function there only as symbols of the real thing. For the atrium, perhaps, there could be myriad cascades of small change and reflecting pools of liquid silver, gold, and copper.

Lifelessness aside, there is an effect operating here which, however subliminal, more or less ensures distraction from any objet d'art or leafy foliage. Unlike museums, which have their own ways of perverting reception, banks are not designed for the leisurely strolling connoisseur. And though it's true that the aesthete's museum delectations transpire near the fitting gaze of sequentially stationed, bohunk guards, this is hardly as prophylactic of a worthwhile encounter as is the sensation of being, at every moment, *under electronic surveillance*. As you look, you are being watched, video-recorded, transformed into an object of corporate scrutiny—with, in the case of ChemGallery, a real live guard thrown in, peering at you from the environs of the elevator bank. Therefore, you unavoidably experience the visual form of your own viewing experience as a spectacle monitored for signs of nonconformity. A curious condition in which to enjoy someone else's nonconformity, to say the least.

The Chase Manhattan Bank has successfully blanded-out this effect in its Soho Branch by turning it into a gallery-bank combo. At last there is a bank that is also an art gallery, with changing exhibitions. This is easier to accomplish with a space that's repeatedly changed hands and lost the flavor of its original function, as this one has. Here there are large, tusk-shaped modern sculptures, kinetic assemblages, jumbo-scale paintings in an array of up-to-the-minute styles and humors, with a sidebar display of Carl Van Vechten's photos of black celebrities from the going-up-to-Harlem period of the 1920s. (Now that the East Village has successfully been raped by the happy gang of art and corporate money, white folks are headin' up to Harlem once again.)

The Chase collection is legendary for its excellence and profuseness (9926 works of art so far), just as Chase is legendary for the amorality of its domestic and overseas financial operations. Indeed, Chase outpaces Chemical in both areas: though the Studio Museum works at Chemical Gallery are first-rate, Chemical Banks' own collection is said to be rather dreary. In art as in profiteering, Chase leads the way. It only remains for Chase to start selling the works instead of just hanging them. This would bring art, the buyer, and the spiritual bond that presently unites them together in their proper home, under the venal and approving stare of the corporate spy camera.

August 13, 1985

O FURNITURE

["**Material Pleasures: Furniture For A Postmodern Age.**" Organized by Robert Janjigian, at the Queen Museum, New York City Building, Flushing Meadow, Corona Park, Queens.]

What is furniture? What is art? What's the difference? The current show at the Queens Museum features several tons of furniture that would like to pose these questions. This is furniture on the cutting edge, so to speak, much of it on loan from such final words in chic as Art et Industrie, Furniture Club, and Dennis Miller Associates. This show makes a strong visual case for the furniture, which is ranged showroom style, in cramped ensembles, along either side of a gallery-length divider. The installation is splendid, playing up the undeniable attractiveness of the work without trying to make it look like the Elgin Marbles or Art Treasures of the Uffizi. Whatever else it may wish to be, furniture is furniture.

How the viewer will feel about this furniture depends on who the viewer is, and where the viewer lives. I say "viewer" with only slightly less reserve than I would "spectator," because there is something a bit odd about looking at contemporary furniture in a museum. Antique furniture answers questions, shows us what the things used in past times looked like. We can imagine the scale and character of people's dwellings and something of their habits of life, without imagining ourselves laboring away to maintain their privileges. We can envy the luxury of the past, yet still feel fortunate when we consider that those who enjoyed it are dead. Contemporary furniture of a certain priciness, however, would seem to provide no such compensatory pleasure for those who can't afford it. In the museum context, one might simply view this furniture as evidence that some people still enjoy greater material comfort than others, with fresh novelties being constantly invented for the amusement of the privileged classes.

Oh, but with this furniture there's a difference, which those who merely view can gloat over to their heart's content while contentedly languishing on mass-produced sofas. Like so much else associated with the easy end of the New Feudalism, the New Furniture looks like fun only from the perspective of the non-consumer. Just as parties with Bianca and Andy tend to be deadly boring but photogenic, so postmodern furnishings look much better than they sit. Living with them must be at least as arduous as feigning perkiness night after night in the same dreary discotheques. Just try emptying Richard Nonas's tubby ashtray of steel slabs every five or six butts in the course of an evening without developing triceps in your wrists. Or, if you aren't gigantic, lounging in Stanley Tigerman's striped, curvy, semi-upright brass recliners without altering the phrenology of your medulla oblongata. Postmodern art may be a yuck a minute, but postmodern living must require an unusually stoical sacrifice of comfort for appearance. Appearance that requires sacrifice tends to be just that.

In certain cases, the postmodern era's waiver of liberal guilt among the undeserving rich has caused the repressed to return in the form of protest furniture. For instance, take Paul Ludick's *Apartheid Chair*, a blocky number with white trim over black support structure, backed with chain-link fence that chews into one's vertebrae. This piece is a double irritant, unsuitable as furniture and a meager, window dresser's idea of an art statement—perfect for stimulating the postmodern consumer's sense of the emptiness of it all, whether the thing is installed in the home as sculpture or deployed as an actual chair. Less overtly political, but no less aggressive, is Anna Anselmi's steel and rubber *Alpha Chair*, with its visually smart, physically gratuitous and spine-bumping red bar running down its back.

The subtle dysfunction of objects like Carlton Cook's squat, unpleasantly assembled *Francis Table* (which is just big enough to hold a glass and just low enough to demand awkward lurching movements from anyone seated at a normal elevation) and Cal Spitzer's checkered laminate *Flag Console* (a sideboard with the stingy width and prissy undershelf of a luncheonette counter) betrays the subversive, sadistic credo of Cynical Design: for a jizzed-up feudal system, jizzed-up furnishings that emulate the physical inconveniences of the middle ages.

As any theater director well knows, one must never underestimate the contempt of technicians. Practical design is an art area where knowledge and vision can be verified or disproven. Ideas promoted as the spokes of a zeitgeist are acid-tested in the "applied" arts, where they're often revealed as mingy, elitist peccadillos and redeemed as enjoyable trivia. The designer can make visual ideas work in ways that deflate their fine art origins, as in Wendy Maruyama's spiffy *Smallboy*, a piece of furniture that condenses every idea Jedd Garet ever breathed on, without demanding an egregious amount of space.

Furniture that aborts or parodies its own function, like David Wiener's *BMW Desk*, asserts itself as a commentary on the lives of people who would purchase it—debutantes, one assumes, who have no real need for a usable work surface but would like a desk as a symbol of some "serious" private activity. Such an object exhibits the designer's identification with the "obsessive" artist who must, because of his/her obsession, create—even if the customers for this creation are hopeless philistines. The object, then, incorporates both the concept of the object and its maker's assessment of the object's potential audience, which thus divides into two groups: those who "get it," and those who habitually copy this cognoscenti and want the same thing. As far as the designer goes, the making of such products represents a fetishism balanced between adoration and repulsion. In this sense, the inventor of classy, impractical furniture applies the myth of the avant-garde to its final frontier: the human backside.

This, anyway, is where work like Richard Snyder's *Loveseat for One* pops up where it should give in, and where Richard Nonas's obtuse *Notched Back Steel Chair* and Howard Meister's nastily jagged-edged *Fury* seem designed for anorectics. These pieces improve it considered as sculpture one can sit on rather than as furniture. The less grandiose chairs in this show are also more practical: Paolo Favaretto's *Kinetics Business Seating*, your basic office roller; James Evanson's *Primazoid*, which combines chunky elegance with genuine comfort; and Michael Braun's *Arc Chair*, an arching reinvention of the Rietveld that puts yielding canvas in the place of rebarbative wood.

The best things in this show are ones that don't involve a lot of body contact below the waist, like Bruce Kaiser's witty glass-topped *Propeller Table K1005* and his *Olympic Torch Lamp K1002* that goes with it. Ditto James Hong's *Tropic of Cancer Table*, Darcy Moore's *Table* that has diagonal and vertical elements supporting its wire glass top, and John Danzer's *I-Table* with its base mirroring its surface: in each of these pieces sophisticated design is sophisticated enough not to make a statement the whole time you're eating.

As for lamps, the more technically daring ones here recommend themselves to people who don't mind large insects. Leo J. Blackman's *Cyclops Lamp* and spiderish, forthrightly titled *Bug Lamp*, David Nelson's *Upwardly Mobile—with Teeth*, and Juergen Riehm's *Ceiling Mounted Halogen Light* all look like things that might fly in the window and settle ominously in some hard-to-reach corner. The postmodern lighting alternative to the thin, angular, and wiggly is the squat and stolid: Charles Pfister's menacing overhead *Pfister Pendant*, Ned Smyth's illuminated birdbath, *Column Lamp*, and Robert Younger's tapering stuccolite *Beehive Sconce*.

As far as I can make out, the fully postmodern home features tartly colored things that are irritating to sit on, tables designed for people squatting on their haunches, and fixtures that look like they've been carved out of sheer rock, or like prehistoric mosquitoes: a modern medieval castle dressed up for a masquerade.

September 17, 1985

SLICE OF ART

["**Gordon Matta-Clark: A Retrospective.**" Museum of Contemporary Art, Chicago, May 10—August 10.]

I got to the Gordon Matta-Clark retrospective at Chicago's Museum of Contemporary Art just before the show was packed up for its subsequent venue. It will travel extensively before arriving at New York's forthcoming Broida Museum in January 1988, but many New Yorkers attending the Chicago Art Fair this spring managed to catch it early—coming away, perhaps, with the same nagging, melancholy feelings I had. Matta-Clark was a prodigious originator and a seminal moral presence. The few years that have passed since his death have blurred the precocity of his work; the retrospective feels like a memorial, not only to Matta-Clark, but also to the fervid idealism from which he proceeded.

The short memory of the art world is diminishment enough in cases where living artists receive less attention than those who've imitated them. When the artist is dead, custodians of his or her legacy are often appalled if the legacy is co-opted without accreditation. It's natural for originality to engender secondary work, but galling that the sources are so often obscured by epigones.

In Matta-Clark's case, it isn't his work that's been copied, but his use of the urban infrastructure as material. One can truthfully claim that Matta-Clark anticipated the aesthetic exploitation of subway graffiti and the derelict riverside piers of

New York City, approaching these phenomena with greater conceptual ambition than those who stumbled upon them in the 1980s. However, this material "belongs to everybody," as the phrase goes. What makes the recent surge of interest in the city's detritus different from Matta-Clark's is the baldly mercantile direction of the later effort. This displacement of raison d'être is mannerism in action, a bit hard for longer memories to swallow but an almost invariable art-historical happening—which we can leave art history to sort out.

In defense of those who've picked up on Matta-Clark's trail with a keener eye for the marketable, the Reagan Years have left artists with little to do besides amuse the idle rich and decorate executive offices. It was not always so. In the '70s, the idea of changing the world, or at least observing some notion of *communitas*, could respectably afflict certain souls. As one of the founding spirits of Soho, Matta-Clark made exemplary efforts to preserve the area's viability as a mixed-income artists' community, a place where the marginally financed might survive alongside flourishing colleagues. Near his life's end, Matta-Clark initiated a Lower East Side community program to recycle useful materials and provide occupation for local young people.

Matta-Clark involved himself in the urban ecosystem with tremendous force, deftly erasing lines between art and life. Certainly his best-remembered works are the "cuttings" he made in various architectural structures, carving through walls and building cores to open revelatory, paradoxical spaces. He sawed a house in half in New Jersey (*Splitting: Four Corners*, 1974), removed grid-sections of another in Niagara Falls (*Bingo*, 1974); he chopped a sail-shaped "clerestory window" through the side of Pier 52 on West Street (*Day's End*, 1975) and cut out a rectangle from a wall and window of Pier 14 (*Pier In/Out*, 1973). Matta-Clark took cuttings from condemned buildings throughout the city; these excerpts were often transplanted to a gallery. Just as often, Matta-Clark sliced or excavated the gallery itself.

Matta-Clark's work embodies a utopian aesthetic. Dysfunctional architecture becomes a site of transformative energy and artistic play, while used space is liberated from rational closure. The cutting device is an audacious form of inscription that uncovers a "ready-made" collage object. Matta-Clark also used it to beautiful effect in making drawings, cutting lines through thick stacks of paper.

The cuttings were an integral part of a surprisingly large, remarkably unified body of work. Matta-Clark did many different kinds of things, but always operated from a coherent philosophical base. On one hand, he made "useless" art with use-associated processes and materials (photographs fried over a stove in John Gibson Gallery, a restroom "house" built inside a dumpster). On the other hand, he reproduced aspects of ordinary life on the symbolic plane of art, establishing an affordable restaurant for artists ("Food" in Soho), offering purified air on city streets (*Fresh Air Cart*, 1972), planting trees and bushes in incongruous locations (*Rosebush*, 1972; *Cherry Tree*, 1971).

The urban universe obsessed him. He created sculpture from piles of garbage and melted wine bottles. He shot films in aqueducts, storm sewers, and subway tunnels. In Paris, as a memorial to his brother Sebastian (who killed himself in 1976), Matta-Clark dug through the floor of Yvon Lambert Gallery and then through the street underneath it, exposing multiple layers of the city's foundation.

Matta-Clark's two most ambitious cutting projects, *Office Baroque* (1977) in Antwerp and *Circus* (1978) in Chicago, scissored up the intricate internal structures of whole buildings. The documentation indicates the monumental scale Matta-Clark was capable of. If he'd lived, he could have done skyscrapers if any were available. The weird floating platforms and perspective-jangling ledges his structural deletions produced were perfectly stable, weight-bearing entities. The artist knew what he was cutting into.

It can't really be regretted that so much of Matta-Clark's retrospective consists of documentation, since the artist deliberately engaged the transient and the biodegradable. All art decomposes over time, and Matta-Clark knew that most of his would vanish fairly quickly. Moreover, most of the documentation in this show is Matta-Clark's own, collaged and rephotographed and blown up in Cibachrome. These pieces multiply the spatial puzzles of Matta-Clark's "performance architecture" and were enlarged with the film sprocket edges showing—playing up the fact that photos are "cut" from reels of images.

This isn't to say that all of Matta-Clark's cuttings have physically vanished. An impressive number survive. Four building fragments from *Splitting: Four Corners* poke up from the floor in this show, like debris from a neatly quartered doghouse. A prow-like wooden sandwich from *Circus* dips downward from the ceiling. An assortment of walls bearing shingles, window and door frames, and the phantom traces of a staircase stretches along at considerable length, interior and exterior metonyms from *Bingo*. The slice drawings are complemented by fine-lined geometric studies and boxy, marker-and-pen sketches of whizzing arrows and whirling curves. Richard Nonas has done a painstaking, delightful reconstruction of *Open House* (1972), Matta-Clark's dumpster/house/performance space. *Fresh Air Cart* still offers relief for clogged industrial lungs, and was recently remobilized on Chicago sidewalks by Charlie Scheips of the Chicago museum.

Matta-Clark became a legend in his time; his time was drastically shortened by cancer at the age of 35. The catalogue that accompanies the retrospective carries testimonials from the artist's intimates (Laurie Anderson, Dennis Oppenheim, Holly and Horace Solomon, Jane Crawford, Alanna Heiss and many others), which are often funny, moving, and informative. A key essay by Robert Pincus-Witten further disperses a widely held notice that the 1970s were a decade in which "nothing happened" in the art world. In actual fact, much of what's happening now happened then, with less publicity: for instance, Gordon Matta-Clark.

September 24, 1985

SHADOWS OF A SUMMER NIGHT

[**The International Shadow Project 1985.** Sponsored by Portland PAND (Performers and Artists for Nuclear Disarmament, Box 10227, Portland, OR, 97240) In cooperation with the Friends of the Earth Foundation USA and the Women's International League for Peace and Freedom.]

Between the hours of midnight and 6 a.m. on August 6, 1985, many things happened that could have happened otherwise. But in the cold light of morning these things seemed fated to be so. *Some people reached the flash point after exhausting calmer methods. Was it the moon, or just a sudden sense of futility?* Among much else, small bands of people in New York and other cities traveled from block to block, sticking vinyl cut-out figures down on sidewalks and fixing imprints of them with faint application of white paint.

Some figures represented people. Others depicted animals. These were intended to suggest one of the many striking visual effects of the atomic explosion over Hiroshima, where the blast fixed people's very shadows on walls. Come morning, thousands, or perhaps millions, of people rushing to work would see the painted shadows and think about Hiroshima, atomic weapons, and death.

Brainchild of Alan Gussow and Donna Grund Slepack, the Shadow Project dates back to 1982, and now occurs, when it does, simultaneously around the world. This year there were shadow painters in New Zealand, Hungary, Nigeria, Brazil, "most of Western Europe and even in remote Mauritius!" This is an impressive organizational feat, akin to the Live Aid festival. The notion of getting many people in many places to do the same thing has been a popular one ever since Unforgettable 1848, when most of Europe erupted in revolution. In the aftermath of Unforgettable 1968, though, such endeavors have played to a passive audience: turn on the TV, or walk down lower Broadway, and you are the world.

The Shadow Project workers used an impermanent latex paint that would fade off in a couple of weeks. *Something looked wrong with the paint. They didn't put enough on, or something had discolored it from white to gray.* I witnessed only a few shadow paintings, in the World Trade Center vicinity. *A dog caught by the fireball. A bunch of people crawling in the street.* Just before midnight, my colleagues and I, members of the dreaded press, stopped for a drink in a glittery fun-filled Tribeca restaurant. There, several dozen exiles from Ibiza were desperately recreating the atmosphere of an early Virna Lisi film. Strolling guitarists, costumed to suggest good-natured Iberian macho, regaled the glamorous crowd with traditional favorites.

I tried to imagine the effects of an atomic explosion on the restaurant: the shadows of pendant smoked hams and dangling mozzarella baubles forever embedded in the particolored ceramic tiles. Irradiated beakers of blue margaritas dripping senselessly amid the wreckage. The dentures of busty socialites and dashing European auto salesmen gleaming amid the charred ultramarine Formica. Not a pretty picture. Where once there was laughter and bright voices, all would be rubble and hardy cockroaches.

Did these milling, flashy, fleshy club lovers realize that less than a mile away, in the heart of the financial district, earnest brigades of earth's friends were commencing to swab the streets with grim intimations of impending disaster? Was even one voice choked in the middle of a gargling laugh by the obscene specter of the mushroom cloud?

In all candor, I doubt it. I tried in the din to think about Hiroshima. *But who, in that week of media commemoration, didn't find him or herself unable to think about Hiroshima?* "Living With the Bomb." "Hiroshima's Grim Legacy." "Is There Hope!" One had seen virtually every archive picture of the Enola Gay, the Atomic Dome, and the chubby little bomb before detonation. Shots of the Pacific tests, graphic evidence of radiation's deadliness, centerfold carnage provided relief from the Presidential nose and the promise of more Hollywood stars with AIDS. After the calming drink we pushed off towards Wall Street and the Shadow Project. Surely this would center one's thoughts on the reality of nuclear weapons.

Several shadows had been painted by the time we got near the Trade Center. The outlines were slapped down with rollers, in milky-thin applications. The resulting figures looked puzzlingly crude, less than human size, with weirdly proportioned limbs and unnaturally tapered extremities. A legend had been stenciled here and there: "Hiroshima 1945, New York 19??" But the question marks disappointingly read like "77," as if we had all bought the farm eight years ago. Whoever had designed the vinyl cutouts had learned nothing from Richard Hambleton, whose homicide-squad outlines and later black shadows really were scary when they first appeared. The stencil, even if the question marks registered, seemed to suggest that after *our* Hiroshima someone would still be keeping track of the date.

Mine was, admittedly, a tiny view of a large project, at an hour when it was impossible to measure public reaction. I'd like to be kind, because the Shadow Project is, at least, redolent of noble intentions and brave hopes. But the execution seemed, from the fractional perspective of midnight, lacking in some essential feeling of transgression. True, two shadow painters informed us sarcastically that we should "get a picture of the cop who just tried to stop us." The project, however, is perfectly legal. And unrealistic. An actual, 1985-vintage thermonuclear weapon dropped on New York wouldn't leave any walls standing for any shadows to congest on. And even if tangible surfaces survived, it's unlikely that such a bomb would discriminate between public and private property, confining human residue to sidewalks and thoroughfares.

To fault this project may be ungrateful. Even so, the whole approach is flawed. It doesn't interfere at all with public order, and public order is precisely what allows the insane proliferation of nuclear warheads. The idea of *raising awareness* of the nuclear threat is unhelpfully tame, since more than half the population regularly experiences nightmares about nuclear war. If showing what nuclear war would do could solve the problem, the problem would no longer exist. Within a framework of legality and nonrisk, dramatizing nuclear war enhances the general helplessness.

The Shadow Project could be improved if its participants actually put themselves at risk of mass arrest, targeting government buildings and real nuclear weapons in transit with more effective graphic messages. Unfortunately, a society that thinks of war as something that happens to other people, on television, isn't likely to get the message until it gets a taste of the real thing.

October 1, 1985

JUST ADD MILK

[John Wilkins, Cash/Newhouse Gallery, 170 Avenue B, through September 22.]

John Wilkins's painting-size watercolor works on paper look like delicate landscapes or bright-colored maps, or abstract fragments of a jigsaw puzzle. Or psychiatric ink blots. Or blotty variations on Cézanne. The methodological build-up of solid background colors in certain of his works gives the paper a subtly mottled texture that evokes some animal's skin, upon which the "figure" looks like a vivid blotch, varicolored epidermal plaque. Often this background color is gold, giving the passages of integumented earth colors the bright relief of Japanese characters on fancy scrolls. To one viewer, Wilkins's new works at Cash/Newhouse looked like "bad imitations of Helen Frankenthaler." Another person thought they resembled very expensive wallpaper.

Wilkins certainly intends his paintings to suggest the things they resemble, but it's important to know what they really are. The pictures now on view derive, first of all, from photographic studies of a Weetabix cereal box, and, secondly, from photographic studies of details in his initially derived paintings. In other words, certain paintings are enlargements of little things in pictures of other paintings, which in turn magnify details in pictures of other pictures. A pre-Weetabix series is generated from the signature image of Ovaltine (a country milkmaid in Luddite-era garb) as viewed from a low-angle, fisheye perspective.

Wilkins's treatment of received imagery reverses the "paradox of infinity" so many people remember from childhood: the product label featuring a figure holding the product, whose label shows a figure holding the product, and so on, and so forth. Wilkins's paintings demonstrate the limits of visual intelligibility, zooming into the microstructure where the ostensible point of infinity reveals itself as the point of closure. That last, teensiest figure in the product-label puzzle is a bunch of colored data.

But perhaps it's more pertinent to consider that the dots resolve into a figure on the label of a product, and function as ciphers in the visual language of advertising. Blown up through several generations, the details operate as works of art. Works of art, mutatis mutandis, are models of the world, paradigms of consciousness. So, in a sense, are advertisements. In the work of art we find the archetypal, the eternal, the grandiose. The advertisement, on the other hand, trades on the stereotypical, the transient, the absurdly hyperbolic. Pop Art's conflation of art and advertising capitalized on the flagrant difference most people seemed to draw between the two. Wilkins's pictures explore the peculiar area where such differences become visually indistinguishable.

This murky field of reception has intrigued many artists. At the perceptual threshold, images succumb to a condition of flux. Giacometti, for example, tried to catch appearances in the ambiguous moment when someone far away becomes equivocally recognizable. The photographer in Antonioni's *Blow-Up* finds the murderer in the trees by hyperenlarging a fuzzy pictorial detail. Early photo works by Sarah Charlesworth transform lurid news photos into cryptic masses of black and white. Work that operates at the nether edge of legibility has something creepy about it, hinting as it does that we don't see things as they really are, and that we're constantly looking at things that we don't really see.

Perception is shaped, and dulled, by environment. Wilkins's pictures destabilize familiar, almost subliminal images from the urban environment he lives in (London), giving them a kind of liquefied mutability. The beauty of these enlargements is a terrorizing mimicry of state-of-the-art advertising in England, which largely dispenses with verbal information. An ad campaign typically begins with a strong visual symbol of the product presented with the product name; subsequent advertisements simply use the visual symbol. A Silk Cut cigarette billboard, for example, consists of a large, almost abstract image of razor slashes in a length of silk. The urban viewer has been programmed to associate the image with the product—but not instantly. The decoding required heightens the viewer's involvement with the advertisement, but sidesteps the rational mediation required for reading words.

This is unquestionably the wave of the future. An environment of image bombardment is producing a sophisticated syntax of visual cues. Wilkins takes the mute pedagogy of ad sequences a step beyond into a paranoid realm where free-floating bits of ad manna bloat to consume our attention. And there they patch into whatever networks of association are set off. As partial glimpses of coherent pictures that are never seen, Wilkins's paintings set off sensory desires and manipulate them towards an imaginary completion. As pictures "on their own," replete with the tissuelike naturalness of watercolor veiling, they stimulate a highly modern fear of the inorganic assuming autonomy, of representation replacing the real—like the cartographic fantasy of Borges, in which a map becomes large enough to coincide with the territory it describes.

QUARTERLY DIVIDENDS

[**Georgia Marsh**. Bette Stoler, 13 White Street, through October 5.]

Reentering the atmosphere of the New York art world after a few weeks in the countryside is like being trapped in a wretchedly ventilated freight elevator with a capacity crowd of amphetamine abusers. Yesterday, a perennially fringe painter materialized in front of me on the sidewalk, breathless with the news that she had just been photographed for the cover of the Sunday *Times* magazine. "Not as myself," she explained, with little rue, "but as part of the exciting East Village art scene."

At this point, "not as myself" might be an appropriate theme for an exciting East Village art show. The ridiculous cover story of the September *Arts* magazine embalms the whole phenomenon, offering group portraits in which the most palpable feeling is the intense resentment of each figure at having to be in the same room with the others. I, lest there be any question on this score, declined the honor—politely at first, politely at second, politely at third, and at last with a certain exasperation. Though one of Viva's greatest lines kept coming to mind ("I'm not *dead* yet!"), I beat it down throughout each telephone call, saving it for use here.

It's my silly guess that the present season will be devoted to weeding out the more superfluous publicity creations of last season. Collectors will unload the conspicuously worthless objects of their scavengings. Certain painters will turn to the performing arts as their breakthrough works begin peeling and dropping crockery shards into the étouffée. The marginal shall become central and the central shall become marginal. A rain of toads shall fall for 40 days and 40 nights. A foul gas shall seep from old spaces that are made big, and from many galleries that have moved, and from critics who have published their diaries.

These, at any rate, are my predictions for the time at hand. Of course there also will be artists who always have been good and get better; not all of them have time or inclination to sit, stand, or recline for publicity photos. One of the pleasanter aspects of art writing is the occasional discovery of interesting work that becomes more interesting as it evolves, work that proceeds from an apparent impasse into something unexpected and fresh. Another pleasant aspect is the liberty to say, without demur or fear of blue pencil, that the cover cuties in *Arts* magazine (with two or three exceptions) shot their wads a long time ago.

Let's turn now to the new paintings of Georgia Marsh. This is an artist who started with grids and segued into acidly bright, blotty abstractions. The latter group of works suggests multiple close-ups of heat X-rays, or details in Impressionist paintings chromatically amplified, with molten colors and swirling under loose patterns of dots and splotches. Marsh's abstract work is wonderfully considered, poised between fastidious control and an appearance of violent spontaneity: in other words, the kind of work that risks failure right up to the last splash of paint.

The abstract paintings Marsh showed last year carry no taint of the representational, yet they do mysteriously convey the immanence of something real—specifically, landscapes seen with a hallucinatory intensity. Marsh's new works are, in fact, landscapes, 13 watercolors on paper and seven vinyl gouaches on canvas; these pictures take as many large chances as Marsh's earlier ones. For one thing, the emotional pitch of a landscape painting is far less ambiguous than either abstraction or pictures of the human figure. If the picture doesn't catch something awful and immutable in nature, it's at best clever painting, or merely academic. At the same time, when successful landscape pictures strike a mood, it's often a bombastic, curdlingly overdone mood. Marsh's landscapes deliver emotion gradually, like a Chopin étude, drawing one into a faintly deepening sadness, or a slowly numbing grief that this moment *now* already is becoming *then*.

Marsh's work resonates with the sense of passing time, registering moments of light, as painting traditionally has, and seldom anymore does. Careful observation of reality is widely considered irrelevant among contemporary painters, which may be why the whole middle range of emotions between orgasm and apocalypse has dropped out of general view. Marsh's fluent, bleedy sylvan glades and spectral clearings may provoke jaded eyes to flit over her watercolor as so many book illustrations, ignoring their complexity (watercolor rarely is handled this richly), and probably oblivious to the fact that the sky really is pink and orange at certain times of the day. Several of these pictures grapple with daylight as it's disappearing, stressing the unrepeatable, fortuitous occasion of empathy between the self and nature.

Marsh's vinyl gouaches are big and ambitious and manage really extravagant effects: a misty space between the trees in *La nuit Américaine*, an almost moiré sky reflected in water in *Mouth* (with a deep blue vapor rising off the darker part of the water), a massing of forms in *The Fall* and *The Sound* that gives an illusion of thick impasto. The most spectacular gouache is *Reflex*: a midnight sky and lake, broken by the darker forms of woods, revealed as the eye adjusts to pinpoints of yellow fireflies and white stars. For all the aching melancholy these paintings emanate, their presence as paintings is as tough as nails.

One could, of course, view Marsh's virtuoso realism as a peculiarly retrograde achievement. Until a few years ago the constraints of realism seemed the paltry argument of mere skill against the grand, untutored, intuitive creative gesture. But now that representational art has returned, with its celebrants asserting its emotive and spiritual significance, the ante of sophistication is steadily being raised. Serious people once again are looking for art they couldn't make easily themselves. Marsh's switch to representation, whether temporary or not, implies a refusal to reduce one's "product" to a salable trademark, and affirms the autonomy of a singular talent. Georgia Marsh is part of an avant-garde of *difficulty*.

October 15, 1985

THE HOLLOW

[**Meg Webster**, *Hollow*, in "Outdoor Installations" at the Nassau County Museum of Fine Art, Roslyn Harbor, through November.]

The outer wall of stucco-colored rammed earth is five feet high; the interrupted circle it forms is 25 feet across. The sloping interior wall runs 10 feet to the bottom. The inclined trench leading into it slices through 90 feet of a clearing landscaped by Frederick Law Olmsted. Meg Webster's *Hollow*, on the grounds of the Nassau County Museum, is a sculptural marvel with its roots in the work of Smithson, Holt, Heizer, Haacke—as well as that of Olmsted, Calvert Vaux, Gertrude Jekyll, and Alexander Pope.

Hollow is an earthwork, a garden, a grotto, a microcosm. Its exterior has the resolute geometry of sculpture that dents the landscape and asserts the intervention of culture into nature, prescribing our physical experience of a surrounding space. Its interior is densely planted with ascending vegetation, a wild variety, everything from Chinese delphiniums to shasta daisies, yarrow, Scabiosa caucasica; tobacco leaf-size weeds and prolific clover add dramatic splashes to the stippled color and deliberately naked fissures between plantings.

Inside, there are two rock seats that face each other across the tapered-down circumference. In the summer, bees harvested the blossoming plants, rare butterflies appeared, oxide-green beetles scrabbled in the red clover ringing the upper wall. In

September, many of the flowering plants reverted to green, leaving an intricate matrix of conical, bulbous, splayed, and bladelike forms, stalks, dissolvent textures and muted colors.

It is not a garden in design, but more like the cultivated landscapes that thrive along the inner gorges of the Amalfi Drive, where horticulture defies gravity and wildflowers jut skyward from cracks in sheer rock, or the Incan farms that wrap around the faces of Peruvian mountains. One thinks of things that might evolve in a volcano crater.

A garden is sometimes prized for effects of spreading color, balance, shape; *Hollow* has been worked up to curtail the dominance of one growth over another, like a specimen greenhouse. It draws your attention to the individual plant species: how it grows, what it looks like, what sort of thing it is. Some parts are poisonous. Others have medicinal properties. Still others, most, are ornamental.

The mixture of botanical types for a formal effect is *like* gardening, but its enclosure within a meditative space has both a pedagogical edge and a gratuitous, distanced quality that makes the spectator curious about the plants and curious about the space, but lulled in quite a different way than one is lulled by a garden. The acoustics are less baffling than one expects, but filter off part of the surprising peacefulness of the surroundings in such a way that, were you seated on one of the rocks supplied, and someone else seated on the other, an unusual silence would occur, as silence might arise in a garden. The humidity is slightly higher than outside, and the air cooler, as in a grotto. However, the processional entrance, the quality of being slightly sunk into the earth, the "natural" environment that envelops you after you negotiate a highly contrived architectural descent, raises your perception of the moment at which *the environment ceases to exist*.

You can find no "normal" within the "natural": in *Hollow*, everything has been arranged to sidestep a received experience of normality within nature. Yet the piece is restorative, tonic, contemplative, Buddhistically at peace with its own contents. As if someone, in the night, had moved the refrigerator into the bathroom, and you woke and got something out of it with no geographical uncertainty.

All successful art dissolves hallucination and erodes the unconscious, even when these are its materials. Webster's *Hollow*, like the best works that have traveled under the umbrella of "environmental art," or Minimalism, or earthworks, addresses the human sensorium grandly, demanding the full scope of the body's attention—and rewards us with a slightly dizzying sense of what we habitually overlook, ignore, don't have time for, take for granted. Besides this, *Hollow* has a discretion in its scale that eschews any macho grandeur in favor of audience complicity, welcoming a slow, considered appraisal. *Hollow* also has a sensual subtlety that acknowledges the spectator's freedom to ignore it. It's a pleasure-oriented work.

If the bulk of painted art in the '80s seems to be about enhancing sensations produced by tabloid newspapers, perhaps the skim eventually will be seen in its relation to other forms of art, like *Hollow*, that connect with universal experiences, submerged feelings, the possibilities of living, continuities instead of crises. The force of this work is its dialogue with nature. The terror that nature produces in the contemporary mind is a highly unnatural fear of an unplanned, nontechnological death: an irrational death unmediated by medical bills, diagnoses, scans, X-rays, doctors, prognoses, death that can't be managed by credit card or predicted by statistics. Death, however rationalized by purchase of the anticipatory plot or acquisition of the predictable disease, takes us all, in the last gasp, straight out of the world of planning. Banishing nature from the inorganic world is a means of controlling life absolutely, abolishing the marvelous. The insurance company that owns the Fuller Building recently prohibited Luhring, Augustine, and Rhodes from installing a Garnett Puett sculpture containing bees, refusing even to consider that the bees could be quite harmless. The company representative, in fact, spoke of "killer bees." Anything natural becomes lethal in a world where everything is dead.

Nature, like an air crash, has become a source of titillation—witness the idiotic news marathon attending Hurricane Gloria—for people who regard nature as a quaint anachronism, superannuated by their VCRs and private blood banks. Yet nature is quite hardy within us, and, more to the point, without us.

Webster's work isn't about death, or morbidity, but it takes the transience of everything, including itself, cheerfully in its stride. All its materials would decompose without tending. In *Hollow*, it's possible to understand the futility of art without giving up on it, because the work is joyful and "irrelevant," hard labor personified and cosmic pleasure. You can scan the grounds of this magnificent place, formerly the Frick estate, and see that its present custodians care nothing for the formal gardens—with their roses demolished and trellis in splinters, trees overgrown with weedy climbers—and nothing for the art, either, with Michael Heizer's zigzag iron wedges overgrown with scrub grass. If you wander long enough on the grounds of the Nassau County Museum, you can feel a detestation and horror of natural death, natural life: recently, the trees were ripped out of the parking lot area, to make it look more like a mall. *Hollow* makes you feel that living and dying are important processes to pay attention to, and that everyone is always doing both. You could die even if you belonged to the country club, and you could live even if you didn't.

October 22, 1985

ENIGMATIC MAKEUP

[**Cindy Sherman**. Metro Pictures, 150 Greene Street, through October 26.]

In a beautiful fantasy by Gottfried Keller or E. T. A. Hoffmann, a young woman with dirt-speckled, honey-colored skin and a fake nose like an Arcimboldo zucchini grows sleepy after drinking a magic potion. She dreams of becoming an odalisque with rotting teeth and detachable breasts, in some emir's psychedelic seraglio. She's menaced by a wart-chinned witch. A harvest ogre blocks her path in a wheat field. She burns her hand plucking treasure from a fire. When she falls asleep, vegetation grows over her and pins her to the forest floor. She prospects for cowrie shells in a riverbed near a decapitated man whose face is beginning to sprout extra eyeballs. She turns into a giant and gobbles people up with a huge tongue. She changes into a pig. When she wakes up, she's much older, and dizzy stars swirl in the air above her head.

Actually, this doesn't happen in Keller or Hoffmann, though something like this does. Probably the dream in a traditional fairy tale would be a little boy who ran away from home in search of ghosts. Gender distribution between protagonists and ogres in folklore is a matter of some controversy. But narratively, fairy tales interest us mainly because they have the structure of dreams: episodic, elliptical, fantastic. Cindy Sherman's new series of Cibachrome photographs is hooked together by dream-logic.

Inspired by the idea of fairy-tale illustration, Sherman has extracted generic resonances for stories of her own.

Like any worthy dream or fairy tale, Sherman's is replete with bizarre metamorphoses, false awakenings, preternatural miseries. The life-size format of the prints invests terrific force in the discrete icon; seeing them all together reveals a dramatic unity. Sherman's work has always seemed suffused with latent horror of *reduction* (to roles, to appearance); one of its tensions (and conceits) is the artist's/subject's difference from herself, played against the viewer's awareness that "they" (the Monica Vitri look-alikes and Italian starlets of the "Untitled Film Still" series, the reclining, emotion-fraught solitaries of Sherman's long horizontal pictures) are all really "her"—the artist, a larger, ironical personality hidden under the makeup, even when there is no makeup.

Sherman's new work gets us much more involved in "her" than any of her previous pictures. The quality of artifice in these is more theatrical than cinematic, obvious yet magically complete. The studio set changes from character to character; Sherman convincingly simulates forests, deserts, the landscapes of reverie. Most of her characters give the impression of having awakened in a different place than where they went to sleep. There is usually an overturned vessel of some type, a goblet or bottle lying around to suggest transformation-by-intoxication, or waking with the horrors.

In at least seven of these pictures, Sherman wears prosthetic body parts: nose, breasts, a warty schnoz, buttocks, tongue, and best of all a welt-bloodied pig snout. Of the buttocks and breasts it could be said that these invite and then frustrate a certain kind of attention: "If you're looking for tits and ass, these come off and you can have them." But these prostheses are potently evocative in a poetic sense and heighten the atmosphere of dreaming. In dreams, parts of one's body can change form effortlessly, detach, and assume a life of their own.

Sherman's work has so often been about movies, has so often arrested glimpses of movie archetypes, that films quite naturally suggest themselves here in her least movie-conscious work. Syberberg's recent films have exploited the oneiric, fine-line possibilities of gel lighting and theatrical camouflage; the dramatic cropping of Sherman's overhead-diagonal witch, and an even more startling shot of a screaming woman viewed from the far end of the yellow wrapper she's been sleeping under, share an enchanted indifference to camera convention with Raúl Ruiz's *The Roof of the Whale* and *Three Crowns of the Sailor*. Like Ruiz (and quite unlike Syberberg), Sherman has a semidetached sense of the visceral that encourages her to go quite far in the direction of shock without risking tastelessness, the grace of a sleepwalker filming her own eidetic images.

Of recent films, the one that comes closest to doing what Sherman does is Nicolas Roeg's absurdly underrated *Insignificance*, which fixates on one frozen moment of a Marilyn Monroe film (the subway-grating sequence from *The Seven-Year Itch*) and spins out its full meaning in terms of cultural mythos and relativity theory. The acting in *Insignificance* is akin to Sherman's acting in her photographs, deliberately wobbling in and out of the archetypal wrapper, sporadically revealing the "actor" (who is still acting) and exposing the machinery of simulation.

Sherman is fascinated by the *appearance* of mutilation, scarring, decay; these pictures stop a millimeter short of total illusion. One is absorbed in the image but not entirely taken in by it. Sherman leaves enough in for us to see how it was made, that it was made—not the whole join, but a bit of the seam, a dob of blatant grease paint here and there. I think she's interested in why we're interested to see a girl with a blubbery pig snout casually ingesting (what looks like) a worm, but *she* wants to see it too. The man with the severed head lying against a gorgeous mosaic of pebbles, whose right eye appears to be propagating in two places, suggests the perverse persistence of the desire to see things, no matter what they are.

Sherman's new pictures don't illustrate old myths, though they represent a woman barking back at old myths quite ferociously. They give a violent female reality to characters that might fit into male fairy tales if Sherman's creations were less ambiguous, less harsh, less obsessed with their own curiosity—or more lovely, more ugly, more recognizably fairy tales.

October 29, 1985

NOW, VOYAGER

["**The Knot: Arte Povera At P.S.1.**" P.S.1, 46–01 21st Street, Long Island City, through December 15.]

Press releases are the purest modern literature. "In the past few years," this one from the Hirshhorn Museum and Sculpture Garden says, "international attention has focused increasingly on the vitality and diversity of contemporary Italian art." It goes on. "The surge of activity is not confined to a particular region of Italy, nor is it characterized exclusively by a single critical camp or position."

Furthermore, contemporary Italian art encompasses a wealth of different styles. For instance "*anacronisti,* referring to those painters whose styles are associated with the use of myth, allegory, and idealized images culled form specific sources of Western art history, and *transavanguardia,* a general designation for a variety of artists whose work often alludes to a more distant, primordial past." Not to be confused with "the formerly prevalent aesthetic of *arte povera,* wherein nonart materials were used to create stark environments, to illustrate ideas or thought processes, or to protest the perception of art as a commodity."

These helpful designations accompany the catalogue for "A New Romanticism: Sixteen Artists from Italy," a show I haven't seen, but an interesting catalogue withal. It contains an essay by Carl Brandon Strehlke that tells us (another quote, excuse me)

"…the profession of art critic in Italy has evolved in such a way that the critic has had his hand in numerous activities…. For the emerging artist, finding the right critic as a champion is more important than acquiring a dealer or being exhibited in a private gallery."

This kind of information is always helpful when a new phenomenon bursts upon the scene, or an old one "emerges" inexplicably. A new romanticism at the Hirshhorn is neatly paralleled by "The Knot: Arte Povera at P.S.1," an immense recrudescence organized by Germano Celant, an associate editor of *Artforum*, whose hand is amply in evidence throughout the exhibition. Celant's musings ubiquitously preface the exhibition rooms, in large type. The catalogue texts for *this* show link *arte povera* with our homegrown Minimal art. *Arte povera* is said to be a reflection of the industrialized erasure of the city/countryside dichotomy, a committed art opposed to Italian fascism, the antithesis of patriotic, retrograde romanticism à la Chia, Clemente, and others who have leapt into myth, allegory, or an even more distant, primordial past.

Of course, one can't ignore that "The Knot," in a rather different manner than the three Cs or the *anacronisti* digs up a fabled past that would like to be the wave of the present. This is a perilous enterprise, as a hard look at any number of recently exhumed, Minimal glories would surely demonstrate. The subtext of any huge contemporary art show is always prescriptive and assumes the supposedly exploded idea of Progress in Modernism. Everyone with a proprietary interest in art would like to proclaim what the next big thing is going to be, declare what's presently valid, what's presently garbage, and how art can be saved from the depredations of the commodity system.

Does *arte povera* "protest the perception of art as a commodity"? I'm curious about this rather flippant, perhaps adversarial description, which is not Celant's but the kind of telegraphic collapse of meaning perfected by the modern press release. But Celant makes the claim in his own way. Most of the work in this show represents the pursuit of ideas that the *arte povera* artists launched 20 years ago, a longevity that suggests some form of accommodation to the marketplace. Springing *arte povera* on an especially moribund art season seems intended to seed a second, American generation of *arte povera*-inspired work, which would certainly generate revenue for the progenitors, in the form of shows, international travel, funding for projects. The perception of art as commodity may well be lowering, but the perception of art as money is anything but incorrect. The trope of the art movement has been inextricably entwined with cash flow for many years, and lately has become so obvious that even art magazines feel obliged to point this out.

The altitude of *arte povera* is considerably higher than that of most recent art movements. Its stance is less crass, more idealistic. Its polemical raison d'être, however, falls into the same hole that Minimalism did. *Arte povera* objects are made from "nonart" materials, true, though what really qualifies in 1985 as a nonart material might be hard to identify. *Arte povera* works do resist the ambient blanding-out that happens to art objects more readily installed in a condominium, prone as this "tendency" is to prod, poke, and proliferate uncontrollably through space. On the other hand, this simply means you have to own a palace to accommodate *arte povera*, or control vast quadrants of public land.

Happily enough, we have P.S.1. It would be hard to know where else in New York to put this stuff. Mario Merz's concentric igloos of glass sheets and Giuseppe Penone's landscape of weed-permeated sculptures and dirt-filled planting tubs would fill quite a large gallery. *Arte povera* per se is obsessed with scale and "uselessness": Michelangelo Pistoletto takes up most of the basement with bales of old clothing, ringed to support sheets of plate glass, with tea kettles on hot plates under the glass forming condensation patterns. Upstairs, Pistoletto has bisected a Versailles-scale gilded mirror. Then there's a gigantic, aggressive piece by Luciano Fabro with a jagged-edged, flat chunk of metal hanging off a pole, the pole supported by two fat piles of 80 pound sandbags. Jannis Kounellis's wall of eccentric wooden shelving and plaster shards likewise strikes the heavy note of Scale.

Overall, the *arte povera* show suggests a paradigm joined at the hip to Minimalism: the artist as a beefy, sweating, blue-collar manqué, heaving massive chunks of raw material hither and yon between vast bowls of spaghetti. (In case this image strikes you as anti-Italian, I got it from a Pasolini movie.) However, in his otherwise elusive catalogue texts, Celant is careful to say that *arte povera* is not, in fact, a coherent movement, and certain pieces suggest more delicate sensibilities: Giovanni Anselmo's little stone pillar with a head of lettuce wrapped to one side by a metal rope and another rock; Pier Paolo Calzolari's refrigeration pieces, particularly the small one, featuring a sculpted flute and raised letters on a frozen metal sheet (*Un flauto dolce per farmi suonare*, or *A flute for me to play on*), and some very disturbing, overhanging whorls of ribboned aluminum by Marisa Merz.

The immensity of P.S.1 is perfect for an exhibition like this; the impression of there being one too many works by each of the 12 artists included isn't nearly as intrusive as it might be if the show was physically cluttered. Celant has made the best possible case for *arte povera* here; the dramaturgy of "The Knot" is, if you will, a poem of force, powerful as any Minimalist sculptural heroics, and similarly redolent of a boy's club scheme of cultural revolution.

November 5, 1985

THE WORLD'S ONLY HYGIENE IN PICTURES

["**The Indelible Image: Photographs of War—1846 to the Present.**" Grey Gallery, 33 Washington Place, through November 16.]

"The Indelible Image: Photographs of War—1846 to the Present" is the kind of exhibition meant to tease out various key problems about looking and picturing. It contains over 200 photographs of "war," the earliest a quarter-plate daguerreotype (1846) of Exeter, New Hampshire, volunteers for the Mexican War, the latest titled *Aftermath of Battle of Tejutepeque, El Salvador* (1984). The show's curator, Frances Lindley Fralin, intends "to make a statement about the absurdity and futility of war…(notwithstanding knowledge of the theories of 'just' and 'unjust' wars or 'good' ones)." Her selection criteria were aesthetic; well-known war images that have become "clichés," "banal" through extensive reproduction, were excluded.

In other words, what has been assembled is an assortment of fresh horrors, plucked from as many wars as possible. Just as Edward Steichen's "Family of Man" exhibition showed us how people everywhere love and laugh and toil in the same way, "The Indelible Image" shows us how they blow each other's heads off, defoliate each other's crops, commit suicide to avoid capture, maim one another's children, test explosives, and execute traitors. We learn that war is not only absurd and futile, but sad, lethal, and extremely photogenic.

The captions that accompany many of the photographs broadly outline the conflicts they illustrate and tell us whom and what we are looking at. The seven naked men in coffins are members of the Paris Commune murdered by royalist troops. The frozen female corpse with its left breast ripped off is Zoya Kosmodemyanskaya, a Soviet partisan tortured and hanged by Fascists. The woman with the shaved head covering her face with a kerchief is a Saint-Tropez collaborator. The kneeling man whose brains are flying out through the back of his head is also a collaborator. The human-shaped hole in the ground is the imprint of someone who fell from a burning zeppelin. The scarred object that looks like the shank and bone of a deformed animal is a *Beer Bottle after the Atomic Explosion*.

It takes a certain dogged faith in Pavlovian response to assemble all this without irony, and on the Pavlovian level, it works just fine: one is saddened, angered, exasperated, and, quite often, disarmed by the formal splendor of the images. You may indeed come away depressed and nauseated by the undifferentiated sensation of having looked death (other people's death, actually) straight in the eye, your sense of outrage at organized slaughter competing with a sense of inevitability and helplessness. But subtler effects are available to the jaded contemporary eye.

As an ensemble, "The Indelible Image" seeks to bring the reality of war close enough to smell. After the visual shocks wear off, however, the image of the photographer, snapping away as the world burns, begins to supplant the picture before one's eyes. This is, evidently, an intended effect; the picture chosen for the catalogue cover shows goggled air force personnel in deck chairs watching an atomic test blast, passive spectators actively irradiated by the spectacle.

On the imaginative level, the generous visceral grossness of "The Indelible Image" melts away, in many instances, into an appreciation of war photography as narrative fiction, contrived for larger psychological effects than mere photojournalism can achieve. In this regard, Margaret Bourke-White's *Dr. Kurt Lisso, Leipzig's city treasurer, and his wife and daughter (Red Cross uniform) took poison as American tanks rolled into the city* anticipates the overhead interior angles and vampiric bathos of Fassbinder's *The Yearning of Veronica Voss* and Visconti's *The Damned*. Yevgeny Khaldei's *Victory Flag over Reichstag* strives towards the panoramic effects of Eisenstein's *Ivan The Terrible*, sixth reel. *The patient's skin is burned in a pattern corresponding to the dark portion of a kimono worn at the time of the explosion. Hiroshima*, by Kimura Kenichi, is a clear precursor of Franju's *Eyes Without a Face*. In these photographs reality has become a fiction, the fiction of objectivity: lower the camera to the floor level, change the lighting, and you've got a whole different kind of truth on your hands.

Since the viewer is being asked to appreciate these pictures as aesthetic objects, one may as well acknowledge that formal beauty is uppermost in many of the photographers' minds, at least in recent decades. The slaughtered Zulus and decapitated Boxer heads of the 19th century may have been pictured strictly for shock effects, but when we get up as far as Harry Mattison's *Interior of the Cathedral, Oct. 1979*, we are unquestionably dealing with art of a sophisticated, self-conscious, 20th-century sort. Five women in sundresses, dead or wounded, lie in the foreground, while a horrified male Red Cross worker and a man in a patterned shirt step over them. In the background, an expressively varied crowd (some looking at a man whose arm points across the extreme upper left section of the frame) includes not only the usual lay photographers but the presiding liturgical presence *craning forward for a dramatic snapshot*. No question about it, this shutterbug priest is the true punctum of the picture, the comic relief at the massacre.

Mattison's photograph bears a certain resemblance to the more coy, more discreet *Gaza Palestinian Hospital—Beirut*

(1982), superficially a study of a naked, bearded man with a heavily bandaged arm and an apprehensive child hooked to an IV bag, their beds facing each other under fluorescent tubing. The eye passes over the suffering presences, coming to rest on a profusion of shock-absorbing sandbags piled in the window, about to spill into the room like detritus in an early Buñuel movie.

Then there's the bespectacled IRA terrorist at home with his artillery, his face completely discernible under a nylon stocking disguise, the utter normality of his surroundings (cheap flowered wallpaper, a framed lithograph of Christ just off the cross, a cozy striped bedspread) underlining the incongruity of the submachine gun, the rifle, the neat rows of bullet cartridges. And the PLO soldier in his rubble-dusted bedroom, holding the weighty phallus of an artillery shell and a pistol, the cheap bedroom set keynoting that atavism of destruction in a world where man's accouterments are so sleekly and easily mass-manufactured.

And then, you know, there's this from the catalogue: "[Penny] Tweedie and several other photographers were recording a scene in Bangladesh, where three suspected Pakistani collaborators were being tortured by Bengali soldiers. Sensing that the drama was being enacted for the camera, Tweedie and a fellow photographer, Marc Riboud, withdrew and tried to dissuade the others from continuing. However, cameras kept clicking, possibly inciting further violence, until three executions ended the drama. Two of the photographers who continue to record the scene received awards for their work there…." In recognition of their exemplary moral restraint, what Riboud and Tweedie managed to snap before things got out of hand have been included here as indelible images.

November 12, 1985

WHERE THE BEUYS IS

I had hoped to find some salient, cheery words about **Joseph Beuys**'s *Capri-Batterie* at Massimo Audiello (436 East 11 Street, through November 24), something that would go directly to the heart of the piece and make it appealing for the reader. If I didn't, the thing could really sound silly—it's not very big, it's a "multiple," and the prototype is installed in engorging isolation as if it were something emerald-encrusted and hitherto unseen by Fabergé. The style of presentation invites deflation by the idle pen; any number of other lone objects, similarly plinthed and glass-encased, would certainly have elicited whoops and shrieks from this quarter. The current hedging sobriety of the art world cries out for some monumentally jejune pretension to provide the season with a hearty cackle; I have the abiding faith that many will turn up soon.

However, the one-piece conceit of *Capri-Batterie* is entirely apt, and elegantly funny by intention: a lemon and a yellow light bulb joined by a socket, the bulb angled forward, culture and nature stuck together in an aesthetic precoital attitude. The work alludes to juice, which the light bulb needs to light up, of which the lemon is presumably full, the plenum of one object intransmissible into the vacuum of the other: a binary opposition of energies that "works" as art because it doesn't work as a bug-lamp.

One could belabor the fragility of the bulb, the stolidity of the lemon, the utilitarian plainness of the plastic socket joining them; this work resists too much verbal attention of an appetitive type. It really didn't take much to contrive it. As is often the case with Beuys, the beauty of the idea is sufficient to carry the offhandedly virtuosic execution. It just manages, in fact, to float in the considerable volume of the space and seem like a witty answer to gallery glut.

Beuys's *Capri-Batterie* is a streamlined metaphor for civilization's ecological balance. It shows an interdependence between artifice and substance, technological artifacts and organic entities. The terms it provides demonstrate the fusion of culture with nature, culture become nature, nature as a fuel source. The light bulb doesn't exhaust itself because it never goes on, but the lemon "battery" requires periodic replacement when it shrivels up. The symbiosis of the two elements is false, in a practical sense, and true, in an artistic one.

The absolute economy of Beuys's work reaffirms the irrelevance of scale as an index of meaning. We can look at *Capri-Batterie* as a fully fleshed art object pitched toward a singular, self-constrained kind of lucidity, a sculptural lucidity that commands an ample vocabulary of abstractions and locates precise physical equivalents. In a similar vein, **Bruce Nauman**'s latest neon pieces (Leo Castelli, 420 West Broadway, through November 16) are pictorial translations of phrases from the bank of neon words Nauman showed last year (FUCK AND DIE, PISS AND LIVE, SHIT AND DIE, etc.), figures in life-size neon outline blinking through sequences of fellatio and stabbing, licking each other's body parts and firing guns, limp neon penises erecting in syncopation with gestures of mechanical violence, all in spectacular, eye-numbing colors. The utter explicitness of Nauman's kinetic panels has nothing at all to do with pornography, and everything to do with equivalence: of image and word, of sex and aggression, of art with the time it inhabits.

Like Beuys, Nauman is addressing postindustrialism's prevailing features. Beuys splices together two salubrious quantities, an organic natural object with a technological contrivance that inverts nature by providing light in darkness. Nauman fuses libido with weapon-augmented violence, alluding, more dramatically than Beuys, to a bizarre interpenetration or confusion of discrete quantities, a cultural linkage of incompatibles. In either case there is nothing especially new in the idea, but the felicity of execution lights up modern truisms with unusual brilliance.

Nauman's new works suggest the uses of technology open to well-focused artists, though these particular works also immediately suggest the limitations such artists are likely to have imposed on them. Nauman has created immensely effective pictograms for technological society's core psychic sewage, and their optimal effect might best be achieved by installing them on the surface of the World Trade Center, or featuring them on television. Things being what they are, one imagines quite a few museums barring their portals to such unambiguous statements.

Vincent Gallo's recent paintings (Annina Nosei, 100 Prince Street, through November 14) look like residue persisting in some future age of rust; in Gallo's work one finds a dichotomy comparable to that of *Capri-Batterie*, nature and representation folded together in a metaphor of mortality and renewal. Gallo paints bunches of grapes and scratches shapes of bowls and furniture into panels of oxidized, peeling metal, the fruit done in the elementary style found in recovered Greek and early Roman frescoes. The decayed industrial surfaces, in other words, carry the imprintings of a vanished culture and forgotten art, and in themselves embody the processes of nature, the action of time on the manufactured artifact.

The end-of-the-world feeling Gallo's pictures transmit is peculiarly calming. What could be called the modesty of the artist's inscription, its complicity with the very rot it faintly colonizes, instills a rather slow-burning appreciation of how well Gallo understands the temporal dimension of his materials, placing what might have been there exactly where it might have been.

November 19, 1985

GENUINE IMITATION ART

[**Richard Prince**. International With Monument, 111 East 7th Street, through December 1]

In Richard Prince's published writings, one seldom encounters the freighted descriptive felicities that persuade a reader to forego incredulity, to enter a fiction, to embrace the author's point of view. The sensibility Prince records seems hardly fictive. It has the unorchestrated realism, instead, of a faintly pointed mono- logue delivered over the telephone. Its measured jitteriness, its rehashings of tawdry spectacles and provisional intimacies, its oscillations of ego register ironic flatness, never drama. Prince's neutral, accepting tone is considerably less sunny than John Cage's, more like the enforced passivity of an airline passenger whose personal disposition has nothing to do with the condition of the landing gear. At 50,000 feet, all you can have is sanguine resignation or panic, and an assortment of beverages.

A book editor recently told me what he found objectionable about a Prince story he'd read in a magazine. "Well, you see, in real writing, one doesn't simply say these things. One *shows* them." Too true. On the other hand, Richard Prince would probably gag at the idea of being a "real" anything, since the various things he pro- duces tend to articulate the terms of a basic refusal. His current show of rephotographed photographs and redrawn cartoons is paradigmatic. The very nature of Prince's work repudiates the accepted contemporary manner of "being an artist," charting a career, coming out every season with something "original."

Granted, Prince is an artist, has a career, and he is, in the most exasperating and perverse sense, original. One follows the trajectory of his attention with continual alarm. His preoccupations are ghastly, and his method of presenting them forces us to locate the artist *elsewhere*, above and beyond his excavations of pictorial banalities. At the same time, Prince's loving attention to detail (his elegant formal thinking in assembling related, found images on single large surfaces in various photographic works) reproduces in the viewer the conditions of Prince's own fascination with particular image genres. One is gradually worn down, won over, and finds oneself thinking *well, why not*, which finally becomes, *of course, what else?*

As far as it usually goes, this kind of seduction is standard artistic strategy; any art production, sustained over time, begins to look inevitable. But Richard Prince's wayward selection of other people's images is, in one sense, arbitrary: the question of "why this instead of that" acquires its true meaning in the display. In another sense, Prince's work is much less arbitrary than that of an "artist." An artist who originates images is usually thought to follow some compulsive inner itinerary, but can in fact choose to stop, or be compelled to by circumstance (neoplasm, brakeless Mack truck). Prince's images already exist in the inexorable flow of media; giving them a different status in a funky hierarchy is as much an act of revulsion as one of homage, an acknowledgment that a picture already in the world can say as much as a new one would.

"Image appropriation" has already passed effortlessly into mainstream artchat as what-to-call-something-quoted-out-of-context, becoming a blurry buzzword for numerous, distinct activities. Prince's new works are displacements, restagings, generic overhauls: punk rock gangs, hot-rod magazine photos, pictures of surf, single panels isolating various cartoons. Each "gang" of images, represented in sufficient quantity or imposing scale, invites consideration of the specific desires the gang caters to. Interestingly, the kind of subart photography Prince reorders doesn't promote interest in the original recording eye, but in the originally intended audience.

Or audiences, plural: specialized magazines have special constituencies. For example, those who enjoy pictures of massive, wheeled industrial equipment are assumed to enjoy a contrastingly tiny but ample-jugged female figure somewhere in the picture. Custom car enthusiasts like the sight of fanged serpent decoration lacquered across hoods and bumper panels. For surfers, a view of powerful coiling waves is optic bliss. These pictures share many formal properties (sinuous forms contrasted with hard-edged ones, etc.) but are unified mainly by the crude libidinal yearnings they were designed to satisfy. In Prince's groupings they function as style specimens that often have an eerie correspondence to the surface diversities of contemporary "fine art."

The cartoons in this show are similarly distanced from their target audience, and bring this audience into the viewer's mind as a subject. Most of them seem to be taken from *The New Yorker*, though one, a fishing joke, is obviously aimed at a lower-income readership. The jokes are more intriguing "ink blots" than the photos. The contemporary art viewer knows every sort of irony to account for scopophilia, but laughter and its absence are comparatively personal, uncontrollable, and at times coldly revealing.

The question of audience carries a dark potency in this show. Unlike mass-media images that address "everybody," these images, originally contrived for smaller demographic groups, have been conceptually transmogrified for perhaps a smaller single one, though having strayed into the art zone they've acquired whatever status of permanence such a migration can ensure. I hesitate to say they've been rescued, because they seem rather to have been gotten rid of—it's Prince's quirky talent to preserve the things that have sidetracked his voyeurism as the physical evidence of his art. His mental itinerary is what really interests us, and its visual and verbal markers always seem, at first, like digressions from some central point. But the real center of Prince's current work is precisely the absence of the author from his self-portrait, "telling" rather than "showing."

Prince's work is a reinvention of surrealism, an uncorrupted and thoroughly modern surrealism in which every picture tells more than it's supposed to, simply because of a change of venue and a change of signature. True, Prince does everything necessary to present what he finds as art. But he also inserts a phantom spectator between this "real" viewer and the uninvented image, maintaining the ambiguous stance of an invisible artist.

November 26, 1985

"GARBAGE, THE CITY AND DEATH," ETC.

Not a week has passed since his death that I haven't wished Rainer Werner Fassbinder were still alive. If he had moved to New York, as he sometimes planned to, I'm almost certain he would have made movies about artists, art, money, and real estate, movies about careerist hustlers and flim-flam promotion men dolled up as critics and dealers, movies about cash flow as the source of aesthetics, and everything else, in our patriotic time. Alongside *An Early Frost*, we might have had a speculative fiction in the manner of *The Third Generation*, about how a major chemical company invented AIDS for germ warfare purposes, and how a biological experiment got out of control, and the means by which the resulting havoc came to be blamed on the most despised minority groups; yes, Fassbinder could have managed a fiction like that quite convincingly, and perhaps uncovered an interesting notion: if the right wing didn't invent AIDS. It might as well have, since it works so well as an instrument of state policy.

Fassbinder understood the modern world in the least deluded terms available. He showed how capitalism organizes all human beings into victims and exploiters, prostitutes and pimps; he saw the historical mechanisms in which victims become empowered by the guilt of their oppressors to victimize others in their turn. This is a central theme of *Garbage, The City and Death*, a play that was banned in Frankfurt 10 years ago and is now being banned again, for alleged anti-Semitism. (One of the two sympathetic characters in the play is called "A Rich Jew.") The most vociferous allegations come from Joachim Fest, editor of the *Frankfurter Allgemeine Zeitung* and, ironically enough, author of the only exhaustive study of Hitler that barely mentions the Final Solution.

Certainly Fassbinder intended to provoke people with his naming of characters in this work, but the internal properties of the characters play against their surface "identities." The tallest character is always called "The Dwarf"; the former concentration-camp exterminator, Herr Müller—instead of going to South America with money from the American CIA like Klaus Barbie—gets up in drag every night and sings in a nightclub. The city of *Garbage, The City and Death* is run by gangsters who carve up the town into zones of real estate speculation, preying on the underclass that serves their libidinal cravings. On the surface, social problems have been solved, because everything has been rationalized. Everyone knows his place; the scum on the bottom will be destroyed, the scum on the top will profit. Fassbinder's play anticipated the Reagan '80s. It paints a world where no one needs to talk anymore because everyone feels the same fear, and even this fear has been turned into merchandise. *Garbage, The City and Death* should not be banned to placate a hypocritical "morality."

* * *

In her unforgettable and long-needed evisceration of Pauline Kael's collected works a few years ago, Renata Adler discussed at some length the problems of daily, weekly, and monthly writing. Adler pointed out that the ante of hyperbole rises in proportion to just how frequently one is obliged to turn up *the newest, the best, the most interesting* thing in one's field. Indubitably, picking over the same turf day after day, week after week, can engender severe perceptual distortions, including a taste for the *most sensational, most mindless, most nihilistic* manifestations. Naturally, one hopes to avoid the creeping philistinisms that recommend themselves to the deadline-pressured during the off day, the off week, the off month: to do so, however, one finds oneself developing all sorts of little phobias. For example, I question any paper object bearing the words "For Immediate Release." What does that mean, immediate release? It suggests a previous incarceration, or something that has built up unpleasantly and needs to spew forth, or an imperial decree issued to a faceless mass of feudal subjects.

The regular contributing writer also faces certain transient personal whims, indulging which can be more than a little dicey. I did hit on one this week, though, which seems almost innocent: I went to Philadelphia. Specifically, I went to Richard Flood's **"Memento Mori"** show at Moore College of Art (through December 18), and urge you to do likewise. This show features work by 35 artists who have addressed one of the few topics that never goes away. Although the breadth of individual approach is, as you might expect, considerable, all the works in the show are unnervingly direct about The Subject, from the two versions of Andy Warhol's *Electric Chair* to Steve Gianakos's four *Dead Girl* paintings (*Dead Girl at Party, Dead Girl in Egypt* and so on), or Robert Delford Brown's gypsum skulls on satin pillows (*Mr. and Mrs. Herman Eutic*), or Juan Sanchez-Juarez's large vertical graphite drawings of skeletons. The show is wittily installed in a big, airy gallery with no endemic whiff of morbidity, but Death is everywhere.

* * *

David Deutsch's new paintings (at Blum-Helman, 20 West 57th Street, through November 30) are gouaches on paper mounted on interestingly shaped canvases. In a show earlier this year,

Deutsch had mainly very large paintings; one group dealt with the internal architecture of domes, and the notion of viewing the outside world from inside by means of lenses, as within a camera obscura or celestial observatory. Another group, of long, thin pictures whose stretchers were distinctly curved, referred to the elongation of the lens-mediated image, while the third showed the landscape-object plainly.

Deutsch's new work advances the investigation. Most of the pictures are landscapes, some richly dark and profusely painted, others built up in a sketchy, scratchy manner. Again, because of the uncommon shaping of the pieces, they suggest a world that can be observed only with the aid of instruments; the dome is a metaphor for the artist imprisoned inside his own sensorium, who reveals certain privileged croppings, faint or muddy representations of whichever chunk of the big picture his tools let him see.

Deutsch has found an appealingly understated way of emphasizing the fact of representation, depicting vision as the floating layer between subjectivity and the world. The paintings in his show also play on the normative appearance of art, making fun of it, in a way. Having been done flat and then affixed to an assertive support structure, they physically embody the metaphor of distortion, partly in order to "look like art."

Barry Bridgwood's extensive show of silkscreened paintings (at New Math, 206 Avenue A, through December 15) are far differently appealing. They're wonderful because they don't look like art, but instead like glistening industrial artifacts of unknown purpose, stamped out in garish, multipocketed enamel with sloshy and puckered textures congealing across indecipherable dot matrix "pictures." Bridgwood made drawings of apples and landscapes with computer graphics and transferred them to silk screens. The resulting canvases vibrate like flowers of evil seeded by some malign decorative technology of the future.

SHERRIE LEVINE AND BETTE DAVIS:

AFFINITIES AND CONTRASTS

[**Sherrie Levine**. Baskerville + Watson, 578 Broadway, through December 21]

Bette Davis is walking down the street in Los Angeles. She's wearing a frumpy cloth coat and sunglasses. She stops in front of an auction hall. In the window there's a glamorous publicity photo of Bette Davis. I don't remember what her name is in this movie, but the poster the picture's attached to says that her belongings are being sold. Just as she's looking at this, her agent comes out carrying a table lamp or candelabra that's covered with noisy crystal pendants.

The subject was Sherrie Levine. My friend said, Sherrie Levine must be the most written-about person, do you realize how many articles have been written about Sherrie Levine? I said no, I didn't, but I suppose I sensed that there had, in fact, been quite a few. Do you think, I said, it would be possible to say something new about Sherrie Levine? Something no one else had said?

Bette Davis snarls at everyone in this movie. Particularly her agent. I can't remember his name, either. It's probably Joe. Picking over the leavings like the rest of them, I see, she says. Come on Joan, he says, or Jean, or Maggie, or whatever her name is, let's get a cup of coffee.

Maybe the point of that work is the impossibility of writing about it, he said, it seems so slender, almost gestural, in terms of what the thing itself actually is (he talks like that, this friend), but then when you look at it and think about it for a while it takes on this whole historical dimension… The conversation was getting nowhere. Fortunately, the new paintings aren't copies.

They go to this outdoor café and she says, If only I could get one good part, Joe. I'd be back up there again in no time. Talk to Selznick, Joe, that property was written for me, you know that, I was born to play that role. An uncomfortable silence. Listen, Maggie, Joe tells her finally, Let's be realistic. When you first came to Hollywood, you had that glow, that dewy quality that everybody loved.

They just look like copies. Some are geometric abstractions. Vertical stripes. Each of the 12 stripe paintings is 24 by 20 inches, made of casein and wax on mahogany. The stripe along the left of each painting is thin. Then three thicker stripes run across to the right edge. The stripes are identically arranged from painting to painting.

Just how long do you expect anybody in this town to stay dewy, she practically spits at him. The waitress walks up to the table and says, Excuse me, I got a bet with the dishwasher—aren't you Maggie X (whatever Bette Davis's last name is)? Why yes I am, Maggie says, gracious to her fans even as she hits the skids.

Some of the pictures have two colors, others three, and one, I believe, has four. I wrote them down: cobalt blue, thalo green, carmine red. Aqua green, warm gray. Chartreuse, plum, thalo green. Chartreuse and eau de Nile (I had help), cerise and chocolate, terra cotta and eau de Nile. Azure and aubergine.

Bette Davis drives home to the dumpy bungalow she's been reduced to living in. As she's making for the door, the lady who collects the rent stops her gently, respectfully. You can tell she's a fan who hates to see a star down on her luck. I'm real sorry, Miss X, the Tacoma Brothers say if they don't get the rent tomorrow you'll have to get out.

Then there are five completely different paintings, all 20-by-16-inch slabs of cut plywood, each with a differently grained, moiré-looking pattern. Where a leaf-shaped knot occurs, by chance, in the surface of the wood, Levine has spilled a thin layer of gold paint. The number of knots varies from plywood piece to plywood piece. And that's the picture, period.

I just need another day, she says, then busts in on her worthless in-laws who've been waiting up for her, expecting their monthly allowance. Her sister is a classic whiner, her brother-in-law a cringing, snuffling cretin who's already eaten everything in the refrigerator and is now ensconced in an easy chair, burping.

The first thing anyone would say is that the stripe pictures, at least, look like they've been taken from somewhere else (Burgoyne Diller? Blinky Palermo?). The gold-knot pictures "evoke." Magritte uses a lot of that wood-grain effect, for example. For that matter, Diller uses it too.

I'm broke, damn it, I've got four dollars and seventy-five cents in my purse, you want that too? Bette Davis is screaming. I'd certainly like to know, Maggie, her horrible sister whines, how you went through all that money. You would, would you? I'll tell you, then. I bought the house you're living in. I paid for the three operations that worthless husband of yours has had in the last two years. I paid for your daughter's braces.

But even though they look familiar, no one has quite done these pictures before. Levine is addressing, or rather creating, a fictional art history; having already excerpted real art history and in some ways inverted it, Levine is now inserting fakes in the form of originals. To put it another way:

She throws all the bills off her desk and kicks her relatives out of the bungalow. Then she grabs her Oscar off the mantelpiece and says, Come on, Oscar, we're going for a ride.

There is a formal way of thinking about art that assumes that perceiving a thing *purely* requires us to strip away all of our learned responses to it. Forget that this or that engraving was made by Picasso, that these clay lumps are Rodins. But to perceive a thing purely is necessarily to perceive it wrongly. In the modern era every created thing has specific information attached to it; every work by Popova or Klee is elaborately codified. Every object emits its own history. In a distinct sense, the relatively short but highly significant history of Sherrie Levine's art infects these nonappropriated paintings with a conditioned expectation: who is she doing now?

Bette Davis steers the sedan with one hand, glugging whiskey from a bottle she's clutching in the other, all the time jabbering and cackling at the Academy Award on the dashboard. She pulls up in front of various Bel Air mansions. "That's the beautiful home of the young Janet Gaynor," she growls. "How young can you be?"

In copying masters like Klee, Malevich, Schiele, and Rod-chenko, Levine has carved out a sizable chunk of art history as "her" history, defined what exists for her, what she wants to look at. Everyone, in fact, assembles his or her own story about the past. Goethe thought every civilized person ought to be able to account for the last two thousand years in elaborate detail, but the modern mind is generally less omniscient. An aleatory, non-linear sense of the past turns history into fiction, but Levine also reverses this effect. Single tendencies in art are imperialistic, in the sense that they propose ideal solutions to "the problem of art." In her "1917" show last year, where she showed Malevich and Schiele rip-offs simultaneously, Levine demolished the thread-tracing model of art historicism. The show's overt aim was to reveal history as inescapable and cumulative, art as the product of its time. "1917" endorsed two mutually exclusive, synchronous forms of art production, reclaiming the idea of history from the fiction of prescriptive methodology.

Similarly, Levine's current show embraces two contrary but esteemed modernist practices (strictly controlled, geometric abstraction/the exploitation of chance) to dissolve the fiction of style, locating her work in the rudderless moment of contemporary art. *Don't be so sure no one said that before, either.*

Bette Davis played a failed actress at the height of her success. Sherrie Levine…

December 10, 1985

MEMORIES ARE MADE OF THIS

["**The Art of Memory/The Loss of History**," The New Museum of Contemporary Art, 583 Broadway, through January 19.]

"The Art of Memory/The Loss of History" at the New Museum, organized by William Olander, is an ambitious attempt to isolate a notoriously slippery theme. A good deal of interesting contemporary art is obsessed with the idea that representational media determine the structure of the human psyche. The act of remembering correctly is thought to conflict with official constructions of "history"; the act of seeing a thing clearly, then, unravels an overdetermined, false version of reality.

Most of the art in this show takes off from these premises. Judith Barry's videotape, *Mirage*, shows an American Indian (according to the notes, a Vietnam veteran) returning to his hometown, where everyone is behaving strangely, and everything is not quite as he remembers it. Ultimately, it's revealed that the town has been replaced by a sort of replicant tourist attraction. Another videotape, by Peter Adair, features three male storytellers. Each describes power conflicts between men; some of the stories are true, some aren't. Bruce Barber's videotape loops together several fatuous TV spots for United Technologies that define, in serendipitous ad blather, what things like technology, history, and life itself really are.

I'm starting with these works first, because they most obviously assume an audience that spends 90 percent of its time in front of a television set, getting brainwashed. And they demonstrate an intimate acquaintance with the sensory condition. I'm not saying these works aren't effective, but effective upon *whom* is a question occasioned by more than a few pieces in the show. You have to have something before you can lose it, and it would be interesting to know which of the artists included here has ever heard of Herodotus, or for that matter E. J. Hobsbawm. In numerous instances, ironies obvious to any reasonably informed person are offered with a souring mixture of enthrallment and condescension. They seem ideally intended for a viewer who has never had a skeptical thought in his/her head.

One shouldn't necessarily look a skeptical thought in the mouth these days, even if it's one you've already had. But if you've already had it, God forbid it should come back to you shrieking *eureka*. While it's true that mass media instill as much amnesia as they possibly can in their consumers, the counsel of perfection is simply to turn off the television set. Few seem capable of doing so, including many of the artists in this show. Of course, even if you've been lucky enough to avoid United Technology's mush-brained TV spots, just open a magazine and there UT is again, "Remembering Vietnam" as none but the memory-impaired could possibly remember it: "As a nation we have always tried to do what is right." A long, lying text, which Bruce Barber has superimposed over gruesome images of the war, adding at the bottom excerpts from "The Winter Soldier Investigation into America War Crimes in Vietnam." The juxtaposition of corporate duckspeak with direct descriptions of atrocities has a starling effect, yes. These photo pieces do revive important historical memories, as if with a sledgehammer. But who, exactly, is supposed to have forgotten these things?

History and memory survive and disappear through language. Several things in this show thrive on the presence, or absence, of contextualizing language. Along one wall, Sarah Charlesworth has photo pieces that reproduce *International*

Herald Tribune front pages from September 1977, with all the text between the news photos deleted; a space of historicizing language is cleared away, and what's left is a blunt visual code describing a world of male power relations. Rene Santos's luscious paintings of square-framed, daguerreotype-toned portraits of 19th-century luminaries, with the occasional figureless square in the middle, emphasizes the white space in historical memory caused by transient cultural fashion; one might know a few things about Daudet, Manet, and Rossini, but who, right off the bat, remembers Adolphe Crémieux, Alfred Musard? Even certain biographical dictionaries are mute. Richard Prince's "Sunset" series of C-prints, in which pictures of beachside fun are enlarged into menacing scenes of imbecility and violence, are similarly cryptic, silent about their origins.

Quite talkative, by contrast, is Martha Rosler's *Global Taste*, a tri-monitor video work. On one monitor, a loop of commercials, mainly kids eating ghastly things, families gushing over food products; another monitor endlessly reruns an interminable Dr. Pepper commercial, while the central monitor offers pictures of Pampers-happy babies, Michael Jackson hawking Pepsi-Cola, *People* magazine's ad for its "The Day Rock Cried" issue, plus analyses of CocaColonialism, Saatchi & Saatchi's plans for global domination, and the cultural imperialism of Hollywood. Here, I'm afraid, the didactic voice of reason, spoken as well as printed out à la *60 Minutes*, sounds every bit as manipulative as the Dr. Pepper jingle—in different ways, both kinds of language speak to a narcotized, mentally inferior, fictitious audience.

Louise Lawler's *Two Wall Displays: Arranged by Mr. and Mrs. Alfred Atmore Pope or their Daughter Theodate, Farmington, Connecticut* features three pictures of art in a "preserved" interior; Lawler's artistic economy is fairly breathtaking, especially in proximity to verbosities like *Global Taste* and Adrian Piper's *A Tale of Avarice and Poverty*, the latter a woman's portrait surrounded by framed, unenticing text. Lawler is never tendentious, and the history/memory theme is hilariously understated in that "or their Daughter" in the work's title. Hiroshi Sugimoto's close-in photographs of nature dioramas effectively obscure the staged, stuffed quality of what they depict, and thus question the historical veracity of photographic evidence; Christopher Williams's Cibachrome prints of city views enhance a picture-postcard kind of representation the viewer recognizes, again, as a sparkling, bogus memory; in *On New York*, this is counter-poised with an image of racial violence in two different sizes.

This is hardly all; "The Art of Memory/The Loss of History" *is* an ambitious show. The catalogue has three excellent texts by William Olander and a smart, funny piece by Tina L'Hotsky on the similarity between Los Angeles and the moon, plus "Photography at the Dock," by the always-prescient Abigail Solomon-Godeau. Besides the video works mentioned already, there are others by Dan Graham, Vanalyne Green, Ulysses Jenkins, and Paper Tiger Television; on the main floor, Troy Brauntuch has a group of Cibachrome prints and a large painting. Brauntuch's images have been culled from obscure sources, among them Hitler's drawings; their unidentifiable quality bears out the fact that images die and then revive without their signifiers.

In a show where shortness of memory is a persistent concern, the presence of so much familiar recent art should not surprise or displease us. Much of this work is first-rate, and if the show overall strikes only a few notes of its attempted theme (the same ones, repeatedly), the attempt is memorable, anyway.

THE AGE OF SILVER

[**Group Show**. Anne Plumb, 51 Greene Street, through December 2]

The group show at Anne Plumb Gallery has a subtle coherence, the clarity of a well-developed argument. The works are arranged with ample breathing room between them; six artists are represented, by various numbers of works. The poise of the art within the space is peculiarly undidactic, firmly balanced and sober yet friendly, unintimidating. It's a pleasure to walk into this show and spend time with it; this is, need I tell you, rare.

Two floor pieces anchor the show. At the near end, Tom Bills's *Dog Legs*: four steel slabs, held together by a geometric form that's been cut through them and then filled with lead. The steel has oxidized to a ferrous earthy color, setting off the glinty lead form like blocky calligraphy burned into a solid wall with a laser beam. *Dog Legs* has a stubby height, a huggable width; the elegance of its lead insert, combined with the weighty force of its materials, gives it an unignorable presence, not unlike a dressed tombstone awaiting a title. Near this work, Bills has a smaller wall piece, *Horsecollar*, in which the linear motif of *Dog Legs* is inverted, serving as a steel armature for a bracketing thickness of shaped lead, curved at the top. This helmet shape reveals, in the inside contour of the "drawing," the razory striations of cut steel.

Across the gallery, John Chamberlain's *Ultra Yahoo* perches on tenuous-looking points, shoulder-high, emitting the wily chortle of civilization-after-collapse. From Chamberlain's galvanized steel period, *Ultra Yahoo* consists of two crushed-in, scored-surface, welded and screwed-together metal sheets that were, I think, fabricated to resemble Judd boxes and then subjected to Chamberlain's ambitious mayhem.

Like the underside of Bills's *Horsecollar*, the surface of *Ultra Yahoo* incorporates the natural scars and erodible quiddities of material into the formal presentation of the work. This assertion of the fortuitous as legitimate material is, of course, nothing new, but it has been less than popular in recent years—so much art is being shown now, and so much of it unskilled, that the look of happy accident produces automatic skepticism. Almost all the work in this show plays with *the given* in convincing, refreshing ways: most particularly, Christopher Wool's *Funnel III*, which looks like a funnel and was produced by pouring silver enamel over paper, and *Untitled*, the same kind of enamel poured over galvanized tin. *Funnel III* has a wonderfully thin surface of biomorphically pocked streaks and velvet-smooth passages; its veiny parts pick up the pink halations of the gallery lights as you walk past it. *Untitled* is full of minute, horizontal streaks, stippled by irregularities in the tin ground that look like graphite notations.

James Nares has two large paintings in the show. *Stone Drum Song* is a three-foot-eight-inch-by-six-foot landscape that looks like African veld growing out of acidic orange topsoil; the vegetablelike blades showered across the picture's upper half are paper-thin fronds of sheet lead, applied over enamel and galvanized tin, in the lower half, Nares has left some stylish, random-looking brushwork, like a Japanese signature. *Spirit of St. Louis* has a galvanized steel ground, with silk layered over it, pentimento forms worked from sheet lead, and an overpainting of coiling orange brushstrokes shaped into a propeller.

Carl Apfelschnitt's vertically imperious *Return of the Priest* also features sculpturally suggestive materials; it's a massive egg form, swelling out from the dark triangular edges of the picture, the shiny palladium surface dramatically cracked and punctured by 10 circular fissures that reveal flat-painted innards and walls of densely piled underpaint. The circles evoke a tree-form lurking behind the bursting surface, as well as an immanent, dammed-up energy.

There are five comparatively small paintings by Christopher Lucas, all on found pieces of wood. What they have in common with the other works in the show, besides glary or metallic-looking surfaces, is a mysterious ambivalence, a tenuous balance between the materials and the work. In Lucas's paintings, elementary forms have been worked onto unprepared ground; whether it's varnish or lacquer on the ground, or something resistant in the paint, colors inside the squares, triangles and circles are drizzled, streaked, thinly clotted; the pictures have a wan, simply regretful quality, revealing their struggle to exist, their completed inscription betraying their fragility.

All the works in this show have complex, variegated *skins*, and evidence not only of artistic willfulness, but the willfulness of materials. In some cases, an appearance of stolidity and weight has been fretted forth from essentially light, frangible stuff; in others, heavy matter is forced to look easily penetrable, to mimic suppleness. Nares uses metal as canvas, metal as wind-blown grass; Chamberlain makes light metal suggest massy volume. Wool's pieces exploit the molten metal look of paint, while Bills uses molten metal to suggest drawing. Apfelschnitt gives leaf metal an illusory, monumental density. Lucas makes paintings that float on wood, that look as if they could easily slip off, like the skin of a tomato plunged into boiling water. These exemplary works have the unfashionable, welcome quality of almost having failed, of having gotten it right after a great deal of disgusting turmoil—in other words, of not having been knocked off the assembly line to meet an exhibition deadline, agree with an established formula, or reduce a pressing waiting list. This is not to be confused with the look of heroic effort, which everyone has gotten tired of.

This column is a trifle short, so I am going to turn over a little space to Friedrich Nietzsche: "Of all actions, those performed for a purpose have been least understood, no doubt because they have always been counted the most understandable and are to our consciousness the most commonplace. The great problems are to be encountered in the street."

December 31, 1985

SIGNS OF EMPIRE

[**Clegg & Guttmann**. Cable, 611 Broadway, through January 11]

Three genres that we associate with Dutch painting of the 1600s—the business portrait, the still life, the bucolic landscape—have survived in more or less their original formal terms since the time of de Gheyn and Rembrandt. The pictorial conventions gelidified by the Dutch, even more than those of the Italian Renaissance, provide an instantly recognizable "look of art," or perhaps merely a look of iconic retentiveness that can serve, in conservative times, as pretty much the same thing. However enriched or decomposed by modern irony, the tropes of Dutch paintings surface in much recent art as earmarks of high seriousness and that ever-arguable thing, objectivity.

Photography embraced the Dutch legacy far less equivocally than painting has; inasmuch as the content of Dutch art reflects "reality" as perceived through the camera obscura, the microscope, and contemporaneous theories of optics, its scientific proclivity anticipates the mechanical picturing of the world. While critical theory and artistic practice in the past several decades have, to some extent, exploded the notion of objective photography, the popular delusion that photographs have some mute, inherent honesty is brutally reinforced by the largely visual, prosthetic sensorium of mass media.

The difference between information and knowledge, like the difference between gossip and truth, is collapsed by the immediacy of the unquestioned. If Dutch pictures had the goal of presenting things as the assisted eye truly sees them, their descendants aim at re-presenting a reality that only exists in representation. The glossy surrealism of the advertising page and the video splice—as well as what Carol Squiers calls the sculpted cream-cheese look of executive portraiture—typifies the homogenous visual idealism that suffuses Media World like a lobotomizing gas. Clegg & Guttmann's work is a strategic assault on the typical. Their Cibachromes replicate the formal arrangements of luxury advertising and corporate self-depiction, but recast them in a classical, demystifyingly artificial Northern light. Human subjects and utilitarian objects "natural" to photography appear as products, bearing the physiognomy of power.

The works in Clegg & Guttmann's current show ensnare our attention with their silken textures and elegant Netherlandish School compositions. But these pictures gradually atomize their constituent parts and deliberately ruin the kinds of representation they imitate. Commissioned portraiture, for example—a double matrimonial portrait, *The Tafels of Stuttgart*, links its subjects with the overlapping edge of a monochromatic photographic backdrop; the figures, which cast shadows across the illusory "interior" perspective, push toward us so emphatically that we read them, not simply as real people, but as living mannequins disporting the uniforms and postures of a privileged class. Cuff links, tie, jewelry, lipstick, and other embellishments float into high relief before an austere, moneyed interior. The Tafels "look the part." However, just as the background interrogates the foreground, the subjects' exaggerated identity with their roles as portrait subjects makes their visible flesh question their clothing. The four bow-tied, tuxedoed gentlemen in *Corporate Music*, poised against a similarly disjointed, *trompe l'oeil* "chamber music" space, also project the visual diction of a stylized, instantly familiar, elite ritual.

Clegg & Guttmann's portraits simulate and theatricalize, in their words, "the most direct way in which power represents itself." In effect, their models portray fictional characters who are posing in the way these characters might like to see themselves. (As far as I know, they also accept portrait commissions, which must complicate matters.) For the past few years, the artists have been searching out the look of "the executive potentially existing in every white male." However, most pictures in this show are arrangements of commercial objects, which more saliently embody a condition of the world than do individuals. Here, the commodity operates doubly as sign and signified; its physicality and its name are conceptually coextensive. The titles of these works are taken from featured lettering on product labels—*Pick-apecka Peppa, Kiwi Neutral, Hirschquelle Quelle, Tabasc-Tabsco*— and in the case of *Arleir Nesore*, from the edge-letters of a largely shrouded Joseph Kosuth work in the background.

Centuries before the umbrella met the sewing machine on the operating table, disparate entities encountered one another in the still life, relieved of quotidian meaning. In Clegg & Guttmann's work, however, the relationship of one thing to another reveals connecting threads of language and commerce; the aesthetic is approached parodistically and recedes before meaning. *Kiwi Neutral* forms a line extending left to right from a pair of straw sandals to a straw basket containing two coconuts and the head of a wooden mallet, the mallet's handle diagonally anchored by a tin of Kiwi shoe polish, which in turn is balanced against a coconut. Without the Kiwi, we could infer, simply, "leisure in the Caribbean." Instead, the packaged cosmetic substance pairs itself with shoes that never require polishing, which share the substance of the basket and the name of the hairy fringe around the coconuts. Further, the specific reference to a sleekly packaged export product identifies the other items as *imported goods*, things that came to one place from another through the power of money.

This implication of an insidious and universal process permeates all Clegg & Guttmann's still lifes: none of the combinations is authentically "organic," since all things empty themselves before the gaze of the consumer. *Quink Quink* offers a beef tongue nailed to a signature "interior" of stolid chairs and monumental architecture; nearby, a tin of Kiwi polish rhymes with three kiwi fruits, two uncapped fountain pens rest against a pair of dry, elongated bath sponges, close to two bottles of Quink brand ink. These objects meet on the plane of an imaginary utility that's also the space of complete uselessness: everything requires an absent moisture to "live"—the dead tongue, the sponges, the pens. The process of consumption commences the moment after this picture, when everything is eaten, irrigated, or inundated, and finally used up and replenished. And, of course, picture-making is itself a ravenous consumption, an emptying-out of the pictured.

Clegg & Guttmann's portraits describe a human reality that's satisfied with a one-dimensional condition, as long as artifice protrudes from it with enough ostentation. Their still lifes are microcosmic studies of planetary exploitation, and describe the domestication of the world through attractive packaging. The economic metaphor in *Echt Kölnisch Kölnisch Wasser* neatly summarizes what the artists call "our present time and age": three not-entirely-fresh herring with lifted tails, sharing a satiny tablecloth with two cheery bottles of toilet water. Our time and age will be remembered, certainly, for throwing perfume over everything that smells.

January 7, 1986

THE PHYSIOLOGY OF TASTE

"So who needs a Brancusi so bad they have to buy one from a murderer?"
>—Anonymous, in conversation

"So then people do come here in order to live; I would sooner have thought one died here. I have been out. I saw: hospitals. I saw a man who swayed and sank to the ground. People gathered around, so I was spared the rest."
>—Rainer Maria Rilke, *The Notebooks of Malte Laurids Brigge*, 1910

"For the so-called man of affairs with interests to pursue, plans to realize, the people he comes into contact with are metamorphosed automatically into friends or enemies…he reduces them from the outset to objects: some are usable, others an obstacle. Every differing opinion appears…as tiresome resistance, sabotage, intrigue; all agreement, though it may stem from the basest interests, becomes support, something of use, a testimony of alliance. Thus impoverishment of the relation to others sets in: the capacity for seeing them as such and not functions of one's own will withers, as does that, above all, of fruitful contrast, the possibility of going beyond oneself by assimilating the contradictory."
>—Theodor Adorno, *Minima Moralia (Reflections from Damaged Life)*, 1951

"In a country where everyone is trying to be noticed, many must believe, and indeed do believe, that it is better to be bankrupt than to be nothing."
—Chamfort, *Products of the Perfected Civilization*, c. 1780

"This sounds like an exaggeration, but it is a fact: the unexpressed archetype of the portrayal of all and everything in terms of universal history that is palatable today is the illustrated weekly."
—Martin Heidegger, *What Is Called Thinking*, 1954

"Hans von Gluck: Is it possible to run for it with a suitcase full of real estate? You get tempted by Siren songs—the houses, the property—and you're back so you can be tortured again and bleeding. And someone exists who is laughing up his sleeve all the while, and he's bought you out even before you've thought of selling. He has the banks and city hall on his side. You give up, and in the next minute you're tightening your grip on the same property which is causing you the pain. The doctors lie to your face, they're all bedfellows, they keep you alive until you've suffered enough, and 'til the gods, whoever they are, have been able to jerk off while watching you suffer. The gods hate you, and they need you to satisfy their perverse desires. They're nothing but witches and fairies, the stuff of children's nightmares, invented to prepare you for life—which is death."
—Rainer Werner Fassbinder, *Garbage, The City and Death*, 1976

"To doubt things which are now believed without any investigation whatsoever, that's the main point everywhere."
—Georg Christoph Lichtenberg, *Aphorisms*, 1789

"The mind industry can take on anything, digest it, reproduce it, and pour it out. Whatever our minds can conceive of is grist to its mill; nothing will leave it unadulterated: it is capable of turning any idea into a slogan and any work of the imagination into a hit…. The mind industry's main business and concern is not to sell its product: it is to 'sell' the existing order, to perpetuate the prevailing pattern of man's domination by man, no matter who runs the society, and by what means. Its main task is to expand and train our consciousness—in order to exploit it."

　　—Hans Magnus Enzensberger, "The Industrialization of the Mind," 1962

"Modern man understands how to digest many things, indeed almost everything—it is his kind of ambition: but he would be of a higher order if he did *not* understand it; *homo pamphagus* is not the finest of species. We live between a past which had a more perverse and stubborn taste than we and a future which will perhaps have a more discriminating one—we live too much in the middle."

　　—Friedrich Nietzsche, *Daybreak*, 1881

"One of the great rules of art: do not linger."

　　—André Gide, *Journal*, 1927

"Art that seemed eminently worth defending ten years ago, as a minority or adversary taste, no longer seems defensible today, because the ethical and cultural issues it raises have become serious, even dangerous, in a way they were not then. The hard truth is that what may be acceptable in elite culture may not be acceptable in mass culture, that tastes which pose only innocuous ethical issues as the property of a minority become corrupting when they become more established. Taste is context, and the context has changed."

　　—Susan Sontag, "Fascinating Fascism," 1974

"Talent was blazing through the columns and onto coffee tables. The physical-assault metaphor had taken over the reviews. 'Guts,'

never much of a word outside the hunting season, was a favorite noun in literary prose. People were said to have or to lack them, to perceive beauty and make moral distinctions in no other place. 'Gut-busting' and 'gut-wrenching' were accolades. 'Nerve-shattering,' 'eye-popping,' 'bone-crunching'—the responsive critic was a crushed, impaled, electrocuted man. 'Searing' was lukewarm…. 'Literally,' in every single case, meant figuratively; that is not literally. This film will literally grab you by the throat. This book will literally knock you out of your chair. 'Presently' always meant not soon but now."
　　—Renata Adler, *Speedboat*, 1971

"The effect of making men think in accordance with dogmas, perhaps in the form of certain graphic propositions, will be very peculiar. I am not thinking of these dogmas as determining men's opinions but rather as completely controlling the *expression* of all opinions. People will live under an absolute, palpable tyranny, though without being able to say they are not free."
　　—Ludwig Wittgenstein, *Culture and Value*, 1937

"They admitted they never really knew what to expect, so they watched each week to see if the saturation would ever bottom out. They knew at least, if they did this,…then whatever they did next, could look as good as the latest color, on the latest page, from the latest magazine."
　　—Richard Prince, *Why I Go to the Movies Alone*, 1983

"It will no doubt be a mighty comfort to our grandchildren, when they see a few rags hang up in Westminster Hall, which cost an hundred millions, whereof they are paying the arrears, to boast as beggars do, that their grandfathers were rich and great."
　　—Jonathan Swift, "On the Conduct of the Allies," 1711

January 14, 1986

NEW AND DIFFERENT

In art and life, things are changing. Some people think we're adjusting well. Others feel positively morbid with dread. Here and there, privileged individuals have come to view themselves as victims. Victims of their families. Victims of their friends. Victims of the press. These walking wounded are beginning to air their grievances, to speak out. *Premature Ejaculator*, the autobiography of an art world victim, has just reached this desk in galley form. Eye-opening is not the word. In the first 20 pages, the artist reveals how he was scarred for life by a spanking his father gave him in 1957. This caused him to become a street whore and to draw poorly, crippling his chance of early success. Instead, he wandered, leaving bad drawings on hydrants and parked cars, *which were not any worse than Keith Haring's drawings*, according to the author. And yet worldwide fame descended on Keith Haring, while all our ejaculator got was *adoration from second-rate people* and, worse, *persecution from the very people he tried to hustle*. It's a torrid account, and that rare thing—a work of the imagination.

Speaking of premature ejaculation, the current issue of *Spectacle: A field journal from Los Angeles* contains an interesting gloss on Rambo as a preemie-ejac victim by Helen Knode, to wit: "He'd come all over the world, with no regret and no warning.... No man, no law, no war can stop him from spilling his used cartridges on the ground." The magazine also carries a good piece by

Kathi Norklun on special effects, and a piquant essay by Joseph Nechvatal, "Superfacts," urging us to accept the condition of sensory overload as a method of transcending it. I'm not sure I agree, but Nechvatal's case is elegantly stated.

It's true that complaints about overload are becoming clichés. Mass media is so diabolical. As soon as a salient cliché can be minted some nuance occurs that disproves it. For example, on Christmas Eve one television station goes straight to underload and displays a crackling Yule log for hours. I spent both Eves, Christmas and New Year's, with the same people, part of the time near a TV set: a learning experience. Besides the Warhol log, there was a stack of rented cassettes, including a gay porno item called *Inch by Inch* that was shot in video. Video porn will undoubtedly replace all other kinds. It has the real-time immediacy that makes video a terrible medium for drama and a questionable one for art. You can almost *smell* the actors in *Inch by Inch*, and through the miracle of direct sound you can also hear all the awkward little noises that accompany Intimacy. This is the kind of triumphant realism *Premature Ejaculator* goes vainly after in prose, that only television can really deliver.

On the other Eve, Art People came crashing in at 3 a.m., but not before *They Saved Hitler's Brain*, a sublime *film noir* about the origins of the Moral Majority. What the art people wanted to do was not really very clear. They had already done quite a lot of something. I wanted to ask someone about the new "interview format" press release, of which I had received two examples. You, reader, may soon find yourself regaled against your will, by printed Q and A sessions between Gallery and Artist like the following:

Saltpeter Gallery: George Plugg, you're having seven shows in one month. I guess you've been feeling pretty productive lately. That must be a great feeling. But then I guess everybody already knows how great you are. What they didn't know, probably, is how productive you are, too.

George Plugg: Yes.

Saltpeter Gallery: Is the reason why everything you do is so astoundingly beautiful the fact that you know more about what you're doing than you once did, more perhaps than anyone, and also that you're doing more of it than you ever did before?

George Plugg: I think that's entirely possible.

Well, you get the drift; I'm afraid yet another dreadful convention has been launched.

During the unnecessary week between the Birthday of Our Savior and January 1, nothing much happens in the art world. I wanted to catch the "Art Treasures of Andorra" show uptown, having heard that this tiny principality, which is hardly bigger than the postage stamps for which it is famed, is in fact the repository of several gigantic, fake Titians and numerous authentic but wretched Rubenses. Casa Andorra, as the seat of this fabled kingdom is called, boasts over a thousand Tiffany lampshades and examples of Lalique crystal vases, plus the world's largest collection of zinc-and-lead paperweights. Alas, the museum was closed for repairs to the atrium.

I did find something downtown at Barbara Braathen Gallery (76 Duane Street, through January) that I didn't expect: two rooms full of fantastic abstract paintings by **Jamie Dalglish**. Some of these are painted on metal screen material, and in the right light cast weird shadow-paintings on the material backing their stretchers. The larger pieces, in the main room, are thickly worked up into whizzy, gooey whorls of color broken into grids of one kind or another, overlays of dots and underlays of perpendicular lines. Dalglish also has some sculpture in this show, including one piece with a television set, the screen obscured under painted shapes.

Dalglish's paintings have a relationship to television; this artist sometimes works in video, and what the paintings do is simulate the sensation of color television viewed close-up, where the constituent electronic pattern reveals itself as the image breaks apart. Imagine this enlarged and frozen and you have something like Dalglish's work. It has the feeling of violent process, paint thrown and splattered on, worked over in huge strokes like Poons. But it also gives an appearance of two physically distinct planes intersecting, one flat, one deep.

Dalglish's pictures come in modules or parts that can be configured differently from one hanging to the next. Even in the aftermath of Conceptual art this sort of alterability makes some collectors nervous. However, the fact that they can be broken up according to viewer whim is perhaps the compensation of modesty for the paintings' overloaded, overpainted pushiness; it acknowledges the problematic silence of abstract painting and the viewer's need to project meaning into it. Dalglish's work has some resemblance to that of Ralph Humphrey and Howard Hodgkin, but it also has an unbridled, relentless, almost insanely didactic bent to it; it was no surprise to hear that many works had been fussed over for several years. The canvases bear the scars of sudden, sweeping alterations and obsessively laid-in patterns.

This show is the only serious thing I looked at over the holidays besides *They Saved Hitler's Brain*; I recommend both to the overloaded.

January 21, 1986

THE GOOD, THE BAD, AND THE TURGID

[*Art After Modernism: Rethinking Representation*. Edited by Brian Wallis. The New Museum of Contemporary Art/Godine, $19.95.]

Broadly speaking, *Art After Modernism* is a textbook, but a revolutionary one. Its essays eschew the customary "servicing" mode of art criticism, which singles out masterworks for celebration, places them historically, and casually isolates them from the circumstances of their production and socio-economic/ideological careers in the real world. Instead, the book urges us to look skeptically at pictures; Brian Wallis, the editor, seems to have seized on any extensive theoretical text supporting a postmodern view of modern art and culture.

The list of contributors suggests an overreaching all-inclusiveness—which is, in fact, the arguable flaw of this volume. Less would have definitely been more, particularly when so many ruminate on the same cud. The first section disestablishes the concept of unique authorship, from three angles: inferentially, via Borges's limpid story "Pierre Menard, Author of the *Quixote*"; abstrusely, in Rosalind Krauss's "The Originality of the Avant-Garde: A Postmodernist Repetition"; and bluntly, in Kathy Acker's "Realism for the Cause of Future Revolution." The second section repudiates modernist clichés—the eternal progress of art, the autonomy of the creative process—at slightly too extensive length, hitting all bases (painting and hype, avant-garde film, art photography, criticism, etc.). Painting is taken apart and put together again in section three, by two university intellectuals and a painter, who also writes criticism. Next, new theories to replace the old, starting with the all-too-inevitable Roland Barthes, followed by the prescient Douglas Crimp on the difference between modernism and postmodernism, the equally prescient Hal Foster on the difference between modernism and post-modernism, and, surprise, the no less prescient Craig Owens on, guess what, the difference between modernism and post-modernism. Thereafter, mass media, the art world, and patriarchy are mowed to a stubble by the unduly generous number of voices, including everyone from Walter Benjamin to Michel Foucault.

Despite the book's overstuffed quality, it's at least an embarrassment of riches instead of the usual blathering pedantry found in art books. Blathering it isn't. Pedantic it is. And the illustrations mirror the intense seriousness of the texts. Artworks are shown outside the "eternal" space of aesthetic savoring, in real space and time. Cropped and arranged by Louise Lawler, the book's black-and-white pictures aptly reflect the polemical widening of critical perspective beyond the picture frame, featuring art *in situ*, and/or extremely tight relation to specific points raised in the adjacent texts. In Robert Hughes's evisceration of the Warhol phenomenon, "The Rise of Andy Warhol," for instance, Lawler has inserted Richard Avedon's picture of the artist's surgical scars. Benjamin H. D. Buchloh's "Figures of Authority, Ciphers of Regression," which links the mid-war return to figurativism in 1915 to social repression, is smartly ornamented with before-and-after paintings by Severini, Carrà, and Picabia. But these are Lawler's most matter-of-fact touches. She makes brilliant juxtapositions of film stills, posters, and art reproductions, the real with the representational; Lawler's pictures enliven this book as too few of the texts do.

Art textbooks have traditionally been celebratory, arranging one or another canon of works into hierarchies of beauty and importance. As several essays in *Art After Modernism* point out, a basic flaw in this scheme is that aesthetic values are at worst arbitrary, at best devised by academic elites, and sustained by fashion-fickle consensus. As practiced by Greenberg and Fried, formalist criticism arrived at the ultimate removal of art (and criticism) from surrounding reality: first by insisting that work in a given medium derives its entire raison d'être from its exclusive concern with that medium's properties and possibilities, and second by defining "real" criticism as the examination of an artwork's internal characteristics only. This was the jail that Rauschenberg and Johns, then the Pop artists, broke out of, only to inspire the loosened-up formalism of critics like Harold Rosenberg, who discovered aesthetic and psychological affinities between works in various media, appreciated mixed-media work, and pursued a conceptual thread stretching back from Pop clear through to Dada and beyond.

But this thread was very much in line with the pattern of modernism: aesthetic shocks, followed by a sifting-out of the minor topical, the boiling-down of movements to a hard core of important works. Importance, finally, was deemed to have lasting aesthetic resonance—"aesthetic" stretched, after Duchamp's embrace as the Grand Old Man of Modernism, to encompass the elegant gesture, the witty *idea* about art.

Art, however, remained serenely self-concerned. Even when it operated (*vide* Rauschenberg) in the gap between art and life, "life" meant a biological experience rather than an ensemble of culturally determined events. That art would "progress," in forever-new, "shocking" forms, remained the unwavering faith of modernist art and criticism. When art-historically logical disappearance of the tangible, salable art object came too shockingly close to the art market in the mid-'70s (with the proliferation of noncommodities like earthworks, performance art, etc.), "pluralism" came to the rescue: modernism could now leap beyond its own demise, and once again flood the market with collectibles.

Where a vast number of the resulting art products seemed uselessly to mimic past art, to flounder in the La Brea tar pit that "progressive" modernism had made of art history, pluralism detected a tonic irony, or discovered a differently sustained, long-standing tradition asserting itself center stage. And if the bulk of "new" painting happened to be atrocious even by the purely aesthetic criteria of formalism, so much the better. "Bad art," it was declared, had always been good art perceived as ugly upon its first unveiling—producing that salubrious shock so typical of "the new," a shock familiar enough by this time for certain keen nervous systems (mainly located in curators, art dealers, and interested critics) to recognize it way before anybody else.

These circumstances led inexorably to regression, 'round about 1981, cuing in neatly with a refulgence of political conservatism. (Buchloh's essay infers a parallel with the resurgence of conventional figuration during the First World War.) Art revived as a safe investment. Since investment had become the primary reason to buy art, a low-risk, high-gain market was established for the work of artists who'd been active for only two or three years. Martha Rosler's essay, "Lookers, Buyers, Dealers and Makers: Thoughts of Audience," takes apart the art consumption apparatus as well as its philosophical underpinnings in the history of aesthetics: "For most of the art audience and especially for buyers who want investment that will appreciate in value, the *certainty* attaching to elevated sentiments, to the Kantian rhetoric of removal and formal values, to the denial of the relevance of subject and context, offers the reassuring familiarity of a discourse that sounds like art-10-years-ago, dishing up again the ruling ideas of painting from the late '50s through the '60s."

The oiling of the culture industry by corporate investment in the art market has clarified the role of the spectacle in reinforcing capitalist ideology. In many respects, the accepted function of art in contemporary society is no different from that of less rarefied mass entertainment, which is why so many authors in *Art After*

Modernism exclude the ostensible qualitative boundaries between the two fields. All cultural phenomena are grist for analysis; drawing lines between "high" and "low" is simply a parlor game for investors. For example, after years of stale debate, photography has at last found acceptance as "art" (in large part, Rosler makes clear, through the efforts of the Museum of Modern Art, and other interested institutions), establishing new departments in cultural institutions and fixing a baseline price ghetto for photographically derived work, which, unlike art photography, raises questions about the aura of originality, the status of authorship, or the tangible functions of artworks in a society where distorted representations of reality in mass media exert far greater influence on consciousness than anything that ends up in a museum.

In somewhat shaky outline, this is the history that much of *Art After Modernism* contends with; although it is a staunchly oppositional, blasphemous history, its endless recapitulations are among the book's more tiresome features. Fredric Jameson's "Progress Versus Utopia; or, Can We Imagine the Future?" is a concise analysis of science fiction; it doesn't need to be followed by the self-swallowing gibberish of Jean Baudrillard ("The Precession of Simulacra"). This book tends to locate a salient point and then pound it into the reader's brain without mercy.

The consistency of outlook is dauntingly persuasive. With the exception of Donald B. Kuspit's "Flak from the 'Radicals,'" (which proves beyond reasonable doubt that Donald B. Kuspit was the first to recognize how the new German painters could be comfortably displayed in *Artforum*), the essays avoid promoting the hypnotic-fetish idea of the art object. The aesthetic power of art isn't negated; rather, it is assumed. These critics know very well how coercive the rhetoric of images can be, and how deeply entrenched the clichés of reception really are. Beauty is the world's oldest whore, seductive even after death—in this connection, Kuspit's self-congratulatory essay provides a veritable mine of regressive eurekas. But one feels, delightedly or not, that *Art*

After Modernism sets Kuspit up to look ridiculous—a few musings from Barbara Rose or Hilton Kramer might've softened this impression, if nothing else.

Unfortunately, most of *Art After Modernism*'s contributors share with Kuspit an etiolated sense of language that is perfectly serviceable in academia but has no chance of attracting a wider public. The most gnarled prose in this book often contains its most valuable thinking—Constance Penley's "A Certain Refusal of Difference,'" and Rosalind Krauss's "The Originality of the Avant-Garde" are prime examples of self-defeating exposition. Krauss:

> *This is the perspective from which the grid that signifies the pictorial surface, by representing it, only succeeds in locating the signifier of another, prior system of grids, which have beyond them, yet another, even earlier system.*

But why pick on women. Here's Baudrillard on TV and nuclear war:

> *The only weapon of power, its only strategy against this defection, is to reinject realness and referentiality everywhere, in order to convince us of the reality of the social, of the gravity of the economy, and the finalities of production.*

This is the kind of writing that makes Rene Ricard sound like Michelet, and *Art After Modernism* is packed thick with its gooey, glottal croakings. There are exceptions: Robert Hughes's deadly accurate "The Rise of Andy Warhol"; Borges's "Pierre Menard, Author of the *Quixote*"; Kathy Acker's vulgar, demystifying "Realism of the Cause of Future Revolution." Hughes's essay—like Sontag's "Fascinating Fascism" and Renata Adler's "The Sad Tale of Pauline Kael"—so thoroughly and hilariously debunks its subject that one can never again listen to a serious conversation about it without laughing. Borges has been roped in to lend literary credence to the notions of aesthetic exhaustion and historical paradox that are favorites with the rest of the volume's contributors. Acker talks about art as if she didn't know any theory, and more power to her: she describes what she sees in pictures with a liberating, combative irreverence and glee. But the lion's share of this book has been given to highly intelligent, turgid writers, people with good ideas who don't articulate them with particularly winning fluency.

It can be argued that students and other specialists who read *Art After Modernism* will absorb its plentiful ideas, and make them available to a larger public—that these ideas will inform the creation of works of art (as they already have). One of this book's many virtues is its incitement to hard thinking, its persistent scraping away of naïve myths clustered around the art-making enterprise.

But it can also be argued that the hermetic language so many of the book's contributors rely on, laden with interreferential buzz-concepts and jargon, demands an unreasonable amount of soporific decipherment, and thus leaves the business of influential art criticism in the hands of less fastidious thinkers who happen to write well. Without recommending journalistic simplicity to anyone involved, I do think people with no special interest in art ought to hear what these writers are saying. Having grossly oversimplified what they *have* written, I'd be relieved to see them do a better job of exegesis.

January 28, 1986

THE NO NAME REVIEW

A man was found driving a car with his wrists slashed.
Malaise was in the air, thick as orange juice with too much pulp in it. Even sanguine people, exhausting their stock of bright chatter, abruptly confessed a profound, low-burning depression. They'd thought it was going to be the real thing, the time of their lives, sparkle plenty. "This is supposed to be the most sophisticated city in the world, and every corny thing that comes along gets blown up as earth-shattering, unprecedented, or brilliant. I just don't get it, even folks in Wisconsin wouldn't be taken in by this stuff." People were turning into "moments." Moments registered as mere formalities. "I've got to go to that opening and show my support," he said. I asked if he was in a body brace. Lives were becoming processed, like cheese.

The culture had long entertained the concept of dread as an ironic aphrodisiac. But no one made love any more—only the copulations of remote farmers and religious personalities were considered safe—so dread itself became the spirit of the culture. It was the worst of times, with no countervailing wind. Every stimulant ultimately functioned as an incitement to suicide. *A man was found driving a car with his wrists slashed. Cancer-causing agents were detected in apple juice. War was declared. This escaped nearly everyone's attention.*

Only the press occasionally asked questions any more: almost invariably, the wrong ones. Is Neo-Cretinism on the decline, it might wonder, fervently, as a hostess might query her dinner guests, Are these quail eggs "enough," or would anyone care for some smoked salmon? And how can the stock market *truly* crash, if the windows along Wall Street can't be made to open manually? *A man was found, driving a car, with his wrists slashed. He said that enemies had done this to him. Enemy aliens.* Is a new surrealism emerging, the press wanted to know, as if surrealism might still be confined to dreams and artistic visions, when waking life itself had long ago succumbed to a surreal condition. Every image was now double-edged. Every image forced you to decide if you were *for or against,* and further defined the imaginary opposition, *us against them.*

People fled the contaminated in droves. They flew to places where venality and pettiness did not, as yet, *entirely* set the tone. Some who stayed realized they were living in the calm before the storm. Others didn't. The discussion of real estate at virtually every artistic gathering inspired a rage for the vomitorium as a postmodern rumpus room. The sight of the word *gallery* was enough to cause shudders. As an icebreaker, "I'm having a show this month" had acquired roughly the same cachet as "Excuse me, I just farted." One began to admire the pathologically shy, to cultivate people who covered their mouths when they giggled.

Paintings and photographs in restaurants began looking just as good as art hanging in galleries. You could switch them around without disturbing anything but cash flow. It depended on what restaurants you went to. Each restaurant had its moment, too. War was declared. Most people continued eating. "The level of antagonism in this room right now," T. said, "is the kind of thing I never wanted to get used to. And furthermore, I'm not going to."

We wondered how it would be if I just did this without mentioning any names. Because names had become, in manifold ways, obstacles of epic proportions. To venture a less than gushy view of an object on a wall was interpreted, quite often, as a full-scale strike against the Grand Duchy of the Name. Some artists had become tiny nations unto themselves, developing intricate defensive systems to protect what they were offering. Slander and innuendo were the least subtle tools in the arsenals. "The ridiculous part," R. said, "is that if you travel 20 minutes outside New York, nobody knows or cares anything about all this." Moreover, printing proper names had become like naming an art movement: you became a salesperson in spite of yourself. I thought if I got rid of the names, then I could get rid of the genders. If I got rid of the genders, I could get rid of the hierarchy. If I got rid of the hierarchy, I would demolish the structure. The problem was, and is, that no one can do this without a lot of help, and like-minded people are always fighting over trivia.

"Every time I turn this television on," S. complained, "I see the president declaring war. Or that awful ad for *The Village Voice*. If they want to sell papers, they should let me do that ad. Fuck the yuppie-in-tweeds image. Get Cyndi Lauper up there, if she'll do endorsements."

I listened carefully to everything everyone said the week the war was declared. *If the car travels at 60 miles an hour, and the man loses blood at a rate of half a pint per minute, how far will the car travel before the man loses consciousness?* I looked at shows. I kept listening. "You know something, those images—well, they're perfect. The champagne glasses. The faces. The pearls draped over the velvety arm of the sofa." "The technique! When I look at that I honestly feel like I'm in Claus von Bülow's penthouse. All that picture needs is a respirator and he'd be committing narrative." "Let's get out of here, I'm suffocating. These ladies with the fur hats and the Dean & Deluca bags don't know how to move around in a crowd. They have no experience of nightclubs." A. said the stock market had collapsed because of Estée Lauder and Polaroid: "See? That's all America is now, commodities and spectacles."

Okay, I said to someone on the phone, what do you really think about it. "Well look," she said, "I would never claim those pictures aren't gorgeous, the guy has incredible skill as an artist. And let's face it, talk about production values, those things are Cibachromes, not C-Prints, they must've cost a fortune. But. You know what I think they're about, are those 'What Kind of Man Reads Playboy' ads that show you twenty thousand dollars' worth of hi-fi equipment and some glasses full of imported Scotch, to give guys the idea they should buy all this electronic stuff, so if they bring chicks up to their expensive pad and put on some groovy music, and get them all liquored up, you know, and get them to, what did they used to call it, *put out*, all this orchestration will enhance that moment when they shoot the big wad. I mean, what's so critical about making that image perfect?"

But what about the antithesis, I asked someone else: those stark black-and-white landscapes of urban ruin, those unflinching studies of slaughtered animals, those serene, elegant, haunting views of dead people and living people who look dead? *If an ambulance is moving toward the car at 70 miles an hour, from five miles away, on a perfectly flat road, how long does it take for the ambulance's headlights to meet the light from the car being driven by the man with the slashed wrists?* N.: "Isn't that what they teach as art photography in college? Not flinching? I'm sorry, there's enough shit right in the street I have to flinch at without having any control over it. He prints better than practically anybody, and a lot of those pictures stick in your mind, when you leave you think, *it really is an evil world*. Like when you see that Eisenstaedt portrait of Goebbels on the lawn, in a wicker chair. I mean I do like being scared by those pictures as much as you do, but most of those people looked like Goebbels. So did the duck. So did the dog. It's too much grim reminder to get off on it these days. I prefer *Pee-wee's Big Adventure*."

"Think about things you'd miss if they were gone," B. said. "Those funny gouache paintings we saw in the colored wooden frames. I don't think anyone has ever painted some of those subjects, at least not in that handmade style. And those big fabric panels, in that place downtown, that looked like she'd covered these huge canvases with her underwear. She'd even wrapped that little aquarium in satin, you never saw that before. And those blocky sculptures the other one did all covered with pennies mooshed into Sculptmetal, and oh, those enormous mythological paintings M. did that look like tapestries, where everything's made up because he's American and doesn't really know the legends. Where would you be without some of that?"

Yes, I said, but that's not American culture. American culture is the death trip and the beauty trip, the dead cow and the seed pearls, and it's all about meaninglessness, isn't it? Empty luxury and nothing to look forward to but death at the end of it all. If you're on the consuming end, the death part shows that you're brave about things, undeluded in spite of material comfort. And the pearls…the pearls are as close as you can approach irony without achieving it.

"G.," he replied, "that isn't American culture, that's American art. American culture is the man driving down the road at 60 miles per hour with his wrists slashed." Pause. "What's all this about a war?"

February 4, 1986

ON THE RIVER OF NO RETURN

[Hanne Darboven. Leo Castelli, 142 Green Street, through February 1.]

Hanne Darboven's *Ansichten 85* is all one piece, in 54 frames, each 59 ½ by 27 ½ inches; each frame contains three images, regularly spaced. The top pictures are photographic views of Hamburg, taken at various points along the Elbe River, ranging from north to south. Beneath these are enlarged picture-postcard vistas of New York City. The bottom thirds consist of calendrical notations: seven rows marking the days of the week. The numerical date is written horizontally below a vertical addition of its numbers; the total is recorded in a box at the bottom.

Over the years, Darboven has exhibited many, many works like this, and one would not be wrong to find them rather dry, though a supremely insidious irony often surfaces in them. Darboven's activity seems quasiscientfic in nature, a prodigious, lifelong research project that logically concludes with the artist's death. It involves mathematical modeling of passing time; it dispenses with the flashier aspects of artistic expressiveness. One could say that Darboven internalizes certain structural givens that art is often thought to deflate or circumvent. She assumes that the world conforms to a logic that includes the artist, that the artist is in some sense beholden to systems that determine the nature of art. At the same time, Darboven stresses the manufactured and inadequate nature of systems by putting them to work in an idiosyncratic and therefore useless, nongeneralizing way.

Many of Darboven's projects have paid homage to system-makers of the past; a 1975 piece is dedicated to Johann Jakob Moser, inventor of the modern filing system. *Ansichten 85* is partly a tribute to Alexander von Humboldt, discoverer of the Pacific current and taxonomist extraordinaire. Between 1799 and 1804, Humboldt and A.J.A. Bonpland explored South America, leaving with a vast collection of fauna and mineral specimens. Humboldt established the interconnection of the Orinoco and Amazon river systems; he recorded important meteorological and magnetic phenomena. There are 30 volumes of his and Bonpland's classifications. In *Kosmos*, Humboldt showed, as Darwin later would, how dissimilar things could have the same organic origin.

Another book named *Kosmos*, by Witold Gombrowicz, is a novel about the intractable human need to impose form on chaos. Between Humboldt's *Kosmos* and Gombrowicz's is a century's leap, with a quantum difference in perspective. Humboldt proceeded from the late 18th century's ideal of humanism and rationality: the world makes sense, if only we look into it. Gombrowicz saw the universe as essentially meaningless, a palimpsest upon which human beings inscribe their compulsive patterns. While profoundly different in feeling, these two ideas are, in fact, the same. In either cosmos the universe is closed, an encyclopedia of secular data. Whether or not its final meaning is nonmeaning, any two of its available facts will suggest a system which in itself is meaningful.

Darboven's *Ansichten 85* acknowledges both the perception of arbitrariness and a real order in things. Each panel asserts Darboven as a subjectivity and as a fact in the world. Darboven locates herself as a monadic being-in-time, trapped in specific dates, her activity circumscribed by material and temporal coordinates. The week passes and "adds up" to an abstract total. The juxtaposition of her own chosen views of Hamburg with pre-fabricated images of New York yields formal similarities despite the overwhelming bucolic character of one, the architecturally packed appearance of the other: this farmer, standing in front of this little house, has something to do with the statue of George Washington in front of the federal building; this dirt road through an orchard is a road, just like that causeway through the South Street Seaport.

Like the botanical wonders that Humboldt revealed to European eyes, Darboven's pictures of New York speak, in their context, of a fantastic accumulation of seemingly alien objects—a proliferation of marvels. But in contrast to the calm, semirural sights along the Elbe, pictured in subdued and often somber light, the neon amplification and giantism of Chinatown and Manhattan-by-Night suggest a mechanical or mathematical principle that has shot out of human control. The simple numbering of days, the tabulation of rational units, the modest industrial appendages of the Hamburg riverside all become ghostly reminders of human scale beside a reality that exists in the same world, in the same moment. Perhaps one thing is the logical result of the other, but only according to an imaginative act of partial comparison.

The New World was conquered and settled by a pastiche of the Old. Since the graft of the Old consisted primarily of mercantile adventurers and religious maniacs, the conquerors had no interest in preserving history, in learning what the New and Old had in common. The concept of unlimited development, with its corollary notion of unlimited destruction, continues to inform social organization in the New World, uninhibited by the Old World's hard lessons. What has "taken" here, to European eyes, is something Americans have to go to Tokyo to discover: a burgeoning soullessness matched by unparalleled growth and technical control of consciousness. The evolving New World Human has a bright, triumphant look, and so does the world it lives in; in Darboven's pictorial ellipses of Hamburg (which is, after all, really a modern city), it's Europe that looks battered, crumbling, and archaic.

Darboven's *Ansichten 85* is by no means a straightforward or hortatory contrast between Europe and America, nor is it judgmental, except by inference. Rather, what Darboven's work does is wonder about conditions. If we wanted to stretch the analogy to Humboldt, we could even call these meteorological conditions: the light in Hamburg is coolish, the river winds along through places that evoke melancholy and reflection. New York is hot, metallic, thundering in scale, a perpetually seething foreground spotted with human miniatures. And then there are these tracings of the hand, the insistently totalizing figures, inserting the idea that both views, both weathers, meet somewhere in the mind, can be concretized by notation, *figured out*. Darboven's work insists on the intellect's ability not only to hold contradictions in suspension but to resolve them elegantly, if not in reality then in art.

The long-view impression of *Ansichten 85* is that of a calendar year broken down into weeks, the calendar pages blown up into icons, time quantified. Darboven's project tells us about the artist's relation to time, how artists colonize time and define it as theirs. Darboven's method is formulaic, and like Roman Opałka's paintings of progressive numbers, Darboven's framed pages of time ensure a continuous production. The theme is unwavering, though the system of notation changes; the project itself demands a kind of eccentric failure, since human beings cannot, in fact, be entirely, systematically accounted for. The failure of Darboven's technique is the success of her art. She is the ample ghost in her own machine.

February 11, 1986

TALKING BACK

[**Group Show**. Metro Pictures, 150 Greene Street, through February 22.]

As it happened, the space shuttle exploded the day I went for a second look at Metro Picture's all-women group show. Gretchen Bender's installation is a grid of color television sets attached to the wall, with the names of artists in the show painted across individual screens (the Metro Pictures logo appears on the one in the center); these are tuned to various stations, and when I saw them last Saturday they were beaming cartoons. On Tuesday, however, numerous grim-visaged male anchorpersons were on view, fondling identical clusters of what looked for all the world like oversized personal vibrators.

While several televisions segued into the, let's face it, spectacular footage of the ill-fated liftoff, Jenny Holzer's LED sign, high up on the adjacent wall, ticked out in red electronic dots OUTER SPACE IS WHERE YOU DISCOVER WONDER, WHERE YOU FIGHT AND NEVER HURT EARTH. IF YOU STOP BELIEVING THIS, YOUR MOOD TURNS UGLY. Parts of the television grid cut away to a close-up side view of the soaring, inexorably thrusting projectile which, an instant later, had become a vast smudge of drizzling cosmic debris. IF YOU HAD BEHAVED NICELY, Holzer's sign continued, THE COMMUNISTS WOULDN'T EXIST.

There is this about Bender's installation: the voice of the television, the veritable drone of the state, is turned off. The names painted over the screens disengage the viewer from the spectacle and preempt the authority, and the authorship, of the spectacle's constituent images. A malignantly cheerful American family creaming over the wonders of fiber in its breakfast cereal becomes an ironic presentation by Sherrie Levine or Nancy Dwyer. Whooping game-show contestants and sinister functionaries of the Reagan administration are transformed into symptoms "brought to you by" Julie Wachtel or Jennifer Bolande.

YOU ARE TRAPPED ON THE EARTH, Holzer's sign says, SO YOU WILL EXPLODE. This is not a nice idea, but there it is. Numerous works here use the spellbinding properties of familiar media to convey distressed messages, harsh feelings, and a sense that things are, most decidedly, not at all what we're trained to think they are. Devastation is a frequent theme. One of Bolande's two pieces, *Sign*, is a small sandwich board with a drawing of burnt-looking trees on one side, a photograph of menacing clouds on the other, planted in a pile of potting soil; like Laurie Simmons's four close-in, black-and-white photographs of damaged-looking dolls in miniature slum interiors, *Sign* has an atmosphere of utter ruin, suggesting what those of us trapped on the Earth can look forward to. Louise Lawler, in *This Drawing Is for Sale*, encloses a framed photograph of a gallery storage room in a much larger rectangle painted on the wall, with a big red dot, and a label. The dot does not represent a successful sale but the 16 megatons exploded in World War II; the painted rectangle represents the megatons currently available for use.

Annette Lemieux's *Home Coming* contains a large oil painting, with a small star at the center of a blue rectangle inside a maroon rectangle. Attached to this, at the top right corner, is a framed photograph of a woman sitting in her living room, and on the wall near this is a framed book cover that's a field of blue with a tiny star in the center. Inside the photograph, behind the woman's shoulder, is a sort of flag repeating the star-in-the-rectangle motif, as well as a framed photograph of a man in military uniform.

Home Coming creeps up on you. The man is dead. The woman is what the government refers to as a Gold Star Mother.

Not everything in this show is elegiac, and the things that are aren't simply so, or lacking in humor; Simmons, Bolande and Lemieux deal affectingly with rather plangent emotional states, meanwhile playing with formal ideas associated with cooler sorts of art. Another angle of approach is a more sardonic, dissolvent sensibility: Holzer, Lawler, Barbara Kruger's immense, hilarious photographs of a girl in braids making a bratty face, with the legend *Money Can Buy You Love* declaring the obvious, ever-suppressed secret of capitalist living. Then too, there are Nancy Dwyer's ambitious combine sculptures, *Diet Lifeforce* and *Don't You Love Sports*, replete with sleek materials like Astroturf, Formica and Plexi-mirror and Cindy Sherman's two very large, very horror-stricken self-portraits. And a painting by Julie Wachtel, a vertical diptych, one panel featuring a greeting-card female dunce, the other a scabbardlike ethnological artifact.

This assemblage of artworks by women is a rather belated curatorial effort, but on the whole a successful one. What's interesting are the different ways in which these artists address power—and the fact that each of them does. Sherrie Levine's small-scale paintings on wood, in which the single mark of the artist is the application of gold enamel on one wood knot, criticize the giantism of contemporary machismo painting and appeal to a sense of proportion, in a manner similar to that of Allan McCollum's surrogate paintings. Lemieux subverts a familiar kind of Minimalist icon by attaching it to an image of real-life tragedy, an image created by power machinations in which humans are employed as tools. Lawler's piece places her own art-skeptical art, firmly and terrifyingly, within a larger context of potential annihilation.

Dwyer's work acquires its point as a closed model of the world, in which consciousness is endlessly shuffled and pushed by lines of force, directed, coerced. Simmons's doll pictures represent the miniaturized, impoverished interiority prescribed for women by the existing power structure; Sherman's photographs show us a nightmare female reality, oscillating between cliché and brutality. Kruger and Holzer, in different ways, empty out modes of didactic presentation, spoiling the channels by which power represents itself.

One should be grateful for a show that's as politically smart as this one. However, a few quibbles. Sarah Charlesworth certainly ought to have been included here; the extravagance of Bender's piece is slightly jejune, despite its effectiveness; Julie Wachtel is an interesting artist, but in this context the anti-aestheticism of her work looks a bit marooned. On balance, though, for a commercial gallery, this show is welcome and, hopefully, precedent-setting.

February 18, 1986

LIGHT AND DEATH

[**Ross Bleckner**, Mary Boone/Michael Werner, 417 West Broadway, through February 22.]

Although I know Ross Bleckner as a friend, Ross Bleckner the painter has always astonished and upset me. It isn't that the artist's prodigious black humor never resonates in his work—it often does—but his saturnine temperament, with its roots in melancholia and intellectual pessimism, disperses itself in social life through self-deprecating humor, and coagulates in the work of art as a condensed, obdurate, and powerful primary narrative. In other words, what people go off and make in private seldom echoes the orchestration of their social life. Effective art invokes a shared reality, but the fact of art inevitably reminds us that each of us comes into the world alone, and goes out of it in the same condition.

The rough geometries and raised shapes in Bleckner's new work are familiar from earlier paintings: Bleckner often starts off with formal devices he doesn't want to lose track of, and if they submerge under multiple veils of paint, as they usually do, the unevenness of the ground causes them to bleed through. *Hospital Room*, with its exuberant, Redonesque bouquet spraying forward out of murky space, has six fleur-de-lis shapes spaced across it, symbols of the representation that partially effaces them. In *Memoriam*, two sketchily defined grids map the background of variegated darkness into a roomlike spatial container for a translucent trophy cup, a gold banner, and flowers. The background of *Damaged Trophy (Former Paintings)* has an insistent pentimento of burnt orange whorls and raking strokes.

These paintings play on the indeterminacy of oddly illuminated, dark spaces. They show objects and halations of light looming forward from necrotic, nocturnal landscapes, occupying several distinct planes. Often the *things* (flowers, goblets, the wrought iron grillwork in two versions of *Gate*) seem to be crumbling apart; specks of brilliant luminosity suggest their imminent extinction. Two paintings titled *X-Friends* (one 48 inches by 40 inches, the other 18 inches by 14 inches) are simply pitch-dark fields pulled open into bright color by streaks and pools of graded white.

One of Bleckner's favorite effects is to make an already deep space deeper, by painting opaque, flat shapes or thick impasto dots in the foreground. *Damaged Trophy (Former Paintings)* and *Crocodile Tears* both feature compass-perfect circles on the points of a starburst; the ones that are shaded in emphasize the background density, while the solid ones bring the viewer's attention to the painting surface. David Salle has done this with profiles of Abraham Lincoln and other cookie-cutter shapes, but in Salle's work the intention (I think) is to collapse illusory space, revealing the equivalence of all images. Bleckner's illusionism affirms, instead, the pre-eminence of subject as the reason for a painting.

The subject is death, as you've probably surmised. But before getting into that, I should mention some pictures Bleckner's show brings to mind. In the late Baroque period, when fireworks displays were common festivities at the palaces of European nobility, master engravers began to represent these nighttime spectacles as fantastic sprays and scallops of light exploding over darkened architectural glories and crepuscular cityscapes; plates from the early 1700s by Amédée-François Frézier, and others by Romeyn de Hooghe from 1692, depict the aftermath of these displays, the stringy lines of smoke and dying fire. In such pictures there often appears a ribbon or banner inscribed with details of the occasion.

Some of Bleckner's new pictures also contain these irregular streaks and trails, often appearing gouged into the surface when in fact they're delicately painted threads slithering over it (while the Baroque estate entrance in the small version of *Gate*, which seems lighter in mood than the other work, really is sunk into the paint). *Memoriam* has a banner, and *Brother, Brother* has part of one, but nothing's written on them. The well-like perspectives of *Crocodile Tears* and the large *Chamber* recall engravings done almost a century after Frézier and de Hooghe, namely Piranesi's *Carceri d'Invenzione*, imagined prisons. True, *Chamber* contains three chandeliers, but they're obviously burning out, and the light they cast ripples across a viscous-looking floor. To the right of this a hooded figure stands waiting in darkness.

These pictures aren't as dark as I'm making them sound. The intense color of a picture like *Hospital Room*, the furred yellows and roses in *Memoriam*, the epiphany of blues in *X-Friends* have the arresting, even numbing authority of Bleckner's recent stripe paintings. Like Beckett novels, though, no amount of bright "action" quite gets your mind off the dark grain of the voice that's talking, or that reality is being disintegrated by the same technique that's making it present.

Well, death: one of the first paintings one sees upon entering the exhibition is a stately arrangement of reds and blacks, with the shiny trophy that appears in several of the works. Numbers painted at the corners, and shapes decorating the sides, give it the look of a multidimensional playing card; the title is *8,122+ As of January 1986*. These paintings mourn and commemorate the deaths of personal friends, specifically friends who have died of AIDS. The trophies stand for ended lives, and perhaps for the good luck that making a work represents when others have lost the death lottery.

While Bleckner's new paintings operate on many levels—especially that of operatic beauty—one pertinent reading necessarily charts the condition of homosexual consciousness in 1986. The spent fireworks of liberation have segued into dimming lights in mental prisons, bright stars have burned out in the cosmos, and we have all become eerily familiar with terminal hospital rooms and continual fear. Bleckner has absorbed this untenable surplus of dread and loss; his new paintings are brave acts of affirmation, proof that difficult creative acts can still be carried off in a milieu of complete alienation.

February 25, 1986

UNDERMINING MEDIA

[**Barbara Kruger**. Annina Nosei, 100 Prince Street, through March 2.]

Many people who think of art as swank decoration find Barbara Kruger's work extremely irritating. Others, who gurgle over any example of art used as a handy political tool, however ineptly wielded, deem this work "incorrect." Kruger is an artist whose answer to any multiple-choice question is "none of the above." Like Hans Haacke, Kruger makes statements in art that attain their peak effectiveness in the context of galleries, museums, collections, magazine reproduction. These works violate the notions of the sublime, the ethereal, the timelessly detached splendor of the art object. They refer the viewer not to some imaginary realm where the human spirit masturbates to the music of the spheres, but to the world we all live in, where exploitation defines the quality of every life.

Neither Haacke nor Kruger needs any defense as an artist. The objects they produce have abundant aesthetic interest. Within the current glut of art production, art that is actually about something, that has a subject, becomes more mysterious and involving than art-about-art or art-about-Me. Both Haacke and Kruger deal with problems intrinsic to contemporary art-making; both recognize contemporary art-making as something implicated in a political system, with far-ranging effects beyond the picture frame. Kruger's work addresses the viewer as a social component, a You standing in front of it completing the terms of its dialogue. It's simplistic to receive these works as accusations, though they are clearly statements by a woman about male power. Kruger's exposition doesn't proceed from an us-against-them, binary model of human interaction. She is, rather, a phenomenologist of attitudes created by sexually determined power structures—structures in which everyone participates, consciously or not.

Kruger's new work reflects a determined amusement at the ongoing circus of inanity and bad faith we call our national life. The most subversive response to this shabby circus is to laugh at it, and Kruger's humor has never been more edgy and analytical grace, more bristly with latent horror. While Kruger glosses specific social issues, she invariably goes after their deeply embedded psychic roots. *Untitled #4443*, a blown-up red-and-black image that is almost certainly a close-up of E.T., contains the caption *Only the unborn have your right to life.* On a green-and-black putting green where the gold ball has just inscribed a vaguely phallic imprint on the grass, *We are your complicated holes* appears in the aimed-for orifice. In a large three-panel black-and-white photograph of wrapping paper shards, it takes a moment to pick out the words: *Promise us anything but give us nothing.*

The prevailing theme is one of exposing empty seductions, labeling their metaphorical equivalents and sometimes appropriating the voices of the powerful. A spectacular two-piece frame console (something like a Minimal sculpture, in bright red) contains eight lenticular-screens, with two images on each. These shift back and forth as the viewer moves, alternating between shiny solid-color overlays and silvery black-and-white pictures: *If it screams,* says a picture of a little boy flexing his muscles for a little girl, *shove it,* says the magenta overlay. This sequence flashes, spectrumlike, across an inventory of innocent stimuli and brutal responses—*If it sighs, shame it. If it loves, buy it. If it moves, fuck it.*

Formally, Kruger's show ranges further than her previous ones. There are several two-color works, one without her signature red frame, numerous lenticular screens, a large full-color picture in a pink frame, and a piece without words. These range from the small (19 inches by 19 inches) to the gigantic (138 ¼ inches by 90 ½ inches), horizontal to vertical to square. Kruger has opened up a style that's been widely copied, adding the jizz of "special effects" to pictures that belie their own attractions.

Ambiguity plays an important role here. If Kruger's work had ever been as crystalline as critics sometimes make it out to be, it might easily subside into the limbo of agitprop. I know this artist "personally," as the phrase goes, but the intention of particular works often evades me, and assumptions I've made about them have often reversed themselves over time. Kruger is a peculiarly cryptic visual aphorist; her work makes a picture of the state of things, but it's neither an incitement to guilt nor a vengeful indictment. Kruger seems to find pleasure in symptoms of general malaise, insofar as these verify a worldview and provide critical fodder; this is quite different from feeling individually abused, oppressed as a class, or raped once again by an implacable enemy. Kruger's stance refuses to nurture misery, instead prescribing intelligent ridicule, pointed outward. Her strategy lies in flushing out the sexual infrastructure, the subtext of domination and submission, however welcoming the social surface. In this respect, *Untitled #4439*, with its about-to-be-stepped-on legend *Don't buy us with apologies* is paradigmatic.

The reversals that occur within specific works erode any definite sense of who speaks and who listens. The double-image lenticular screen provides its own distancing editorial space along with the "dazzling" sheen of technology. *Read my lips*, invites the dusky face inside, peering at you through torn netting: *My tongue is in your mouth*. There are voices that preempt other voices, speech that's contingent on the silence of others. Power allows only certain voices to be heard. But there's this, too: power always says the same thing, no matter whose mouth it's using. In the multipanel lenticular piece, a ventriloquist's dummy illustrates the proposition *If it sees, blind it.*

Kruger's work recommends, among other things, the abolition of either/or—the reactive mentality that divides the world and the genders in it. The untitled lenticular piece without an inner caption shows an overhead picture of people in rows, college or high school students in identical sweaters and sneakers, which dissolves into a grid of knitted yarn: the social fabric, surely. But whether this bright image is tomorrow's hope or the prelude to a goose step has been left to the viewer's imagination.

March 4, 1986

THE ENIGMA OF URANUS

It was certainly too good to pass up, the idea of the Emperor's message and the two, possibly three, things that would verify it. Events suggested the impending realization of Kafka's fable about the message on its way from an infinite distance. An unmanned space vehicle was transmitting perfectly splendid photographs of Uranus, long a pariah among planets because of its pronunciation. But now they were pronouncing it differently, with a watery emphasis. The Emperor is sending us a message, the column might start. Across the vastness and mystery of outer space. And so on.

I knew that **Taylor Mead**, himself a legendary figure and my frequent co-star in *the theater*, thank you, had done a painting of Hitler, and went to P.S.1 (46-01 21st Street, Long Island City, through March 23), where it's hanging with other Taylor Mead paintings, as a kind of sidebar to a show called "About Place: Contemporary American Landscape." Taylor Mead's Hitler is a very wan-looking yet gruff personality, a brown study of an emperor. Mead's telegraphic treatment of this figure is the opposite of monumental. His Hitler is a little man, albeit with big ideas. (One could say something here about the *size* of ideas as a basis for aesthetic inquiry. Taylor's idea about Hitler is expressed on a modest, quiet scale, but it refers to the loud, important ideas people find so impressive.) Mead's paintings are charming examples of an American *povera* that's perfectly content with Woolworth's pre-stretched canvas and the impasto knife that comes with painting kits. He has one thing called *Money* that shows people lounging around the Mike Todd Room, with an excellent little ochre dog at the foot of the table. A sketchy, perky treatment nicely encapsulates the subject, and the background Basquiat is just as toothsome as the original, if not considerably more so. The labels in French, with English translations, are a high point—e.g., "Le Coq (Rooster)." But *Adolph* is the turn-on.

One often loses the thread while trying to weave things together. The world of modern art is so sprawling, so various. Just like outer space. Taylor Mead makes a painting of Hitler, then someone sends the strangest press release of the season. *This exhibit differs from other art exhibits in that it contains a plot*, it claims rather artlessly. *In the exhibit Mr. Rockefeller slowly emerges as an ancient Egyptian Pharo* [sic], *perhaps Ramses II*, it really was too good to pass up. The Emperor was sending us a message, in this case through the person of **Joseph Gourdji**, a jewelry designer whose show, the release said, is at the Carol Mjaanes Art Gallery at 1050 Second Avenue (through February 28). And so it is, in a building that contains several hundred antique dealerships and tchotchke vendors. In the gallery window, a photograph of Mr. Gourdji "wearing the amulet of Ra," along with the amulet of Ra itself, featuring an exquisitely wrought silver visage in the center: *the face of John D. Rockefeller*.

That's not all. There are also these...*shrunken heads* of John D. Rockefeller worked out of clear plastic, mounted on cardboard. And a drawing of John D. Rockefeller, superimposed on the profile of Pharaoh Ramses II. And another small silver mask of John D. Rockefeller, mounted with precious Egyptian-looking jewels and surrounded by arcane emblems. The resemblance between the late Mr. Rockefeller and this much later Pharaoh is indeed uncanny, possibly even amazing. Gourdji modestly proposes two potential messages: "That Mr. Rockefeller emerges as a cult figure. That Mr. Rockefeller was the reincarnation of Ramses II." These conclusions seem inescapable. I'm convinced, anyway. But then, we are looking for the figure in the carpet, the beast in the jungle, the signal from Uranus, the message from Planet Debby.

Where would it be? Possibly at **Terry Winters**'s show at Sonnabend (420 West Broadway, through March 1): lots of pods, bugs, things that look like volleyballs and cell clusters, fading in and out of the paint. The work is astute, loaded with painterly mannerisms, and indefinitely repeatable. It's the right look for a truly enlightened corporate office. Biomorphic forms thrive best in an institutional setting.

Ed Ruscha's pictures at Leo Castelli (also at 420 West Broadway, through March 1) are no more encouraging vis-à-vis the Emperor's message. Paintings of flapping American flags; paintings of words looming up out of bleary skies and cartoon sunsets. Ruscha is a graceful artist, perhaps too graceful for his own good. Flag-waving is unattractive even when ironically performed, and chronic wavers of the flag would not be uncomfortable with these Old Glories. On the other hand, Ruscha suggests that a message is on its way, about to flare across the picture tube, traversing unimaginable distances to get here.

The Emperor was sending us a message, and I lost it. It could be somewhere in the current show of **Rebecca Horn** (Marian Goodman Gallery, 24 West 57th Street, through March 8), where a huge needle hanging from the ceiling flies back and forth above a metal pool full of black water, barely scraping the surface and stirring up a few bubbles. Another needle narrowly avoids grazing the point of a needle planted on the floor. A mechanical set of wings fashioned out of bird feathers flaps open and shut at the top of a thin metal rod. A motorized pick chips away at tubes of charcoal in a metal cylinder set high on the wall, dropping flakes onto a fake gold bar. And there's a bulb thermometer you can cradle in your palm; its rising mercury will tell you if you're emotionally tepid, full of passion, or verging on insanity.

Horn's constructions are metaphors of vulnerability and dreams that go sour. They allude to fatal sensitivities, sensory antennae so finely pitched they risk disaster with every move. So it was not *The Emperor's Message* after all, not entirely, for there was something there from *In the Penal Colony* as well, something else from *The Great Dictator*—and a third thing from the tomb of Ramses II.

March 25, 1986

FORMAL WARES

["**Time After Time**." Diane Brown Gallery, 100 Greene Street, through April ?]

Of contemporary sculpture in contemporary space, the most salient public work currently on view has been achieved by a simple painted addition to construction hoardings on either side of 11th Street at Third Avenue: NYU WE DON'T WANT YOU HERE, in white letters against blue-painted wooden panels. WE DON'T WANT YOUR BORING YUPPIES. This graffiti transforms the twin construction sites, formerly parking lots, into sculptural performance works in which the scaffoldings, the squat and ever popular "workers," as well as the enervating, incessantly pounding pile drivers exemplify the brutal rape of a community by the power of money. The finished state of these erections, as can already be seen in a companion piece at the corner of Third and 10th, will be matching examples of hideous architectural expedience. It should be of great comfort to those whose environment is being poisoned by NYU to consider how many temporary jobs these monstrosities have created, and how many students will find it easier to shop in the East Village next fall.

Less imposing, but more distinctly welcome sculpture is featured this month in "Time After Time," curated by Collins & Milazzo, at the Diane Brown Gallery. This show's explicit concern with modes of temporality roughly differentiates between primary forms and simulated forms—that is, between work with an organic, familiarly sculptural focus and work that proceeds from an arch awareness of "the duplicit reality of consumer products, media-effects and science fiction."

This dichotomy between the protean and the intellectually sly is one version of familiar polarities: heart versus head, inspiration versus calculation, sincerity versus wit. Much of what's in "Time After Time" inhabits a fortuitous creative interzone where an object's self-conscious status, or lack of it, doesn't inhibit the pleasure of looking at it; but most work here undoubtedly falls into one or the other net, and a few pieces fall with a thud between the two.

Broadly speaking, objects in the "simulated forms" camp recommend a distanced view, and display a ruminative or joking relation to the art context, while "primary forms" resonate as self-contained, reified, reinvented archetypal or historical artifacts. In the former category, the most aggressively ironic piece is Haim Steinbach's *lead part*, where mass-produced objects are ranged on colored Formica platforms: an orange hose coiled in a plastic container, several identical digital clocks, and two novelty-shop Dracula heads. Steinbach's combinations of shopping mall wares and sleek geometric shelving add the grotesquely quotidian object to the flattened, cleared ground of Minimalism; each is a sort of hyper-rationalized Duchamp urinal, an inventory item set down in pseudo-heroic relief. Jeff Koons's *New Jeff Koons* has a relatedly abrasive effect, using a Judd-derived box structure to frame a Duratrans blow-up of the artist as a child, playing with crayons. Between the elegant form and the coy, almost fatuous content, the sheer imperiousness of artistic will becomes a material property of the work in a rather old-fashioned, modernist way: *This is a sculpture because I say so.* (And it is, strangely enough.) However, a much more pointed statement about sculpture and its ostensible purpose is made by Allan McCollum's *Perfect Vehicles*, identically formed Chinese ginger jars, ranging spectrumlike from red to violet. McCollum transposes the redundancy principle of his familiar painting surrogates (which are themselves sculptured objects) to the three-dimensional commodity art object; the different colors indicate the consumer's "range of options."

Works that are more conciliatory toward precedent strike a more poetic tone, though they purposely deflate ordinary expectations of sculpture: Annette Lemieux's *Portable World*, a Royal typewriter sitting on the floor with its "text" (a Photostat of an immense aerial photograph) running up to the ceiling; Joel Otterson's *Designer Nucleic Acid*, a tall copper-pipe structure rising from a racing wheel, crowned with a finial that appears to be a bronze detergent bottle. Gretchen Bender's black-lacquered wood sculpture, tapered to a point from a three-legged base, has a deceptive look of metal, and plays off three silk-screened tin panels behind it, one of them picturing a massive, magnet-shaped Max Bill. Like the lapis-colored column of Richards Jarden's *Allen Ginsberg Desk*, Bender's piece appropriates the appearance of heavyweight sculpture and lightly mocks its material ponderousness. Joseph Nechvatal's tear-shaped Plexiglas pool, its bright pink floor inscribed with an intricate drawing, is a whimsical-looking answer to the usual solemnity of floor pieces, especially ones with liquid in them.

On the organic, historicist—or, if you prefer, hand-crafted—side, Gary Stephan's *Leda as the Swan*, Not Vital's *Wheel Animal*, Michael Zwack's *Bronze Heart*, and Joel Fisher's *It*, which differ radically in form, represent in abstract and semiabstract forms mutations of mythological and allegorical tropes of traditional sculpture. At the same time, each of these works resists a naively mythic function, being pervaded by psychological modernism (Freudian in Stephan's case, Jungian in Vital's—to put it more vulgarly than they do). Contrastingly, the drapery effect of Maureen Connor's *Robe de Jardin*, which segues down from the ceiling on a wire, and Ricardo Regazzoni's deco phallus in gold leaf, *Obelisk*, as well as Kenji Fujita's wall construction of painted wooden gasket forms, *Oxen of the Sun*, compress the more decorative effects of Modernist and pre-Modernist sculpture into antisymbols, dysfunctional excerpts, and memory traces. In either situation, the uselessness of myth and symbolism in contemporary art—except as ironic shards and recovered synecdoches—is frankly acknowledged. This is where the two strands of this show fuse together: historical forms consume themselves and turn into each other (*Leda as the Swan*), while posthistorical pastiche equalizes *all* forms as comparably mythic and comparably meaningless. The varicolored patina of John Newman's *Mother Tongue* suggests a calcification of Modernism, an amorphous Lee Bontecou piece turned to stone, or rather bronze. In Edward Allington's *I, You, We are Crime #2*, a doilylike chunk of ornamental bronze is punctured by a blunt, flint-headed object.

This show traffics in the ideas of time embodied in synchronously produced works of sculpture. Its plurality, as well as its exclusivity, suggest that we are occupying several kinds of time at once: bucolic, urban, nostalgic, anticipatory, cumulative, and posthistorical. It questions how one can usefully think about art when all art is present to the mind and available for reference and bowdlerization, imitation and debunking, consumption and exhaustion. So far, no one has invented a plausible answer.

LIQUID MEMORY, SOLID OBJECTS

This space became a trifle pinched last week, owing to certain vagaries of style. I'd intended to discuss the show of Arte Povera works at Barbara Gladstone Gallery (99 Greene Street, through March 29) in connection with Collins & Milazzo's "Time After Time" group sculpture show at Diane Brown. These shows seem related, and they're conveniently across the street from each other.

If you'll recall, the Collins & Milazzo show draws a broad and often-abrogated distinction between primary and simulated forms which reflect different constructs of art-historical time. One set of things could be said to exist "within history," reflecting primarily sculptural concerns, while the other deals with the altered status of sculptural objects in an inorganic, largely artificial environment.

This general difference expresses itself in materials as much as in iconography. Here one can borrow some terms from the painter Peter Halley and substitute "real" for primary, "hyperreal" for simulated. Real sculpture tends to employ traditional materials like bronze and wood, and more recent materials like fiberglass and aluminum, with emphasis on malleability. The chosen material yields to a sequence of artisanal processes, and the physical evidence of this yielding comprises part of the work's signature. Hyperreal sculpture generally dispenses with such evidence, instead presenting a smooth, industrially crafted surface that relates to modern packaging and mass production techniques.

Arte Povera is one of many middle links between real and hyperreal sculpture. It repudiates classical notions of sculpture, though it often pays homage to them in the form of parody—as in Giulio Paolini's *Intervallo*, where a mass-produced classical statue of male wrestlers is bisected and each half placed flush against a different gallery wall. The figures are therefore seen being absorbed by, and re-emerging from, an imaginary plane, like science-fiction characters liberated from the constraints of physicality. More typically, Arte Povera's materials range between the elemental and the ultramodern, the real and the hyperreal. But in Arte Povera these materials are fused together differently than in the gleaming, ironically Apollonian realm of the contemporary hyperreal. Arte Povera views the industrial substance as essentially dysfunctional, ripe for scavenging. Jannis Kounellis makes heartbreaking visual poetry from architectural debris, cigar boxes and espresso pots as well as piled rocks and weathered steel beams. Mario Merz's *Hagoromo* combines glass sheets and polished steel with beeswax slathered over wire screening; pale blue neon handwriting is planted in the wax. Pino Pascali's *Quadrifoglio* exploits the evocative properties of fun fur, Piero Manzoni's *Achrome* the giddy effect of fiberglass feathers.

To borrow some language from another contemporary American artist, the remarkable thing about the Arte Povera artists is what they've given themselves permission to do. Undoubtedly there is something tempered by a rich, awful experience of history in Arte Povera's approach to technology and modernity; this approach reflects a sense of living in tomorrow's ruins and using today's materials for melancholy monuments to the future past. The current American hyperreal in sculpture seems like a weird grafting-on to the work of Donald Judd: clear the decks, then add kitsch. This is, perhaps, an unavoidable intellectual response to the American culture industry, but its bite is often toothless, overly coy, and emotionally etiolated. At its worst, the hyperreal is simply reactive to media inanity and commodification and rather grossly infatuated with both at the same time. While the Collins & Milazzo show mainly featured resonant, ambitious pieces, it must also be acknowledged that *the look of critique* has begun to exert the same undiscriminating, hypnotic effect on exhibitors and collectors that *the look of expression* did a few years ago. The most memorable works in "Time After Time" are, like the Arte Povera show, corrective to the idea that any palpable emotion in a work of art already amounts to some regressive Cult of Feeling.

* * *

I hasten to add that regressive Cults of Feeling call for relentless deconstruction and careful scrutiny, particularly in the visual arts, where such cults have endured through the eons in emblem form. In **Sarah Charlesworth**'s current show of laminated Cibachrome photographs (at International With Monument, 111 East 7th Street, through March 29), various religious artifacts appear on solid-color fields, sometimes ornamented by border designs and incidental motifs (leaf patterns, beetles, fish, birds, a halo, the moon). In the extreme relief of a Charlesworth print, the associative charge emitted by the fetish object is neutralized, or rather, gathered into itself and fixed within its physical boundaries. There is a Madonna, an intricately painted medieval crucifix, an African (Gabonese?) mask, a pre-Columbian deity, a lotus floating above a golden bowl, a *Super-buddha*, an Egyptian bull, a red-shading-to-white circle in a red-edged ground of solid black; most interestingly, a Muslim woman in purdah, that is, totally covered in a white burnoose. (In an earlier Charlesworth series, exposed parts of bodies were subtracted from found photographs, leaving only body-contoured clothing.)

I've avoided looking up the specific provenances of each of these images, which were culled from magazines. It would be easy enough to do, but Charleworth's procedure is essentially unpedantic, and in this particular series seems to play on the somewhat misted quality of "posthistorical" memories: *Superbuddha*, I think, is a Hindu statue, not a Buddha, but in present time signifies the same kind of otherness, just as the red-and-white circle on black suggests Zen contemplation, the green mask "Africa" and primitivism, and so on. Charlesworth's treatment stresses the lavishly designed character of the artifacts, their bombastic qualities as mystical clichés, and also, because of their dramatic foreground isolation, the paranoid-hysterical nature of their original function.

I won't presume to say that "we no longer know" why these images activate networks of profound meaning, because they still do, however hazy our reception of them happens to be. In fact, the replication of this haziness, a kind of listless stirring of metaphysical longings, is an antidote to contemporary revivalism, with its demagogic appeal to vague stupidities no one really believes in. Charlesworth's "Objects of Desire" objectify the seductive emptiness of the symbolic: in this case, "faith."

April 8, 1986

NOTES FROM THE SNAKE PIT

[**Robert Hawkins**. Patrick Fox, 56 Bleecker Street, through April 19]

The American Dream is a curious and embarrassing thing. Its overt form is the pursuit of greatness—not goodness, or equity, or excellence, but greatness in the sense of large dramatic effect. Greatness as impact. The American Dream is deeply fatalistic: when major, destructive things happen, their inevitability sometimes has a "tragic" edge. But later we are told that it really couldn't have happened otherwise. Just now, forces purportedly beyond our control call for a show of American greatness. We resume nuclear testing. We send a military fleet to provoke an attack from Libya. Our presidential Ahab invents a "massive" Sandinista invasion into Honduras to jimmy a hundred million plus out of Congress. (When the Germans invaded Poland, they first dressed up some corpses in German uniforms as evidence of provocation.) The president, departing from the avuncular homilies of his prepared scripts, begins speaking in his own voice and turns out to be a rather nasty, deranged piece of business.

As our elected representations rush to drop their pants for the administration, we would do well to consider the other side of the American Dream. If our greatness is half glad-handed innocence, the other half is certainly murder and madness. The country was born in a blitz of exterminating energy. Its vastness induced spiritual vertigo in sensitive souls, venality and self-absorption in coarser spirits who smelled opportunity in America's detachment from civilization. Our literature is full of melancholia and guilt, ghosts and devils. So is our truly indigenous art, especially that of the late 19th century. If the ideally Europeanized, well-mannered American painter is John Singer Sargent, surely the quintessentially American one is Albert Pinkham Ryder. *The Race Track (Death on a Pale Horse)* condenses the American Dream into a bucolic treadmill of mortality, replete with blasted tree, smashed fences, and the pestilential snake-in-the-garden.

Robert Hawkins's paintings are very much in the tradition of Ryder—and of Thomas Cole, who painted overgrown ruins to depict "The Course of Empire" in the 1830s, and Elihu Vedder, whose *The Lair of the Sea Serpent* (1864) shows an enormous snake draped across a sand dune. The sinister, explicit content of Hawkins's work is hilariously out of whack with the contemporary mainstream, a refusal of artistic good behavior. Hawkins is a terrorist in the manicured bourgeois Eden where Alex Katz and Jennifer Bartlett while away the long afternoon of Empire painting the scenery; he envisions a time when all the summer homes and cocktail-hour mavens have been swept away in a radioactive gale. In fact, Hawkins pictures the future in terms of the past: an early, biological past, where the terms of survival precede morality and social organization. Some round, gold-framed works in Hawkins's current show, formally reminiscent of ancestral portraits, immortalize simple organisms: the amoeba, the paramecium, the bacterium. The little things that have always meant so much.

Hawkins is not an apocalyptic artist in any usual sense. A disturbing aspect of his work is its unexcited, often cheerful view of the irremediable. A series of small graphite drawings on birch bark show gravestones inscribed with legends like "Why Why Why" and "Mistake," eerily appropriate in an era of grand death. The larger works, generally in oil, are good-natured, ghastly metaphors for the marginality of "the human" in a world where both macroscopic and microscopic forces run out of control. And "the human" is indexed as a weird scattering of futile, pernicious, uncontrollable obsessions and impulses. Storage tanks marked URINE and DUCK SAUCE loom up out of rural landscapes. A faceless bride in a frothy wedding gown stands beside a faceless groom cloaked in an executioner's outfit. Earlier Hawkins works celebrate the guillotine as the apogee of human invention.

In Hawkins's cosmology, mutation is the salient fact of history. His expressive portraits of cavemen suggest a lack of meaningful development in the past few millennia. *The First Pretty Girl*, Neanderthal in a leopard skin, promenades on a beach that would fit right into an Eric Fischl painting. *The First Ruler* is a long bone, with inch markings. Nativity wears a look of bright surprise; the thing being born, however, is usually a snake, in one instance popping from an egg, a frangipani lei draped around its head. Hawkins's predators slither into life with keenly focused energy, yuppies of the animal kingdom. Symbols of treasure come wrapped in certain doom: *Safe Underwater*, possibly dropped from the *Titanic* and glowing evilly from within; *Underwater Statue*, circled by patient, pink-mouthed sharks; *Mamba with Ruby*, the snake's neck firmly collared by the gleaming jewel.

Portraits of ghosts in haunted mansions, eyeballs sprouting from odd patches of human flesh (labeled as arms, legs, asses), snakes, cemeteries, microbes: Hawkins's sensibility obviously owes something to Edward Gorey, Gahan Wilson, and Charles Addams; he sometimes handles paint with the quick dash of an illustrator. But Hawkins's work often reaches heights of the old-time sublime, and carries truly menacing conviction. His approach to presentation is consistent with a disintegrating reality—using chipped, smashed, or peeling frames and shards of antique furniture; lighting parts of the gallery with candles. This show's trappings propel us back to a simpler but no less lethal, spooked-out time in America. Its largest piece shows an old lady in bed, startled by the collapse of her ceiling. According to the gallery checklist:

Mrs. Winchester, the widow of the inventor of the Winchester Repeater, believed that as long as there was building going on around her, the ghosts of the Indians and other victims of her husband's rifle wouldn't get her. She built a house in San Jose, California, and she slept in a different room every night to confuse the spirits. When the San Francisco earthquake of 1906 struck, it took them three days to search the hundreds of rooms to find her. But she lived, though.

We should all be so lucky.

April 15, 1986

NEW YORK COMMONPLACES

Ambition. Everything has been done; everything remains to be done perfectly. This is the decade of perfect artists: perfectly docile, perfectly domesticated, perfectly comfortable on the wheel of Society. A person achieves celebrity by displaying a mild, forgiving irony toward massive insults to intelligence, grace, compassion, feeling. It is best not to feel anything, or to feel everything at once, in a kind of neutralizing synesthesia. Art should refer to "the jumble of impressions" available to the abbreviated attention span.

The artist should be a bright boy—white, comely, well-mannered, *sportif.* He must be eager to part with his products, to send them flying to whatever capital-intensive walls beckon. His best shot at immortality: his works will be purchased en masse by the head of a giant advertising firm, who will then reproduce them in authoritative-looking catalogues. Another member of the firm will describe the creative ferment of the artist's lifestyle in expensive magazines. The artist's skiff is well and securely launched on the sea of ordure. Next come the summer place in Montauk, the German and Italian retrospectives, the Manhattan building purchase.

The *great* artist becomes a landlord. Ideally, a landlord of artists. His position in the hierarchy of culture is underlined by his economic domination of less creative types. The *great* artist bridges many realms. He lives in the metaworld of publicity and the bogus world of professional occasions. He also lives, at conspicuous advantage, in the real world of others. In the morning he poses for photographs, amiably seated before one of his giant canvases. He dresses like a bright undergraduate. The message of his publicity: anyone can obtain what I have, if they aren't fussy. Imagine that a brain as big as mine lurks beneath this housebroken exterior. In the afternoon, he trades consumer homilies with his wizard dealer and a couple of vulgarian collectors over lunch. Conversation turns on sales: his own, other people's. Who bought what. Or rather who *got* what, as in "The Xs got three pieces from Dizzy's show." The implication of Hun-like plunder goes down easily, like the luncheon itself. I am bought, therefore I am.

The artist's own labor can be consigned to an assistant, and often looks "more like him" when it is. This leaves him little to do besides collect rent. He does this with a self-ironic air of deep humanity. He'll wait, though not beyond reason, for the tardy tenant's swag. In idle hour, he decides to lease part of his building as a storage space for works of art. An ideal economy evolves. His work is purchased as a tax write-off by collectors who will then pay him to warehouse it. Once the work starts to function in the money system, no one really needs to see it. Successive owners simply exchange bills of sale.

Ideas. Everything has been done; we live in an exhausted time; soon everything will explode; history is finished. Because history is finished, we can only repeat, picking things out of the parched riverbed with quotation-mark pincers. We cannot improve on the system. Nor can we improve on the past, which is fictional anyway. We are allowed to withdraw into formal pursuits and fractional nuances. Originality is impossible, but perhaps it can happen by accident. Overproduction equals optimism, as when one of infinite monkeys at one of infinite typewriters tosses off *King Lear*. But infinity isn't what it used to be. At best, once upon a time, we'll get Cordelia's first few lines of dialogue, a word or two from Gloucester, mixed in with a lot of concrete poetry and utter nonsense.

If some proliferations cause hope, others cause despair. As in: things have never been this bad, people have never been this craven, this desperate, this lacking in idealism. And since nothing opposes this skidding crash into barbarism, there's nothing for us to do. Look here, there are too many more homeless people than before for my single quarter to make any difference (as if, not long ago, the same quarter would have changed the world).

Life doesn't live, after the first compromise. No need to offend anyone. The rich are human, after all. So are corporations. They employ people, don't they? And the man who collects for Company Y is a perfectly civilized fellow, has a wonderful eye. Of course they won't let him buy *certain* things, we're talking about a corporation. But for the most part, the artist benefits. His work gets bought, and even seen. Not just by executives, but by their secretaries and their business associates and, once in a while, by the public, too. These people are affected by the art, they relate to it. It lifts them out of the world of tawdry commerce, into the world of higher things. Is it really so necessary to be confrontational all the time? Shouldn't the artist benefit? Don't forget, he's *special*.

Or: we want to maximize Z's exposure. His work's good, therefore important. Important, therefore salable. Why should Z limp along, with all his financial difficulties, when A (a talentless fraud) and B (an empty creation of the media) and C (who really hasn't done a decent piece in four years) continue to flourish, give interviews, get on magazine covers? Q is interested, definitely interested. He came in, looked at some things. And he's actually very self-effacing, almost humble when he sees a work of art. At one time, the whole idea of Q buying Z's work would have been, well, grotesque. But these are difficult times. Refusing an opportunity is suicide, career suicide. Even an opportunity from Q. In fact, especially an opportunity from Q. We won't sell him *everything*, just enough. To maximize Z's exposure.

Windows. One is inside, safe, looking out the window. The other is outside, supposedly in peril, looking in. The person inside is suffocating. The person outside is merely cold. The contemporary persiflage of opposition is the person inside telling the person outside: Better cold and breathing than in here, trying to scream where there's no air. The contemporary pretense of opposition is the person outside screaming. Let us in. We want what you've got. We want shows in your galleries. We want the house in Montauk. We want the magazine covers and the shopping trips to Paris. We want to die the way you do, observed by millions, smiling while the oxygen gives out, our names and faces registered in the media. You've sold out completely, but we won't. We'll only do it a little bit. You can't really call it selling out if you give more intelligent interviews. We can change things. And if we can't change anything at least we'll continue to know what's wrong. And even if we grow tired and eventually bored with saying what's wrong, in the face of so much that continues being wrong, better wrong with us than right with you.

The air is thin behind the glass, and disappearing. And though there's lots of space, too many nostrils will definitely ruin things. Faces pressed to the glass outside believe they're not allowed in because of age, sex, race, content. They're right. Being right has certain limitations. It's made them obsessed with getting in. The people inside really can't breathe freely, although they exaggerate this difficulty to make *inside* less attractive. On either side, breaking the window is the obvious, drastic, dreadful step no one even contemplates. One would then have to continue smashing things and throwing things out. Not just the teensy proscenium of art stardom, but the rest of it—the complicity with money and power, the schizoid double and triple standards, the horse blinders that come with the career.

Value. Everything has been done; nothing new under the sun. Perhaps things were always like this. Then someone says: I really don't think in the '50s, '60s, and '70s people thought about nothing but material success. Someone else says: The alternative to material success wasn't as hideous in the '50s, '60s, and '70s. Translation: Art and society have nothing to do with each other, except when they do. Everything being highly questionable, it's not a good moment to question things.

Motto. "There are no worms in the door hinges." (H. M. Enzensberger)

April 22, 1986

SOHO SKETCHES

I have always envied people who take notes, carefully organize their thoughts, and know exactly what they will write when at last they settle down to that miserable occupation. I do, from time to time, take notes: scribbly, illegible notes, accompanied by numerous wretched drawings. But real notes, notes you can count on, notes to live by, so to speak—such notes are not mine. My notes are a disgrace to the concept of note-taking, and yet I must take them. This week, however, I hit on the expedient of having someone else take them for me—to draw the things and write down the colors.

I tried to draw them myself at first, and did about half of the Metro Pictures **"Signs of Painting"** show (150 Green Street, through April 26), starting with Philip Taaffe's *Queen of the Night*, a long vertical in dark blue acrylic with a lighter blue lino-print rope motif running down it in a stripe. This was easier than *Block Island*, a smaller picture with blobs and wavy forms in it. It's a sort of diptych and I messed up the proportions, so the red-on-blue parts compressed. Allan McCollum's enamel-on-hydrastone surrogates were easier, since they're basic rectangles within rectangles or squares within squares. (If you have lined paper in your notebook, it's simple to do edges.) The only problem was deciding what to call the colors, which I have here as periwinkle (ha ha), green (grass green, could be) salmon, violet, and—this was not my idea—light pumpkin.

Walter Robinson's spin paintings are impossible to draw. They are whirly splatters of acidic colors. I think these are done with the kind of machine they have in the window of Unique Clothing, but I'm not sure. The one on the right is a "green and red iris-burst" according to these notes. Then, three narrow John Miller paintings in murky brown and black, staid and somber. One of these contains a grid of black squares, and another, a thin yellow strip. Peter Halley's rectangular work is white on top and Day-Glo orange on the bottom with a right-angled strip of black. What you miss in a sketch is a stuccolike stubble on the white part, unless you're good at drawing stubble and little knobby protrusions. Then, two tiny Gerwald Rocken-schaubs, cadmium red lines on gold. Lots of geometry in this show abutting lots of spinning effects, as in Jack Goldstein's box-mounted piece, where there are precise colored shapes at the bottom and top, and a sunspot or something in computer-enhanced colors in the middle—alluring in an *Omni* magazine sort of way.

My companion drew the Goldstein and everything from then on. I could have managed the four Sherrie Levine stripe paintings, though here there's trouble naming the colors because they're actually mixed, mixed very subtly. They resonate. They glow. She's terrific, period. (I've already recounted an epic Sherrie Levine color-naming episode. What we have here, without benefit of consensus: light green/light orange, light green/light cobalt blue, red/sepia, light forest green/gray.) Next to Levine, Ashley Bickerton: a rectangular box structure with industrial colors, bolts at the edges, shapes that look like glossy machine parts painted against light red, decorated with black strips on which the word "coconut" appears in white. This impeccable-looking piece reminds me of Eduardo Paolozzi's in the '60s, as did everything in Bickerton's recent show at Cable Gallery. Whereas Goldstein's new work reminds me of Bickerton's. Artists influence each other in such mysterious ways!

The Metro show contrasts a handmade geometric look with art that mirrors industrial processing, so it's a natural, short step to **David Mach**'s "Road Show" at Barbara Toll Fine Arts (146 Greene Street, through April 26). If I had kept a notebook last year, an entry would have read: "Saw this very strange floor piece, hundreds of bottles clustered together, some filled with colored liquid. The filled bottles formed the outlines of a person and a shark." The kind of person who takes notes intended for publication would probably add words like "fascinating" and "intriguing," but this would be of no value here because that piece isn't in this show. However, there is something compelling about an 80-cubic-inch Harley-Davidson motorcycle hanging on a wall "with a dozen black drafting lamps whose shades are cut into hand shapes, touching the bike" (friend's notes) and (friend's notes again) a "full-size Nitro-methane dragster called 'Public Enemy' whose rear is raised about 10 inches off ground, seemingly held up by about 50 black Barbies ('Miss Mary') and 2 dozen white child dolls."

This is one current show that can justly be termed striking, full of humor and menace. The dolls beneath the roadster look like they're carting it off to a Luddite bonfire; the cut-metal bands grasping the motorcycle suggest the legs of an enormous spider, hoisting the machine up into its web. There's also a somewhat unsuccessfully modeled head fashioned from dozens of plastic soldiers; Mach has made others from wooden matches. Mach has a playful grip on the expressive potential of technological reproduction, using multiple objects in nonbinding accumulations (cars and submarines formed from piles of books and rubber tires, a sphere made with hundreds of shoes). His work involves a mediation between the industrial and the human; it implies that we can do whatever we want with the stuff we produce in such insane quantities, "humanize" it by adapting it to imaginative needs. Broadly speaking, this reflects a European humor and sensibility (Mach is British). American artists (again, a generalization) tend to excite themselves with the destructive potential of technology. A great deal of interesting recent art seems content simply to mimic the nullity of meaning produced by mass media and mechanical reproduction, confronting the same hypothetical spectator who hasn't yet heard the bad news.

It takes all day to draw a motorcycle. We moved on, instead, to **Chris Macdonald**'s massive wooden sculptures at Diane Brown (100 Greene Street, through April 26): heavy, aggressively (and inexpertly) chained-sawed blocks of timber bolted together into vehicle forms. The largest looks like a wagon on the scale of a tank, with a thick, weaponlike cylinder mounted on it. Macdonald's work has a rugged, blocky power, a palpable air of menace, and a desperate need to develop a sense of humor. His smaller works have less force but more grace.

IMITATION OF LIFE

"Confusion/Order," a photographic installation by the **Starn Twins** currently at Stux Gallery (411 West Broadway, through April 30), is an arrangement of 58 photographic objects, radically varied in size, shape, and mode of presentation. Some pieces are elaborately framed, others fixed to the wall with pushpins; the central work, *Christ (Stretched)*, reposes under glass in a raised, segmented sarcophagus of black wood. The immediate impression of visual sprawl and overinclusiveness, heightened by the damaged appearance of most of the pictures, is misleading. The Starns' work is a meticulously ordered, thoroughgoing assault on photographic convention, thematically unified and visually thrilling.

It would be wrong to confine the Starns' accomplishment to the field of art photography. It is part of the contemporary co-optation, or rescue, of photographic media by artists. This rescue has taken a number of forms: the re-presentation of existing images, either through contextual displacement or by scale alteration, captioning, cropping, and juxtaposition; the creation of original photographs in which the traditional "objectivity" of the photographer is abrogated, the image staged for the camera or manipulated in various ways; and photographic work that ignores the conventions of virtuosity. "Photo art" is an art of inquiry. It examines the twin zones of photography—both the fetishized, compartmentalized region of art photography, and the much vaster, more sophisticated area of photographic media used for mass manipulation.

Photo art attempts to locate the self in relation to images, to meditate on what images do, and to undercut visual seduction with a built-in, Brechtian distancing. It rejects the worship of the polished print and the ghoulish aspects of connoisseurship. It jettisons inanities about universality, detachment, and "the recording eye." The Starns are, as it happens, technically fluent photographers in the traditional sense, but their work evinces the dubiety, vigor, and heightened consciousness of photographic art as practiced by Richard Prince, Barbara Kruger, Sarah Charlesworth, Benno Friedman, Cindy Sherman, Clegg and Guttman, Lehndorff and Trülzsch, and numerous others.

Like Barbara Ess, whose astonishing pinhole-camera prints derive their emotional power precisely from qualities considered defects in art photography (blurriness, edge darkening, the registration of dust and flaws on negatives), the Starns enlarge aesthetic possibilities partly by working up darkroom mishaps and mechanical flaws. They use intermediate artifacts of printmaking such as proof sheets and test prints as raw materials. Finished prints may be methodically crumpled, scored, torn apart, and reconfigured. Several prints are sometimes used to form a single work, and in many cases a single image is fractured by projecting it on many pieces of photographic paper, developing the fragments, then taping them together.

While standard photographic practice searches for the singular, "perfect" version of an image, the Starns use every image multiply, in many states. A professionally seamless black-and-white picture of a rose hangs near its pinkish-sepia, fretted-edged double. Between them appears a chemically mottled version of a portrait, echoed in a larger, more readily legible print of the same portrait on the opposite wall. One *Portrait of Doug*, dark and crinkled, suggests an image rising from murky water; another, in high contrast, reversed, slightly cropped, and seamed together in Constructivist taped lines, evokes dementia.

The use of a single image to engender numerous objects inverts the stigmatized "reproducibility" inherent in photography, and operates as internal joke, formal device, and querulous theme in the Starns' "mirror" pictures, where the image merges with its double. *Double Stark Portrait in Swirl*, with its dizzying network of tape splices, is a signature work (in a manner of speaking), its fractured surface like a cracked glass, the bedraggled figure doubled as if standing at a waist-high reflecting pool. The Starns are identical twins, and this circumstance has much to do with the soul of their work. Doug and Mike Starn aren't simply collaborative artists, they're as close to being the same person as two persons can be. Their doubleness, and their difference from each other, mirrors the photographic issues their work addresses.

An image may be reproduced, but an object, like a person, is always itself. Even duplicate objects occupy different space and exist "uniquely." For the Starns, every photograph is both an image and an object—and not necessarily a photographic object. They frequently use imageless, exposed photographic paper and photograms as collage parts and self-contained art objects. One of the most beautiful works in this show is a completely blackened print, inscribed with needle-thin white fissures.

Some works contain fragments of other works, or consist of detail blowups; a "whole" image often appears in miniature, while a detail from it becomes a larger object. A portrait of the artist Mark Morrisroe is dramatically cropped, in two different developed black and whites, to feature a sliver of face and torso, while a huge, multisectioned, green-tinted blowup of the complete image conceals the face in dense shadow. Synecdoches and shadows have particular eloquence in the Starns' work, as features of a general theme of blurred identity. Several studies of a '50s chair make use of a half-oval shadow as a key element in what becomes, from picture to picture, an expanding geometric design; the shadow replaces the chair as the main subject. *Double Cat Shadow* repeats, in violet and blue, a shadow that's fuller than what we actually see of the cat.

The Starns' dualism pervades this show in many ways, including the combination of radical practice and allusions to classical formal order. In a gigantic picture of a marble bust, the taped sections form a fairly rigid grid, as they do in another work that monumentalizes a gargoyle on the Place St.-Michel. A vari-toned, less regularly partitioned picture of a gowned woman refers to the Venus of Milo in its concealment of the subject's arms. Here and there, discreet *homages to art* photography, lovingly framed, have slipped in between formal audacities: a startlingly composed but hermetically presented horse's head (*Luther*), two milky, time-haunted domestic interiors (*Stairway, Kitchen*), a tiny cityscape (*I-95*).

The Starns' work complicates the notion of an "original"— as, in its way, being an identical twin does. The enlargement and multiplication of details and shadows, the fracture and recompo-sition of complete images, act as metaphors for a complex psychic equilibrium in which the Other is also oneself, claiming half of a shared ego. A crackled, elegiac study of a pair of boots becomes a meditation on identity and difference. The tonal and scale variations each image undergoes also play on the instability of memory: photographs are about remembering. The Starns' photographs enact the idea that memory has no fixed state, no ultimate corresponding image, but functions like a fluid that expands and contracts with stress, like the ego.

* * *

Izhar Patkin's "The Black Paintings" at Limbo Gallery (647 East 9th Street, through May 4) are a painted enactment of Jean Genet's play *The Blacks: A Clown Show*, which had its American premiere at St. Mark's Playhouse in May 1961. The gallery vestibule is decorated with white-on-black stencil paintings of the cast, which consists of people the artist knows personally, except for the Maid from Manet's *Olympia*, who plays Augusta Snow, and Al Jolson, who plays the Valet. "The Action," as the accompanying imitation *Playbill* notes, "Takes Place on Rubber."

And so it does. Patkin has depicted the key scenes of the play on drapery folds of black rubber enclosing the four walls of the gallery; these were stencil-painted exactly as they hang, and so behave less like theater scenery than a rippling hallucination that can turn black with the stirring of a curtain. These curtains are fairly heavy and don't stir by themselves, but the pleated effect wonderfully evokes the fragility of theatrical illusion.

Genet's play was written for a black cast, partly in whiteface, to perform for a white audience, and Patkin's stenciling carries this idea perfectly. His use of Olympia's black maid, as well as Olympia herself (as the shrouded corpse that rots and stinks throughout the play, but is finally revealed as nonexistent), extends Genet's paradigm of political colonialism to encompass cultural colonialism, inferring the status of blacks in white culture.

Like the Starns, Patkin has given grand articulation to a core idea; both shows make intricate use of doubling motifs, shadows, things being at once opposite and the same. And in both instances the scope and integrity of the work convince us that art really can be the mirror of life.

May 20, 1986

UNITED STATES

I couldn't appear, as advertised, at the Cooper Union panel on "Gender Discrimination In the Arts." But since I was denounced by an audience member as a ringleader of a homosexual cartel, I've decided to punctuate this column with pieces of Roland Barthes's *A Lover's Discourse*. A cartel is only as good as its propaganda.

"I encounter millions of bodies in my life; of these millions, I may desire some hundreds; but of these hundreds, I love only one. The other with whom I am in love designates for me the specialty of my desire."

In the meantime, **Meg Webster**'s *Circuit* is currently transpiring at Art Galaxy (262 Mott Street, through May 31) in successive excerpts, and if you missed the first one you shouldn't fail to catch the other five. Webster's overall project had 14 components; the parts appearing in the gallery have a fine theatrical edge transforming the space in biweekly episodes.

"Despite the difficulties of my story, despite discomforts, doubts, despairs, despite impulses to be done with it, I unceasingly affirm love, within myself, as a value. Though I listen to all the arguments which the most divergent systems employ to demystify, to limit, to erase, in short to depreciate love, I persist: 'I know, I know, but all the same…'"

Its emphasis on process, unfolding over time, invites the spectator to get involved with something active and changeable.

Circuit opened with the brightly lit gallery office jammed full of potted flowers. A narrow path between the pots led up to the desk, which was obscured by a jungle of varicolored blossoms.

The adjacent exhibition space was dimly illuminated, occupied by a vertical steel triangle filled to the rim with water. This cut into the space dramatically, yet it took up little more room than a person would. You could walk around it, but because of the lighting it never completely revealed itself. The water rested flush with the structure's edges, a physical mystery, repeating the form that contained it.

"Waiting is an enchantment: I have received *orders not to move*. Waiting for a telephone call is thereby woven out of tiny unavowable interdictions *to infinity*: I forbid myself to leave the room, to go to the toilet, even to telephone (to keep the line from being busy); I suffer torments if someone else telephones me (for the same reason); I madden myself by the thought that at a certain (imminent) hour I shall have to leave, thereby running the risk of missing the healing call, the return of the Mother."

In one room the profuse, sexual heads of flowers brushed against the viewer's legs, insistently touchable, while the steel piece's delicately balanced liquid seemed to ask for a certain distance—again, like a person.

The current installment of *Circuit* is an eloquently molded cone of potting soil, the circumference of the base nearly touching the two walls. It can't be walked around, or shouldn't be. In effect, Webster here inverts the proscenium scheme of landscape perspective, bringing the outside indoors and into the foreground. This cone is like a Magritte painting come to life: cryptic, funny, and rather disturbing (like finding Sydney Greenstreet in your hotel room). The next cycle of the work will contain a prodigious array of animal life.

"Language is a skin: I rub my language against the other. It is as if I had words instead of fingers, or fingers at the tip of my words."

Webster's theme in *Circuit* is the enclosure of nature by culture; her work investigates our social alienation from organic processes. It raises awareness of our dependence on nature for survival, and most to the point, nature's dependence on us for survival. Like Garnett Puett's sculptural collaborations with bees, Webster's work slightly erases the line between art and life, arguing for a less dehumanized, more broadly participatory, and finally more logical culture. While Webster's work extends the practice of environmental intervention found in works by Heizer, Smithson, Serra and others, hers represents a feminization of earthworks, if you will; Webster doesn't want to assert herself over nature but to arrive at a mutually acceptable understanding. What's especially striking is that *Circuit* has no commodity dimension; its quirky mutations require a "working audience" to keep up with them over the span of the usual gallery month.

"Sometimes the world is *unreal* (I utter it differently), sometimes it is *disreal* (I utter it with only the greatest difficulty if at all)."

Nancy Dwyer's new work (at Josh Baer Gallery, 270 Lafayette Street, through May 17) seems like an extreme contrast to Webster's, technologically brusque and snappy-looking, using synthetic matter such as Formica and mirrored Plexiglas. But Dwyer's work also examines the inorganic way we live now, with appealing sarcasm and smartly pointed energy.

Dwyer's constructions often look like they've been reflected off a satellite camera, and their discursive properties function in the gap between reality and abstraction. While they resist the sense of touch, they also resist the condition of decoration. Dwyer uses the vocabulary of high-tech as its own dissolvent, for instance in *Sins of Omission*, a huge Formica letter "O" that could've rolled off a façade in the financial district. The corporate-scale word always says something definite and authoritative; the corporate-scale letter is permeable, multifaceted, and empty. O can be orgasm or zero or "Oh?" or whatever.

"The moral tax levied by society on all transgressions affects passion still more than sex today. Everyone will understand that X has 'huge problems' with his sexuality; but no one will be interested in those Y may have with his sentimentality…"

Inside is a box, with its sides on hinges. Open, it shows a black-on-white spiral. Inside the spiral is the word "Inside." When you close the box the sides read "us," "you," "me," and "them." Dwyer locates us, here, as social units attached to a cultural artifact; we are also parts of language. The simple nominatives Dwyer isolates are distressingly flat, cold elements in this context, identities that label what is boxed in and inaccessible to us.

"The space of reverberation is the body—that imaginary body, so 'coherent' (coalescent) that I can experience it only in the form of a generalized pang."

Much of Dwyer's work heightens the unreality of abstraction, simulating the weird equalization of everything that happens in mass media. In *Your Name*, a map of the United States, angled as in TV hypergraphics with the East Coast jutting forward like the snood of some recrudescent dinosaur, is encircled by a sharp yellow halo; YOUR NAME HERE splays across it in victorious-looking letters.

"What echoes in me is what I learn with my body…"

Dwyer's immaculate presentational style mimics the laminated presentation of America we've been bludgeoned with for years. Her subversion of the symbolic indicates the loss of the human being in certain constructions of social identity; Dwyer links this to the loss of language in visual culture, as Webster does to the loss of nature.

"I say silently to who is no longer or is not yet the other, *I keep myself from loving you.*"

May 27, 1986

INSOMNIA

You might think this is picky, but a stretch of prose that has to be interrupted to give the name, address, and end date of a gallery show can never achieve elegance, so let's get it out of the way: **Louise Bourgeois** has a show at Robert Miller Gallery (41 East 57th Street, through June 7), and **Michele Zalopany** has one at John Good Gallery (39 Great Jones Street, through June 7). There.

I can't even consider writing about these two artists without discussing insomnia: the prolonged, ravaging kind of insomnia that settles in for months at a time and alters the texture of reality. In the current issue of *Grand Street*, the brilliant Romanian writer E. M. Cioran explains the important role insomnia played in his early writing; it's a certain fact that large numbers of artists and writers are hapless insomniacs. And something in the work of both Bourgeois and Zalopany correspond to the experience of sleeplessness.

Bourgeois's current work is full of biomorphic forms and anatomical parts growing out of dense gnarls of matter; one piece is a kind of showcase for shelves of oddly larval-looking clusters of marble. *Articulated Lair* is an environment of foldable metal panels in which flaccid strips and bulbous lumps of black rubber dangle from cords. It's like a dream, you could say, but no, it's like your apartment when you haven't slept for a week, when objects appear to shift around by themselves, perch on top of the refrigerator or hide beneath the bathtub.

Perhaps the most horrifying song of recent years is "We Are the World," a Kantian nightmare of global pretension. It's our assurance that the world really exists, that it's not simply our projection or our dream, that keeps us from going insane. The solipsistic manipulations of dreams would be intolerable as waking conditions. But this is exactly what insomnia accomplishes. The temporal dimension is demolished, everything occurs in the same static moment. Matter becomes flabby, even fluid. Sounds disconnect themselves from their source. Architecture begins to melt. Solid things buckle and warp. Two of Bourgeois's *Nature Studies* are carved out of Greek marble, an almost obscenely soft marble that you can cut with your fingernail.

These *Nature Studies* look like umbilical growths coiled around stylized phalluses, mutating at one end into fingers, hands, and arms—life forms nudging their insidious way out of stone. They're beautifully formed and charming, but also sinister in the manner of insomniac hallucinations. Insomnia animates dead objects and eliminates the boundaries of living ones; the chronic insomniac is used to seeing arms and legs growing out of walls and furniture.

Then too, the vivid-smelling rubber items in *Articulated Lair* have this strange, deceptively yielding, unsettling tactility associated with insomnia. In dreams, the pliability of things is effortless, guided by an internal narrative devised by the dreamer. But in insomnia the friability of objects is a source of distress, even terror, as real things acquire the qualities of things dreamed.

Viewed as simulations of insomnia (there are, of course, many other ways to view them), Bourgeois's sculptures suggest insomnia's ambulatory, energized phase, in which the nonsleeper goes about the business of daily life, encountering objects and people through the distorting lens of his malady. Michele Zalopany's large charcoal and pastel pictures in black and white, illustrate insomnia's other pole, where the exhausted body is kept awake by the mind's inexorable churnings.

Zalopany's drawings are derived from archive photographs. Several in this show are taken from the New York Public Library file on "Houses." However, Zalopany doesn't simply draw enlargements of the pictures she finds. She plays with the details, enhances various creepy effects of light, leaves things out. *Without Them* shows an elongated thatch barn with several black doorways, with pigs rummaging near troughs; the original photograph contains farmers, and without them the picture becomes a foreboding, even ghoulish, setting, something out of *I Walked with a Zombie* or *Cat People*.

It's interesting that Zalopany sifts through available images to work from, since she draws freehand instead of using a slide projector; her work betrays the *stare* of the insomniac, fascination with *the horror of images*, even innocuous ones. Zalopany's work is about finding the hidden threat in things, a threat which is always palpable and present to the insomniac imagination. And rather than drawing "from life," Zalopany works from stasis, like the nonsleeper who lies awake and conjures landscapes on the wallpaper, for whom an hour feels like a minute, and a minute like an hour.

In such a state, a sensation of placelessness colonizes the mind, while exhaustion sharpens the contrast between light and dark. The terminal gloom of a house in the woods (*Addressee Unknown*), a squat administration building (*Memento*), or a forest lake (*All the World Is Not a Stage*) issues partly from suppression of certain details, partly from chromatic starkness, but mainly from the absence of location. The extreme frontality of the picture's subject, like the scale-juggling in Hitchcock movies, induces the paranoia of insomnia, insomnia's third term. It's of no help to know exactly where the house is, in what forest, near which lake; Zalopany's work is too grim to be described as "oneiric," too vivid to be other than insomniac. People don't really dream in black and white, even if they think they do. But the long-term insomniac often does see reality that way.

This is, of course, pure speculation. It could very well be that Louise Bourgeois and Michele Zalopany have blissfully fallen asleep on time every night of their lives, but those who haven't will feel an immediate attraction and sympathy with their work.

June 3, 1986

AFTER READING BERNHARD'S *GARGOYLES*

[**Oskar Schlemmer.** IBM Gallery of Science and Art, 590 Madison Avenue, through July 5. Organized by the Baltimore Museum of Art.]

In mid-May, when things were again becoming disagreeable, sticky, importunate, and distressing, I found myself standing behind Joris in the IBM Gallery. Chance has thrown us together too many times, I considered. Everywhere I go, he goes. It's as if he had read my appointment book. And since I don't have an appointment book it's as if he knew the workings of my inner mind, which is worse. Of course he turned before I could flee to another section of the gallery, grabbed my sleeve with an affection that made me shudder, smoothed his hairpiece with his free hand, and started talking. I like Joris. I don't know why he repulses me.

"If you would finish reading Bloch," Joris said, maniacally, "then you'd understand Oskar Schlemmer. The human being throughout history has been looking for utopia, for 'home.' Each utopia put into practice becomes an oppressive purgatory. It's all there in Bloch, *The Principle of Hope*. Now Schlemmer. Schlemmer was a purist and therefore an idealist, part of the Bauhaus utopia which ended so tragically. Look at the way he represents the human body in space. Here for instance. All the body's forms are rounded off, simplified, reduced to linear and volumetric clarity. Schlemmer depicts the body performing basic motions.

Going upstairs, taking steps, bending an elbow to hold the ban-nister, knees bending, the hands turning this way, that way.

"And see how Schlemmer situates the figure in space, how the space is defined geometrically, a rationalized space. In many of these pictures it's the space of Weimar Bauhaus. But not all, not all. Note the lack of embellishment, the etched-out perspectives, the mathematical order of both the figure and the space. The light-saturated secondary colors and their unconfused harmonies. The person is defined in terms of architecture, in terms of elementary and universal movements, such as turning the head or walking forward, or bending at the hip, stretching out the arms, one foot flat on the floor, the other foot bent, one leg extended forward, the other leg retracted, or the other leg straight, the shoulders bent, one arm upraised, the other arm extended sideways or outward toward the viewer. Or in this self-portrait, with the hand raised to the chin, with the fingers straight against the chin, the thumb tucked under the chin, and so on. Almost all these movements, by the way, are culture-determined, you wouldn't see babies making them in the wild or anything. No, these movements are con-ditioned by architecture and social organization.

"And here," Joris went on, blowing his nose and pointing, putting his Kleenex away while his other hand continued to point, his finger to wave, "are the costumes for *The Triadic Ballet*, which are carnivalesque but absolutely geometrical, this one with hoops of wire mounted on the head and around the waist, that one a stacked arrangement of balls and oblongs, with masks, notice, which completely stylize the dancer's form. To see *The Triadic Ballet* is to understand all of Schlemmer's paintings as ballet studies, or at least theater studies, of figures in an ideal architecture, on an ideal stage." Joris blew his nose again, pocketed the tissue, gestured toward a distant alcove. We started walking. I walked a little ahead of him and paused. A woman with a lorgnette passed between us, stopped, went forward three steps, stopped, turned. A man in a blue suit caught up with the woman. They stood in front of a painting. He put his hand on her shoulder. She raised her chin. He took his hand away and brought it to his mouth. Joris stopped in front of another painting. He raised his arm. He put his fingers under his chin. Then he placed his forefinger over his lips. Then he dropped his arm. A woman with brown hair, wearing a white blouse, came up and stood next to him. As I moved forward, the woman moved away. Joris took a step backward as I stepped forward. After a moment, I stepped back. Joris stepped forward.

"This idealism of rational form," Joris continued immediately, "and spatial order, and the worship of mechanics, and the notion of man as a monadic architectural presence within a community of other presences, comes out of the disorder of the Weimar Republic as it collapsed, the chaos of the '20s, and also, partly, as a reaction against Expressionism. The Bauhaus emanated from Expressionism but was also a reaction against Expressionism. And the precise, logical forms of the Bauhaus architects derive from Loos, from Constructivism, De Stijl, you can see a lot of El Lissitzky in an architect like Gropius. Architecture is *the most utopian and the most corrupt art form that exists*," Joris asseverated loudly. "All we see today, throughout Manhattan, is *a disgusting debasement of architectural utopianism*.

"And in Schlemmer's writings, to say nothing of Schlemmer's work, the artist expresses a *longing for order*. The whole Bauhaus period was nothing but a *chaos*, a *chaos longing for order*. The Bauhaus represents a longing for a liberal democratic order, but the Bauhaus period ended in the perversion of this longing into a Nationalist Socialist order. And the Bauhaus, in my opinion, *played into this perversion without wishing to*, and then became its victim."

Joris walked a few feet and stopped in front of Schlemmer's portrait of Paracelsus. "You see that the ideal order, Schlemmer's concept of the ideal order, is a spatial order. Schlemmer had a horror of politics," Joris said, "and therefore a love of the rational.

But life isn't rational, life is political. Schlemmer's notion of the perfect dance, Schlemmer's whole conception of dance, is based on the dancer as marionette. The marionette has no consciousness and so its movements have the perfection of animal movement. Schlemmer had read Kleist's essay *On the Puppet Theater,"* Joris said, "in which it is said that grace, *having traversed the infinite, will return to us once more and so appear most purely in that bodily form that has either no consciousness at all or an infinite one, which is to say, either in the puppet or a god."* He turned on his heel, reached into his jacket pocket, took out a packet of chewing gum, held it out. I moved my head slightly to the right, then the left, then to center. Joris extracted a piece of gum, unwrapped it, brought the gum to his mouth, opened his mouth, put the gum in, chewed, rolled the gum wrapper between his fingers, and put the resulting ball, and the gum package, back in his pocket.

"Paracelsus, whose real name was Philippus Aureolus Theophrastus Bombastus von Hohenheim, from Einsiedeln, of the Swabian Bombasts though illegitimate, was of course the greatest physician of the Renaissance, and he believed that the human being's inner constitution reflected that of the macrocosm. For Paracelsus, the macrocosm was the natural world, and God. Well, in Schlemmer's milieu, the Bauhaus scheme of things, the macrocosm is the social order in which human beings interact. That is to say, the technological universe, where nature is the mechanical ordering of life.

"Obviously," he continued, inexorably, "this Bauhaus conception was disagreeable to a National Socialist Weltanschauung, because on the one hand the Nazis needed to implement technology, but on the other hand had to encourage irrationalism in the populace. The Bauhaus conceived an enlightened order where everyone would understand technology, but the Nazis wanted a medieval order where only a few people would understand it, and the rest would be afraid of it. It would determine the whole nature of their lives, and they would be ignorant of it."

Joris chewed his gum. "But," he said, "the utopianism of the Bauhaus and the dystopianism of National Socialism, while they are two entirely different things, both assume the possibility of engineering the human soul, one for a presumed good, the other for a demonstrable evil.

"After all," he said, "Kleist's essay presumes the existence of a master puppeteer. In the utopian puppet theater, everyone is integrated into a structure. And being integrated, almost everyone can dispense with consciousness, which originates in man's alienation from nature. Once culture becomes nature, only a few managerial leaders need to remain conscious; everyone else can become a marionette. You could have a society where everything functioned rationally, and life was spatially organized with the mathematical grace adored by the Bauhaus, and still have a population *controlled by ignorance*. Such a population would have to know *almost nothing* to function. You could accomplish this technologically, by putting something, some appliance, for instance, that emitted image-models of everyday life, in every person's home. This appliance would prescribe what reality should look like, and tell people what to consume, and constantly assure them that they are living in Utopia.

"And whoever controlled this appliance, let's say financed its images of culture, would necessarily control the puppets, and orchestrate the theater. And those of us who take such pleasure in the thought of our mental sovereignty," he concluded, "could find ourselves gravitating to spectacular cultural exhibitions in Bauhaus-derived buildings, presented by the masters of technology."

Joris lifted his palm to his mouth. He coughed. I shifted my weight from the left leg to the right leg. Joris scratched his nose with his forefinger. I rubbed my left eye with my left thumb. I coughed. He coughed. I scratched my nose. Joris pulled at his earlobe. He smoothed his hairpiece with his fingers. It went on like that all afternoon.

June 10, 1986

[**Joseph Kosuth: "Zero & Not."** Leo Castelli, 142 Greene Street, through June 14]

Here in newspaper land, it's customary to justify, or somehow apologize for, writing about the same thing, or the same person, twice, and, in this department, to avoid writing too often on things at the same gallery. Having once written on Joseph Kosuth's work, and having paid attention to many shows at Castelli in the past year, I can only justify doing it again by saying that Castelli has had an unusual number of significant shows, and Joseph Kosuth's new work surpasses even his last exhibition in fervor, intelligence, and wit. And I am going to delete this paragraph from my collected works.

"Zero & Not" works as a play on words, "not" and "naught" being Boston homonyms: looked at this way, zero equals "not" numerically, and the meaning of Kosuth's installation would be a cancellation, the addition of nothing to nothing. The reverse interpretation of the title is "zero and not zero," or "nothing and not nothing." Kosuth has covered the gallery surface with 31 copies of a paragraph from Freud's *The Psychopathology of Everyday Life*, printed in sections. The paragraph reads on a vertical scheme, but because the text follows the surface of the architecture—that is, does not cover the recessed spaces, except those which are part of the out-facing planar surface of the gallery—it doesn't run consecutively, since the parts of the space that define volume (including air-conditioning grilles, alcove sidewalls, the elevator, light sockets, windows, and so on) break the text in numerous places. Discrete phrases repeat on frequently interrupted, horizontal lines, therefore, the continuous text scans downward from the ceiling in an irregular pattern.

The linear reading of repeated lines is further interfered with by the varied height of the surface, the rear clerestory windows making the rear wall considerably lower than the others. But I've so far mentioned only the least obvious ways in which the integrity of the Freud paragraph has been ruptured; every line of text is traversed by a thick black deletion-line, which crops the letters into equal upper and lower fragments. One can read the lines, with slight difficulty, mentally filling in the missing alphabetic parts, and hence "canceling" the sign that indicates that the text itself has been canceled.

Kosuth's paragraph numbers are in color, the colors corresponding to a designated wall letter: wall A's numbers are red, B yellow, C blue, D green; in various places the numerical distribution of the text's pieces is indicated by a color bar underlining passages, so that if a given passage appears more often on wall B than wall C, the underscore contains a length of yellow greater than its length of blue. These kinds of notations enhance the impression of a nonarbitrary system, and break the monotonous black and white.

The Freud paragraph comes from a chapter on "Slips of the Pen," in which Freud discusses receiving a telegram that reads, "Provisions received, invitation X. urgent." His publisher had sent a telegram acknowledging receipt of a preface and requesting a promised introduction. "We may assume," Freud says in the antecedent passage, "That it had fallen victim to a revision by the telegraphist's hunger-complex, in the course of which, moreover, the two halves of the sentence became linked more closely than the sender had intended."

Kosuth's choice of this text, which deals with transcription mistakes impelled by unconscious desires, is a way of mirroring the transaction between artist and work, work and audience: the work itself is never more than the echo of its process, and once it is shown it's delivered to misunderstandings based on preconceived wishes. These discrepancies are the very problems the artist tries repeatedly to overcome; hence a normal, left-to-right reading of the text yields endless repetitions of scored phrases, redolent of continual production, vexed by incessant error. Freud devotes much of *The Psychopathology of Everyday Life*, of course, to examining his own unconscious writing errors, particularly in *The Interpretation of Dreams*. The ruminative, cyclical, often halted voice created by Kosuth's horizontal fractures also evokes the self-masticating prose of Beckett, Bernhard, and Kafka— writing that eats its tail, issuing from an inexhaustibly self-critical consciousness.

As in Kosuth's previous "Fort! Da!"—annotated photographs of the Castelli West Broadway location—"Zero & Not" is site-calculated in numerous ways. Freud's reference to his publisher becomes Kosuth's reference to Castelli Gallery; Kosuth's visual rendering simultaneously asserts and negates Freud's text on errors, and this rendering leaves itself open to caesuras and erasures created by the space it's intended for.

At the same time, Kosuth has made his work's surface strictly congruent with the surface of the gallery walls, so that the architectural features that define the gallery's volume are thrown into really startling relief. What is strictly spatial forms a series of windows inside Kosuth's work, as do certain blank passages created within the text by the architectural disruptions. The initial effect of the ruled-out text, as in book galleys and other manuscripts, is to make the text a visual object rather than a text-to-be-read, a two-dimensional picture, a language-skin. Kosuth has adhered this skin to the skin of the gallery; if the text ran across every surface, "Zero & Not" would *become* the gallery, whereas deletions effected by the carved-out spaces define the separation of the art from the architecture. Kosuth's work so overwhelms the uncovered spaces that it miniaturizes the functional components of this environment, vivifying a structure that's usually in plain view but repressed from attention by the desire to see only *art*.

This desire, like the telegraphist's hunger-complex, is typically the hunger for an object which obliterates its context. One could compare it to being in love, in the sense that a person in love no longer sees the love object as it is, but as an ever-present blankness on which the lover projects his own hopes and anxieties. Kosuth's art, it seems to me, has always pointedly revealed the lineaments of aesthetic desire without refusing to gratify it altogether; his work *detoxifies* aesthetics.

To put it another way, Freud says that the telegraphist's errors joined the two phrases of the telegram "more closely than the sender intended." *Preface* became *provisions, introduction* became *invitation*. If we view Kosuth's activity as the reflection of a way of thinking—about the meaning of art, about how that meaning is made—then Kosuth's tangible production should be regarded as investigatory, "Zero & Not" as prefatory to a true reading of how things mean. But the inevitable and necessary context for this preface is a gallery, which is, after all, a kind of store, for certain kinds of provisions.

However, nothing is on sale in this case. While a gallery show invites an audience to witness and buy the aesthetic commodity, "Zero & Not" cancels the possibility of instantaneous consumer gratification; it implies the urgency of an introduction to different, more demanding models of art. The terms of Kosuth's message, transcribed by the gallery and its architecture, are brought closer to the language of unexamined craving and delectation. But they can still be read as intended, because the artist crossed them out.

June 17, 1986

TRAVEL PIECES

["**Bon Voyage: Designs for Travel.**" Cooper-Hewitt Museum, 2 East 91st Street (at Fifth Avenue), through July 13.]

To travel: as in, to split, to get out, to scram, to take off, to go from one place to another. "I hate traveling and explorers," begins the most beautiful "travel" book of our time, Claude Lévi-Strauss's *Tristes Tropiques*. "The wall outside my window is enough," wrote Kafka, who so hated travel that an out-of-town appointment inspired reams of flustered, apprehensive correspondence and finally a cancellation. In "Self-Reliance," Emerson notes that the person traveling for amusement (as distinct from an artist or scholar) "travels away from himself, and grows old even in youth among old things."

These examples mainly decry a modern sort of traveling: travel as a purposeless, frivolous, hedonistic ritual. Modern travel evolved from the Grand Tour, an ostensibly educational rite of passage prescribed for young English aristocrats of the 18th and 19th centuries, and from Thomas Cook's more plebian invention of the package tour in 1841, made possible by the new railway technology. But people have "always" traveled—as nomads, pilgrims, soldiers, exiles, merchants, and convalescents, among other things; before the advent of mass tourism and its service industries, the prudent traveler had to carry most of what he needed with him.

"Bon Voyage: Designs for Travel," at the Cooper-Hewitt Museum, is essentially a survey of the history of luggage, containing a prodigious number of actual travel items as well as far-ranging illustrations, including Dürer's woodcut engraving of St. Christopher, an Edo period woodblock print of Japanese travelers, pages on case-making tools and luggage from the Diderot Encyclopedia, a surreal Dutch illustration of Magellan's chronicle, and assortments of stickers and baggage tickets from steamship lines and grand European hotels.

Among the earliest artifacts are long, curve-top leather and metal trunks, intricately decorated with studs or carving, shaped to deflect rain, as they were generally carried by hand or else rested, exposed, on the roofs of carriages or the backs of horses. (Travel trunks became flat-topped when rail travel superseded coaches.) One especially stolid piece belonged to Marie de Médicis, and has the date 1617 (the year her son, Louis XIII, banished her from court) worked into its decoration; another sturdy trunk, decorated with crown and cipher patterns, belonged to George III. When royal personages moved from placc to place, the paperwork of administration as well as household chattels had to be hauled along; this show features several ingeniously devised portable desks, trunks that open up into marquetry cabinets, and early versions of the briefcase or business portfolio.

The larger trunks are interesting for their contrast with the modest luggage of religious pilgrims—tooled leather missal cases, tapered sacs for utensils that were worn from the belt, and so on. What becomes fascinating, chronologically speaking, is the increasing complexity of luggage design as the experience of travel expands. As coach travel made it possible to carry more of one's personal environment for greater distances, things like eating kits and dressing cases became more elaborate, bulky hat boxes and other idiosyncratic items came into general bourgeois use. Specialized travel kits—for doctors, surveyors, scholars, and soldiers—begin to appear as items of craftsmanship and eventually of mass production.

The genre of military luggage, for example, becomes refined with the eventuality of the seasons-long campaign, in diverse weathers. Here there are suitcases that turn into camp beds, a collapsible mahogany bidet, cases for epaulets, cases for chapeaux, cases for plumes, Marshal Ney's personal dressing kit with numerous, ingeniously stacked oval trays. For the itinerant surveyor and the doctor on horseback, there are cases full of snug compartments for instruments, medicines; for the musician in transit, a case that converts into a three-stringed violin.

My favorite is a tilbury carriage that comes apart and can be folded up into three trunks—designed, as many things in this show are, by Louis Vuitton. There's also the ultimate traveling environment, an astronaut's space suit covered with movable Velcro pockets, containing its own supply of oxygen, luggage your life depends on.

While this exhibition is physically appealing in its variety, and amply demonstrates how practical design has been modified by new travel technologies, its principal interest lies in what it shows about travel itself evolving from a necessary procedure into the prerogative of certain classes, and finally into a mass medium. When travel was arduous and unpleasant, one went somewhere with a particular purpose in mind, packing whatever would ameliorate the worst inconveniences. For example, the pre-modern inn did not necessarily have lamps, or utensils, or bedding available. That was what you packed. Later, as travel became more painless, the idea that one should do it, to "broaden oneself" and gain experience, gradually spread from the aristocracy to the middle-class. And like many such ideas, this one has been corrupted to the point where "consumption" has replaced "experience" as the raison d'être of mass travel.

The mass media tourist, like the astronaut in his space suit, doesn't ever really get outside the cocoon of his own luggage.

Whatever he needs from home awaits him elsewhere: American Express, English-speaking natives, experiences that coincide exactly with the descriptions in the guidebooks. He and she (they always come in pairs, which travel about in groups) find everything, everywhere, extremely odd indeed, unnatural, vexing, even insulting. One hears their braying voices in every world capital, like children who've wandered into a vaguely frightening playpen, indignant and at the same time strangely docile, throwing currency around like politicians during a campaign. They do not understand the hostility that gathers around them whenever their nationality asserts itself; the modern tourist travels without ever really being there, addicted to the idea of exoticism and repelled by the reality of it, despoiling the world while unaware of being in it.

TI SHAN HSU: A CHAT

I thought it might provide some relief for both reader and writer to run an interview this week. The reader has had to hear my ideas and opinions every week for over a year, and I have had to come up with them every week, often with a deep sense of embarrassment over having quite so much to say about things that may not, in many cases, finally be worth entertaining an opinion about. So I decided to pick a New York artist, Ti Shan Hsu, who is currently showing his work at the Pat Hearn gallery, and find out what this artist is thinking: whatever that happened to be, it would come from a different voice than my own. (A writer who never tires of hearing his own voice must be singularly blessed or cursed. Not I, not I.)

Gary Indiana: *A lot of attention is being placed on abstraction of a certain kind. Some of the titles of your pieces refer to things like conduits and circuits. Peter Halley, for instance, operates with all these ideas he has from Baudrillard about circuits and so forth. What is your relationship to someone like Baudrillard, or an artist like Peter Halley?*

Ti Shan Hsu: What I've read of Baudrillard and Lyotard, the sort of vision they present is very interesting, very contemporary; they have a lot to say. My work is intuitive. It developed over a number of years, according to a certain sensibility. It really had no words directing it. It came from a direct experience of everyday life. So when I became aware of Lyotard's and Baudrillard's writing, it seemed to describe something I feel much more internally, physically. I'm interested in something that's not necessarily illustrative of an idea. I would have to step a little bit away from the current moment, so to speak—

For instance—

There's a lot of talk about "Neo-Expressionism is dead," or something like that. I don't really see much difference between the underlying content of Neo Expressionism and the New or Neo-Abstraction or whatever you want to call it. In the art world generally, there's this kind of time frame we're all slotted into, five years this, then five years that, then five years this, and it's gotten to the point that a dealer can predict, "This is gonna go five years and then something else—" and it's just so simplistic and unnecessary. It becomes so expected that it's short-changing what art could do.

My feeling is that a lot of current discussion has been about loss of faith, a sense of failure, a sense that there's nothing vital that can really be done any more, and that life has become somewhat deadened and empty and lacking any real vital impetus. That's understandable—we're at the end of a rather traumatic century, and we are tired, especially tired of new forms. In that context, I think we're tired of the myth of Modernism. It's clear things aren't better, progress wasn't necessarily made in the last 50 years. However, to say that nothing new is going to be done, that this is the end, is extremely egocentric, not of a person, but of our time: that our time is so particularly special. I'm not so sure that it is.

The particular construction of culture we deal with in the art world—what you said about being slotted into a moment—as far as I can tell, what's going on in this very restricted little art world paradigm is that the kids who were making Neo-Expressionist paintings, which were dumb, have been replaced by the smarter kids who think they're intellectuals or something, in the playpen. That's not a cultural moment for me, really. That has to do with social life—which smart kids will get good grades in the magazines this year. It's boring.

I guess that's putting it a bit more strongly. Even that, you know—I think there are new things going on in the world now, I don't mean this year, or this season, but we're moving in a new context, and I think these French philosophers are interesting because they're addressing a much broader framework, it's much newer than we may even be aware of right now. I don't feel the art world has really dealt with it in a substantive way, and in fact to deal with it may take longer than the three years it would take for it to be "in," understood, and then dropped.

I think we've become so enslaved by the idea that the new always means a new form, and formalism is dead, so let's not go that road—it's so simplistic to look at it that way. I mean, form is there whether you want it or not, and maybe the mistake was to consider form the be-all and end-all. Form is the means to something else, to say something. I can look at any work, and I can talk about form. I don't think form is the essential thing, however. I think the world is changing, there are new things to be dealt with. Not that the world is going to be any better. I think that, as opposed to the modernist vision, the world may get worse. I think life will be just as tragic, as painful, and as difficult as it always has been, but that doesn't mean there isn't something new to talk about. Maybe the emphasis will be different. Or how we feel pain will be different. Or the sense of tragedy will be new—that, to me, is exciting.

The relationship of consciousness to technology hasn't really been explored very ambitiously by visual art. I think literature has done it.

Visual art that wants to talk about this isn't so developed. It's one rea-son why so-called Neo-Conceptualism has been so disappointing. That work should be more generative than it has been. At the point where it takes on that capacity, the people making it can't wait to become part of the art establishment, and thereby lose the possibility of going on.

I certainly feel a bit of that pressure myself. Market forces are a temptation, but in many ways a negative temptation. Maybe as artists we need to be aware of what market pressure is doing to the work—sometimes you're so much in it that you're not even aware of what you're potentially losing.

I'm interested in multiplicity rather than singularity, some-thing inclusive rather than exclusive. If we talk, for example, about going from expressionism to abstraction, or this pattern from cool to hot which is so well understood now, to a fault, by artists—is it possible, that maybe there's something else, let's call it X, that may not fit into the categories of cool-hot, or expressionist-minimal—that maybe, this wasn't always the case, you know, 200 years ago people didn't talk about art being cool or hot, or expressionist or minimal. Maybe a whole different paradigm needs to be constructed or dealt with.

In connection with your own work, you've referred to The Body in Pain, *Elaine Scarry's book.*

I found Elaine Scarry's book fascinating, because, first of all, I've been very frustrated by the way the art world has dealt with deconstruction. People deal with it in such a simple, appropria-tive, legitimating way, to make their work seem current, and deconstruction is actually very complex, a complex way of looking at reality. Elaine Scarry's book is radical and brilliant because she uses deconstruction in a deep, substantive way, going from pain and war and torture into creativity and making. It's not that she—for those who haven't seen her book—talks about one and then the other, but in a deconstructive way turns one into the other and back again. It shows you that something very negative can, underneath, actually be very positive, and what's positive can be negative. It goes back and forth between opposites, and she covers a wide range of experience, managing to illustrate how one thing can be turned into another. She looks into the world, not just into literature—she's not just taking a text and showing how each word can turn into another word in a mechanical way. She's looking at the world deconstructively, and using texts, and words, to get at that. But it's very much about direct experience, and I feel that direct experience is somewhat lacking in a lot of the work that we see now.

July 1, 1986

MONO

[**Olivier Mosset.** Tony Shafrazi, 163 Mercer Street, through July 11.]

It would probably be too easy to say that the churnings of art fashion this year were fated to culminate in an effulgence of solid color works and shows on the theme (if it is one) of color. Nevertheless, it seems far from accidental that June, the month when the art world typically delivers its closing remarks for the preceding year and its premonitory ones for the season to come, is replete with so-called pure painting.

What, you may ask, might pure painting be? Perhaps it is nonanecdotal painting, or painting whose subject is painting. Of monochrome painting, it could be said that exegesis is everything. One black painting might be a statement on race relations, another about despair, another about the absence of light; perhaps the painter ran out of every other color, or decided that black was the only *real* color, and so on. Intention and context are the keys to interpretation. Information around and about monochrome paintings provides whatever "meaning" they have that's peculiar to a particular artist. Quite a few artists, for example, have made monochrome paintings, stripe paintings, and color field paintings, artists as diverse as Yves Klein and Larry Poons, Sherrie Levine and Brice Marden, all for different reasons, and, arguably, in different contexts.

Olivier Mosset, who has been doing this sort of thing for many years, currently has a large show at Tony Shafrazi gallery. He also has a work in a show of European painters at Barbara Gladstone gallery, and another in a show called "Red" at Massimo Audiello gallery. He's in the group show at Cable Gallery, too. Mosset also had a two-man show, with Alexis Rockman, two months ago at Jay Gorney Modern Art. These are a lot of contexts, even though they are all galleries: Shafrazi's establishment has primarily been devoted to fun art, of a broadly accessible sort, since it opened in Soho; Barbara Gladstone's usually offers extremely serious European and American art, as does Cable; Massimo Audiello shows slightly whimsical, clever, often topical things of high quality; and Jay Gorney Modern Art, a comparatively new gallery, has acquired a lightning reputation for efficient salesmanship of "difficult" work.

Mosset's paintings seem logical in all of these contexts, though they don't necessarily look different from one to the other. Are they "signs" of painting, functional expanses of colored canvas, substitutions of blankness for images? If this were the case, the work in the Shafrazi show would be a departure, since Mosset has included two-color paintings and stripe works. These are, in fact, the most recent works, but Mosset has done stripe paintings before. Perhaps some clue to Mosset's intentions can be gleaned from the titles: *Challenger*, *Bandwagon*, *Lobby*, *Greene Piece*, *K.A.L.*, and *Stranded*, which do give the nonmonochrome pieces anecdotal properties, whereas the three extremely large monochromes (two white, in oil, one red, acrylic) are untitled.

It may be that the two thick black stripes on heavy gray in *Challenger* have some sort of funereal chromatic relationship to the explosion of the space shuttle, and the turquoise T-shape on cerulean blue of *K.A.L.* refers to an object flying through the sky. However, looking for these kinds of meanings in Mosset's work is a much too literary procedure. Pure painting, strictly speaking, resists interpretation: it makes a picture, let's say, of the color red, or two varieties of the color red (*Bandwagon*), and this picture is presented in and of itself as an event. In its way, this event can have as much impact on the spectator as the representation of a disaster on television—maybe greater impact, since the viewer comes into direct personal contact with the painting. (If it weren't for the 1986 date of *K.A.L.*, of course, we could also speculate that the titles refer to what happened to be going on while the paintings were being made.)

Certainly Mosset's paintings have the capability of registering as events. They are sometimes heroically scaled, so their appearance in certain contexts tends to wipe out everything around them. The color is usually flat, evenly applied, "the hand' more or less extraneous—though the fact that these pictures are arduously hand-painted is important. The slightly fuzzed edges on Mosset's stripes are intentional signs of hard labor, of seriousness.

The pictures themselves, appearing in the context of an art world that has become more parochial than it was last year, signify rigorousness and the autonomy of the art object. If Mosset's work is concerned with anything besides "painting," it's other painting. Even a small solid green or pink square looks reproachfully clean, and relieving, in a room full of busier art; Mosset's pictures *en suite* recall the iconoclastic reductivism of almost two decades ago, and suggest that being *really serious* about painting means doing nothing *except painting*.

Mosset's art has an undeniable strength as painting, because it is obdurate and distinct most of the time. But the limitations of the idea of painting it represents are extreme, because these are not original with Mosset and seem to reassert worn notions of painterliness. Perhaps these limitations are appropriately severe, deflating the bombastic claims recent painting has made in the area of soulfulness and self-expression. Mosset scrapes away most of what engages painting with the world, paring it down to an investigation of color and scale. On the phenomenal level, the result has considerable optical allure and an appealing air of sarcasm. It demonstrates that nothing can be the content of something and still hold our attention. This has been done before, hilariously by Duchamp and in a steadily souring manner by Warhol. It conceivably needs to be done again, or to be done all the time by a few artists like Mosset. A parallel activity in literature has not been especially generative, e.g., concrete poetry and "language writing," but then, the audience for literature is considerably smaller than the audience for art, and less in need of radical ablution.

July 8, 1986

HOME

["**Eminent Immigrants.**" Newhouse Gallery at Snug Harbor, 1000 Richmond Terrace, Staten Island, through August 31.]

> *Your voyage has not yet terminated; the most important part of it is yet before you; there are quicksands, concealed rocks, whirlpools, and yawning gulphs. There may be a darker, severer, and more terrific storm, and a more awful warring of the elements still in reserve for you, than any through which you have ever passed— you may yet be hopelessly wrecked, and left to sink into the deep and unfathomable abyss. Have you prepared your bark for this last part of your voyage, and are you sure it is all right?*
> —Reverend W. W. Phillips, inaugurating the chapel at
> Sailors' Snug Harbor in November 1855

Between art and life, June 1986: This column is my last one until much later this summer. Since New York is afroth this week with "liberty," I'm taking the liberty of airing some opinions that may seem extraneous to my assigned context. Consider, though, that our quality of life is the only pertinent subject of art, and we must now and then go over it with a magnifying glass. Context, as more and more recent art single-mindedly demonstrates, is everything.

Despite the heartening news that Roy Cohn has lost his license to practice law, it's an immense pity that he's been disbarred, not for destroying countless lives during the McCarthy era, not for corrupting national morality, but simply for defrauding the rich, which the rich do to one another (and to those less fortunate) at every opportunity—once again demonstrating the truth of the Alan Price lyric, "We all want justice but you got to have the money to buy it." Nearly every news story about Cohn, who really is monstrous seven ways to Sunday, has, in recounting Cohn's crimes, hinted blithely that he has AIDS, as if that were crowning proof of his perfidy. On the contrary, this is the single charge that would make Cohn seem human, and the only one that is none of the public's business.

If you skim the papers this week you'll learn that an AIDS cure isn't even being contemplated by "experts," because the condition hasn't spread very dramatically into the white heterosexual population. If it ever does, it will become the nation's health priority, down at the bottom of a list topped by nuclear space weapons. Also noted: 11 million tourists will turn up in Manhattan for Independence Day, to gawk at the Statue of Liberty, spread litter, and harass our native nonconformists. Then there's the report that a hole in the ozone layer the size of the United States appears for one month every year over Antarctica.

The first and last of these stories are obviously more compelling than the second, at least in the long run. Taylor Mead wrote some beautiful lines about the Statue of Liberty. To paraphrase: "Is lesbianism something new? I don't know, but there's been a very masculine-looking woman holding the torch for somebody in New York Harbor for over 60 years." In realpolitik terms, however, this symbolic object should be rechristened the Statue of Limitations. America is befouling the planet with suicidal abandon, yet Americans seize any paltry occasion to congratulate themselves over abstractions like "liberty" and "freedom." As Norman Mailer once stipulated, freedom consists of being able to say *shit* in the *New Yorker*, and to my knowledge no one ever has. (In this connection, I would like to express my solidarity with C. Carr on the Karen Finley "eat shit" issue: if

The Village Voice wants to become the *New Yorker*, it should pay us *New Yorker* wages. As things stand, *The Village Voice* is half a parody of *The Village Voice*, and it isn't our half.)

It's depressingly clear that with a Supreme Court headed by William Rehnquist we can kiss whatever "liberty" we have good-bye. The citizen of the near future will have the liberty to salute the flag like an imbecile whenever it passes, to sleep with the same person for the rest of his/her life, and to express, on all occasions, opinions identical to those of his/her neighbors. The citizen will otherwise risk getting his or her head bashed in by a bunch of straight guys worried about the size of their dicks (some of whom obviously write for this newspaper). And with a hole in the ozone layer as big as America the Beautiful, this citizen can count on getting cancer. The upper atmosphere does not go on vacation for 11 months out of 12. If a large hole appears in it every December above Antarctica, you can be certain this hole travels everywhere during the other 11 months.

Americans have sentimental reasons to be moved by the Statue of Liberty. But after receiving at least two dozen announcements, posters, and press releases for events and art works devoted to the exploitation of the vulgarly touted "Lady Liberty," I find that any representation of this object positively stinks of some malignant advertising agency. I even have a particular agency in mind. The most nauseating aspect of the current circus is the complete identification of "liberty" with venality on every level, with Battery Park City residents leasing their flats for thousands of dollars per night, while the Staten Island Ferry is docked for the holiday, to avoid giving anyone a 25-cent seat for the fireworks. If this is liberty, give me communism.

* * *

While liberty hysteria reaches its flatulent crescendo, a calm, well-selected homage to American immigrant artists is on view at the Newhouse Gallery's Main Hall, in Staten Island's Snug Harbor. A better location could not be dreamed of: founded in 1801 as a home "for aged decrepit and worn out sailors," Snug Harbor's complex of crumbling Greek Revival buildings (under gradual restoration as a landmark) now serves as a cultural center, set back from Richmond Terrace in woodsy desuetude.

The Main Hall is in the original Snug Harbor building, from which the complex grew to include farms, a music hall, a hospital, numerous cottages, and a one-sixth-scale replica of St. Paul's Cathedral, the latter demolished in 1952. The Main Hall housed the original sailors, administrative offices, and common rooms; it features a rotunda with murals, painted inscriptions ("Rest after dangerous Toil," "Port after stormy Seas"), and colored attic windows inscribed with constellations and starbursts. The side room ceilings have nautical decorations like ship wheels and sailor's-knot borders. Even with everything flaking, chipping, and gone to seed, the atmosphere is rather grand—redolent of another age, another world. It transports you to the period of Sarah Orne Jewett's *The Country of the Pointed Firs*, the world of our grandparents.

The current show, "Eminent Immigrants," curated by John Perreault (Director of Visual Arts at Snug Harbor and an occasional contributor to this section), contains a mixture of things that look incongruous but somehow appropriate to the setting—centrally, Gillian Jagger's bulky, curved expanse of cement-and-urethane foam chunks resembling shoreline boulders. The Main Hall also has a large dusky oil painting by Komar and Melamid (*Portrait of S.C. as Siren*), Christo drawings of giant umbrellas in landscapes, Picassoish vertical sculptures in painted wood by Italo Scanga, an "altered bicycle" with Duchampian rotorelief wheel spokes by Eduardo Costa, and three shaped-canvas geometric abstractions by Lydia Okumura. In addition, there's a three-panel excerpt from Sylvia Sleigh's realist painting called *Invitation to the Voyage*, a work that evokes the wilderness landscapes that still exist, in dwindling pockets, on Staten Island.

Les Levine has one of the side rooms, the walls papered with the same family album images that appear on a billboard Levine's done on Bay Road. In another side room, there are Justen Ladda gouache drawings; several gnarled, skeletal-looking porcelain forms by Rina Peleg; Bernar Venet's C-shaped steel *239.5° Arc* (along with a pastel drawing of the piece); and an intensely realistic Naoto Nakagawa still life, *African Queen*.

Other featured work includes the late Ana Mendieta's highly tactile, dark, brittle-looking bark drawings and female forms executed in twisted vines, branches, and dirt. These are hard, poetically inconsolable presences; the most disturbing one is a floor piece in two charred, cracked wafers that look like patted-together volcanic ash. Mendieta's work is situated near a big mixed-media painting busy with tree branches and surface fractures, by Zigi Ben-Haim, and a maquette of Ben-Haim's *Rising Path*. The full-scale *Rising Path* stands on the Snug Harbor lawn and looks like two razory, thalo-green teeth sharpened to points.

Among the Komar and Melamid paintings in the front room is *First Drop of Blood*, a deft synopsis of patriarchal history. A commissar has just chopped off somebody's limb for the first time; a young girl, hunched over with cramps, contemplates her first drop of menstrual blood. Over both panels, a skeleton carries a scythe and a (functioning) clock.

Are you making daily observations, watching the clouds and the winds, and the tides, and are you habitually ready to launch at any moment? Above all, have you engaged Him who alone can pilot you safely through the dangerous sea into the haven of eternal rest?

    —Rev. W. W. Phillips, *op. cit.*

SOCKS MAKE THE MAN

[*Dick Clark's Easygoing Guide to Good Grooming*. Dodd, Mead, $15.95.]

Virtually every book on male grooming contains the same basic information: how to shampoo, how to clip your fingernails, what style of clothes to wear for your body type, what kinds of foods to eat, how to stay fit. Most feature, as illustrations, incredibly comely, well-developed dudes, preening in their underpants before luxurious full-length mirrors, or striking poses of provocative indifference at the beach, their scant trunks stuffed with excelsior. *Dick Clark's Easygoing Guide to Good Grooming* is different. It contains numerous photographs of Dick Clark, in various outfits, along with many simple line drawings that show, for example, how to knot a tie, the difference between an endomorph and an ectomorph, and what the classic-mode suit looks like.

If you've never picked up a grooming book before, you may be startled to learn that skin has a pH factor, that blacks scar differently from whites, that a good sunscreen necessarily contains PABA, that frequent jet travel dries the skin, that "the number of suits you own usually depends on the kind of work you do," or that clothes purchased in Asia are generally smaller than American clothes. Perhaps it will surprise you to hear that there are two kinds of sweat, eccrine and apocrine. Then again, it's hard to imagine anyone in need of such information who doesn't already have it, and easy to imagine millions with no particular need of it.

This book seems to be written for two kinds of men: the straight workaday schlub who needs butch assurance when using cleansing cream instead of soap, and the fast-lane junior entertainment mogul whom Dick Clark might find himself interviewing for a job. The *Easygoing Guide*'s advice on self-presentation aims for a dynamic blandness of the sort we associate with Clark himself. He doesn't advocate flashy dressing, unless you're a celebrity like Willie Nelson or Johnny Cash—Clark admires them tremendously—in which case anything goes. For less exalted males, he prescribes fitting in, dressing "appropriately": "A second basic principle for dressing well is to *not stand out in the crowd.*" You can take a meeting in "non-conformist" Hollywood wearing an open shirt with a sports jacket, but God forbid you should set foot in an "exclusive" New York restaurant in anything but a pinstriped suit. Jewelry is out, except wristwatches. Ditto saggy boxer shorts. Clark becomes almost vehement on the topic of loafers worn without socks—it's one thing to be undistinguished, quite another to be really out of it. If he were to encounter someone wearing loafers without socks—for instance, in a job-interview type of situation—Clark would surmise, "He is not keeping a fresh outlook on the world, is stuck in his ways, or perhaps...is trying to emulate a social class to which he doesn't belong and so is not totally honest with himself and may not be with others." To which one can only retort: Don Johnson.

There is, in fact, a little too much West Coast board-meeting semiotics sprinkled through this book for Clark's easygoing manner to sound very natural. It's nice that he credits blacks and gays as trendsetters, but his guide is clearly written for neither. It lacks the homoerotic allure typical of such books, and the well-groomed male it describes is seriously deficient in *cojones* of any persuasion. Clark does avoid, for the most part, making explicit assumptions about the reader. (I had to stop for a minute after reading that "only two people are going to see you in your underwear—you and your lady," but such lines are infrequent.)

On health, Clark informs us that the foxtrot burns up 5.2 calories per minute, the rhumba 7.0, the Charleston 8.06. The diet section cautions against salt, sugar, and saturated fats, and offers Dick's recipes for Pasta Primavera and California Lemon Chicken. My favorite part is the Holmes-Rahe Social Readjustment Rating Scale, which tells you numerically how much stress you should experience at various times—Death of Spouse rates 100, Jail Term 63, Death of Close Friend 37, Mortgage or Loan of Less Than $10,000 a mere 17. Dick also tells us how we can know if we're under stress: "You have to pay attention to yourself."

The basic message of *Dick Clark's Easygoing Guide* is moderation in all things. This message can be had elsewhere for considerably less than $15.95.

August 5, 1986

VENICE AS USUAL

VENICE—The two things everyone saw during the opening days of the 1986 Venice Biennale were not, properly speaking, art objects, though they were similarly useless in context and produced widespread irritation, like modernist art. One was called *Trenton*, the other *Portland*; both are massive American navy ships used to transport helicopters. At the outset of the Biennale (June 29 through September 28), they anchored in the Grand Canal, squat gray tubs that obscured the view of S. Maria della Salute from the Piazza San Marco and rubbed out the landscape from myriad other nautical and terrestrial vantage points.

No one seemed really to know what the boats were doing there. Many said it was an ugly show of American force intended as "symbolic protection" for the American ambassador (whose speech at the official U.S. dinner, slurry with provincial chauvinisms, unhappily reinforced the idea). Meanwhile, Venice was becoming infested with hundreds of boorish, sexually desperate, drunken American sailors, many of whom amused themselves by reeling into various canals. This all produced an especially adverse cultural impact in terms of American presence, as if the Noguchi installation in the American Pavilion (Henry Geldzahler, commissioner) had not already gone improbably far in this direction.

If the American ambassador required such heavy security, it was a very telling circumstance that I and some Spanish friends were able to lunch at a tiny Giudecca restaurant only a few tables away from President Mitterrand, without first being strip-searched or interrogated. *Vive la différence.* But then, for Europeans, the idea that "terrorism" is anywhere near as ubiquitous and menacing as Ronald Reagan provides endless amusement; for Americans here, the ritual of dissociating oneself from Reaganism is the invariable icebreaker. By the same token, one now becomes wary of Europeans who too quickly claim to "love Americans," reflexively wondering which Americans they mean.

Hardly anyone loves the American Pavilion, devoted as it is to a blocky marble kiddy-slide and numerous other minor works by Isamu Noguchi. The pavilion is crammed with those banal rice-paper and wood lanterns often found in on-campus housing for associate professors at Columbia; here they cohabit with some bronze maquettes for uninteresting architectural garnish. The only substantial Noguchi work on view is *Ends*, a topographically compelling cube of Swedish marble, which is, in fact, the stone residue of another work.

It is of course true, as Mr. Geldzahler notes in his catalogue statement, that the wire ribbing of Noguchi's lamps reflects a deep preoccupation with the helix structure. So, indeed, do the marble slide, and the scale model for Josef von Sternberg's swimming pool. However, what this rather mingy collection of decorative odds and ends has to do with current American art is hardly apparent; as a tribute to Noguchi, the selection could not have been worse. While the technical cleanliness of these works agrees with the "Art and Science" theme of this year's Biennale, the U.S. might have done with a less plodding pavilion, and perhaps a less predictable choice of commissioner.

Alternative American work hangs in the "Aperto 86" show, located off the Giardini grounds where the main pavilions are, in the Arsenal's narrow rope factory. This space, chopped into dozens of tiny galleries, has the look and feel of a convention hall, housing art from countries that don't have pavilions and sidebar entries from ones that do. Most of the U.S. works—by Kevin Larmon, Sarah Charlesworth, Mark Innerst, and Rene Santos—are either too small, or too adversely placed, to avoid being swallowed in the general jumble, though Mark Tansey's pieces hold their own in the central corridor. The circus atmosphere of the Biennale doesn't really invite serious appraisal of context; everything has been thrown up in a frenzy wherever there happened to be space, at least outside the Giardini.

The top awards were handed to Sigmar Polke and Daniel Buren—Polke for the best art, Buren for the best pavilion. Someone remarked that Buren's several rooms of variegated wall stripes need only a bidet and some other plumbing to represent the perfect bathroom for a villa in Nice. Polke's installation, looking quite at home in the Speer-designed German Pavilion, features several monumental paintings, essentially nonfigurative, with wan surfaces as cold and glistening as porcelain. They look like artful smears of light maple syrup on the walls of well-scrubbed trench urinals. Less enormous, earlier Polkes, in his more familiar lap-dissolve style, augmented these imposing yet strangely vacant works.

Opinion on Polke, during opening week, was crisply divided—that is, opinion as it circulated, late at night, at Florian's and Harry's Bar, opinion greased by the gourmandizing, alcoholic *ambiente*. Has Polke segued to abstraction from expedience, or is it a logical, even salubrious, move? And what of Frank Auerbach, representing Great Britain, whose dark, slathery portraits and landscapes, though "serious" as painting in a sense that Polke's work isn't, are almost irrelevant to the cherished belief that "world art" is headed somewhere it hasn't already been? This notion, after all, is the implicit premise of the 1986 Biennale, linking art with science and progress, mystery and wonder—mainly in quotidian, fun-fair exhibits like "Art and Alchemy," "Color," and "Art and Biology." Only two of these extravaganzas, "Space" and

"Wunderkammer" (the latter a particularly beautiful historical survey of cornucopias) transcend the overall mediocrity.

Events like the Venice Biennale are primarily staged for those whose fortunes fluctuate according to consensually perceived "developments" in art, secondarily for the general public. The contents of the Biennale comprise its least festive aspect. What most visitors really get off on is the novelty of Venice itself—the notorious difficulty of getting from one place to another, of finding anything in the maze. The mood is quickened not by the art (which everyone agrees is worse than ever, excepting their favorites), but by the eccentric hours kept by restaurants and bars, the ever-present threat of transport strikes, and by running into people one avoids like the plague in one's city of origin. It is the ancient spectacle of Venice, a city whose watery disposition makes it feel both eternal and fragile, like a fata morgana floating on the Adriatic, that gives the Biennale more glamour—and far less seriousness or real clout—than the other periodic art conclaves. Since spectacle is the main draw, the American warships become part of the entertainment. But most spectators wished that America had come up with something more amusing.

August 19, 1986

CASTLE TO CASTLE

> *Once the populace begins to reason, all is lost.*
> —Voltaire, letter to Damilaville April 1, 1766

SOMEWHERE IN ITALY—"*We* are the new aristocracy," brayed the American painter, one wheel of a duo that another guest had dubbed the "Tupperware Gilbert & George" shortly before their arrival at dinner. The more recessive of the two was distinctly more amusing, but the other livened things up in his way, issuing provocative fatuities about restoring the servant class, Jesus Christ and the Apostles as gay orgiasts, and the painter's "mission" to cure Neapolitans of the reproductive urge. We were on a terrace in Capri; the horizon had dissolved in mist hours earlier.

The dinner was a cunningly contrived mésalliance of American art people, its host a German art dealer who, somewhat later in the night, trapped my companion in a downstairs bathroom and declared his wish "to make luff." The American painter was singing "You're a Grand Old Flag," in magnificent voice. A songfest ensued. The art dealer was ensorcelled into several choruses of "*Deutschland Über Alles*," which he and his secretary delivered with gusto until, suddenly remembering that one of the artists present was a Jew, they abruptly pretended to forget the words.

The evening's tensions are easily explicable. American artists, critics, and dealers lay down eccentric stakes in Europe and guard them as zealously as their reputations at home. One may be hugely famous in Europe, moderately or only slightly so in America. In the art field, the opposite can also be true. Artists of massive visibility in New York are typically less than household words over here, and Europeans do not defer to American estimates of those who are known. The movies belong to Hollywood but art…is another story. Americans here scrabble over limited turf. Internecine rivalries exported to European dinner parties break into mayhem all by themselves, as if at last the proper ambiance had been struck. While New York, in season, opts for asphyxiating decorum, Europe still expects art people to be crazy, argumentative, even violent.

Nearly every guest on Capri had some readily fingered interest in what current American art gets to fly in Europe in the present period, and rallied into one or the other camp immediately after the dessert course. One conspicuous bone of contention (though hardly the only one) was "Rooted Rhetoric," a show assembled by Gabriele Guercio, which had opened at Castel dell'Ovo in Naples the previous day. Castel dell'Ovo is a hive of eroding ochre tufa stone at the end of a sand spit that juts into Naples Harbor. Pliny the Elder lived there, as did a succession of Neapolitan princes.

"Rooted Rhetoric" is, among other things, a survey of recent American art rather at odds with what's been presented by the Neapolitan dealer Lucio Amelio, who occupies a position comparable to Leo Castelli's in New York—with the difference that Amelio pretty nearly runs the only game in town. In this respect, Guercio's show was partly provocation, releasing new energies into a narrow field. Working closely with Lia Rumma Gallery, Guercio presented work by Barbara Kruger, Louise Lawler, Joseph Kosuth, Clegg & Guttmann, Hans Haacke, Richard Prince, Jenny Holzer, Allan McCollum, and Thomas Lawson, artists known but seldom shown in Italy, along with nominally "second generation" work by Mark Dion, Gregg Bordowitz,

Peter Halley, Meyer Vaisman, Stephen Prina, Peter Nagy, Christopher Williams, Haim Steinbach, and David Robbins.

I don't intend to describe all the work; anyone who's followed the last several seasons in New York has seen most of it, with the exception of Dion's and Bordowitz's. The names alone indicate a confluence of sensibilities quite far to the intellectual left of the American art most familiar to Europeans. The political designation recommends itself here because this art, like Italian Arte Povera, makes considerable claim to address its social context with greater integrity and directness than, say, American Neo-Expressionism à la Schnabel or the Italian Three Cs; it's an art that exists not merely to be admired, but to be comprehended, even to be used polemically.

To paint it with a broad, old brush, this kind of work is called Conceptual, neo-Conceptual, deconstructive, photographic, media-conscious, and other things, since it must be called something. I would call it symbiotic, or even ecological, if such words weren't the kiss of death, since it refers to its own condition as art but also refers outward to the world of things, mental actions, and sociopolitical processes in which it, as a specific thing and event, occurs. Since it speaks a secular, nonallegorical, historically rooted discourse, often using verbal as well as visual language, it is indeed rhetorically active in several directions. The most salient, in this particular context, are its methods of raising consciousness about the phenomenon and the reception of art: by miniaturization (Lawler's plaques of art-decorated interiors), mimicry (Clegg & Guttmann's "Dutch Still Lifes" with products like Tabasco sauce and Kiwi shoe polish), enlargement (Prince's magazine-ad cowboys), subtraction (McCollum's blank surrogates; Bordowitz's captioned, empty picture planes), parody (Vaisman's "designer painting" with limp-penis motif; Steinbach's Judd-shelves-with-mall-purchases), exhortation (Kruger's photographs, Holzer's message machines, Kosuth's neon sentences), and reduction-to-diagram (Halley's "cell module" paintings;

Kosuth's annotated, upside-down, b-&-w repros of classical paintings; Nagy's Xerox cartography of "intellectual history"; Dion's re-sectionings of decaying paintings, with proposals for restoration; Prina's mixed-media structural analysis of a Glenn Gould recording; Robbins's augmented-Op sociological montages; Haacke's slides of gallery-goers' houses; Williams's archetypal city views). In effect, Guercio assembled objects to be looked *through*, materially dissimilar, resistant to quick categorization. This kind of art isn't new to Europe; one could argue that it was invented here. But it has been marginalized, in recent years, by the conservative re-reification of older, market-compliant forms like "straight" painting.

"Rooted Rhetoric" clearly means to break down the American/European dichotomy with different dissolvents than "classical" painterliness and cryptomythological iconography—that is, the stuff that's ingratiated the School of Schnabel, if not to the European public, at least to the contemporary museum circuit. Presenting an art of ideas from New York was itself a daring move. Guercio countered the ambient notions of what's going on in New York, but this would be standard procedure for any enterprising curator. "Rooted Rhetoric" went against the nap of a more intractable cliché: the indulgent fondness Europeans extend to the crudest manifestations of American culture. Guercio's selections are poised, intelligent, witty, playful; not at all the Mack truck that art from the Empire usually feels like here in Italy. Paradoxically, this very difference courted disappointment.

It's a matter of practical fact that Stupid Art from the East Village enjoyed a wild, if brief, vogue throughout Europe for the same reason that books by horny toads like Henry Miller and Charles Bukowski are piled up near the cash registers of Italian bookshops. These rough-hewn, aggressively uncomely products confirm the "exhilarating" violent energy and anti-intellectualism of America, and hence the superiority of European culture. No one would deny that such things reflect the pathology of

American society, but few Americans could defend them as the most accomplished, or even the most truthful, examples of American culture. The European embrace of things American is curiously similar to the Japanese, though the latter is even less discriminating. In any event, the Parisian gigolette who "adores" the East Village, the German director who locates the "real" America in the plays of Sam Shepard and the Japanese graduate doing his thesis on water imagery in the novels of Pete Hamill merely exhibit different degrees of obtuseness.

"America is quite an extraordinary accomplishment as what it is," the writer Gregor von Rezzori told me recently, "but I'm afraid it shouldn't be exported." If one generally finds less and less in this to disagree with, it's interesting that the excluded discourse, or antiestablishment rhetoric, embodied in so-called neo-Conceptual art from America, travels as well as it does. Perhaps its appearance of relative statelessness derives from its overt concern with Western cultural history as a shared human fact rather than an American sell-out sale of exploitable iconography; then, too, it is strongly linked to contemporary European sentiment vis-à-vis the United States and its omnivorous mass culture. Since this culture is now everywhere, impacting on everything (today's *la Repubblica* reports that the Soviet Union's first subway ads will promote Coca-Cola), an American art that tracks its nuances and exposes its underpinnings (psychosexual, economic, philosophical) looks less American than art that wallows in—and celebrates—the condition of being that culture's victim. To put it differently, "Rooted Rhetoric" succeeds as an American show precisely because it does not "reflect" America with the vanity mirror of alienation, doesn't embody the clichés of American national character, mentality, and artistic ego that Europeans have traditionally cherished and are now, perhaps, learning to be scared of.

September 30, 1986

THE DEATH OF PHOTOGRAPHY

> *In the utopian state it would impossible to take*
> *a bad photograph.*
>
> —Clegg & Guttmann

The past is one kind of utopia: completed, perfect, dead. Old photographs interest us regardless of their quality. "This is what the past looked like." Here is a copy of *The London Illustrated News*, dated September 13, 1958. Some of the pictures are sepia, others black and white, many of them badly registered. "Completely Successful At The First Attempt: *Black Knight*—Britain's Ballistic Missile, Which Was Fired At The Woomera Range, Australia, On September 7." "England's First Riots Between White And Coloured People." "Portugal, The Individual Champion In The Skin-Diving Contests: The Frenchman Jules Curman, With A Fish As Long As Himself." "The Han Dynasty Brick Tomb At Wang-Tu: Some Of The Fine Murals." "The Largest Of All Living Lizards: Komodo Dragons Of Eastern Indonesia."

This is all strangely uninflected, matter-of-fact, "a window on the world" crowded with miscellaneous views. Most of the advertisements are drawn, rather than photographically illustrated, as if some conceptual barrier between recorded reality and the promises of commerce were still being observed. Perhaps for this reason, the somewhat bizarre compositions of the photos, their promiscuous juxtapositions on the page, the magazine's earnest, relatively unsophisticated devotion to pictorial novelties, all suggest a distant ancestor of the modern news magazine, a relic from the late 19th century rather than 30 years ago.

These pictures tug our attention because they depict the recent past. But their real fascination lies in the fact that they look fictional, fantastic—at the very least, they're much more remote from us in time than descriptions of British life in the novels from the same period. Even the grainy, grim Cold War London of *The Golden Notebook* seems more contemporary. Nothing dates faster than a new photograph. Not just because news is temporary. Information media have evolved much faster than we have. The world according to *The Illustrated London News*, 1958, is merely lumbering toward the Apocalypse; its residents have time to weed their vegetable gardens and grumble about the weather. Magazine photos favor Awesome Views, vertiginous long shots, perspectives that titillate with the promise of catastrophe. But as the disaster draws near, the intimacy of the tight shot will make it seem imaginary, a harmless digression in life's little film loop—like the press pictures of Chernobyl which, though taken from a helicopter, make the plant look like a miniature golf course, or the "laser enhanced" video-game coverage of the Tripoli bombing.

Here is the Queen Mother, receiving a bouquet. The faraway puff of an atomic device in the American desert. Nesting bats. Horticultural hints. A bitchy review of a fizzled drawing comedy, with a still that looks 400 years old. These pictures are dead as doormats. But all photographs lead a double life. As photographs age, the fact that they are objects becomes the most interesting thing about them. In time, photographs begin to picture not only the world they were made in; they also reveal the conditions of consciousness that determined their style and content.

This second life of photographs is an embarrassment to traditional notions about photographs as art. Since the beginning of photography, the partisans have made increasingly desperate efforts to distinguish art photography from more vulgar kinds, on the basis of technical differences, the authorial eye, types of subject matter, compositional niceties, and, ultimately, when every "difference" had been smoothly absorbed into commercial practice, on the basis of ethereality—hence Stieglitz's attempt to make photographs equivalent to music, believing that the world would be dissolved into gaseous abstractions. If anything, Stieglitz's *Equivalents* look more archaic than his other work. "Oh look, a cloud." People who look at photographs want to see something, the more something the better. A crumpled amateur snapshot of a certain vintage can hold much greater interest than any number of photographic masterworks. And this interest is hardly naïve.

Every photograph manipulates the reality it discloses. All photographic media prescribe versions of reality, inculcate and reinforce the existing patterns of man's domination by man. The spread of mass media has made it necessary to view all photographic images skeptically, to see them first of all as objects emitting messages into the environment rather than as reality transcripts.

While some critical writing of the past two decades has concerned itself with debunking representation, the technical management of consciousness through photographic media has become ever more sophisticated and inescapable. People have become voracious, if passive, image-consumers, citizens of an illusionistic global "culture." Every action that controls life is condensed into a photo opportunity for the rulers. The most important appliance of the unconsciousness industry, the television, sells consumers the status quo in a literally stunning array of packages. The omnipresence of photographic images in daily life comprises a duplicate universe, a metaworld of appearances, with its own deafening soundtrack, its own hologram geography. The conflation of reality with fiction is the premise of contemporary mass media: nothing is true, but everything is "real." The media discourse shapes consensus from difference, delineates the fanatically manufactured "enemies" of the rulers, reduces the world's complexity to a set of easily manipulated symbols.

The importance of photography in our everyday lives ensured the doom of a hermetic "art of photography." We do not have to live with paintings; painting can engage in an endless dialogue with itself without bothering anybody. But a photography that claims, on one hand, superior insight into reality, and, on the other, transcendent indifference to it, cannot compel serious attention when other photographies virtually flood the collective sensorium. In art, the shift in interest from the unposed, naturalistic photograph to the elaborately staged tableau, the "defective" print, and the emphatic deployment of photographs as objects, reflects a widespread disbelief in "innocent" representation.

Contemporary artists who use photography are critical, if not openly contemptuous, of traditional photography's polemical mise-en-scène, particularly the mystical fetishism of Stieglitz and Minor White. The photograph is now regarded, a priori, as a spectacle contrived in the subjective proscenium of the viewfinder, and therefore available for further manipulation or use as an *objet trouvé*: in effect, flexible in the manner of advertising and other commercial images.

The most recent effulgence of photography in art ignores the technical codes of classical photography and deconstructs the ideological codes of media images. It would be difficult, though, to gather it all under one umbrella, or assign it a single lineage. The photograph as admissible substance in "art work" dates back to Picasso's and Braque's collages; but it becomes important in a contemporary sense only in the 1960s, when Rauschenberg, Warhol, and other Pop artists began using photosilkscreens to make works about consumer products and mass media.

If photographs had previously functioned as aesthetic materials in art works, in the '60s and '70s they became bewilderingly active objects of critical scrutiny. Artists such as Joseph Kosuth, Jan Dibbets, Douglas Huebler, John Baldessari, and Ed Ruscha made works investigating the semiotics of photography and language. Photography had a broad, different importance in the '70s, too, in the documentation of land art projects like Smithson's *Spiral Jetty* and Michael Heizer's *Nine Nevada Depressions*; in Gordon Matta-Clark's architectural "cuttings," and other ephemeral works; in video and performance art; and, naturally, in Photo-Realist painting. The idea of a temporary artwork destined to end as a photograph or a temporary photograph destined to end as an artwork, encouraged the decay of photographic naturalism.

Throughout the '70s, numerous artists worked with photography in ways that objectified and augmented the "pure" images produced by the camera. Gerhard Richter's paintings, precisely copied from "bad" photographs in many cases, emphasized the aesthetic arbitrariness of images in circulation. Benno Friedman printed partial negatives and drew in the left-out parts, sometimes extending this procedure through several print generations. Valie Export drew human body parts over landscape photographs, rephotographing the altered prints. Vera Lehndorff and Holger Trülzsch made dye-transfer pictures of trompe l'oeil paintings done on Lehndorff's body. Gilbert and George drew explicit attention to their gridded photographic combines as objects by titling them sculptures, the framing apparatus being integral to the works.

Various hybrid photo objects began to appear in galleries in the late '70s: Mac Adams's crime scenes, using photographs and installation elements; Jim Collins's pictures of voyeurs in action, shot from behind; Bill Beckley's alternated text-and-image panels. In the same period, text-and-image works by Barbara Kruger, rephotographed magazine ads by Richard Prince, and Sarah Charlesworth's photographs of *Herald Tribune* front pages, minus their news photos, appeared in alternative spaces. The 1977

"Pictures" show at Artists Space, featuring photographic and photographically derived work by Troy Brauntuch, Jack Goldstein, Sherrie Levine, and Robert Longo, was pivotal in establishing photographic work as part of contemporary art practice.

Probably the greatest influence on photographic art in the '80s is the avant-garde film of the '70s, and the staggering volume of film theory (feminist, structuralist, Freudian) produced in the same period. Even someone who casually absorbed the theory or randomly viewed the films came away with a keener appreciation of photography's subliminal voodoo power. Certainly films like Jean-Luc Godard and Jean-Pierre Gorin's *Letter to Jane*, Yvonne Rainer's *Lives of Performers*, and Peter Wollen and Laura Mulvey's *Riddles of the Sphinx*, for example, suggested the possibilities of montage and annotation within the still photograph. Similarly, the films of Michael Snow, Paul Sharits, Hollis Frampton, and many others revealed the aesthetic interest of blurred, scratched, streaked, or indecipherable pictures, of "imperfect" photography.

A common theme in much of this work is the strictly cultural nature of representation: images don't fall from the sky. Photographic images occur, invariably, in an inorganic culture of artifice. (In the bogus film stills and magazine spreads of Cindy Sherman, James Casebere's fictive landscapes, Sandy Skoglund's dreamtime interiors, and William Wegman's anthropomorphic portraits of his dog Man Ray, the morbid closure peculiar to photographs becomes an active element of picturing instead of a dreaded by-product.) How images produce meaning depends on their context as well as their content; the linguistic or architectural setting of a picture tells us how to read it. "Nature," as imagined by photography's early practitioners, has yielded everywhere to culture, precisely because of its mechanical transcription in the camera lens. The images provided by the culture industry prescribe models of behavior, sexual attitudes, compliance with the power structure. By way of so-called high culture, which makes money and is therefore valued in American society, images with contrary messages can slip into the media stream. Photography's much-stigmatized reproducibility is ideal for this purpose.

The new photographic art defines itself as an active, critical practice. It invites the view to evaluate pictures in terms of meaning and function instead of purely aesthetic gratification. It is, in fact, dissolving the aesthetic of the old photography, locating "the beautiful" in the bleary, oneiric pinhole photographs of Barbara Ess and the ripped-up proof sheets of the Starn Twins. It embraces the phobias of the old photography, disseminating images on matchbook covers and wall posters. The unique producer is now, sometimes, a pair of Conceptualists (Clegg & Guttmann, Ulay and Marina Abramović), sometimes a gifted pirate of existing images, often someone who "hates photography."

After depleting its imperative of Beauty by revealing it in every conceivable spider web and splash of milk, art photography spun itself on the dime of Diane Arbus and commenced using up Horror and Repulsion. It's always possible to go a step further in that direction, but the thrills are becoming increasingly scarce—and, more to the point, quickly consumed. It was art photography's misunderstanding of its own medium that proved fatal: the assumption that some images—the pedestrian ones—get emptied out while others, lavishly produced in limited editions, retain their original impact. (And fatal too that other assumption, utterly alien to inhabitants of modern cultures: that holding up a static mirror to the visible is somehow a desirable achievement....)

The unconscious fiction that served as the truth of art photography has been supplanted by the deliberate fictions of photographic art. For the most part, art photography has entered Clegg & Guttmann's utopian state: it is never "bad." Every new example of it resonates with the same pathos. It doesn't even need to age; it's dead on arrival. One would prefer a live utopia for images, but this would need a living one for people.

October 7, 1986

CHAOS PLUS

In a cursory way, without any scientific acumen, I can relate the show of fractal photographs called **"Frontiers of Chaos"** (at Goethe House, 1014 Fifth Avenue, through October 18) to many things that have seeped into our lives as if by capillary action. The fractal photos are taken from computer visualizations of mathematical sets applied to irregular structures. The math theory that accounts for them was developed by Benoit Mandelbrot. If you take a piece of something like a coastline or a potato and describe its structure mathematically, you will get a picture that resembles the whole coastline, or the total potato.

Let's say the three-dimensional model on the computer screen is this beautifully colored semipotato. Or, a metonymic space photo of Jupiter with one of its moons. With fractal geometry you can punch up the image and get an idea of what the potato is really like, or an enhancement that looks like what a moon and a planet would look like.

With the computer, you can blow up your potato chip and zoom in on its surface with a little square cursor (this is the other trick), thereby producing a blowup. If you ever saw *Blow-Up*, you recall what happens when you do this with regular photographic equipment. But, because the computer can figure out the structure of things that would normally lose definition, these successive images are sharply defined. But along with symmetries, you get sprouts. You get strands. You get "devil polymers." Deformed sets. You get chaos.

The fractal photographs at Goethe-Institut are gorgeous, something between microphotography and spin paintings. Lots of whorls and islands and spirals and curlicues. They look like beautiful natural things: jewels, sunspots, snowflakes. It's nice to just look at them without thinking anything about them.

However, the makers of these pictures seem a bit defensive, anticipating objections from art critics about the value of such artifacts. The catalogue contains an essay called "Refractions of Science into Art" by Herbert W. Franke, which begins with the forthright claim that in the future, "Most likely the painters and sculptors esteemed today will nearly have been forgotten, and instead the appearance of electronic media will be hailed as the most significant turn in the history of art." Mr. Franke is probably right; the curious thing is, he seems to think this is highly desirable. Moreover, "…the proverb 'a picture is worth a thousand words,' is supported by arguments from the psychology of perception. Not only can the visual system handle an information flow approximately ten times that of all other sensory systems together, but the information processed can have a two- and to some extent even a three-dimensional structure."

Some of the combative statements in Franke's essay are simply meant to claim art status for fractal photographs. He sees the main obstacle as "the uncertainty of the experts, the art historians and the critics, and above all the gallery owners." This is really a quite minor issue. Art in the institutional sense is indeed whatever this list of gargoyles says is art. But if the computer experts who make fractal photographs painted copies of them they could probably sell them right now; I could give them a list of galleries. Anyway, if they really are artists they shouldn't be in such a hurry to crash the marketplace: it's crass.

It's normal for underappreciated scientific minds to assume that what they do is art: after all, isn't art about the beautiful order in things, about harmony, and particularly about harmony's symbiotic partner, dissonance? Well, yes, and especially, no. I am sorry to bring this up, but applied science itself has created a situation in which such ethereal notions don't much apply. Just as fractal geometry reveals the element of disorder in mathematical picturing, art (and I really do hate using the word) for the past 50 years has reflected the failure of science to genuinely improve our lives. We are slaves of state-exploited scientific research. Even a small child presented with a new scientific marvel will readily imagine its application in some incredible weapons system.

The scramble for innocent technological products is always meritorious and usually deluded. If we are disinclined to regard scientific novelties as more than decorative effluvia, perhaps it's because the scientific mind so readily leaps from a criticism of the art establishment to a wholesale dismissal of language as an unnecessary "sensory system."

You could certainly do something with fractal photography in art—James Welling and John Wilkins both have—but the thing by itself, as issued off a computer, is *merely beautiful*. I mean, in the same way a mushroom cloud is merely beautiful. True, it shows the miraculous hidden structures of things. But it doesn't produce meaning as art does. A fractal photograph can be "interpreted" ("This is a picture of a teeny corner of a potato chip"), but it can't tell us anything except what something looks like to a computer. In a structural sense, a cadaver looks just like a living person, which may suggest the limitations of a mathematical picture of reality.

Recent memory research has discovered that the human brain is not, in fact, very much like a computer at all, a notion dear to scientists. So computers cannot really function "like a brain" and brains that learn to function like computers will eventually find themselves shorting out. In any case, you can feed all sorts of things back; it doesn't bother me as a *critic* if you want to call it art. But as a person, I've always found that art is *perversely erotic*, and I know by my terminal that this is one thing a computer, by nature, isn't.

October 14, 1986

INFOMANIA

If your idea of a good time happens to be staring into an assortment of color television tubes embedded in a variety of sculpturally piled cabinets, with myriad abstract patterns flickering on them, you still might find the **Nam June Paik** show at Holly Solomon (724 Fifth Avenue, through October 25) a little hard to stomach. Aside from the robotic and totemic TV clusters, which might have occurred to any competent window dresser on 57th Street, this show offers an unhealthy amount of Fan Club Art that desperately wishes to impress us with its wacky cuteness and its irreverent use of sophisticated technology.

Those familiar with Paik's output will recognize the grim inevitability of numerous electronically generated portraits, framed in offbeat ways and sometimes hung at funny angles, depicting John Cage, Merce Cunningham, Allen Ginsberg, Laurie Anderson, and other members of Paik's extended family, hereafter known as the Club. Paik's work usually carries the assumption—also to be found in Cage's writing—that the public is inexhaustibly fascinated by the members of the Club, that their every sneeze and yawn is memorable and endearing. For quite a long time now, the masturbatory frivolousness of our official avant-garde has been a source of amused irritation in the art community: *My God, these people think they're movie stars!*

In Paik's cosmology of flickering Americana and stale performance art, the notion of a global village linked by telecommunication goes hand in hand with the idea that this village is culturally dominated by old copies of *Evergreen Review* and a few people Paik knows personally. We are expected to recognize the faces, and, what's more, to wish we were as cool as they obviously think they still are. Isn't that bald head with the glasses, in that painting-transferred-from-TV-scan-lines…Allen? Or John? Or Merce? What's Laurie trying to tell us, making that weird scrunchy face? Is that—could it be—*Burroughs*? Look, here's Laurie again, in these teensy-tiny frames at the bottom of this picture!

After a mercifully brief look at this show I felt embarrassed for these people, and for Paik—after all, they've each contributed something to world culture. But even if the contributions were as gigantic as they imagine, it wouldn't excuse this ridiculous posturing, as if they were godlike presences peering down at the peanut gallery from some Grove Press Olympus. This is 1986, and Grove Press is primarily a reprint house these days. Someone should tell Nam June Paik that the parade has moved on.

The Global Village idea, the we-are-all-one conceit, at least in most of its practical applications, is hardly the mind-expanding tool its devotees in the art world take it for. As the vicissitudes of the world economy transform citizens of advanced countries from active producers to passive consumers, they all become "the same" in the sense of gross diminishment. Freedom of choice becomes freedom to buy different products and watch different TV shows. The airwaves and outer space have been colonized to expand the department store. If you try to use a satellite to interrupt the flow of controlled information and send a substantially different sort of message into the pop heart and mind, you will be prosecuted by the federal government. If you do it in cooperation with the information controllers, your message will necessarily be deformed into something innocuous.

Global Villagers place a premium on "information," which is often confused with "communication." Communication occurs when the receiver of a message is able to respond to it. However, the existence of the Global Village depends on the silence of its permanent underclass. The exploitation of the Global Underclass is what makes the Global Village go around. We can only all be one if those of us who happen to be different have no voice in the InfoSystem.

AT&T's "**InfoQuest Center**," a four-story fun-house-cum-science-fair in Philip Johnson's atrocious AT&T building (550 Madison Avenue), "explores the technologies that are reshaping our future." Reshaping. InfoQuest is not, strictly speaking, an artwork, but it is a cultural entity that offers a simulacrum of "life in our time." Its picture of the Global Village is dowdier than Paik's, but its presumption of a Universal Spectator or Consumer isn't all that different.

InfoQuest starts talking at you in the elevator and it doesn't quit until you exit. There is a talking robot named Gordon and lots of talking video panels in beige plastic cases. There is a Corridor of Light. Lasers. Chips. Valium-smooth voices gurgling about "lightguides" and "hair-thin glass fibers." InfoQuest employs a special genre of voices peculiar to this sort of corporate entertainment, the TV commercial voice-over voice with slightly higher grain, addressing a generic You: The second you hear this voice, you know what kinds of questions it will never answer.

At InfoQuest you can " have a conversation with a computer," but the computer sets the terms. The language games it knows how to play determine the form of expression and consequently dictate what is expressed. The pretense of "participation" masks the totally closed nature of the InfoModel at hand: you can ask all day what happened to the AT&T strike, or questions like that, and the voice will keep telling you that beams of light carry phone calls. InfoImperialism only requires a consensus among the speech impaired.

There is a floor devoted to Lightwave Communications, another Microelectronics. The floor with the robot demonstrates

Computer Software. The displays are activated by inserting a personalized "access card," which you "personalize" upon receipt with a touch-sensitive video alphabet display. Along with personalization comes infantilization—first names only.

You're then led to an "orientation exhibit" which lets you know which inhabitants of the InfoAge make up InfoQuest's target audience: the Sacred Nuclear Family, ranged like George Segal sculptures in the Sacred Living Room and Kitchen Unit. Mom's gazing into the TV. Junior's playing chess with a computer. Dad's rummaging in the fridge, radio headphones clamped to his ears. Sis is squealing into the telephone: "I'm sorry, marshmallow pizza sounds gross." An unexplained red light plays over the top of Mom's head; it's possible, I suppose, that this fully wired family is being irradiated against bacteria, like contemporary vegetables.

Your Name travels down a sloped wall-length LED board, as you descend past video InfoScenery and scale models of Info-Hardware: chips, satellites, the works. Now you arrive at the "hands-on" material, three floors of special effects and "fun" educational equipment. You can "help make a microchip." Or "direct your own music video." You can freeze your face on a monitor and then bust the image into jumbled-up squares. Or ask a computer to make up a "zany" story. A robot arm will play a synthesizer for you with a glass rod, and spell out your name with children's blocks. (On my first visit, someone had gotten it to spell out "SMEGMA.")

The noise level at InfoQuest is far too debilitating for the visitor to pay very close attention to anything. Most of the displays are basically video games; while it is possible for one to learn about certain technical processes, InfoQuest's main purpose is not to teach the curious, but to reinforce the idea that information technology is entirely benign, "linking people together" in the glorious Family of Man. Certainly there is no suggestion that "instant communication" helps concentrate capital in fewer and fewer hands, or that the primary impetus for InfoSophistication is the state's need for InfoSurveillance of both its proclaimed Global Enemies and its own citizens.

In the Information Age, art can only perform as insane decoration unless it resorts to a kind of InfoTerrorism. Instead of going through the proper channels to homogenize the slightly eccentric into "the universal," like Naim June Paik, artists need to discredit every paradigm of normality as it wobbles out of central casting. We need SMEGMA where the system says BILLIE should be. The question is, who will become InfoEntertainers, and who will be the InfoCriminals?

October 21, 1986

SQUARE ROOTS

It seems to be the usual thing, at this time of year, for the regular art writer to offer an overview of the scene and the season. I'm not going to, but I will venture this: art is now being made by collectors. Not all art, but lots of it. The typical collector's taste has been formed by the practice of buying things for the home, principally furniture. The typical career artist no longer feels begrimed or compromised by learning what others want and adapting his or her production to suit. Therefore, this season, we will see a plethora of *art du jour* that resembles furniture.

Perhaps the only thing to be deplored about this is the pretense that the situation is otherwise—that the mid-'80s versions of Pattern and Decoration need to bore people stiff with ponderous theoretical backup. If Mr. and Mrs. F. want it in red they'll get it in red even if they have to wait for it. The reflectively inclined among the art audience already will have read Baudrillard—and, unlike his American acolytes, other things, too. To everything there is a season, and to many things there are two or three, but even good ideas begin to pall when attached to too many press releases, or too many pieces of custom furniture.

There has been too much written about **Donald Judd**—a good deal of it by himself—for much of general interest to be added. Judd's current show at Paula Cooper (155 Wooster Street, through November 1) contains several kinds of Judd pieces, or rather, one kind in several variations: boxes. Some in plywood with colored Plexiglas laid across the inside back panel. Others in aluminum, also with Plexiglas. One in Cor-Ten. Then, in the rear gallery, a shelf piece and several box/shelf pieces.

The largest piece rests on the floor, an open-ended aluminum rectangle from 1968, to which Judd added a blue Plexiglas panel in 1985. All the other work is new or recent, and on the wall. Six of the plywood boxes range in two horizontal rows, six aluminum ones in vertical progression. Where the pieces are grouped, they operate like values in a math formula or notes in a musical scale: this space is half that space halved.

Judd's aesthetic is foolproof. The Pythagorean ordering of material creates a familiar, closed visual system. This is intrinsically pleasing, possibly sublime, since it incarnates a classical abstraction found everywhere in the inorganic world. Perfection, even when it is the perfection of nothing, appeals to the desire for absolutes, finalities, ideal standards.

The fabrication of these objects represents the most rigorous and expensive craftsmanship available to the contemporary artist. On this material level, Judd's work prescribes a guild approach to making things with industrial substances. The integrity of an artwork should be apparent in all of its parts; moreover, it should exist "for itself" and be situated in an ideal space. This object is a box, but what a box: the best of possible boxes.

What interests me about Judd in relation to certain other artists—especially ones he denigrates in his writings—is how keenly he's concerned to delimit the cultural space that historically exists for "art": that is, how intensely his work seeks to curtail that space, how deeply it resonates with a preciosity identical to the museum experience. I mean this in the best as well as the worst sense. Just as his boxes preclude the possibility of use, Judd's definition of cultural space is essentially negative, conservative, defensive. He doesn't regard the privileging of "art," or the social deformation that exists around art making, as a dynamic anomaly in an ever-narrowing control system, but as an island whose frontiers are forever being menaced by the untalented and by "commerce." Judd is "an artist," and, given the desiccated entertainment factor in his production, a "cultural worker" in the Calvinist manner of Godard during the latter's Kino-Pravda period. At the same time, Judd's austerity doesn't at all exempt his objects from the commodity system; the special values they embody simply presume aristocratic patronage as a worthy alternative to middle-class consumption.

The present liquidation of the middle class will oblige us to acknowledge that some values we attribute to art retain their character in almost any social configuration. This has less to do with "the eternal" than with the weight of history, and perhaps with anal retention, too. In any case, Judd's work is continually appealing because its will-to-order is consistent with centuries of received form. And it is so rigorously and unbudgingly what it is that it just begs to be taken up and done to.

Judd's influence on numerous younger artists has been mainly formal, though the notion of series inherent in his work has inadvertently encouraged a factory approach to production that's usually blamed solely on Andy Warhol. If the asceticism and occasional dry humor of Judd is echoed by a lot of new art, more explicitly campy recent work looks like **Richard Artschwager's**. Artschwager's current show (at Mary Boone, 417 West Broadway, through October 25) belongs to an expanding genre of exhibition we could call the Neatly Timed Flashback. The NTF is a legitimate corrective to the progressive amnesia endemic (and necessary) to the art world, though "amnesia" is a flattering condition when attributed to the latest species of art collector. (As in "Oh, I'm *re*-reading *The Man Without Qualities*.")

This kind of show has a pedagogical function, and an economic one. It establishes conceptual and physical affinities between currently produced art and earlier art. In this case it redresses the unfavorable positioning of Artschwager vis-à-vis Pop Art and the 1960s. If we look at his work through the lens of 1986, we see that what Artschwager did between, say, 1963 and 1968 (the dates of the work here) was premonitory, and passed into the thinking of other artists, many of whom were born between 1963 and 1968.

On one hand, the chronologically inverted déjà vu produced by these Artschwager pieces, which are based on furniture forms (tables, chairs, cabinets) and function as ironic sculptures, normalizes the idea that hard-edged colored objects in Formica, however radical such things may have looked a year ago, have actually been art for a long time, depending on who does them. This is, of course, true. Like most truths in the art business, it is also quite arbitrary. The expansion of the art world in recent years has left its inhabitants as well as its tourists with a longing for coherent traditions, verifiable pedigrees; this expansion itself guarantees the periodic squelching of one tradition in favor of another. The invention of tradition assures the collector that an acquisition is safer, and smarter, than it would otherwise have seemed.

On the other hand, some rediscoveries are better than others, some recrudescent ideas more genuinely complex and engaging than the rest. The framed monochrome idea, the negative space defined by color idea, the object-brooding-on-itself-and-the-room idea—all these ideas that Artschwager explored 20 years ago have been brought forward to good effect by younger artists. One effect of Artschwager's influence (and Judd's) that shouldn't be minimized is the replacement of impulse with thinking, gesture with craft, spontaneity with difficulty. Even if these substitutions merely promote some bottom-line quality control in the marketplace, they will lower the incidence of visual botulism as well.

October 28, 1986

WRITING IN PUBLIC

[**Jenny Holzer: "Under a Rock."** Barbara Gladstone Gallery, 99 Greene Street, 431-3334, through November 1.]

The possession of a public voice is one of the few fortuitous embarrassments available to the modern citizen. The public voice is ultimately judged by what it said, but while it is still active the fact that it says *something* remains a remarkable fact. Depending on its sphere of activity, the public voice may have the chance to influence consciousness in its time, and even to be preserved—whatever it said—as a telling historical artifact.

Writing in public is the least equivocal way of having a public voice: there are many others. Politicians, pop stars, sports figures, artists of all kinds, fashion designers, terrorists, religious leaders, and anyone else with access to mass media can say things in public, either directly (for instance, in interviews) or indirectly (in their work, their personal style, etc.). Indirect discourse is the dominant form of public utterance in our time. When visual culture overshadows the culture of literacy, most kinds of public expression have little to do with language.

The space of language has constricted; the public use of language (as propaganda, advertising, entertainment) reflects the spread of second-order illiteracy, wherein "language skills" are strictly implements, useful in negotiating verbal obstacles (traffic signs, bureaucratic forms, and so forth). Yet language retains, at all times, a disruptive potential exceeding that of other media. It is the ideal medium of self-consciousness. It is also the only universal art material.

The use of language, especially writing, in works of art is often thought to dilute the power of one medium by borrowing energy from another. This is sometimes true, sometimes not. The conventional segregation of one system from the other has no inherent value, since the written verbal system is visual. Jenny Holzer's work generates meaning by combining verbal and visual codes. It cannot be reduced to writing because its effects are achieved through a different kind of reading than the kind applied to literary texts.

In Holzer's work the site of language, its method of production, its physical appearance (scale, typography), and often the reading time it requires, are important, nonliterary elements. Holzer exploits the pictorial qualities of letters and words as well as the process we use to make sense of them. In "Under a Rock," texts are engraved on granite benches in uniform capital letters; the same texts appear sequentially on three light-emitting diode signs. It's characteristic of Holzer's work that while location influences the meaning of her texts, the same text can have many locations and its words don't need an invariable visual grounding. What's important is the circulation of messages through the urban environment, where writing is normally inscribed either for commercial purposes or to speak for authority. A work may appear in one form in a gallery, another in the street.

The installation of this show suggests a drive-in movie in a cemetery, with the benches ranged in front of the largest LED board, set in high isolation on one wall. Each of the boards runs essentially the same program, differently timed, with individual variations in color. The boards use red, yellow, and green lights that fizz over a grid of tiny glass bubbles. Holzer has programmed these machines to do just about everything they can do. Words loop backward across the grid in one color and flatten out in normal order in another, slide into view from an imaginary space above or below the board, switch color with the background, roll off screen. Sometimes a yellow cursor flashes across a red word sequence, changing it, or a nimbus of red dots crackles and drifts behind words. In one pattern, light rolls vertically like windows in a slot machine, braking suddenly to form a letter, another letter, another. In these pieces, Holzer's manipulations of imaginary space allows words to pass in front of words, to drizzle up from solid color fields, to flip backward and forward.

The continuous strobing of Holzer's signs produces the same hypnotic effect as the giant message boards in Times Square. Her messages reveal themselves with an air of high drama, often very funny simply for their technical ingenuity and their self-evident power to manipulate attention. Holzer's programs guarantee a certain amount of quizzical straining, anticipation of the next phrase, the next effect: the viewer is doing two things at once, reading and staring. Holzer is doing at least four things at once. First, she deploys a familiar, complex technological device in a somewhat incongruous setting. The LED machine is, generically, a public-address system, and by its nature "speaks" to a broader audience than we associate with an art gallery. Second, Holzer supplants the language of advertising with the ruminative, subvocal speech of hypothetical characters, addressing persons instead of consumers. Third, Holzer imposes a precise duration on the reception of messages, breaking them into small, psychoactively enhanced units (nonverbal areas are enriched with suggestive effects). Fourth, Holzer uncovers the sexual dynamic at work in everyday public address.

On this latter point, the literary impact of Holzer's work is crucial to its effectiveness. And in fact, if Holzer did not possess literary originality, it wouldn't much matter what medium she used: her work would be spectacularly decorative, but bleeding at one end. While Holzer's writing is, perhaps, less striking on the printed page than anywhere else, it still has considerable power, there, as boldly compressed thought. Holzer's writing ranges from the aphoristic to the lyrical, and the texts from "Under a Rock" are hard-edged little fictions and passages of remarkably focused poetry.

Holzer's public voice assumes many identities. Some of them are probably her, but rather like Jonathan Swift, Holzer taps into the brains of strangers and others, mimicking their private thoughts—rapists, racists, killers, public-spirited citizens, the rich, hedonists, intellectuals. The point of view encountered in her statements is sometimes one of plain uncommon sense, but is just as often tilted to reflect a certain kind of interest or pathology. In "Under a Rock," the texts suggest a world of male violence viewed through a child's eyes, registered in blunt, vivid language. There is a strong posthumous feeling in this writing, as if a dead world were being evoked by one of its few survivors. The granite benches do have a memorial quality, though I liked what a friend said about them as well: "I thought if I sat down on one of those things that message might crawl right up my ass." Jenny Holzer's work has that effect, too.

November 4, 1986

STAR SEARCH

[**James Turrell**. P.S.1, 46-01 21st Street, Long Island City. Permanent installation, but by appointment only: 718-784-2084 or 212-233-1440.]

James Turrell's *Meeting*, a site installation at P.S.1, has been seven years in the making, which may seem strange at first because this environment is so straightforwardly and simply wrought: a trapezoidal chamber with a rectangular opening cut in the ceiling. Seating is provided along the base of tall, sloped plywood benches, behind the upper perimeters of which run orange lights. The floor covering is a neutral gray carpet; the plywood exudes a pleasant, resinous smell that heightens the outdoor effect of the open ceiling.

To get this room exactly right involved massive structural changes in the building, including movement of support beams. The roof had to be carved out and replaced, within the sight lines afforded by the chamber, with paper-thin metal; a bulky garage-door-like covering rolls out of sight on the roof when the piece is being viewed. Turrell has been concurrently busy with other projects, chief among them *The Roden Crater Project*, which entails reshaping parts of an extinct volcano in Arizona and installing celestial observatories around and in the crater. (Several large, worked-up drawings of his project were just shown at Marian Goodman Gallery.) *Meeting* is a prototype of one of these observatories.

Perhaps it's inexact to say that one "views" this piece. Turrell properly distinguishes between space that's occupied by looking into from outside and space that's experienced by physical occupation. Although both kinds of space possess numerous atmospheric qualities, we reflexively translate distant or "external" space into form, while Turrell's work disintegrates perception of form into an experience of light. The rectilinear shape of the "window" is the ideal neutralizing format. Since it's the most used shape for picturing things, it doesn't intrude as a shape.

One does, of course, experience the dimensions of the room, and the skylight is framed by the ceiling. In a literally cosmic sense the frame determines what we see and the room determines how we see it. But *Meeting* essentially removes extraneous phenomena from the perceptual field so that physical matter recedes from our attention.

The work is activated by celestial transitions, which are most dramatic during the passage from day to night. The artificial light in the room operates on our perception of the natural light outside; even with the lights off, however, normal daytime sky becomes a tightly bracketed event. The ovoid sprawl of normal vision is recontoured. As a result, the colors and shape of the heavens undergo surprising changes.

The architectural effect is very different from that of a window, or for that matter a normal astronomical observatory. Here the outside space is drawn down into the room, or appears to flatten out against the opening. Before daylight begins to wane, the flux of clouds or bland expanse of clear sky may give the impression of extreme distance, but the framing eliminates the normal sense of concavity. Objects in the sky don't indicate distance in the usual way, especially given the auditory ambience of this location: for instance, watching a commercial airliner passing thousands of feet away, I could hear a closer helicopter "out of frame," and the sound matched the image with cinematic plausibility. A helicopter that did pass overhead looked closer than it was.

As sunlight drains from the sky, the air becomes a solid light blue. The interior lighting creeps over the walls as exterior light diminishes, turning the chamber a bright orange, which in turn compresses the light blue. For perhaps a half hour this color darkens almost imperceptibly and seems pressed against the sky-light, at times resembling a smooth sheet of Mylar that one could peel from the ceiling. At dusk this turns a deep ultramarine, while the walls become progressively lighter in contrast.

Throughout these color changes, the volumes of external space shift according to natural tricks of vision. The opening itself looks like a trapezoid from one vantage point, a rectangle from another; the pulling-in and flattening effects often make the outer atmosphere resemble a solid, with imaginary cubic volumes extending into the chamber, suggested by the lines of the frame.

Turrell's inspiration for this work, as well as the larger desert project, came partly from Mayan ruins and other archaeological sites which simply exist as constructed spaces, removed by time from their original function. *Meeting* is a paring-down of the work of art to an arrangement of perceptual signals, something which exists as a diurnal process, its contents as variable as the sky. This reduction of things to elemental terms, to primal process, is very much in the American vein: strip away the world's exigencies and encounter Nature, and ye shall be saved.

The cosmos often offers the only real untainted view left on earth. Nature has moved to outer space. Turrell's work offers a palpable, tranquilizing, grand experience of the world minus its unpleasant sociological and physical detritus. On a clear day in Long Island City, you will still get an earful of not very ethereal buzz from air traffic, but at night you can see all the satellites. When Turrell's *Roden Crater* piece is finished, it will probably provide an aesthetic experience that can justly be called awesome.

There are some limitations inherent in this approach, limitations that circumscribe most gigantic art projects. These are evoked somewhat airily in an essay on Turrell by Count Giuseppe Panza di Biumo, a noted patron of contemporary art: "We do not know that our desire for total happiness can be fulfilled, but it can be. In the middle of *Roden Crater*, this belief seems possible. If everyone were able to have this kind of experience, the use of drugs would disappear, no one would commit suicide, and violence would stop. Unfortunately, few people will make this journey—if they did, the world would change." This is an enchanting delusion, written by one of the few. As another of the few once said, "I want the best of everything for everybody but it costs millions."

November 11 & 18, 1986

JANET MALCOLM GETS IT WRONG

When Janet Malcolm commenced research, two years ago, for a *New Yorker* profile of *Artforum* editor Ingrid Sischy, she let it be known that she knew nothing about the art world: it was, for Malcolm, exciting new territory. The profile has at last appeared, in two consecutive *New Yorker* issues, October 20 and 27, and perhaps its most impressive quality is how ingeniously Malcolm has protected her ignorance over such a long period of time.

Ostensibly, Malcolm's intention in Part I is to show how *Artforum* has changed under Sischy's direction. She calls on a number of the "old guard," by whom she is frankly intimidated. Rosalind Krauss, for example, the Zhdanov of *October* magazine, is depicted in her home environment, which from Malcolm's description sounds like a display window in Conran's, yet "is one of the most beautiful living places in New York." "No one," according to Malcolm, "can leave this loft without feeling a little rebuked…." This may be perfectly true. One feels further prepared to believe that Krauss is "fearlessly uncharitable," though whether her unpleasant characteristics make "one's own 'niceness' seem somehow dreary and anachronistic" surely depends on the degree of submissiveness, or obsequious niceness, one brings to the encounter.

Grumpy Krauss has nothing but disdain for *Artforum* in its current incarnation. Even back in the glory days when she and Annette Michelson sat on the editorial board, they had to endure the importunate existence of other people and their bothersome opinions: "Lawrence Alloway was forever sneering at me and Annette," "Max Kozloff...was always very busy being superior," "Neither Annette nor I would buy into this simplistic opposition that they set up between formal invention and the social mission of art." After the Lynda Benglis Scandal of 1974, when the magazine accepted a sensational ad distasteful to most of the editorial staff, it seemed clear to Krauss and Michelson that *Artforum* and its editor, John Coplans, were pandering to the art market, favoring commodity objects like painting and sculpture over the more ephemeral, "advanced" art enjoyed by Krauss and Michelson. "Yes. That's how we felt." Krauss and Michelson are full of unanimous sentiments and thoughts about the old *Artforum*: "one of the things Annette and I have done," "our theory," "which was certainly why Annette and I thought," "various projects of ours." But Krauss reserves her fiercest lack of charity for the new *Artforum* and its writers: it, and they, are stupid. This verdict is so unequivocal that it's surprising Krauss could formulate it without assistance from Michelson, but perhaps in matters of stupidity we can assume they are as one.

For the Westchester County audience, the thrillingly Minimal decor of Krauss's loft is probably enough to establish her credentials as an important thinker and art swami; nothing she actually tells Malcolm rises above petty spite. ("On the one hand, you had [William] Rubin and [Kirk] Varnedoe sounding like complete assholes... [Thomas] McEvilley doing his hideousness...never been able to finish a piece of McEvilley...seems to be another Donald Kuspit....") Actually, Malcolm's technique ensures that anyone with sufficient floor space and a reliable cleaning service will sound more credible, or at least more "intellectual," than those who live amid the squalid clutter of normal life. Malcolm's gaze sweeps over the surfaces of people, places, and things, calmly categorizing them according to the inner logic of an intractable bourgeoise. Poor John Coplans—his home "has the look of a place inhabited by a man who no longer lives with a woman." You know already that Coplans will be an affable old geezer who loves spinning tales about the past, that he will seem less decisive, more conciliatory in his opinions than Krauss, and therefore slightly… well, pathetic. Robert Pincus-Witten, former art buyer for collector Emily Spiegel and professor of art history at Queens College, is spared the trial-by-interior, having been encountered at a cocktail party. He provides pregnantly diplomatic hiatus between Coplans and Malcolm's next imperious loft dweller, Barbara Rose.

Like Krauss, Rose senses Decline—not just in *Artforum*, but in the art world generally. Like Krauss, she seems to have made out quite handsomely for one so embattled. Her place "looks more like a Park Avenue co-op than a downtown living space…." But she is forlorn, haunted by memories of bright laughter and happier times, when people like herself were taken seriously. She wistfully recalls those halcyon days in the '60s when, with then spouse Frank Stella, she entertained "major intellectuals" like Barnett Newman and Ad Reinhardt. "There's nobody like them today," Rose opines. Today's art world, well, "it's middle-class, it's bourgeois." Not like it was when it was all about "the agony and the ecstasy." Which is to say, not like when it was like the title of an Irving Stone novel.

If truth be told, Rose's rueful blather about the high standards of the past is something of a running joke in the art world. It has only become more vehement each time that Rose has failed to interest her vanishing constituency in "new art." Here, she attributes the decline of cultural discrimination, and perhaps of Western civilization as a whole, to the influence of Harold Rosenberg and Susan Sontag, of all people—and, with an air of disinterested exasperation, feebly tries to settle scores with Rene Ricard over a few withering sentences about her he published years ago in *Artforum*. Malcolm doesn't mention that that's what Rose is doing. Perhaps Malcolm just didn't know; if she didn't, she should have.

More to the point, one of the two redeeming presences Rose spots in an otherwise hopeless Sischy-run *Artforum*, critic John Yau, happens to have lived with Rose's daughter for years. Since Rose is quick to accuse other people of lowering standards, it might also have been useful for Malcolm's readers to know that a few years ago, Rose was removed from her job as curator of exhibitions and collections under William Agee at the Houston Museum of Fine Arts after it was disclosed that the museum had recently purchased works from the collection of her then husband, lyricist Jerry Leiber. Malcolm also neglects to mention that Rose's principal activity in the art world for 20 years has been that of a publicist, sporadic contributions to *Partisan Review* and her column in *Vogue* notwithstanding.

This kind of detail interests Janet Malcolm not at all when it pertains to "respectable" people, though she gives the financial murk of the art world a bit of play when describing people with whom she doesn't identify. But of course, respectable people read *The New Yorker*. Like Malcolm, they tend to glaze over in the presence of opulent surfaces and pushy individuals, and become assertive only when they sense another person's disadvantage. The ugliest moments in Malcolm's article—and there are many—occur when Malcolm's personal feelings creep onto the page; these are inevitably activated by people she feels secure in sneering at. Interestingly, most of them are artists rather than administrators, critics, or editors.

Near the conclusion of Part I, Malcolm describes an unpleasant confrontation between Ingrid Sischy and the sculptor Richard Serra at an opening at the Marian Goodman Gallery. What happened was this: Serra made the assumption that Sischy supported his position in the controversy over his *Tilted Arc* sculpture. When Sischy felt it her duty to inform him otherwise, Serra became enraged. Before getting down to particulars, Malcolm sets the reader up so that opinion will fall on Sischy's side—not with reasoned argument, but with a physical description of Serra, which she uses against him much the way she uses other people's apartments against them.

This was the first time I had seen Richard Serra, and he didn't fit the image I had formed. From his massive, thrusting sculpture...I had imagined a large, dark, saturnine man——a sort of intellectual-conquistador type, emanating an air of vast, heroic indifference. The actual Serra looked like someone from a small American rural community: a short man with a craggy, surly face, receding gray hair, and pale eyes rimmed by light eyelashes.

In other words, Malcolm contrasts her personal fantasies about Serra and his "massive, thrusting" works with the actual person and finds the real thing..."rural" looking. How better to convince the "sophisticated," cosmopolitan audience of *The New Yorker* that Serra is wrong-headed?

Malcolm's reporting is studded with such novelistic details, which twinkle class assurance from reporter to reader: never mind what X thinks, he or she lives alone in an apartment so messy you and I would never dream of living there. So-and-so makes weird looking objects, so naturally I didn't want to find myself alone with him in his flat. These people are Russian émi-grés who serve refreshments in a slobby manner, so I guess you understand how exasperated I felt.

When an "eccentric" person gains Malcolm's sympathy, she projects upon him every cliché of *la vie bohème* that springs to her impoverished imagination; thus, to the utter incredulity of anyone who knows him, Rene Ricard is likened to Prince Myshkin, the Christ figure in Dostoyevsky's *The Idiot*. Malcolm is so oblivious to the world she's describing that the publicity value of her own activity eludes her: she can't *imagine* why Ricard repeatedly prevents her from leaving his table at the Palladium, regaling her with one juicy story after another.

Were Malcolm's investigations of the Freud Archive similarly tainted by her fascination with appearances? Is it possible that one of *The New Yorker*'s star reporters is so transfixed by surface impressions that she consistently mistakes them for reality? Does the vulgarity of Malcolm's article reflect *The New Yorker*'s transition from the Age of Shawn to the Age of Si Newhouse? The maiden appearance of the word "asshole" is the least distressing infelicity in Malcolm's article, but in the context of *The New Yorker* it seems portentous of the shape of things to come.

* * *

"I knew nothing good was coming," said artist Sherrie Levine, "when the fact checker from *The New Yorker* called to ask me if it would be accurate to say that my bathtub is in the kitchen and I live alone with my cat." This is all the quote Levine would venture, since she was already feeling weird about her depiction by Janet Malcolm. "Maybe you could put, 'Levine said *drearily*,'" she added. "Oh, he also asked me if I could define 'a railroad apartment.'"

Susan Sontag, asked if she endorsed the idea, attributed to her by Barbara Rose in Malcolm's article, that "you could just love everything that was going on, you could be positive and optimistic and just love it all," fainted.

"She's not very shy," Alexander Melamid told me when I asked him to describe Janet Malcolm. "Very regular. Gray. Not very special. I was surprised to meet someone from this big intellectual magazine, having such a gray personality. And then, she made a mistake—there's nothing in Chekhov like what I told her. Vitaly and I even spoke to a great expert on Chekhov at Columbia University. I'm sure we're idiots like she says, but she's an idiot herself. Americans mix up everything Russian—Chekhov, Gogol, Tolstoy, Dostoyevsky." Vitaly Komar piped up in the background: "In *Star Trek* there's a driver of a spaceship, they gave him the name 'Chekhov,' so it's clear he's Russian…. Janet Malcolm got Chekhov from *Star Trek*."

Star Trek is only one of the sources for the composite picture of the art world that Janet Malcolm inserts in the yawning gaps of her profile of Ingrid Sischy—the first *New Yorker* profile in which the protagonist is almost entirely drowned out by the chorus. Or rather, choruses: in Part I, the banshee chorus of the pre-Sischy *Artforum* editorial staff; in Part II, the with-it-and-for-it chorus of current *Artforum* writers, augmented by occasional solo numbers that are not so much dissenting as distracting.

Malcolm's piece is rich with implications, and she does strike little notes of skepticism here and there, usually after regurgitating enough bunkum to drive any other reporter to the telephone. She brings to the art scene a dogged determination to find "bohemianism" of one sort or another, and when it arrives in the person of Rene Ricard, Malcolm allows him to hijack the rest of her article. Not only does Ricard pirouette repeatedly before our eyes, he also does an offstage ventriloquist act with Malcolm as the dummy. So we get Sherrie Levine's "bleak little conceits" and "reverent little thefts"—Malcolm sounding very like Ricard on a generous day—microscoped beside Julian Schnabel's gigantic, heroic energy, his three studios, and…his safe, where Ricard's latest poems purportedly reside. We're told by Malcolm that Bill Rice's "chief subject is homosexual black men"—the same unhelpful, inaccurate characterization Ricard used in his *Artforum* article on Rice. Malcolm also treats us to a reprise of Ricard's oeuvre, or much of it, anyway; we hear again the piercing whine that emits from the pages of *Artforum* on those rare occasions when some portion of the art world needs slapping down in the name of cosmic Art Love:

> *When I wrote about Julian Schnabel's last show at the Mary Boone Gallery for* Art in America, *I became so embroiled in a distasteful episode with the gallery concerning my request for an exclusive on the picture I wanted to use as an illustration that I vowed never to cover any painter represented by that gallery.*

Malcolm quotes this, and a few paragraphs later alludes to it without qualification; eventually, after quoting Ingrid Sischy (whose independence of mind is a continual theme) to the effect that "Whatever Rene says is true," Malcolm does get around to mention that one of Ricard's poems records "a litany of … acts of bad faith" and ends with the line, "I made a lot of this up, but a lot of it is true." But by this time, Ricard has sounded off in several directions.

The opening lines of Ricard's best-known piece of art criticism are not true. There was no "distasteful episode," except in his mind, and furthermore, no "request for an exclusive." One afternoon in 1979, Ricard asked me to accompany him to Soho to look at some paintings being stored in a third-floor viewing space on West Broadway. These were the first Schnabel plate paintings. (I remember Ricard asking me, as we stood in front of them, "Aren't these the ugliest things you've ever seen?") Another art critic was present. He mentioned that he was writing about the paintings and intended to reproduce one of them. "Oh, but I have an exclusive on that picture," Ricard told him. The other critic looked puzzled. The idea of an "exclusive" on a work of art had clearly never crossed his mind—or anyone else's mind, for that matter. When the critic failed to fall in with this ukase, Ricard threatened *not* to write about the art. Then we left the building and crossed the street, encountering Mary Boone in the vestibule of 420 West Broadway. Ricard told Boone that he would be writing about the Schnabel show, and that he "had an exclusive" on one of the paintings. Boone let the remarks go by and hurried off. Her recollection confirms my own: "Rene came in and announced that he was going to have an exclusive. I didn't argue with him about it because he's psychotic."

Malcolm's fascination with Ricard is understandable, since her real area of expertise is psychiatry rather than art. However, it leads her to credit Ricard with a much larger role in *Artforum*, and the art world, than he actually plays. But perhaps he saved her the trouble of thinking about a milieu that she found disorienting, acting as an all-purpose Downtown Person and automatic opinion dispenser. Malcolm's interviews with other *Artforum* writers set them up as straight men to Ricard's Monty Pythoness; they also offer hints of something Malcolm is either too dense, or too protective of her subject, to notice.

The customary *New Yorker* profile—not that it is so wonderful in its pure form—*is* a profile. The subject is on camera the whole time. In Malcolm's piece, Ingrid Sischy tends to bland out when others are present, and often she's not there at all. It's as if Malcolm were torn between describing Sischy and describing *Artforum*, with *Artforum* usually winning out. One could argue, of course, that Sischy is *Artforum*, having taken responsibility for the magazine in an unprecedented way. As someone who likes and admires her, I find this overidentification a bit unfortunate. It makes it almost impossible to criticize *Artforum* without seeming to criticize Sischy personally.

However, it's impossible to ignore a certain pattern of description woven through Malcolm's article which, on one hand, laudably praises Sischy's fierce integrity, her fervor, energy, and modesty, and on the other, trivializes or occludes some important issues about editing and writing raised by *Artforum*'s current approach to both.

From Malcolm's accounts of Sischy's all-night editing sessions, various writers' description of their work with *Artforum*, and from Sischy's own mouth, there emerges an appalling notion of art writing as something necessarily unreadable, barbaric, and worthless. The unremarked assumption is that what a writer turns in to *Artforum* is not writing in any literary sense, but an undifferentiated clot of words needing to be sliced up into colorful little slabs in the editing, worried over by editor and writer in eerily protracted deadline frenzies, every sentence pulled apart and reassembled, its ultimate form a sort of collaborative artifact bearing no resemblance to the original. *Artforum* is not a daily newspaper, but a monthly magazine whose writers, according to Sischy, sometimes work on a piece for a whole year. How peculiar, then, that they need such elaborate editorial first aid.

Critic Carter Ratcliff tells Malcolm that "from reading the magazine, one gets the sense that Ingrid is encouraging individual voices." But do these voices belong to the people whose names they appear under? Ratcliff also says that "when I'm writing for *Artforum* I feel free to write in a way that is more direct and more responsible to what I feel and less responsible to some standard of rationality," and that this sense of permission comes from Sischy's encouragement of writers like Ricard to let it all hang out and "strike illuminating postures in the vicinity of things." In effect, the *Artforum* writer is asked to leave his sense of responsibility, organization, style, rationality, and what have you at the door—and why should the writer feel responsible for what appears in the magazine, since he can hardly feel that he's written it himself after it's been put through the *Artforum* mangle, livened up with bold, thought-killing ellipses, made "a little choppier" (Ratcliff) to suit "art-world readers," who are assumed to be in some fundamental way different from "literary readers." Ratcliff reports that Sischy "feels that it's not a problem if something sounds silly"—but then, it isn't really *her* problem if something does. Ratcliff seems to believe it isn't his problem, either, but that is a different can of worms.

One wonders about writers who require, every time, and often well into mid-career, line-by-line revision, particularly when the editor they work with admits, "I've never in my life been a reader." One could either suppose that Sischy, who as a nonreader would have little feeling for written language, still has more than they do, or that language is not being used in *Artforum* as an instrument of thought, but as something akin to the *garni* associated with fashion magazines and promotional literature, striking "illuminating postures in the vicinity of things." In either case, the idea of a written language as this alphabetic gunk used to slap together "texts," which are then used to service art careers and egos, is rapidly becoming the art world's *only* idea of language—which is why any clear, unequivocal, skeptical, or negative assessment of anything has come to be viewed as a gross violation of propriety. It's widely supposed that artists should enjoy immunity from the kinds of harsh judgments routinely given authors, say, who've brought out a bad book, or performers who've launched a flop. The neutering of art-critical language has ensured the smooth functioning of the art world's financial base; most critical nuances of recent years, linguistically speaking, have done the Orwellian job of removing the sting from words like "selling out," "unoriginal," "cynical," "hype," and so on.

This is not, by the way, the exclusive fault of *Artforum*, and the problem of dead "text writing," as Sischy points out, was there before she was. In 1973, *Artforum* editor John Coplans rejected a submission from Les Levine with a memo (incorporated into an artwork by Levine) that read, in part:

> *Hey, Les, don't you know we're an art magazine. We publish lots of pictures of artist's [sic] work with a lot of remarks written in bad English (somewhat Latinized to gain a pompous and serious effect). You're not supposed to read the articles, not unless you're a masochist or anal or desperate for something to read and don't care.*

Sischy brought to *Artforum* an infectious, workaholic enthusiasm, a winning personality, and an altogether admirable, highly developed political consciousness—as Malcolm's recounting of the McEvilley-MOMA-Primitivism controversy demonstrates. Sischy opened the magazine's pages to many young artists and writers, including myself, who would never have had a chance with the previous regime. But part of the excitement Sischy generated around the "new" *Artforum* was fatally linked to the notion of hitting the number every month, catching all the straws in every seasonal wind, *being there when it happened*—and finally, inevitably, *making it happen. Art in America* could never disappoint if it ran a Juan Gris or a Fairfield Porter on the cover: it would just be a pretty cover, usually corresponding to an interesting article. Under Sischy, *Artforum's* covers became Delphic pronouncements, or the art equivalent of *Rolling Stone* covers, events in themselves, often boosting a little-known artist into superstardom, or intimating some imminent shift in the zeitgeist. The problem is that the zeitgeist's flutterings have become altogether too frequent for anyone to take them seriously anymore, and the only logical way of measuring them, in the absence of focused criticism, is by quanta. For quite a long time now, the editorial content of *Artforum* has been a slim wafer wedged between lardy hunks of advertising, and most people can't read it even if they manage to find it.

Malcolm concludes her article by saying that Sischy's "vision of contemporary art is shaped first by societal concerns and only secondarily by aesthetic concerns." Fine, admirable, good. As refracted in *Artforum*, however, that vision often seems blurred by a certain dalliance with anti-intellectualism, philistinism, and the occult opacity of various familiars who have definitely stayed too long at the fair. It was a courageous and timely move to put "cheapness" into *Artforum* when Sischy did. It would have been a good idea to take it out a long time ago, and perhaps even now it isn't too late.

THE JOY OF KILLING

[**"Children's Drawings of the Spanish Civil War."** The Spanish Institute, 684 Park Avenue, through December 31.]

You can come away from "Children's Drawings of the Spanish Civil War," a show at the Spanish Institute, filled with a lot of heart-tugging feelings. War is terrible, especially modern war, and the worst of it is that in modern warfare, civilians—innocents—get slaughtered, or become orphans and displaced persons. *December 28, 1981—Approximately 15 contras invaded the Miskito community of Bilwaskarma, kidnapping four people, including a woman doctor, Myrna Cunningham, and a nurse, Regina Lewis. The contras took the women to Honduras, where they were gang-raped.* You can see in these precociously fine drawings (European children learn to draw well as a matter of course) the horrendous impression that aerial terror bombings made on some of the one million or so child evacuees.

Or can you? Look closely. *March 16, 1982—Union leader Timoteo Velazquez was shot outside of Nueva Guinea, Zelaya. On the same day, a campesino belonging to the union in Rama, Zelaya, was murdered and found with his tongue cut out.* Here and there, as in Félix Sánchez del Amo's *Guerra*, there's a strong elegiac feeling. A woman stands over a bleeding male corpse. *April 26, 1982—Contras murdered four farmworkers, a woman and a nine-month-old child in El Recreo, Jinotega.* But we learn that the artist was 14 years old. And we see that the woman's stance has been copied from Millet's *Angelus*. We're already in the realm of conscious art; the picture is a *statement* about war. *October 28, 1982—Contras mutilated and assassinated 6 peasants in the community of La Fregua, near El Jicaro, including Ricardo Blandon, a Delegate of the Word, and his four children. The same day, contras slit the throat of Leonilo Marin, near German Pomares, Jalapa.*

In other pictures by children from 7 to 16 years old, the clusters of variegated aircraft expelling their bombs over landscapes of houses, cattle, trees, and people often look like part of the natural order of things. *March 18, 1983—Near Rio Blanco, contras kidnapped education administrator Maria Martinez Alvarez. Her body was later found with her throat slit and her breasts cut off.* In drawings by Juanito Durán Gratacós and Carlos Serrano Ilérvias, we sense the artists' detached pleasure in exact rendering of the aircraft, and can see the special effort they took to convey the impression of energetic movement. *May 3, 1983—Contras kidnapped three people, including Digna Barreda whom they raped 60 times and a campesino who they tortured and killed. In a separate incident, the bus traveling between Jalepa and Teotecacinte was ambushed. The contra forces opened fire on the bus, wounding a ten-year-old girl and her mother.*

An especially fine drawing by Antonio Sánchez Taños shows airplanes ranged above a mountain landscape, with ground artillery firing up, a tank perched on a mountaintop, and a big, busy-looking tank in the Liberty or Deco style commanding the foreground, the composition unified by the telegraphic dashes of ammunition. *August 19, 1983—Contras ambushed a pick-up truck used for public transportation at Valle Los Cedros. Of the 18 people riding on the truck, 15 were assassinated.* An aerial dogfight pictured by Luis Estébanez features a massive green biplane with red markings closing in on a smaller, burning plane, with miniature aircraft behind them. The dynamic effect of this picture is heightened by an open parachute in the foreground, echoed by a smaller one in the distance. *March 2, 1984—Contras assassinated two workers in Ruben Dario, cutting out their hearts and feeding them to dogs. March 4, 1984—Approximately 50 contras kidnapped five campesinos in San Pedro, near San Jose de Bocay. March 6, 1984—Contras and Honduran troops attacked Santo Tomas del Norte, Chinandega, killing one-year-old Carina Cardenas Rivas.*

There are many scenes of evacuation, of people boarding trains and ships, ubiquitous figures holding luggage; and other scenes, of children jumping rope and playing ball in rural refugee colonies. The human figures are not especially expressive, faces generally have the dotty eyes and J-shaped noses and po-mouths typical of children's drawings. *March 14, 1984—Contras attacked San Jose, Rio San Juan, killing an eight-year-old boy and wounding four other children. In a separate attack, contras killed three campesinos and burned the entire village of El Copalon, Rio San Juan.* What's unusual are the compositional qualities of these pictures, the intelligent ordering of space, and sometimes the color: for instance, Ramón Luis's drawing, *Boys combing their hair in the washroom*, a deft use of blue gives us the exact temperature of the washroom. *March 16, 1984—San Ramon, Jalaguina, Matagalbpa. Contras kidnapped, mutilated, and beheaded eight farm workers, including Francisco Gonzalez Guevarra, a teacher; Arturo Calero, local school director; and Jose Zavala Casco, head of the local Sandinista association.*

It's probably antithetical to the purpose of a show like this to individuate the artists: they're "children," generically, and presumably the interest of the works has to do with the relatively unlearned and completely helpless way they receive information. *April 3, 1984—About 1,000 contras attacked the village of Waslala, central Zelaya, and surrounding areas, killing 37 and kidnapping at least 210. Among the incidents: A family with a newborn baby was taking cover in a ditch. The father was dragged off, tortured by having his fingertips and then his right hand cut off, and then killed with bayonets. Finally, the contras beheaded him and carved a cross on his back.*

They don't know why the war is being fought, or why people are being killed. They're innocent. *The contras also shot the wife and threw a grenade into the ditch, lodging shrapnel in the woman and her children. On the same day, three children were kidnapped, and the bodies of five campesinos, too disfigured by torture to identify, were found in the nearby hills.* But notice, please, that this innocence is not necessarily inclined toward humanistic sentiments: except in rare cases, there's no polemical brief *against war* issuing from these pictures. *Three teenage boys, returning home after hiding in the hills all morning, were attacked with bayonets. Two of the boys, one 14, the other 16, died from their wounds. The third, who had been stabbed five times in his stomach and all over his body, survived.* You, the adult witness, have to read it into them. If anything truly disturbs us in this exhibition, it isn't the evidence of war—kids everywhere draw fighting soldiers, planes, bombs—but our knowledge that these particular kids witnessed warfare directly, rather than learning about it from comics and TV, and absorbed it in the same interested way that other kids absorb the consumer lifestyle and the shopping mall experience. For the immature human all these things interchangeably represent "normality"—people can adapt to anything, and do.

In nearby El Achote a band of contras dragged an agrarian reform worker from his home, and in front of his wife, 11-month-old son, and three-year-old son, cut him into pieces with their bayonets. And they don't need to be children, either. Spain was the testing ground for indiscriminate civilian killing by aerial bombardment, superpower intervention, and illicit arm sales. The American government has embraced all these innovations with the fervor of a nursing baboon. *The man's wife was then shot, but she lived to watch them behead her 11-month-old baby.* But baboons aren't vicious and their children grow up to be beautiful.

All italicized material is from Contra Terror in Nicaragua, Report of a Fact-finding Mission: September 1984-January 1985, *by Reed Brody, South End Press, 1985.*

December 9, 1986

ENCLOSED BY SYSTEM

As everyone knows by now, a good deal of recent art deals with the elephantine roles played in our lives by corporatism and mass media. This art assumes, no doubt correctly, that much or most of what many or some people think and do is shaped by those who manipulate the flow of capital. Art, which once reflected values aloof from simple (or complicated) greed, has been insidiously absorbed into the economy of commercial products, and functions, to an unseemly extent, as a sort of black-market counter, its cash worth determined by dicey variables unlike the ones fixed for ordinary commodities.

Art that includes this perception in its aesthetic procedures has proliferated, alongside art that doesn't. Art concerned with its ideological and economic functions would seem to preclude art primarily concerned with itself, but in reality both kinds of art coexist. Both rely on the traditional autonomy they have. This autonomy derives from a still very active belief that human life offers imaginative possibilities that are higher, or anyway different, than the options depicted and provided by the engineers of mass consciousness and the corporations for which they work.

Art addressing the present system of social control faces some unique risks. As it intends to embody analytical thinking about issues that are, arguably, rather vaguely framed in many people's minds, this art hazards to become accessible only to a small, initiated circle. Insofar as it compensates for the sophistication of its ideas by wrapping them in more generally appreciated formal aesthetic blandishments, there is every chance that its critical dimension will be missed or ignored by the public. There is also the chance that the artist himself, or herself, overestimates the intellectual significance of the work, or the extent to which the work adequately carries his or her ideas. The paintings of Peter Halley exemplify this problem.

Quite often, of course, artists have used theoretical concepts as expedient tools for making formal breakthroughs. Art historians are often avid to explain the difference between what an artist thought he/she was doing and what he/she actually did. However, many contemporary artists whose works explicitly reject a strictly formalist reading seem stalled between fealty to ideas they cannot develop and derivative formal strategies.

Anyway, this is the impression I get from two current shows. The first is **John Knight**'s "MCMLXXXVI," at Marian Goodman Gallery (24 West 57th Street, through December 6). Knight has replicated alphabetic and symbolic corporate logos in knotty pine and set mirrors into their blank internal spaces, so that when looking at them the viewer sees his/her image framed by the corporate design. A postcard announcement for the show features a Little-House-on-the-Prairie picture which was, it says, used in advertising for Wells Fargo Bank.

It isn't so important that the corporate-typography device has been put to sharper use by, among others, Hans Haacke, Peter Nagy, and Nancy Dwyer, or that the postcard's Western image would have no existence as a conceptually active object without the previous work of Richard Prince. But it is important that the little ideational twitch that occurs when the viewer grasps the point of this work amounts to a familiar tickle. Yes, we're all enclosed in the system. And then what? One waits, and waits, for the next perception to unfold. At last the question intrudes: how much do I like knotty pine? Many people who encounter a work by John Knight on the stairwells of Documenta 7, featuring traveling poster imagery covering his joined initials, automatically assumed the "JK" stood for Joseph Kosuth. What I've seen of Knight's work has the unhappy knack of bringing to mind other artists who don't exactly suffer by comparison.

Gretchen Bender's "No Death OK" (at Nature Morte, 204 East 10th Street, through November 28, and reviewed by Kim Levin in the last issue) looks a lot like her last show: too much like, I think. Again, there are big panels, this time of shiny aluminum instead of dark Plexiglas, with celluloid strips horizontally inset in two works, with words on them, tinier this time: "Revolution" and "No Death OK"; and vertically inset, in one work, with two strips of scrambled images instead of words, resembling the vertical-roll imagery Bender has also produced on paper strips directly from television images.

Bender's work has what I take to be a deliberately flimsy, tossed-off quality. Her primary interest is in video, and her gallery art feels like a research by-product, whipped up from outtakes of something more important. Like her frequent video collaborator, Robert Longo, whose primary interest is in film, Bender seems increasingly unconcerned with the physical quality of these objects, as long as they look materially hefty or daringly fragile; and totally indifferent to the messages they emit, so long as they convey an impression of monumentalism and chaos and the scrambled quality of life in a media-jangled world. Something has gone gravely askew in both artists' cases, perhaps the result of convincing themselves that half-hearted art can be used as a stepping-stone to work in mass media without reeking of this ambition. Bender's show has plenty of visual intelligence (so does John Knight's), but because she is an artist of large talents it would be nice if she dropped Leni Riefenstahl as a role model. Like Longo, her work exhibits an enthrallment to modern forms of power that increasingly resembles corporate evangelism with a plastic face.

A scarred, reconditioned, upturned, glass-fronted billiard table; a long rectangular platform with three little battered-looking stools in one corner; three tall, framed, black-and-white photos of suburban fascist architecture; and three multipaneled photographic studies of industrial furnaces and tanks: this is the current show at Luhring, Augustine & Hodes (41 East 57th Street, through December 20). The objects are by Reinhard Mucha, the photographs by Günther Förg, and Bernd and Hilla Becher respectively.

This show will appeal to anyone for whom the postindustrial world and its glut of sparkling images have some historical link to industrialism's empty promises and idle amusements. The works included venture into modes of feeling that encompass nostalgia, rue, morbidity, and ironic resignation. Mucha's objects recall the world of the smoke-filled Saturday night pub and the homely "modern" kitchen of 30 years ago (the piece with the stools contains a heartbreaking chunk of patterned linoleum). The Förg photographs give the taste of rationalized block housing and enlightened design à la Mussolini. Bernd and Hilla Becher's works evoke the sprawling architectures that once were symbols of unlimited progress, and now signify the betrayed dreams of the labor movement.

The emotional dimension of these works hasn't much currency in the hard-edged, media-bedazzled, politically self-enraptured (but ultimately self-neutralizing) recent work of Knight and Bender (and Bickerton, and Vaisman, and Donner, and Blitzen). Emotional vacuity is a legitimate theme of the art of a generation without emotional depth; but if this capacity is truly lacking in the world of the under-30, how account for an Annette Lemieux?

December 16, 1986

LANDSCAPE TODAY

["**The Manor in the Landscape.**" Lorence-Monk Gallery, 563 Broadway, through December 20.]

One notable aspect of "The Manor in the Landscape," a show organized by Saul Ostrow, is that hardly anything in it closely resembles landscape painting as our parents or grandparents knew it. Like portraiture and still life, landscape is a self-conscious genre, sited in quotation marks. And today, the quotes occur within other quotes. The works at hand reflect our contemporary relationship to nature, which is framed by our distance from it. Nature no longer serves as a source of the sublime. It exists as a variegated substance continually acted on by the human presence. A large factor in its present emotional appeal is our awareness that benign nature has, effectively, disappeared.

This show's title is ironically meant. It summons bucolic vistas punctuated by staid, stable habitations. But the modern manor is simply the drift of culture across the devastated realm of the organic. This is evidenced in what's pictured, and in how things are seen. Gary Stephan's early *Untitled*, painted on an irregularly shaped piece of Masonite, shows a tiny motorboat churning between two bluntly humped islands, on an unemphatic green sea, under a dour gray sky; an integral part of this scape is a sequence of painted-over nails or flat-headed screws ranging along the upper edge of the Masonite, and a handle-like bracket affixed to the top. In Sylvia Plimack Mangold's *The Nut Trees*, a border of yellow masking tape runs across the top and bottom of the picture and interrupts it near the left edge. Strokes of paint radiate over the frame of John Beerman's *In the Heart of the Seer*, heightening the garish artificiality of an orange sunset on a purple sea.

In their scale, many pictures emphasize the friction between landscape's traditional sublimity and modern perception. Joan Nelson's *Untitled*, a hazy oil and wax rendering of (I think) the terminus of a canal or river-lock, with an expanding gale of light at the horizon, is drastically compressed. Dennis Masback's *Cascade* is a cinematically cropped version of a waterfall smashing along its course—a medium shot where tradition dictates a panorama. More extremely, David Deutsch's *Landscape Recessed in Aluminum* features an intricately modulated, furrowed orange field, its perspective almost aerially flat, the size of a very large postage stamp, affixed to the dwarfing square face of an aluminum trapezoid. *The Mississippi (New Orleans, LA)*, by Mark Innerst, encloses its low-slung nocturnal horizon and distantly glittering river view in a comparatively enormous, white wooden frame chipped and pitted with scars.

These works bear a feeling for landscapes as an alluring memory, translated into modes of picturing peculiar to post-industrial eyes. There is never the lush, full palette of early American naturalism; we can no longer celebrate nature's raw grandeur as if the planet were humming in tune with a cosmic symphony. We're used to seeing the landscape from cars, trains, airplanes, or in bits and pieces on TV, in movies. In some places nature has become something else, softened by cultivation. Postindustrial consumers live in hysterical fear of the untrammeled, like earlier barbarian tribes, deriving their sense of mastery from the proliferation of cluster housing and sparkling plastic. As a result, they possess the ugliest landscapes on earth. Here nature is overlaid with the murk of our cluttered senses and spiked with ghastly monuments to ourselves, as in Thomas Lawson's *Spirit of Sculpture*, where a clearing in a dense blue woods reveals the generic phalluses indigenous to rural art foundations. You can almost smell the sewage in Freya Hansell's wonderfully lurid *In the Canal*, where light from the canal's opening causes its greenish-yellow underside to slither into the water in oily reflection.

The spectral quality of Tracy Grayson's *The Big House* (which does, in fact, contain a manor in a landscape), where a monochrome veil places its subject in the distant past, evokes a vividly felt but only dimly visible place. So do the indistinct and disturbingly quiet compositions by Troy Brauntuch and Michael Zwack, both in pastel, and Ross Bleckner's creepily phosphorescent forest floor, where a black vegetable sprouts malignantly. Nostalgia of the Andrew Wyeth type is conspicuously absent from this exhibition. A really effective landscape painting necessarily reminds us that we're physically bound to the organic world we've destroyed; standing in for the sublime is the paranoid apprehension that a world of clean toilets could back up at any minute in a major way. The flame-spotted, looming orange planet of Georgia Marsh's *Riddle (Iapetus)*, the menacingly wide-open plain of April Gornik's *The West,* Jack Barth's nightmarish *Ruined Bridge in Central Park*, and the dazzling white nuclear explosion in Steve Maslin and Alice Stepanek's *Untitled* locate the reality of modern landscape, somewhere between a largely forgotten past and a dystopian future.

Diagonally across from each other are John Bowman's riotous painting of harborside shelling and twinkling hills, *Shores of Tripoli*, and Mark Tansey's blue-and-white *Halls of Montezuma*, a recasting of Frederic Church's *Heart of the Andes*—the same majestic forests, valleys, and mountains, crossed by B-52s and helicopters, with mobile radar units and tanks nestled in the vegetation. These paintings add a narrative dimension to this show, and make the strongest allusions to earlier landscape styles.

December 23, 1986

EASY PIECES

This doesn't have anything to do with art, but last night I was walking home and noticed a Rolls-Royce Silver Cloud parked at the northeast corner of my block, which is a well-known prostitution area. The driver of the Rolls was talking into a car phone with illuminated push buttons, and because of the illumination I happened to see that he was also jerking off. As I got to my door I remembered that I needed coffee, so I walked back to the corner and across Second Avenue to the deli. Coming out of the deli I noticed that one of the regular hookers from my block was talking into the pay phone at the corner. "Uh-huh," she was saying, "and then what?" It suddenly occurred to me that she was talking to the guy in the Rolls, and that he would just be able to see her legs in his rearview mirror. I thought I would share this with you.

"Where in New York," asks the catalogue, "can you rub elbows with Alexander the Great, Napoleon, George Washington, Henry VIII, William Tell, Marie Antoinette, Uncle Sam, Buffalo Bill and GI Joe?" If you answered Queens Cemetery, think again. "At the FORBES Galleries where 12,000 miniature figures are on parade!"

The FORBES **Magazine Galleries**, located at 62 Fifth Avenue, serve as a showcase for part of what Malcolm Forbes, one of the world's richest and certainly one of its silliest men, has spent his money on since the earliest days of an eternal childhood. You, humble commoner, can view Mr. Forbes's loot most days from

10 to 4, during those off-hours when Forbes and his cronies, who party it up in the galleries at night, repose in their respective boxes of earth.

And quite a collection it is, a mixture of the homeliest sort of Americana, antique military toys, trophies, mutually fawning correspondence between members of the Forbes family and famous people, paintings of an eclectic and generally inferior nature, and a staggering assortment of Fabergé eggs, brooches, lorgnettes, cigarette cases, pins, buttons, and what have you. The latter examples of jumped-up kitsch were originally crafted for members of the Russian royal family, including—the catalogue notes—"Nicholas II, his wife and their five children," who (boohoo) "were brutally murdered in Ekaterinburg in 1918." An attentive visit to the FORBES Galleries will give even the least class-conscious viewer some idea why.

The current special offering, "The Painter Was a Lady," is an insensible jumble of women's paintings from the Victorian and Edwardian period, most of them so bland and unremarkable that the gender specificity of this show will offend women. In the permanent displays there is something to offend everyone. Not the objects themselves, necessarily, but their juxtapositions, everywhere, with Forbes family memorabilia: labels and placards full of fatuous references to Malcolm Forbes, his stupendously privileged childhood, and the tasteless noblesse oblige he wields as an alleged adult. There is something obscene about an incalculably wealthy man who assembles an entire minimuseum in his own honor, during his lifetime, especially when so much of the collection celebrates warfare, an activity in which people of Forbes's class generally reap vast profits from the slaughter of the lower orders. It really is something to see, not unlike watching somebody beat off in a Rolls-Royce.

There are plenty of slick, fifth-rate photographers devoted to flattering celebrities, but **Annie Leibovitz**, who currently has a show at Sidney Janis Gallery (110 West 57th Street, through December 27), breaks new ground in the direction of total obsequiousness. Her pictures are valentines to the *idea* of famousness as the supreme human condition; she coaxes her subjects to mug and preen for the camera, acting out fanzine fantasies of themselves in fabulous clothes and arty settings. Leibovitz has a truly peculiar talent: she makes even people who have accomplished something look like empty, narcissistic assholes. Leibovitz could give these gruesomely overstaged, unenlightening portraits some jizz by adding new titles, viz.: *Mediocre Nightclub Comic in Bathtub, Meryl Streep Has Ugly Feet, Famous Guy I'd Like to Sleep With If He Really Looked Like This, Junkie Rock Star Who's Had His Blood Replaced Before Learning They Hadn't Screened It*, etc.

Tyler Turkle isn't showing anywhere at the moment. He had a show last February at White Columns. A few months ago at Cable Gallery I noticed this rectangular *thing* stuck to the side of a file cabinet, a sort of very thin plastic pillow, which readily peeled off and adhered to other surfaces, including a cylinder of bubble wrap. Evidently, Turkle has been making things with soft plastic paint for a long time. In some of his work he fills in magazine and textbook illustrations with a plastic skin that adds body to an outline while eliminating detail; he's done this, for instance, with anatomical charts. Lately he's also done anatomy sections which can be placed on windows or glass doors, and thus appear to float freely in space.

Turkle's current series consists of rather large, two-color rectangles, derived from the cover scheme of *The New Criterion*, minus the title and table of contents so that the work will be more purely formalist. Tricia Collins and Richard Milazzo showed me one recently, in black and blue, mounted on a Plexiglas stand. It's the wittiest geometric painting I've seen all year, and arrived with a charmingly practical letter from the artist that reads, in part:

I think you can place the work on almost any surface that will accept it. By that I mean anywhere it will stick and peel off without damage to either the surface or the piece. I have tested the following and found them to work: 1. any wall (surface) painted with latex or enamel paint. The flatter the paint the less the piece will stay put. Stay away from "chalky" walls and bumpy walls. 2. refrigerators and all enameled metal surfaces like — 3. stoves. 4. microwave ovens. 5. cupboard doors (painted and metal). 6. bathroom walls (tile). 7. windows. 8. doors. 9. Formica countertops. 10. toilet (and seats). 11. car doors. 12. TV screens. 13. desktops. 14. baby cribs. 15. mirrors. 16. vinyl wallpapers. 17. plastic floor coverings. 18. leather briefcases. 19. glass shower enclosures.

To place the work simply press it against the surface with the heel of your hand and gently smooth it flat from the center. A gentle stroke is preferred so as not to stretch the plastic too much. Then press firmly all over.

To remove the piece just peel it down starting at a corner. Placing and removing can be repeated indefinitely.

Cleaning is only a matter of wiping it off with a damp sponge or cloth. The only precaution to take is to avoid leaving it in direct sunlight or near very hot lights.

And finally, the most implausible and ominous show title of the year: "Out of the Sixties," photographs by **Dennis Hopper** at Tony Shafrazi Gallery.

January 20, 1987

RUMMAGING AROUND

Pollution is the necessary result of the inability of man to reform and transform waste—the transformation of waste is perhaps the oldest preoccupation of man.

—Patti Smith, "High on Rebellion"

Dearest Diary,

John Perreault recently observed in these pages that any object costing more than the median annual income is not aesthetic. Even if he was joking I agree with him. You could say the same about any object costing more than the average annual income to make. One of the most numbing effects of hanging around the art world in the past year was becoming inured to the idea of inflation as a positive value. Lots of artists went on record saying that they wanted to make big money so they could work on a grander scale. I think this is stupid. Unless you work in photography or cinema there is no excuse for a huge overhead.

The best trick you can do is make something out of nothing. Even in capitalist terms this is cleverer than dumping money into production. Writers are the happiest artists (though they are all personally miserable) because all they need to work is a pencil and a piece of paper. Whatever you make is gravy, though of course writers don't make anything. Artaud said that all writing was garbage. (Pigshit, actually. Depends on the translation.) All art is ultimately junk in its supreme form. The transformation of quotidian garbage into expressive garbage is the function of the artist. Of American artists, John Chamberlain seems to me the smartest because smashed-up cars are what America is all about—what better material to use? We will never run out of them and they're cheap. People understand debris and dirt and maybe these provide the most direct route into the imagination. The English sculptor Bill Woodrow was in town this week and I went with him looking for useful junk. Our streets are bulging with garbage, it doesn't cost anything.

Right next to Pat Hearn Gallery on 9th Street between C and D a building has been torn down and the rubble looks like it's been put through a shredder, even the bricks. Behind several mounds of sawed-off wood and crumbled plaster is an alley full of auto-body parts and demolished home furnishings, shattered windshields, office chairs, a gutted jukebox, the cab of a truck, and a lot of other vivid detritus. This site is for Woodrow what Conran's is for Haim Steinbach, a veritable gold mine. He finds a disemboweled humidifier, a car hood, a collapsing set of shelves, an aluminum double sink. ("This looks like someone's already had a go at it," he says, extracting some goo from one of the basins.) I find a congealed novel by Chuck Scarborough and a cracked copy of *The Best of Tommy James and the Shondells*, a punctured tin of Perma-King antifreeze, a drop-forged bicycle brake. These objects already suggest an ideal configuration. Woodrow packs his discoveries up in the van (artist Royce Weatherly is helping him, also driving); we unload them where he's staying and then drive into Brooklyn.

Atlantic Avenue, Flatbush Avenue. An empire of signs and an empire of garbage. The signs are particularly evocative, you could make a story out of them with a sprinkling of verbs and adjectives. Fu King Food Shop. Chung Hwa Plaza. Ebony and Ivory Beauty Supplies. Diaz Tirado Travel, Bergen Tile. Karate University. El Gran Castillo de Jagua. The best is a wall-mural ad that says, "When you're dining out, insist on a plate. National Clay Board."

When you walk out of a great film by Antonioni or Bresson or William Wyler the world looks like the movie, and the same is true of good "static" art. The only reason to write about art is that people have stopped making great movies. And bad movies aren't bad in the grand manner any more. One reason why video will never be an art form is that it looks slightly worse than real life. The movies are dead because everything's lit and composed with the idea of future cable sales and video rentals. Art can still have the visual force of Greta Garbo's face because it isn't made to be shown on television. Bill Woodrow's stuff is usually made from strips of metal peeled away from common objects and simulated ones that branch out from it or penetrate it or nestle inside it; if you look at a lot of them the metallic city world takes on their appearance of warp and fragility.

We rummage through some thrift and antique stores on Atlantic Avenue. In one of them the proprietor wants to charge $20 for a scratched Elvis Presley single. When Bill tries to talk her down she says, "You aren't going to believe this, but I had a copy of 'Walking My Baby Back Home,' somebody'd laid a hot iron on it and it had this burn from the middle right to this edge, and this policeman down the street paid 30 dollars for it. No way he can play it either." She's not letting Elvis go for less than 20. Royce points out a lot of metal things—a coffee urn, some standing ashtrays—but Woodrow rejects these. Instead, in the third place, he finds a strange sort of tin suitcase, painted a dullish gold.

This is all he picks out in Brooklyn, but we learn a lot from driving through various neighborhoods about the disposition of waste in the area. People's garbage gives you a poetic sense of how they live. Woodrow's work reflects this experience of rummaging around, the process of hunting through what people discard and making sculpture from familiarly resonant things.

I asked him if garbage was different in London. "No," he said, "not really. There's a sort of common denominator throughout the places I've been in the Western world, but they change from country to country in certain ways, in terms of design, or style, and also age; if you go to a fairly rich country like Germany, you can find things that were thrown away that are comparatively new, whereas, if you go to Italy, there people use things for a much longer time. The condition of things is very different, but basically they're the same things, furniture to car parts; things in America are bigger, things in Italy are smaller; you can't drive through an Italian town with a big American car. Those are the nice kinds of differences. And then occasionally, there are little things you find that have very much to do with a particular area. One of the classic ones, for me, was the yellow Checker cab parts…When people see the work I made with Checker cab parts, it's an immediate evocation of New York.

"Going out today, I had some things in mind mainly because on Saturday I found one item which has colored what I wanted to find, and that was a cartwheel, it was such a strange thing to find on the street in New York that I wanted to use it. I've been more selective than if I were going out to find material I could use for a month's work or so. Several things today were made of steel but had this painted imitation wood-grain surface; I picked them up because of that, it suggests some possible play with the real woodenness of the wheel and this sort of craft element…"

Some of his favorite recent discoveries have been slot machines, the new ones that work like video games. Also, in Italy, "A wooden frame, which was a bed warmer, what happened is they heated up a brick in the fire, then hung it inside this thing that looks like a very open-weave lobster pot. So the frame would keep the sheets and bedclothes off this hot brick that warmed them up…And, they had this very nice slang title, *il prete*, the priest. The priest warms the bed for you."

MODEL PRISONS

If you've tired yourself at least occasionally with monthly art magazines, you've probably noticed the ubiquity of certain writers whose production of an opaque, nervous-looking jargon typifies what's widely known, and dreaded, as art criticism. I have closely examined the recent outpourings of several such opinion-pushers in hopes of finding out what makes these people tick so incessantly. In the case of one particular virulent graphomaniac, a psychoanalytical explanation suggests itself. The writer, an art historian, is subject to frequent—how shall I say it—*visitations* by another personality, a personality that he has imperfectly assimilated from another person. During these spells, or trances, he is "taken over" by this alter persona, a shadowy figure who forces him to write down its thoughts. Psychics refer to such visitors as "walk-ins." It didn't take much investigation for me to trace the source of this writer's turgid, self-besotted style, especially since the walk-in's actual name, as well as the word "regressive," appears at least 50 times in everything he writes. *Aha!* (I thought.) *His walk-in is Theodor Adorno!*

It isn't unusual for a graphomaniac to welcome a regular walk-in into his or her prose, since graphomania is characterized by an uncontrollable compulsion to write down virtually anything that comes into one's head. We can thank graphomania for the novels and plays of S. I. Witkiewicz, but also, alas, for Joyce Carol Oates. In art criticism, graphomania ranks as a catastrophic illness. The very writer I've described, for example, has lately drooled out a harsh, microcephalic attack (his 15th or so) on various artists whose work deals with social issues, essentially asking *where these people are coming from*. Yet it is obvious to people who enjoy the work of Hans Haacke, Jenny Holzer, and Barbara Kruger—three of his myriad allergies—that these artists are coming from the real world we live in today, as opposed, let's say, to some night class they once audited at the Frankfurt School in 1955.

If we had to describe this real world to a visitor from outer space, we might call it an invisible jail whose walls consist of energy vibrations we call money. Money is a sort of nonsterile lubricant that facilitates the human male's penetration of three-dimensional space. Life in the resulting jail is constricted and psychically damaging. **Nancy Chunn**, whose paintings are currently on view at Ronald Feldman Gallery (31 Mercer Street, through February 7), is a shrewd geographer of the world's prison colonies and victim states. Her pictures have a calm, somber pictorial authority, a decorative astuteness that fools the eye into seeing them at first as meticulously composed, dark abstractions.

Some works of art succeed if they effectively resist looking like art. When the goal is to free oneself from the history of forms, the aimed-for result is an initial ugliness that later becomes accepted as beautiful. Another kind of art smuggles inappropriate content into recognizably aesthetic contexts. Haacke has often done this using familiar Minimalist sculptural conceits as vehicles for politically charged information. Chunn uses chromatic effects similar to those found in "purist" AbEx (excuse me) with eccentrically defined, organic shapes, overlaid or interrupted by industrial shapes done in a more illustrational style.

The subversive element in Chunn's strategy is that her abstractions are also representations, the organic shapes being maps, the mechanical ones having associations with containment, imprisonment, and violence (chain-link grids, harvester blades, metal clamps). In several new works the chains are painted in black enamel and so jump into the foreground. *Guatemala*, the map done in the fabric colors of tourist Central America, is entirely fenced in, so to speak, while *Nicaragua* interrupts the nexus of chains surrounding it. *Kampuchea* appears as a procession of bone or meat slabs impaled on spokes obtruding from warped metal wheels. *Afghanistan* has a sort of trailing veil of chains stretching across it, *Chile* a chain-mail hood draped over it.

The power of Chunn's work is its matter-of-factness. The beauty of her arrangements, the formal restraint and obvious involvement with "painting issues" give permission to make blunt political observations. This is not a misuse of painting but an enlargement of a specific practice beyond the boundaries of formalism; it stands up as good art. Chunn makes a concrete picture of the state of things by combining two kinds of abstraction: the painterly abstraction we routinely accept as high aesthetics, and the more pedestrian abstraction of maps. Chunn's maps resemble living organisms, whole objects—the kidneys or lungs of the living jail we call home. These works are not didactic; they don't lay out a program but simply ask us to be conscious that art and life are inextricably connected—that we all live in the same world, which is not a happy place in most places.

Perhaps critics who oppose so-called political art believe that art should simply examine subjectivity and traffic in navel-staring. But as Theodor Adorno himself would tell you, our insides are reflections of our outsides. The enemy within is the *simulacrum* of the social beast without. **Julie Wachtel**'s new paintings at Diane Brown Gallery (100 Greene Street, through February 7) reproduce the kitsch imagery of joke greeting cards, on canvases that alternate with monochrome pictures of primitive effigies. I've always found these pictures extremely unpleasant to look at, but Wachtel's use of them isolates a widespread phenomenon worth examining. The greeting card figures are unwholesomely cute, physically grotesque, and their symbolization of the person who sends the cards reads like this:

here I am, this lumpy, dumpy schmuck who can't do anything right, unattractive, stupid, twisted up inside myself, but even though I'm nothing, Happy Birthday. Or, Get Well Soon. Or, I Love You.

Wachtel's placement of these uncomely, buglike creatures beside idols and effigies suggests, of course, that the latter correspond to the former, formally and perhaps functionally. Although it would be hard to say what a *normal* expression of feelings might look like in comparison, the fact that the links between people are routinely conveyed by such unappealing images manufactured in bulk indicates a severe prolific stunting of emotional growth. And from them we can infer the quality of the social system that progresses from the training jails of our schools to the full-blown penitentiary, bulging with commodities and enlivened by bloody spectacles, that comprises the theater of American adult life.

February 3, 1987

ILL MET

[**Lila Acheson Wallace Wing for 20th-Century Art.** Metropolitan Museum of Art, 82nd Street and Fifth Avenue, opens February 3.]

The opening of a new, contemporary wing at the Metropolitan Museum has prompted the obligatory featurettes in various papers and magazines. The issues cited here and there are not really issues, but the sort of questions that follow in the wake of any huge capital investment. Will the Met become competitive with MOMA? Will Met donors rush to fill the cavities in the museum's modern collection? Will the word "lacunae" appear in every journalist's account of the new wing?

All accounts so far seem to accept the Metropolitan for what it claims to be, namely an "encyclopedia" of art history. The Met's press kit is subtly revisionist with respect to modern art, claiming that the museum "has held a firm commitment to the art of the day since its establishment in 1870." In reality, the Met has collected interest on certain endowments for contemporary art, made numerous unadventurous purchases, and accepted an embarrassing number of unimportant works as gifts. These have languished, or festered, in the Met's basement until now, on cryogenic hold, just like Walt Disney at Anaheim.

The Met's PR strategy aims at transforming a sow's ear into a silk purse, or rather, a sow's purse into an important cultural entity. The spotty collection is being offered as an enlightening detour around the landmarks of modernism, with a few indisputable Masterpieces strewn about like Halloween pumpkins. This is rather audacious: the cult of the Masterpiece is nowhere as entrenched, yet the Met now offers the contents of its storage rooms as thought-provoking surprises.

Before speculating on what "ought" to be on display—a line of inquiry that implicitly endorses the museum's pretensions—we should consider, first of all, those aspects of the Metropolitan Museum that bear comparison with a cash laundry or marketing outlet. If your eye happens to skip over the detail that Lila Acheson Wallace, for whom the new wing is named, was the cofounder of *Reader's Digest*, you have already accepted one of the Met's more questionable standard operating procedures. For decades, Mrs. Wallace's magazine has coarsened American minds with chauvinistic swill, McCarthyite anticommunism, and juvenilia ("I Am Johnny's Pancreas," etc.); at the same time, the Met has industriously cleaned Wallace's money, transforming her into a maven of the highest culture.

Although all museums are endowed by the very people who despoil the general quality of life outside the museum, the Met has an inflexible policy of accepting money from almost anywhere. Even certain bordellos in the Patpong district of Bangkok are more fastidious. As a result, the Met has become a public relations servant for Mobil, Exxon, and other corporate entities whose logos proudly flap above the museum's entrance during special exhibitions, welcoming the shills. In the Reagan years, the Met has pooled its talents with the grotesque Diana Vreeland to market Ralph Lauren and Yves St. Laurent fashions, mounting "historical" costume exhibitions that coincided with sales campaigns for identical costumery at Bloomingdale's.

It would not be unusual, then, if the future held in store such additions to the Met as the Adnan Khashoggi Wing, the Ivan Boesky Collection of Stock Certificates, and special events from the Bechtel Corporation. The tone has been permanently lowered at the Temple of Culture. Still, an operation of this size and complexity cannot be expected to simply disappear; the Met will always be with us. The Wallace Wing is, at least, one more place where contemporary works of art can be seen, albeit in neutralizing bulk.

The debut installation cannot be considered auspicious. "The installations are not fixed," says the Met's chairman of the department of 20th-century art William S. Lieberman, "and those for the museum's collection of painting and sculpture will change about twice a year." The wing itself, a squarish silo that Richard Meier might have designed as a wastebasket, offers the physical effects of an underground parking garage and a hotel atrium. The exhibition space has the hard look of a Park Avenue dentist's offices. The track lighting scheme in current use bathes the walls of each room in glare and plunges the circulation space in a weird dimness. None of these spaces has any character at all.

Especially unfortunate is the mezzanine ghetto for photography, with a ceiling as squat as an East Village tenement's. The gallery actually feels as if it's being squashed between floors. The Met's acquisitions in this area are rather less adventurous than what one finds in modestly funded private collections. There are untroublesome photographs by important names, nothing confrontational, erotic or frightening—even the Weegees are boring. Robert Mapplethorpe is represented by his portrait of Doris Saatchi, which speaks volumes about this museum's priorities: why get a *great* Mapplethorpe, when you can show a merely clever one that flatters a major collector? The Cindy Sherman is tiny. The four-panel Warhol self-portrait is a particularly jejune inclusion, since a gigantic Warhol *Mao* has been hung in the sculpture court.

The sculpture court is another peculiarly unpleasant space. It simply doesn't feel good to be there. Again, the objects have a generic emanation, as if someone had plucked them from a catalogue. What exactly does that *Mao* signify in this context? Why does a tedious Louise Nevelson "chamber" take up so much room? Why not remove everything except Al Held's *Greek Garden*, the Tony Smith, the Matta painting, and the Louise Bourgeois? Not that the other contents wouldn't look good elsewhere; the point is, they would, and fewer objects would hold the space more effectively.

If it really were the Met's policy to enlarge perceptions about "the canon" of modernism, one could welcome the promiscuous juxtapositions of obscure works with famous ones, forgotten painters with brand names. But the current arrangements of paintings are merely expedient, the museum parading its poverty to solicit better donations. No matter what anyone tells you, it is not a joy to behold "a survey of American painting between 1905 and 1940," especially the one the Met is offering. The first floor also contains a jumble of mainly second-rate furniture and textiles, several Georgia O'Keeffes, and a micro "survey" of "currents in 20th-century art." All very thin and forgettable. One area, the Helen and Milton A. Kimmelman Gallery, is stuffed with Robert Rauschenberg's "continuing visual autobiography," *¼ Mile or 2 Furlong Piece*, about which the best that can be said is, it should stop.

On the second floor, we find quite a generous amount of first-generation Abstract Expressionism, with a disproportionate number of Clyfford Stills. And a smattering of Kitajs, Twomblys, a big Alex Katz, and so on. As far as I can make out there are no paintings by women on the second floor, and this is the ultracontemporary section. There are wonderful Picassos and one of the best Dalís, and of course many of these pictures have women as subjects. But you know, there have been a lot of women artists around in recent decades. Too many, really, for a gallery full of "recent paintings by younger artists" to contain only works by: John Alexander, Luis Cruz Azaceta, Georg Baselitz, Peter Booth, Richard Bosman, Frederick Brown, Roger

Brown, Steven Campbell, Julian Schnabel, Donald Sultan, David True, and John Walker.

The peculiar medley of works, many of them ghastly, seems unified exclusively by gender. If the Met wants to be truly competitive with MOMA by being truly different, it has made a mingy though welcome start by leaving paintings in their original frames. The Met could go a lot further and put the stress of its contemporary acquisitions on art by women, who are producing just as much valuable work in all media as men are. Don't hold your breath.

THE FEAR PROBLEM

["**Homo Video: Where We Are Now.**" Organized by William Olander. The New Museum of Contemporary Art, 683 Broadway, through February 15.]

I'm hesitant to generalize about the program of videotapes by gay men and lesbians, "Homo Video: Where We Are Now," currently running at the New Museum. Reactions to these tapes will undoubtedly differ according to one's sexual orientation and experiences. All works in the show are recent, and most are by younger artists. Therefore what's offered are perspectives on sexual difference in a period of crisis, at a generational distance from Stonewall and the first years of gay liberation.

What's most immediately striking is an absence of rhetoric and a sobriety of tone that makes itself felt even in tapes that use satire or broad comedy. But perhaps it's more accurate to say that these tapes connect the situation of the homosexual with the general condition of society; earlier "gay art," "gay theater," and other artifacts of the '60s and '70s often contained a large element of wish fulfillment and celebrated a life-*style* that became for many people, an empty mimicry of middle-class consumerism.

As one of the actors in Peter Adair and Robert Epstein's *The AIDS Show* says, the relief of opening the closets after Stonewall led many homosexuals to equate identity with sexual acts performed. And as others have pointed out, the masculinization of male homosexuality in the mid-'70s, and a related fashion for self-abandonment and excess, posited homosexuality as a *taste*, trivial in itself, that lent itself to commercial exploitation. In many ways, the '70s created a false sense that homosexuality had been normalized, assimilated into the fabric of American life. It was widely believed that the assertion of gay economic power in places like San Francisco ensured continued tolerance and promised real political power.

The boat has turned around, obviously. Homosexuality has become a much heavier fact of life, and the construction of identity in the current situation is deeply problematical. The homosexual has to define him or herself in opposition to a social system that seemed, for a time, willing to add sexual difference to its menu of commodities. The AIDS phenomenon has devastated the sense that we have a right to our desires; several of the "Homo Video" tapes perform a therapeutic function in separating disease from sexuality. Gregg Bordowitz's *"...some aspect of a shared lifestyle"* parodies the slanting of AIDS reportage, showing various authority figures reciting increasingly garbled and contradictory statistics. Captions and other graphic devices emphasize the battering rapidity of media information and the general lack of reasoned analysis.

Bordowitz shows how AIDS has been packaged by American media to bolster the phobias of the so-called general population. John Greyson's *Moscow Does Not Believe in Queers* deals partly with the opposite phenomenon, describing Greyson's visit to the Soviet Union, where no information about AIDS was officially available. Greyson uses a split screen to juxtapose footage of his trip with a conversation he's having in bed with a lover; explicit shots of the two men fucking act as a fissure in the wall of silence Greyson describes.

Adair and Epstein's *The AIDS Show: Artists Involved With Death and Survival* documents the revue-style work of Theatre Rhinoceros in San Francisco. At first, the vignettes presented recall the stereotypical bent of early gay theater and its camping, body-conscious, middle-class characters. But then, with unexpected humor and genuine emotional electricity, the company shows real people coping with illness and death, in the process learning hard lessons about themselves and the world.

Dealing with difference, negotiating complex realities, facing up to things—these themes have acquired texture in the AIDS years, but it was never especially easy to be gay outside certain urban enclaves. Some "Homo Video" tapes discuss and dramatize the perennial problems that go with the territory. Suzanne Silver's *You Know, Something* compresses a lesbian relationship into eight minutes of scattered encounters, demonstrating the incompatibility of a romantic sensibility with the demands of work and practical goals; in the end it hints at reconciliation of conflicting desires. *Just Because of Who We Are*, by the Heramedia group, offers a series of interviews with lesbians who recount harrowing, typical episodes of harassment, political rape, suicide attempts, and disastrous psychiatric intervention.

Richard Fung's *Chinese Characters* examines gay pornography's predominantly white male imagery and its psychological effect on nonwhite gays. *Here in the Southwest*, by Joyan Saunders, shows a group of women discussing "parthenogenic lizards" and speculating on how a woman-hating parrot in a pet show differentiates human males from females; this is followed by a spectacular illustrated lecture on the origin of genitalia. In John Goss's *Wild Life*, we follow two 15-year-old Latino boys, Carlos and Cesar, as they romp around Los Angeles, remarkably comfortable with the idea of being gay—although, for them, this consists mainly of dressing up and adoring "cute guys."

Wild Life's uncomplicated emphasis on pleasure makes it especially welcome in a program that delves, however entertainingly, into so many varieties of pain. In this connection, the sophisticated montage of Lyn Blumenthal's *Doublecross*, where the story seems less important than the visual wit, is a relief from a surfeit of headshots and standard video framing and cutting.

How To Seduce a Preppy, by Rick "X" [Rick Shur], is the funniest tape, reminiscent of Curt McDowell's films. A voiceover accompanies the step-by-step ravishing: get him drunk on good Scotch, throw in some grass, etc. It also explains what safe sex is, in case you were still wondering.

Many of these tapes are artistically uneven—video is notorious for highlighting bad acting, mistakes in phrasing, wrong beats. The resurrection of Alexandra Kollontai on a talk show in John Greyson's tape is a particularly unfortunate invention, though it's somewhat redeemed by the information she offers about sexual freedom in the early Bolshevik period. But sometimes even the awkwardness of a scene works in its favor, as a contrast to the slickness with which heterosexual images are jammed down our throats, in virtually every medium. The absence of the formulaic is, cumulatively, tonic; so is the general lack of obedience to a party line. Greyson's tape contains the "shocking" image of two splendid males (in Toronto) fucking without a condom. This is politically incorrect and medically dangerous. I was still glad to see it.

February 17, 1987

SHORT MEMORY

Columbus's failure to recognize the diversity of languages permits him, when he confronts a foreign tongue, only two possible, and complementary, forms of behavior: to acknowledge it as a language but to refuse to believe it is different; or to acknowledge its difference but to refuse to admit it is a language...
— Tzvetan Todorov, *The Conquest of America*

Lothar Baumgarten arranged his photographs of the Yanomami Indians at Marian Goodman Gallery (we break up this sentence to say: 24 West 57th Street, now closed) after dyeing the walls a rich red by crushing annatto seeds on them. The Yanomami use the annatto dye to paint their bodies. Sentences or phrases appeared near each photograph, marked off by bracket-ended black lines. When the photographs were taken, the Yanomami were returning from a hunting expedition and unusually vulnerable to attack. We see that the women carry all the household materials on backpacks that are actually strapped to their heads, so each woman's head is supporting up to 200 pounds. The men are only encumbered by their weapons.

Their possessions are no greater than the might of their shoulders, says one motto. *The dwelling of our advantages are others' chains*, says another. This is addressed to us, perhaps. The Yanomami live in the upper Orinoco region of Venezuela. They are threatened by extermination because this area is heavily exploited by mining. In a show two years ago, Baumgarten placed the names of minerals adjacent to the names of species endangered by mining.

This installation had the quiet dignity of an elegy. Baumgarten's work is a continuous act of mourning and remembering. In much of his work the native names of things supplant the language of conquerors. He brings to mind the deadly cost of white civilization: the destruction of human diversity, the ruin of the biosphere. (As I write this sentence, someone delivers Sue Coe's book *Police State*. On the back cover it says: "To think and act as a human being in a system set up for profit is to be classified as a criminal. To protest innocence is to become subversive."

The prod to conscience in Baumgarten's work is a reminder that the banished Other will come back to haunt us, no matter what we do. Forms and languages expelled by the relentless march of avarice have mysterious ways of returning. In **Elaine Reichek**'s show at Carlo Lamagna Gallery (50 West 57th Street, through February 28), the artist has blown up and retouched ethnological photographs of body-painted Tierra del Fuego Indians; next to them are woven figures modeled after the originals. These daubed and feathered Others conduct an erotic charge from a forgotten world. The appeal of Reichek's aboriginal images is their inherent sense of *other possibilities of life*, outside the homogenized, carcinogenic system we live in.

There is *Tent Man*, to start with, shaped like a tent, with bright dots painted up the center of his peaked hood, thick lines and trails of dots running down from the base of the headpiece like jellyfish tendrils. *Blue Men* are naked except for their headdresses and patterns of blue and violet paint; Reichek's versions look like colorful terrorists. (I use the word "terrorists" to denote the fairy-tale figures of modern mythology.) *Feather Man/Striped Man* wear differently tapered head coverings; Reichek has modified the overall-feather pattern of the former but retained the latter's zebralike design. *Horned Man*, my favorite, has broad stripes painted over his body and a headpiece something like a jester's cap.

These Indians perished before ethnology could record much about them. The original pictures, considerably altered by Reichek's enlargements, were taken around 1908. There were three tribes, with different body types, living on islands: Yaghan, Ona, Alacalufe, each having its own language. Magellan named Tierra del Fuego, or Land of Fire; the islands too have European names. Londonderry, Navarino, Wollaston, Staten Island. The photographs show the male Indians, in masks and body paint, enacting the Kina ceremony. The males enter a hut and reemerge as spirits. Their dance supposedly ensured the good behavior of the women.

When the Europeans came they gave the Indians clothing, which carried smallpox and measles. They were all dead by 1930. Darwin says very little about them. "The language of these people, according to our notions, scarcely deserves to be called articulate," he writes. He notes their talent for mimicry. But Darwin is mainly interested in bats, mice, foxes, and birds. He spots a white-tufted flycatcher, a wren, a black woodpecker.

Darwin writes that the "perfect equality among the individuals composing the Fuegian tribes, must for a long time retard their civilization." He says that animals who select a chief "are most capable of improvement." Most damningly, in Darwin's view, "even a piece of cloth given to one is torn into shreds and distributed; and no one individual becomes richer than another."

But we should hear other voices on the blessings of civilization:

Cholera and influenza germs from the ships began the work. By 1780 black corpses were a common sight, huddled in the salt grasses and decomposing in the creamy uterine hollows of the sandstone. These epidemics were not meant to happen; the days of arsenic and the infected trading-blanket were still far off.
　　　　　　　　　　　　　　—Robert Hughes, *The Fatal Shore*

The disease exterminated a large fraction of the Aztecs and cleared a path for the aliens to the heart of Tenochtitlan and to the founding of New Spain. Racing ahead of the conquistadores, it soon appeared in Peru, killing a large proportion of the subjects of the Inca, killing the Inca himself and the successor he had chosen. Civil war and chaos followed and then Francisco Pizarro arrived. The miraculous triumphs of that conquistador, and of Cortés...are in large part the triumphs of the virus of smallpox.
—Alfred W. Crosby, *Ecological Imperialism:*
The Biological Expansion of Europe, 900–1900

That which led the Spaniards to these unsanctified impieties was the desire of Gold, to make themselves suddenly rich, for the obtaining of dignities & honours which were no way fit for them...they used them not like beasts, for that would have been tolerable, but looked upon them as if they had been but the dung and filth of the earth...the Indians never gave them the least cause to offer them violence, but received them as Angels sent from heaven, till their excessive cruelties, the torments and slaughters of their Countrymen mov't them to take arms against the Spaniards.
—Bartolomé de las Casas, *The Tears of the Indians*

I try to fight the idea that the gay men are giving us AIDS. I explain that we probably gave it to the gay men to start with, by inoculating them with infected gamma globulin, which is probably what happened.... It must have occurred in the early '70s, and in those years, industrial companies—not the not-for-profit blood centers, but the for-profit blood industry—were buying blood from prisoners and from overseas, including Africa and the Caribbean.
—Dr. Mathilde Krim, in an interview with
Larry Kramer, *Interview*, February, 1987

Freedom is neither a legal invention nor a philosophical conquest, the cherished possession of civilizations more valid than others because they alone have been able to create or preserve it. It is the outcome of an objective relationship between the individual and the space he occupies, between the consumer and the resources at his disposal. And it is far from certain that abundance of resources can make up for a lack of space, and that a rich but overpopulated society is not in danger of being poisoned by its own density, like those flour parasites which manage to kill each other at a distance by their toxins, even before their food supply runs out.
—Claude Lévi-Strauss, *Tristes Tropiques*

February 24, 1987

IT'S A PLEASURE TO SERVE YOU

[**Richard Milani**. Baskerville + Watson, 578 Broadway, through February 28.]

I have to write this down: this morning, just before leaving the house, late as usual with my column, which I thought would be a snap this week, I called a friend who told me Carlos Clarens—film historian, author, tireless champion of films worthy and unsung, mentor, friend—died on Sunday. You know, the way we live now, especially here, you don't get even an hour to sit quietly in a room and simply think about someone: *I'm late with my column.* A bright morning in January three years ago, I walked from the Louisiane to the Café de Flore and there was Carlos, looking like a subtly aging matinee idol, and we talked, as we always did, about movies—what Werner was doing, what Chantal was doing, had I seen Jackie and Sid, yes, Jackie and Sid were staying at the Louisiane. Then Susan came into the Flore, and the three of us ate breakfast, Susan was going to Rome that night to mix her film in Cinecittà. *You never returned that photograph*, Carlos reminded me: Carlos, the omnivore of film stills.

   It was a picture of Carlos dancing with Magdalena Montezuma, someone had taken it on the set of Werner Schroeter's *Flocons d'or.* I had borrowed it from Carlos long before Magdalena became my friend, because I adored her, and Jackie and Sid told me that Carlos had actually been in a movie with her. I was thrilled and envious: did he have any pictures? As a novice film writer, I was amazed by Carlos's collegial generosity, his willing-ness to share his erudition, to make time for me. With his usual, uncanny graciousness he lent the still, after digging around for it for weeks. *Please be sure to give this back to me, it's the only one I have.* Carlos in a white tuxedo, his head tilted back and slightly turned for the camera, dancing. Magdalena has an orchid in her hair. Carlos's boyish eyes and his rake's mustache. *If you hadn't missed your plane,* Magdalena told me, years later in Berlin, *perhaps we wouldn't have seen each other again.* And a few months after that, at a crowded party at the film festival: *let's hope we meet again.* But we never did. A few months after Magdalena died, I saw Carlos again at Sid's funeral.

In the mail, at the office, a friend in Paris has sent me the program of Ingrid Caven's recent concert at the Théâtre de l'Europe, which Ingrid has signed for me, adding, *I'll see you.* This seems to complete something; there's a libretto inside of songs by Fassbinder, Enzensberger, and Jean-Jacques Schuhl. Carlos was one of the few people I could talk to about Ingrid Caven. *I'll see you*: such an optimistic expression. He would have liked Richard Milani's paintings; in fact it's a very strange irony that I have these particular slides for reference this morning.

If you grew up with the movies as your main defense against tele-vision culture, and European movies as your special protection against American culture, Richard Milani's paintings strike an immediate sympathetic chord. They're complicated as objects, and what Milani is actually trying to do with images has an obvious relation to what David Salle does, with found images laid over each other, often in a diptych format. But there, I think, the resemblance ends. Salle's work commemorates an exhausted Surrealist sensibility, the collapse of all images into paradigms of heterosexual repulsion. In Milani's pictures, the specific images have a different psychological temperature, a certain autonomy of meaning transferred from their place of origin.

Since these images are usually taken from film stills, they retain something of the aura of an *arrested flow of time*, a suspended narrative energy unique to motion pictures. Comic books and TV shows don't have it and neither do masterpieces of art history, photography, or sculpture. This isn't to say the stills remain intact, or even particularly recognizable; the viewer often has to unscramble an image spread out across others, as if peering through several photographic negatives. And they aren't invariably film stills, but often mixed with different kinds of pictures. Duchamp's *Rotorelief* turns up in one, in another a *Life* magazine photo of an African political prisoner.

The scattery patterns that appear are often in black and white, or distributed over spectrum blocks of color based on the text bars used in filming (and as leader on VCR rentals). The images are painted, usually in Flashe, on plastic screen mounted on aluminum. If you've seen Izhar Patkin's anamorphically contorted images painted on screen, where the paint sits on the surface in bright gouts with a texture like crumb cake, imagine the opposite sort of surface, almost flat and peculiarly transparent: as if several projected images had frozen on a silver screen, with the paint density *behind* various negative spaces that define figures and objects.

Milani also uses anamorphic techniques, sometimes as a visual foil for a main image. For example, in one picture's upper half, the winglike torso of Ingrid Bergman in *Joan of Arc* is flanked by smaller, curved distortions of the same form. Picture surfaces reveal the supporting screen, which in turn presents a mottled surface, in places a dark gray that colors sink into, elsewhere shiny and reflective, where colors are thrown forward. The fairly large scale of these paintings accommodates a lot of surface variation, which the bleed-through of the metal stretchers pulls into neatly compressed order.

How Milani's pictures play on a viewer's memory depends, of course, on what the viewer remembers. One of the more curious features of these extremely attractive works is the elusiveness of images that turn out to be quite familiar. And since there are often things we've stored in a positive place, so to speak, the fact that they resist recollection when placed in a slightly different visual context may indicate that no image can ever be appropriated whole. For instance, Jean Seberg's sunglasses from *Breathless*, Sterling Hayden smoking a cigar in *Dr. Strangelove*, Monty Clift's face, in *Freud*, stretched out across the screen like a streaming glob of taffy.

Almost all Milani's new paintings are titled *It's a Pleasure To Serve You*. This refers, I'm told, not to coffee cups from the Greek deli, but to recent press statements from various Reagan administration popinjays who *serve at the pleasure of the president*. The all-purpose title makes sense, since the president lives in a dimly remembered movie, *Knute Rockne* or *Bedtime for Bonzo* (or the one we all remember him in, *The Killers*). But I think Milani would prefer it if we all remembered Monica Vitti in *L'Avventura*, or the miraculously exploding loaf of Wonder Bread in *Zabriskie Point*.

FUTURE PERFECT

And secondly, when Wittgenstein asks, "Who has the concept, 'tomorrow'? Of whom do we say this?" We can suppose that he is questioning the systems of the future imagined by the present. In the projections of science fiction we find the unhappy past thrown forward: future lives dictated by yesterday's capital. For example, a few years ago, a report appeared in the newspaper, to the effect that a government study had found *it was perfectly feasible to extend the human lifespan by 40 years*. And further, that the government commission studying this issue had *recommended against pursuing* the health practices and environmental improvements which would make this possible, since a general prolongation of lives would *wreck the capitalist economy*.

Of course, if we enter this problem on its own terms, we will find ourselves inside an opera by Janáček. Is it even desirable to see the future, if it will only be another version of the past? Can it possibly be different, considering what human beings are? (Jenny Holzer: *The Future Is Stupid*.) Even the Chinese experiment has failed to realize a different future: the march of a thousand miles ends at the door of Bloomingdale's where Pat Nixon is holding a bottle of Coca-Cola and a pair of chopsticks…But maybe art can find a better future in the past.

Collins & Milazzo call their show at Massimo Audiello Gallery (436 East 11th Street, through March 22) "**The Antique Future**." In antiquity, the perceptible world was thought to be an imperfect copy of ideal forms. Matter struggled towards form, which was a substitute for something else. Today, at the other end of history, form and matter have a difficult equilibrium; everything moves in the direction of an ideal, scientific solution to the problem of consciousness, yet at the point of realization a process of decomposition begins, a kind of refusal on the part of life itself. (In mathematics, this happens just beyond the threshold of chaos.) The work in this show exhibits this tension: for instance, in a sled frame mounted on the wall above two geometric panels (Salvatore Scarpitta, *Boom Sled*, 1974), where the structures are wrapped in thickly textured canvas. The sled oval echoes the more streamlined rubber matting that runs through Ti Shan Hsu's *Low Band Width* (1987), in which the industrial form is softened by curved patterns of drizzled paint flowing around it.

Scarpitta's *Boom Sled* could be cross-referenced with certain works by Joseph Beuys. It's partly about cultural artifacts used for survival (embedded in the canvas folds is a tubular form resembling a spear); Ti Shan Hsu's painting engages the kind of stare we focus on television but resolves the image into a more mysterious, implacable site of attention. In the same room, paintings dealing with expressive geometries (Gary Stephan, *The Wall*, 1986; Lucio Pozzi, *Castles in the Air*, 1977; Ross Bleckner, *Untitled*, 1976) are counterpoised against the geometrically paradoxical: a classical *Bust* (1984–86) photographed by the Starn Twins, hyperenlarged to extend over a rough grid of image fragments; the hypothetically endless simulation of a mantle-size Aphrodite by Edward Allington (*Tamed Time/Aphrodite Ad Infinitum*, 1986), ranged on a perfect curve, the series limited (and therefore turned in on itself) by pedestal-shaped boxes at either end; Annette Lemieux's *Sonnet* (1987), an A-frame wooden bookshelf with a rustic decorative molding, in which the book titles, variously stacked, transform the sculpture into a piece of writing.

A shrewd dichotomy has been achieved in the placement of Not Vital's *Einhorn, Zweinhorn, Dreihorn* (1986) and Saint Clair

Cemin's *Untitled* (1987). The first is a white marble sculpture extending upward as a bevel-ended, flat-sided post that terminates in a flamelike mass of black animal horns; the second is a blobbily biomorphic shape sprouting a very exact rectangular metal frame. Aside from their aspect of paradox, these rather stolid pieces speak in different ways of a certain vulnerability—perhaps one could say they work in the threatened area between form and matter, with metaphysical poise (as do the works by Scarpitta and Lemieux, particularly). This is also a characteristic of **Abraham David Christian**'s untitled white sculpture, which looks like marble, or at least plaster, but is actually gessoed paper: a gingerly balanced stack of funnel and diamond shapes with its imaginary weight disguising its fragility.

(Christian's current show at Diane Brown features several more works of this type, along with some startlingly fine works on paper—100 Greene Street, through March 11.)

In **Glenn Branca**'s show, "Classical Space—Forms of Infinite Regress Within a Finite Field" (at Cable Gallery, 611 Broadway, through March 7), the preoccupation with classical form is articulated in a number of large drawings, in this case as a way of picturing sound. Branca's drawings are visual analogs for the division of auditory tones produced in space by a harmonics guitar. This instrument (which Branca invented in 1982) is a flat piece of wood with strings mounted on two sawhorses, displayed in the gallery and playable by the viewer/listener using a glass tube and a guitar pick.

The harmonics guitar produces tones that move simultaneously up and down the harmonic scale. The harmonics are most densely clustered when the extreme ends of the strings are played and become more clearly differentiated as one moves the glass tube from left to right. Many sounds can be heard only by the player.

The distribution of tones can be represented mathematically, and this is what Branca has done, using various numbering systems of Pythagoras and Leibniz (Branca explained most of this to me; if I had had him as a teacher, I might have learned mathematics in school.) Certain lines in his drawings correspond to modes, which are places where the strings of the instrument won't vibrate when it's played. Since the numerical representation of a tone's distribution through space is hypothetically infinite, the corresponding lines or marks, if made within a finite space (a rectangle, say, or along the first line plotted in the series), will begin to generate various forms: waves, triangles, and so on. To put it another way: if you make marks on a piece of paper corresponding to the Fibonacci series, you might begin with a dense cluster that will spread out further and further, using the series of natural numbers: one plus one is two, two plus one is three, three plus two is five, five plus three is eight. *But*, if a limit is set, the markings will begin to double back on themselves, having nowhere else to go. Lines and shapes will become thicker as they fold in on each other.

Depending on his initial choice of how to graph the tone, Branca may arrive at a spiral form, or a set of interdigitating circles (like a Slinky wrapped around itself), or spraying lines; in some of these drawings he has combined two separate graphs, finding that two distinct numbering systems yield points of visual correspondence. Certain pictures suggest microphotography and crystal structures, and it's not a coincidence that these look a lot like the fractal photographs generated on computers. The principle of self-similarity at work in fractal geometry obtains in Branca's graphs, even though what's being plotted is the sound of a musical instrument rather than, strictly, the behavior of numbers. As the tone, or the marks representing the tone, constrict in space, the picture (which is a picture of a number, really) becomes so dense a cluster of marks that it passes through the line of chaos. *But the resulting form* will resemble the original form. Because of their scale, Branca's drawings would be impossibly expensive to do with a computer; they are, in a manner of speaking, handmade technological artifacts. And very beautiful.

March 17, 1987

LIVE WIRE

[**Keith Sonnier.** Nature Morte, 204 East 10th Street, through March 29.]

A head-on approach to Keith Sonnier's work really doesn't appeal to me: a Sonnier piece typically suggests mobility, a free-ranging use of materials and technology that reflects a global perspective. Sonnier's peripatetic sensibility is well known. His works assimilate crafts and symbols indigenous to places he visits (India, Bali, Japan, Brazil), but it clearly belongs to a supertech world where all these places link and movement between them is an everyday procedure.

The only thing that has really dated about the works shown at Nature Morte, all from the middle and late '60s, is the language that was used to describe them in various art magazines of the same period. For example, the word "issue" tended to affix itself to any perceptible surface. You had issues of redness, or issues of fluffiness. There were also issues of influence, and issues of affinity.

And then there were the questions. Questions of luminosity. Questions of coloristic saturation and saturated colorism. The infamous question of gesture. Some of the questions were, simultaneously, issues. If someone in the '60s, for example, *dumped a bucket of paint on the floor*, the question would arise: *is it a painting or sculpture?* But, depending on whether the paint was white or green, an issue of color might arise. And certainly the issue of gesture in this case reared its naughty head.

Today's criticism would probably insist that the dumped bucket is primarily a *critique of our commodified culture* and that dumping it on the floor is an *act of simulation*, the repainted floor being a simulacrum of the previous floor. A different sort of mind might insist that none of these issues or questions matters because *the floor paint is beautiful*. Still another would tell us that dumping a bucket of paint on the floor in 1987 is an ironic historical gloss on the celebrated bucket dump of 1967. And then a grumpier type would asseverate that today's younger artists lack the heroic élan of an earlier generation, that they're a bunch of pansies and candy-asses trying to dump paint buckets with the best of them and failing miserably. (A kind of genteel ladies-club homophobia has lately been heard from a certain female art reviewer known to cohabit exclusively with guys who've got balls of steel, real guys, the ones who can really dump the paint around or push the finished product. No condoms in *their* medicine cabinets.) Even more imperious is the academic who points out that the commodity critique aspect *is actually complicit with the thing it purports to criticize*, that simulation *negates originality*, and *the new floor isn't really beautiful*, or if it is, it's *too beautiful to be great art*.

The most popular question or issue afloat in our day, however, seems to be whether or not a thing is—I'm not entirely sure how to phrase this—*just exactly the right thing for the moment, kind of what you'd expect but somehow new*. An object might come in for heavy criticism, for instance, if other objects using the same materials, or similar imagery, happened to be shown somewhere last month. Though it is unclear what issue or question gets settled by proclaiming something similar to something else, many critics today derive an unwholesome pleasure from telling you what they've seen before that makes something new less new than it thinks it is.

I haven't said a word yet about Keith Sonnier, but since I had to bone up on his work, so to speak, I thought I should vacate some issues raised in the things I read. Certain "younger artists" galleries—specifically, Nature Morte, Jay Gorney Modern Art, International With Monument, Josh Baer, and Cash/Newhouse— have quite intelligently avoided the generational antagonism that characterized the now-defunct E-Ho Neo-Doodyhead Movement, a fact that partly accounts for the critical success of these galleries. Moreover, shows like this one, highlighting work two decades old, help our eyes, removing from vivid objects the encrustations of dated polemic.

I don't mean to suggest there is anything ignoble or particularly wrongheaded about old criticism. Some critical writing ages better than its subject, though that circumstance carries its own peculiar pathos. Mainly, criticism reflects the preoccupations of its era. But one thing criticism unavoidably does: it organizes the Cult of the Name. The Cult of the Name produces a hierarchy of *importance*. In any given year of an old art magazine, you can extract the okay list with no difficulty. Because of the eccentric manner in which art objects circulate, names begin to stand in for them as a kind of shorthand historical sense. Over time, people who saw them forget what things looked like, and people who didn't see them feel like they have.

This can apply to the work of an artist like Sonnier, whose early neon pieces are quite distinct from his later video work, the bamboo sculptures he made in India, his felt-pen drawings of runic inscriptions, and so on: the diversity of Sonnier's activity, his willingness to move on from making one kind of object, has perhaps obscured the rather startling vitality of the '60s neons until now. The drastic economy of design in some works is off-set by their whimsical Dacron veils, the suggestion of a breeze blowing through them. And in a sculpture like *Make-up*, in which green and violet bars of eye-shadowy neon augment an arrangement of skin-thin rubber and a mirror whose bottom half is coated with yellowish "invisible" fluorescent paint (Night-Glo, a familiarly smeary shade of yellow that immediately brings a specific substance in its dried form to mind), we begin to apprehend *content* of a kind that formalism tends to perceive as a figure-ground issue at the best of times.

It's exciting to see "problem materials" like foam rubber, satin, and auto-body filler used with Sonnier's flair for ventilation. John Chamberlain's crashed cars emit the same disregard for what art is supposed to look like and the same certainty about how the object has to be. Sonnier's '60s work has little of the solemnity and heaviness of its equally radical sculptural contemporaries. Like many of Dike Blair's paintings, it carries undertones, sometimes overtones, suggestive of a cocktail lounge in Key West. As I've already indicated, it has an agreeably playful sexuality, rather than the more straightforward, homicidal thrust of conventional Minimalism. This show makes it clear that Sonnier has, in fact, been a seminal influence on a younger generation of artists, not least because this latter "issue" is resolved with exemplary grace in his practice.

March 24, 1987

TRIUMPH OF THE CUTE

[**The Dazzling 1987 New York Flower Show**. Organized by the Horticultural Society of New York. Pier 90, Hudson River and West 50th Street, closed.]

Had you gone to the New York Flower Show last Sunday—The Dazzling 1987 New York Flower Show, as it's called—and again on Tuesday, you would have noticed two striking differences in context worth thinking about in connection with flora and fauna. On Sunday, the high temperature in New York was 76 degrees Fahrenheit. On Tuesday, it was 15. On Sunday, Pier 90's 100,000 square feet of display space was so jammed with visitors that one could hardly breathe, let alone see the exhibits; there wasn't the slightest trace of a fragrance anywhere to be smelled. On Tuesday, a full range of olfactory and visual sensations was available owing to the comparatively thin attendance.

The Flower Show bristled with the kind of contextual nuances and intrinsic absurdities that contemporary art has sensitized us to. This celebration of terrestrial nature was staged in an entirely artificial environment, a building without skylights, flanked on either side by cargo ships docked in the polluted Hudson. The pacific associations of horticulture were jumbled by the close proximity of the aircraft *Intrepid*, its foredeck visible from the ramps of the parking garage. Chief sponsor of the healthful, oxygenating plant life on display was Philip Morris, promoters of self-induced lung cancer, heart disease, emphysema, birth defects, and related illnesses.

During the run of the flower show, Dr. Susan Solomon of the National Oceanic and Atmospheric Administration reported to Congress that the ozone hole over Antarctica may have been caused by chlorofluorocarbons. This principally man-made ozone depletion may have resulted in 83 percent increase of malignant melanoma over the past seven years. Meanwhile, the Vatican has restated its position on birth control and abortion, condemning prenatal diagnostic testing that could lead to the elimination of defective fetuses. *Why* does the temperature zag from 76 to 15 these days? *Why* have we ceased hearing the world "overpopulated" in public discourse, when its effects are so obvious at events like this?

The Horticultural Society of New York is an invaluable resource for our city, maintaining its gardens and encouraging small-scale urban agriculture. But its annual flower show, perhaps necessarily, caters to a public so entirely divorced from the natural world that its main perception of plant life is that flowers and plants are pretty and cute. Many exhibitors pander to the kitsch aesthetic, which detaches the organic object from any ecological context. Visitors learn nothing about our interdependence with plant life, especially in the weekend crush. The flower show could be a propitious occasion to dramatize, for example, the complex ecology of the world's rain forests, which are being destroyed to the tune of fifty million acres a year. Which is probably why the temperature was 76 on Sunday, 15 on Tuesday. (And here, let me recommend Catherine Caufield's comprehensive, heartbreaking account of ecological rape, *In the Rainforest*, University of Chicago Press.)

Aboriginal life in South America will soon disappear, along with the forestlands where it has survived for 10,000 years. Vicious groups such as the New Tribes Mission, serving the interests of American companies such as Teton Exploration and

Mining, forcibly convert the forest-dwelling aborigines to the cult of Jesus Christ, and the ensuing development infects them, often fatally, with measles and influenza. Those who survive are indoctrinated into capitalist exchange and put to work in religious concentration camps. The aboriginal land is then deforested by the logging and mining companies.

Deforestation results in the extinction of whole species of birds, insects, trees, amphibians, mammals, and plants. It satisfies short-term greed and in the long run produces both flooding and drought. And other disasters. The rain forest ecology is densely layered: certain viruses and disease-bearing insects have their natural habitat high in the trees. When the forest is cleared, they find their way down into human populations. The Central African rain forest has been widely destroyed in recent decades, wiping out thousands of species and promoting entirely new diseases among Central Africans. While self-revulsed queens parade around the Vatican in gold lamé gowns and ridiculous headdresses, "the banquet of life" increases in toxicity.

But nothing of this in the empire of simulacra. The effect of an aesthetic view of life, finally, is that fake does as well as real, so long as it's just as pretty. At one gleaming booth at the Flower Show, one could learn how to chop up fruits and arrange the pieces into the shape of a bird or a fish; the same vendor sold a device for making "square eggs." Nearby, decorative structures for the home garden featured stuffed birds, with spread wings, dangling from wires.

One passed numerous ideal environments redolent of suburban affluence. A gazebo, with embroidered cushions plumped just-so along its seat; a garden where flora of all seasons bloomed simultaneously, with twin cupids embracing atop a marble pedestal. Tri-State Gunite/Landscaping offered a riot of leafiness ranged around what proved to be, on close inspection, an orange hot tub. I found myself trailing a group of artificial-dogwood bearing young people; the Dogwood Parade invariably stopped to admire the video monitors ubiquitously embedded in the sometimes organic, sometimes artificial vegetation.

While the displays by the large nurseries attempted an atmosphere of Connecticut gentility—the calmly planted, fastidiously tended profusion of bloom, so often resembling the set of a morning talk show—many marketplace stalls proletarianized the Joy of Gardening, dispensing bits of nature as knickknacks: teen cacti, souvenir annuals, the ominously named Iron Cross Begonia, treated with "Nature's Miracle" (a liquid fertilizer). Another miracle consisted of white, soapy-smelling beads in stapled plastic bags: the little sign read "Plant Essence in a Can." (In simulacraland, "can" and "bag" interchangeably signify "package.") From the Golden Leaves of America, you could buy for $5.00, "any 24K Gold dipped REAL leaf, shell, or other object from Nature."

The fate of many plants sold at the flower show must certainly resemble that of those hapless baby alligators who died slow, painful deaths in the terrariums of Florida tourists in the '50s. But in America, we don't feature the concept of animals feeling pain, or the idea that vegetation has a natural habitat developed over centuries. We have pseudotopiary, such as ivy grown over the form of a stuffed bear holding a tambourine. We have Macy's, which installed two adorable, gigantic bunnies and a huge flower-painted Easter egg with a TV set in the center. We have stuffed birds that never die and square egg sandwiches, real nature-objects dipped in 24K gold, summer in the morning and winter in the afternoon. And skin cancer. Let's face it. We've got cute.

March 31, 1987

CHRONICLE IN BLACK & WHITE

Today there were people screaming at each other in the street outside the office. A van had plowed into a cab. There was a mother with a baby in the cab and I guess the father was the one screaming at the driver of the van. I took a walk. I saw a girl I know punching a tall guy, maybe her boyfriend. Her boyfriend had a rolled-up newspaper and every now and then he slapped her with it. Yesterday was St. Patrick's Day. I went uptown to see **Christopher Wool**'s paintings at Luhring, Augustine and Hodes (41 East 57th Street, through April 4).

These paintings are panel-sized, white on black; some look like millions of dripped dots and others look like wallpaper. The drippy ones have strangely regular surfaces, like cell clusters under a microscope or stars on a very clear night in the country. The enamel paint makes a glossy flatness against the metal ground. The wallpaper pictures have monotonous leaf and flower patterns interrupted by glitches of white paint. These were made with a special roller that slum landlords use to make hallways look wallpapered. You just put color on and roll it across. So these paintings, using only black and white, are like bleached-out walls in some severely depressed neighborhood. Samples of etiolated interiors. Then there's a gleaming all-black painting that catches flecks of light when you move in front of it.

I felt slightly dizzy looking at these things close-up. They offer nothing to hold on to, yet they're full, like a noise penetrating your brain and driving out your thoughts. Because of the metallic surfaces they have the physical aura of machinery or architecture. They echo the surfaces that ribbon past from a taxi or a subway window, the smooth glass and polished steel of the city world—but more condensed, pressurized into a heavy portable object. Their decorative qualities are deceptions. The eye doesn't linger in one place or rove over them registering choice bits, but locks into contact with the surface and freezes into a numbed stare. They exercise an almost hideous power, like real mirrors of existence. Perhaps they are Zen objects, surfaces that absorb the spectator into nothingness, enamel rock gardens without rocks.

In the streets, many people were wearing green. An acidic green, louder than the red of a clown's nose. Some wore green pants. Others had green hats, or green carnations in their lapels. A man selling green balloons wore a button that said, KISS ME, I'M IRISH. I went downtown and hid from all this Irishness at a matinee of *Angel Heart*, then saw **Marilyn Lerner**'s show at John Good Gallery (39 Great Jones Street, through April 4).

It's strange to find your taste accommodating things for reasons you don't understand. I know why I like some of Christopher Wool's paintings, but I don't know why I like *Angel Heart* or Marilyn Lerner's work. On what's probably the negative side, Lerner's paintings have an historicist rectitude, a polished self-control that's the astuteness of a disciplined painter: no high-wire leaps or calculated badness, just virtuosity. Which one mistrusts, perhaps, for good reasons. You can look at these pictures and see Popova and Lissitzky and Elizabeth Murray, and feel a fairly tight schematic enclosing Lerner's activity. The lyricism of the titles—*Stargazer, Azimuth Circles, Floating Garden, Spirit Catcher*—shows a traditional abstractionist's hermeticism. The juggling of curves, whorls, and rectangular swatches on canvases shaped like targets and surfboards, with thickly impastoed surface areas, poses and resolves familiar formal puzzles.

But given the formal limits Lerner has set herself, it's surprising how *unlike* other things her paintings seem to be, after the first wave of associations recedes. The spatial tricks accomplished with sweeping gradations of black-to-white, the radical balancing of fractured volumes, the intricate black-and-white reductions of Constructivism's full palette: painterly numbers, yes, but difficult, well-considered ones. They have a brittle sort of poetry, like Christopher Lucas's increasingly weird paintings on warped wood. I confess, though, that none of the above is what I like about these pictures; this is only a language ready-made to describe them. I came out of the movies and walked into a gallery without a thought in my head except "avoid McSorley's on your way home." This is the story of that sort of day. *Angel Heart* is the kind of movie I hardly ever enjoy and these are the kind of paintings I often blank out in front of. They surprised me. Being surprised in New York is almost never pleasant, but this was.

April 7, 1987

NEGATIVE SUBLIME REVISITED

[**Philip Taaffe**. Pat Hearn Gallery, 735 East 9th Street, through April 12.]

The *sublime* was the topic of a special *Arts Magazine* section last March. Philip Taaffe contributed a brief essay, discussing Barnett Newman and "a sublime of dissociation, a Great Refusal of the Sublime." According to the dictionary, *sublime* is an adjective: "a. lofty, grand, or exalted in thought, expression, or manner. b. of outstanding spiritual, intellectual, or moral worth. c. tending to inspire awe usu. because of elevated quality (as of beauty, nobility, or grandeur) or transcendent excellence." *Sublime* can also be a verb: "to cause to pass directly from the solid to the vapor state and condense back to solid form."

There is usually much to be said in favor of refusing *the sublime*. There are those, for example, who think of sublimity as a dimension of spiritual superiority of certain souls over others. The discourse of sublimity, in the context of capitalism, comes attached to the notion of extraterrestrial values. "Grand," "exalted," "elevated," and "transcendent" are words that don't simply raise works of the art-making enterprise to a place far above life itself. To acknowledge *the sublime*, we should be ready to say that the pleasure we get from art is altogether different than the pleasure of a well-crafted risotto, the pleasure of sex (as opposed to Love), or the pleasure of watching Anita Ekberg in *La Dolce Vita*. But is this true? Do we have special organs for digesting art, that never brush against others?

We can live without certain foods, but we can't live without eating. We may need art in our lives, but only a certain kind of art participates in the concept of *the sublime*. From "nobility" and "grandeur" it's a short step to heroic *size*, heroic *scale*, and occult notions of value. Meanings devised by an arbitrary consensus give the mark of eternity to an object; the object enters the realm of inexorable market forces under an umbrella of sainthood. However, a different deployment of *the sublime* can be detected in very private ideas about *justice*. In the art world, one frequently encounters a ruined version of sublimity that goes like this: It's unfair that some things *make money* when others don't. Artists should be idealists, spurning the blandishments of material success. Those who don't are merely *commercial strategists*.

I mention this in connection with Philip Taaffe only because he's one of several contemporary artists who regularly gets mauled in the art press for successfully going about his business. This morning, a request for an article from a Dutch magazine arrived, which reads in part: *More and more artists are employing market strategies to become a success in the marketplace. Especially in New York (Koons, Vaisman, Taaffe, Steinbach, etc.)...a pragmatic tendency is strongly perceptible: artists are carefully directing their careers. In some cases the success in the market seems to be an end in itself.* To which, I suppose, the *sublime*-minded aesthete can only reply, Really? Gee whiz! What a bunch of whores! Reading on, however, one arrives at the proverbial bottom line: *As for our commercial strategies: needless to say we are just a miserable magazine with great prestige.... We cannot pay our writers, to be short. We can imagine though you get a little tired of this art-world virus of not paying writers. We are not happy with it either, but...*

The *sublime* writer, then, must be the writer who *donates* his work. And the *sublime* artist labors away in obscurity, penniless, until some blessed day in his or her old age when the greatness of his/her effort is discovered. Here the concept of *the sublime* merges with the delusion of life after death. You get your reward when you're no longer around to claim it. The cult of lifelong suffering that exists around these ideas is plainly out of whack with current reality—quite enough suffering goes along with daily life without taking a vow of voluntary poverty—but it seems to hold tremendous charm for those who participate in it vicariously, at arm's length.

The language of *the sublime* has been thoroughly co-opted by those cultural powers that ensure, at the apex of artistic mastery, a full complement of *white heterosexual males*. We should distrust "great," we should look askance at "major," and definitely bristle at the word "important." Whenever these terms appear we should ask, "According to whom? According to what?" If we're honest about *the sublime*, its true associations are ravishment and obduracy, conquest, the implemental use of fear. The *sublime* is an especially phallic use of aesthetic power. One simultaneously enjoys it and deplores it.

For Philip Taaffe, I will substitute the verb *sublime* for the adjective. In his earlier work, Taaffe appropriated the design structures of earlier art and passed them through the mangle of his own techniques. What looks from a distance like a Bridget Riley or a Barnett Newman is in fact a kind of viral mimesis, an obsessively reconstituted look with an entirely different physicality. For the cool of Riley's flat pictures, Taaffe substitutes the heat of laboriously self-effacing thickness. In place of Newman's purist zips, Taaffe puts wittily figurative ropes.

Like other closely approximate art "copies," Taaffe's ruminate upon an insoluble linguistic problem: no two things can be genuinely identical, unless they occupy the same space, in which case they are one thing. This picture cannot have *the same* color as that one, since this color is over here, and that color is over there. The problem is, more importantly, also an historical one. The copy is not the original, but something else; the original itself becomes something else when viewed through the lens of a later time.

Taaffe's appropriations or simulations could be said to have caused the art they refer to "to pass from the solid to the vapor state and condense back to solid form." His pictures of other pictures bring them out on the other side of modernism, holding them up to the light of historical inquiry. The timeless *sublime* anchoring Taaffe's models shrinks down to a set of parentheses. The relevant questions become, What does this object look like now, and what does it mean now? Or, what does an object that looks like it look like now?

This procedure has admitted patricidal/matricidal implications. Like Sherrie Levine, Taaffe has paid gently murderous homage to what he admires, working his way towards an originality his previous work seems to refuse. I say "seems" because what's visually unoriginal can claim originality by winning a fresh context for itself, or by undermining the established criteria of originality—this has been proven repeatedly by the contemporary *antisublime*. Taaffe's new work, like Levine's recent stripe paintings, leads away from historical reconstruction and operates in a freer zone. One finds in these pictures Taaffe's usual, ironic references to the past—but the latter occur in a fragmentary state, with swatches of Action Painting and Twombly-like scribbles, Color Field and hard-edge abstraction included as "samples" within complex designs, sometimes on shaped canvases.

Taaffe prints bits of "style" on repeating paper forms and arranges them in regular patterns; the kind of brushwork or marking that connotes spontaneity thereby becomes a token, or pendant, acknowledged as one among many elements rather than the whole thing. Interestingly, several of his new works have an overall symmetry, or near-symmetry, that suggests alternative methods of hanging. *Rosette*, an enormous circular work based on a stained-glass window design, will look the same however it's turned. *Acrab*, with five clusters of macaroni-shaped curves, can be hung by any edge. Taaffe's use of symmetry gives these works a deceptively open-ended quality, an imaginary lightness. Despite the evident playfulness of his compositions, Taaffe is the kind of artist bent on total control of his material, and his work can be airless when it isn't energetically inventive. But it usually is. If George Condo is the Godard of the painted canvas, Philip Taaffe is its Alfred Hitchcock, and possibly its Bresson.

April 14, 1987

FUTURISMS:

A CONVERSATION WITH PETER NAGY

[**Peter Nagy**. International With Monument, 111 East 7th Street, through May 16.]

Peter Nagy's work conflates art with other elements in the environment: electronics, mass-produced consumer products, commercial design. By implication, Nagy erases the boundaries between the utilitarian and the purely aesthetic. Underscoring the notion of the *replica* as a central factor in contemporary perception, much of his early work was produced in Xerox form. A recent series of black-and-white paintings depicts hyperenlarged cancer cells, commercial logos, and technological objects. His latest works in aluminum reflect his fascination with the proliferating design forms that crowd the urban environment. The following interview took place in a Japanese restaurant.

Peter Nagy: There are three ideas in the show. The first is that there's all this doubling going on. You have objects made out of steel, and they're etched in the metal. So it's also like a bomb blast, like after Hiroshima, where people's shadows were imprinted on walls. You have doubling there, but then, each picture's a hybrid, two-part thing. Satellites are double satellites, antennas are doubly antennas, lights are double lights. There's a double doubling going on. So then it's about how all these objects are abstracted through overdesign and engineering, the Bauhaus gone berserk. Like the lady's hand holding the building, but it could be a vibrator, or high-tech salt and pepper shakers, or an electric razor. Everything's amorphous and ambiguous. You don't know what it is any more.

Gary Indiana: *Some are reliefs and some are flat. The reliefs are—what is that process?*

The reliefs are photo-etched magnesium, the way you'd make an old-fashioned etching plate. I never did that kind of printmaking, so it was new to me. The big ones are sandblasted aluminum, the little ones are done photographically. For the big ones I gave them pictures, stencils were cut, and they sandblasted around the stencils.

So it's all one piece of aluminum, basically.

Yes, held by an aluminum frame.

What's the third idea?

Oh! The third idea is that there's always a place for the human being, and there's human scale. But that's the most abstracted, because, for example, in the gun picture, the human goes in a car, which is where the bullet should be. There's still this place for humans in regard to all these overdesigned products we're surrounded by. But that place is all over the place. It's infinite at one moment, microscopic at the next. Half the time we're like completely amorphous amoebas in this maze of fabrication.

Maybe everything will be like that from now on.

It already is. It's not like that for me 100 percent of the time, but it seems like those things like the semi-vibrator-electric-shaver are so similar to works of art—to how, for instance, a Jeff Koons functions. You're not really sure what it is.

Where did you find the designs?

I wrote lists of the objects I wanted and then went to technical manuals and found them, played with them.

So they take photographs of the illustrations?

Of the pictures I made from them, the Xeroxes. Nobody will see those black-and-white Xeroxes, these images won't work that way. These pictures really have to be metal, they're all about the metal they're in. The last cancer paintings were about the condition of cancer; and this body of work is more about the fact that, trying to cure my father of cancer, they injected him with gold and platinum. Which I thought, they inject you with the most precious thing in the world to try to cure you from this scourge, you know? So science becomes alchemy again.

I've never heard of that.

Gold has become quite common, platinum is experimental now. For the brain, too. I think platinum is important, for brain cancer.

So these paintings—well, they're not paintings, but…

I started looking at them at one point and they looked like the Gerhard Richter gray monochromes, when the light hits them a certain way they're nothing, the flat ones.

The works have some relation to Paolozzi.

The construction of the image is really Picabia-esque, too. It's more a result of reading design magazines and looking at furniture and architecture books. I sort of wish it was more about disease.

Everything's about disease now.

It seems that what man tries to do is stop the disease by making metal things, or something. We took the works to this hospital in Long Island City; we took the gun one, it was hanging in an operating room. And I thought, people had come into this room having bullets taken out of them, but also after being in car crashes.

I think the work is related to Paolozzi just in his relationship to J.G. Ballard, and that whole science fiction/Pop Art interface. The way the banal object changed from Surrealism to Pop Art; the way it lost a lot of psychology in the process. That's why the Nouveaux Réalistes like Spoerri were so important, they made that moment obvious. Because the Surrealists knew what they could get out of the banal, really tapped the banal and used it for all these mystical things. But at a certain point the banal didn't signify all the mystical stuff. It became concrete.

What are some of those objects, again?

Antennas, stethoscopes, watchbands, guns, cathode ray tubes, gears, lighting fixtures, satellites, space hardware—lots of information-gathering electronics.

So it's a collapse of all the technology.

That's the nature of technology, it's not like I had to collapse it.

I told you about these collectors, they talk about Baudrillard now. They were trying to make the point that, "When we go to Florida, yes, it seems entirely simulated, because people don't get out of their cars, they don't really interact. Whereas here in New York, no no no, we're not entirely simulated, because just walking over here, we met a man that has dogs, and we talked to him about the dogs, and he really made an impact on us, but we'll never see him again, and that doesn't happen anywhere else."

But the very fact that they'll never see him again is also...

...completely simulated. They act as if, just because they met a man on the street, and it actually had the appearance of a real-life, one-to-one encounter, that...that's what it was, authentic somehow. I didn't go into it with them. They think talking to people, meeting people...I don't think it has to do with that at all, it's the fact that we're all so displaced anyway. People don't really want to see each other.

Too true.

It is a sign of the times, that collectors talk about Baudrillard.

That was a good discovery for the art world, though a lot of Baudrillard is simply restatement of things that have been around a long time.

But sometimes those ideas are still valuable because they're realized visually rather than linguistically. It's interesting and valuable to see that the same things can be said visually that people always connected with writing. There's some excitement in that.

I've been reading about the new phones. What I like is that "call blocking" will be the most sought-after feature to get on your phone, call stoppage. The phone is going to tell people, "Your call will not be accepted at this time."

The phone will tell them?

The phone will tell them you're blocking their call.

Great. So it's a Freudian thing. "You're blocking." The technology will externalize your hang-ups. It's really quite a Utopia, when you think about it. What more could you hope for? Everything will be externalized, bureaucratized…Collins and Milazzo's new thing is radical consumption. That's really good, I think. What else is left to us?

The government will try to figure out if you're a good consumer. I used to think junkies were the ideal consumers, because they reduce everything to one commodity.

That's true. I find I'm splintering into even more of a schizophrenic because my consumption, my *avarice* for consumption takes place on so many different levels simultaneously. You're not happy eating the food unless you've got the magazines on your lap. Someone called me "The Raging Aesthete."

April 28, 1987

ANOTHER REVIEW OF THE WHITNEY

I had only been writing for the *Voice* a few weeks when the last Whitney Biennial unleashed itself upon a weary world. It was obvious that covering the Whitney was part of the game of writing art criticism and I did not intend to play that game the way other people did. If everyone was going to say something about the Whitney, why should I? Everyone said basically the same thing then, with varying degrees of vehemence. And everyone will probably say the same thing this time, in various registers of approval. The show is good, a vast improvement in taste and a real leap in seriousness. But since occasions like this are all about never being satisfied with anything, even people at the Whitney don't feel comfortable. One person who works there told me they were getting worried about all the good reviews. They're afraid fewer people will come if the show isn't a public outrage.

Well, how could I possibly give it a *bad* review, since a great deal of the work in this year's Biennial was first written about in my column? On the other hand, I have a horror of repeating myself because writers repeat themselves endlessly without even being aware of it, so the very worst thing is to *consciously* repeat oneself. Since the Whitney has been so gracious to me by confirming my own taste, I will try to oblige the Whitney with at least a *mixed* review, to help draw in those who are attracted only by horror. The reader will have to excuse me for resorting to the irritating *Voice*-writer device of referring to things I wrote in the past. As a saving grace, I do not have these old columns right here in front of me and only remember them vaguely.

The lighting on Ross Bleckner's Oceans *is not sufficiently even for the viewer to read the undertext.* This is really inexcusable, a public abomination. Whoever lit this corner of the room should be fired immediately. Has any museum, anywhere in the world, ever displayed such indifference to the grandeur of a masterpiece? Have standards really sunk as low as this?

I really *don't like Alan Saret's fuzzy wire sculptures.* These things look like pubic hair from outer space or some sort of horrible growth on the floor. This is yet another demonstration of the Whitney's arrogance, its glacial indifference to what the public wants. Yes, once again, the Whitney descends to frivolousness for lack of anything better to do.

Who the fuck is David Bates? Some sort of lumberjack Max Beckmann, I assume. Is this some not-very-subtle attempt on the part of the Whitney to sneak in the kind of *Expressionism* we're all so sick of we could throw up? Or what? My hair stood on end when I saw this stuff, and I had just paid $80 to have it done.

Judy Pfaff. Dated beyond belief. I can't believe they put her thing in the same room with Barbara Kruger and Jeff Koons. I mean it just *takes over* the whole place. The Krugers are big enough to hold their own but the Koons tanks really suffer. Another example of the Whitney's ineptitude at installation.

Julian Schnabel. Ugh. Don't you just hate him? What's all this "Mimi" business with the cattle horns sticking out of it? And that little pennant with "Virtue" printed on it hanging in the middle of that huge brown canvas? I don't get it, *at all.*

Ed Ruscha and Richard Prince. This was a good idea, the two of them together, but then the Whitney, with its typical flair for the obvious, sticks in two Neil Jenneys, one of them not even slightly interesting, the other one *too* obvious.

Donald Sultan. Yech. Give it up. Go home.

Louise Fishman. Oh, *really.*

The two Willem de Koonings in the same area with Joseph Kosuth's cancelled-out-text hallway and three magnificent George Condo paintings. De Kooning has really hit rock bottom with these vapid linear fantasies, one in blue, the other in red. Leave it to the Whitney to choose an American master at the very moment he hits the skids.

Nam June Paik's two robotic sculptures of antique TV and radio sets with video monitors set into them. I can't tell you how much I resent the Whitney for making these pieces look interesting when I said very clearly they were *silly* when I reviewed his show at Holly Solomon.

The Starn Twins. See? I *told* you they were fabulous artists, and at least one deeply embittered ceramist who also poses as an art critic quoted what I wrote as an example of *hype.* Well, phooey on him.

Annette Lemieux. See? I *told* you she was what Estelle Schwartz calls "majah," not in the *Voice* but in *Art in America,* which is just as good. I hope she remembers once she's rich and famous that I was the one who put her there.

Bruce Weber should not be in the same room with Ross Bleckner and Annette Lemieux. He should have his own room. It should be in New Jersey. An all-too-predictable Whitney lapse in taste. This photograph is obviously stranded at Studio 54, circa 1975. If he were a real artist he would've pasted paper bags over the model's faces.

Robert Greene. At first you think he belongs in the same room with David Bates but anyone silly enough to paint all those poodles and collies is an artist to watch. Was the Whitney's decision to put him together with David Bates a deliberate conspiracy to make his work look less interesting? I wouldn't be surprised.

Robert Ryman really got the Whitney shaft this time. Three of his works are crowded together on one wall and everyone knows that each one needs its own wall for the viewer to *get the point.*

But what can you expect from an organization that has a committee hang a show instead of a single, focused sensibility? I can't tell you how heartbreaking it is to a critic to see an important artist treated in this shabby manner. It depressed me for three days. I even contemplated suicide. Not my own, fortunately.

Jim Lutes's three paintings in the room with Nam June Paik, and putting Philip Taaffe together with Roberto Juarez. It's refreshing to see that the Whitney got a couple of original ideas without elaborate help from me. But don't forget that I wrote a catalogue for Roberto Juarez last year and my column on Philip Taaffe *came out the week before the Biennial opened.* It wouldn't surprise me to learn that I'd written something on Jim Lutes without being aware of it.

Robert Helm. Another artist seemingly redeemed by his fondness for dogs. Except the dog in his painting *Night Window* happens to be a pit bull, the most vicious and unnecessary breed of dog the world has ever known. Leave it to the Whitney to conflate a noble dog like the collie with a vulgar dog like the pit bull. I was repelled by Helm's dog, but not surprised. Helm's pit bull, like David Bates's lumberjack, is a thinly disguised metaphor for the *Expressionism* secretly adored by the Whitney curators, don't you think?

Tina Barney's large color Cibachromes of upper-middle-class families in their gracious homes. I won't say whoever picked these things out should be shot because I am opposed to capital punishment, but here the Whitney has, in its usual manner, gone too far. Even the announcement for the Guerrilla Girls' alternative Biennial at the Clocktower has more going for it than this. But then again, Tina Barney is probably what the Guerrilla Girls would want the Whitney to fill the Biennial with.

Richard Artschwager. Not his best work.

David McDermott and Peter McGough's painting "A Friend of Dorothy." Should have been on the cover of the catalogue.

May 5, 1987

I'LL BE YOUR MIRROR

A thorny, twisty subject: Andy Warhol. The Andy Warhol Phenomenon. The vacant but obdurate public presence—relentless, in fact—famed from the outset for its entourage. At first the entourage consisted of amiable lunatics, charmingly damaged heiresses, beautiful street boys, miraculously loquacious speed freaks, fallen Catholics, people with a flair for "suggesting ideas." Later the shimmering mask surrounded itself with buttoned-down professionals, social climbers, dewy millionettes. Since the new people risked nothing, and felt nothing much about anything, they provided few ideas. The product lost its quality of selective inanity. It became an example of surplus vacuity. The Presence no longer wondered at his inability to feel.

Then the death. The private duty nurse, who sounds like someone who might have changed her name from Valerie Solanas. And the incredible obsequies. Years ago, Taylor Mead told me that Andy's problem was that he wasn't content with being a genius, he wanted to be a saint, too. And so, the speakers at his memorial service stressed his unflagging Christian spirit, his charity. How he multiplied the loaves and fishes. One speaker made the curious argument for sainthood: it wasn't for Andy to be his brother's keeper. The understatement of the century, surely. As further proof of Andy's intense spirituality, his eulogist quoted the line about wanting to be reincarnated as the ring on Liz Taylor's finger. Clearly, Catholicism is exactly what it used to be.

One former superstar put it quite succinctly: "I'm going to Andy's funeral, but I doubt if he would go to mine." Outliving Andy must be, for some, a surprise. As usual, excellent timing. The culture was becoming weary of Andy Warhol. The inanities had ceased to charm, having reached brutal apotheosis with the picture book *America*. Lately, Andy had resorted to flirtation.

Although his influence is pervasive in the best contemporary art, the best contemporary artists were having none of him. The inspired, breathtakingly easy Duchampian gesture can only come off against a background of resistance, of entrenched tradition. When it works today, the background it works against is precisely the seduction of the glamorous surface. Richard Prince had already inverted Andy's best-known, most-misquoted maxim. In the future, no one will want to be famous. A nice twist on Dorothy Parker's line: "If you want to know what God thinks about money, just look at the people he gives it to."

"Either wear a work of art or be a work of art," said Oscar Wilde, an aesthete with an attractively messy private life. Andy Warhol became a much less convincing work of art after the demimonde clasped him to its jeweled bosom. His eerie gift, until then, had been the ability to confer celebrity—on a soup can, a Port Authority rent boy, or a whacked-out socialite. The Factory was a church. The Church of the Unimaginable Penis, or something. Andy was the father confessor, the kids were the sinners. Which is why he didn't need to be involved with them when they finished confessing. The sanctity of the institution and its rituals is what's important, not personal salvation. Maintaining the eternal surface.

After turning his back on the zanies who'd been his inspiration, Warhol no longer bestowed celebrity, but instead sustained his own through increasingly ludicrous associations, chiefly through his magazine, *Interview*. The upscale *Interview* chewed its way through acres of glossy trash at Studio 54 before arriving among such "interesting" people as George Will, Nancy Reagan, Jerry Zipkin, and the Shah of Iran. Whatever Wahol was trying to do, it didn't "read" as anything except venality.

For example, the I'll-paint-anybody-for-$20,000 approach. Art critics committed to the myth of Warhol-as-bellwether suggest that Warhol has simply done the same thing Goya did, or other court painters in the past. But an artist of Warhol's affluence isn't faced with starvation if he turns down a commission, say, from Idi Amin, or the Sultan of Brunei. Contrary to the Warhol philosophy, modern life still does require choices. Quite a few people with money wouldn't piss on Nancy Reagan if her guts were on fire, and many of them commission portraits. At any rate, the "court paintings" are Andy's weakest work— unless you look at them a certain way, and think their very lack of depth tells you something about their subjects.

They're bad as paintings. This is of less concern than the fact that they're bad as images. One of the usual objections to Warhol's paintings is that he's not a "painterly painter" in the traditional sense. People who cling to this kind of distinction miss the point that Warhol, long ago, brilliantly made about mass culture. Robert Hughes, for example. Hughes's essay, "The Rise and Fall of Andy Warhol," is one of those luminously nasty pieces of writing that clears the air of accumulated piety. But to ignore the importance of Warhol's art, especially in the '60s, simply because it isn't *arduous* the way a Francis Bacon is, negates almost every worthwhile development in art in the past 20 years. Painting and image-making are sometimes the same thing, and sometimes are quite distinct. The emphasis can be here, or there. They don't have to have a hierarchical relationship. Hughes seems to believe that some aesthetic utopia existed in the past, a utopia that art will return to after the current, doleful period. Many people think this way. Warhol understood something hateful but true: we aren't going to lose the past in quite the same way as before. And we're not going to find it again, either.

Nothing Andy ever said was true, but that is beside the point. There are less cogent objections to Warhol than Hughes's, less respectable ones. Sometimes they're mixed up with valid ones. Homophobia was one of the first reactions to Warhol, especially from the Cedar Tavern set, the Abstract Expressionists. You could be a fag back then, like Frank O'Hara, as long as you could pass, and understood you were supposed to suffer over it, lusting after those *real guys* painting their heroic, tortured canvases. Andy was a swish.

A swish was somebody who couldn't hide it. It was just the way you were. Something from the '40s and '50s and before, when gays were either butch or femme. You find less and less of this when sexual role models disintegrate, as they did in the '60s and early '70s. Andy wrote somewhere that he exaggerated his swishiness, because it wasn't something he thought he should change.

One of the most liberating experiences of my life was seeing *Bike Boy* at a theater in Cambridge. I was with some ultrastraight but *sensitive*, tolerant Harvard boys who froze in horror after the first two minutes. Viva was in a bathtub with a man, telling him if he wanted to make plastic sculptures he should just do it and shut up about it. "We're into other things, now," she whined. As I watched this film I thought: "That's for me."

It's bizarre that Warhol's films have been out of circulation for so long. Or perhaps not so bizarre. When Warhol said, in his last interview, that the films "are better talked about than seen," it occurred to me that a certain crust of the haute monde might have been less welcoming to Andy if it had been exposed to his movies. Which, I believe, compose his richest body of work. Who will ever forget Ondine, with his face buried in Joe Dallesandro's underpants, in *Loves of Ondine*? Or Ingrid Superstar's recipe recitation in *Bike Boy*? The draft dodger's soliloquy, or Viva's epic monologue, in *Nude Restaurant*? Taylor Mead scampering about in *Lonesome Cowboys*: "Oh you jingle, and you jangle, but you seldom wrangle…" I haven't seen those films in 20 years, and I remember every frame. I've already forgotten *E. T.*

Warhol's films are gloriously erotic, as sculpture is erotic. They're honest. Pornography—which every American should enjoy at least as much as having Edwin Meese for an attorney general—is dishonest. Perfect faces on perfect bodies do not blissfully couple without any problems, in real life; they only do that in California. When Ondine's about to get into Little Joe's BVDs, the bathroom door flies open and in walks Brigid Polk, demanding to know what that cheap little hustler is doing with her husband. Sexual pleasure is immanent in the Warhol movies, a possibility; but pornographic fulfillment is always shown as a deluded ambition. Real people are too complicated.

We should be wary about praise and damnation of Andy. He helped open thousands of closet doors. If the things he lent himself to in recent years fill me with distaste, I still admire the frosty slap he gave America before he became America's favorite vanity mirror. One should especially mistrust portraits like the concoction in *Edie*, a book compiled by George Plimpton and Jean Stein—surely two of the most privileged individuals in America, born with silver spoons, and zealous defenders of their class. Andy was a working boy. He worked hard, he made his money, they buried him with the blessings of his church. A saint for all the wrong reasons. And isn't that what America is all about?

May 12, 1987

HOT DOGG

[**John Dogg**. 303 Gallery, 513 East 6th Street, through May 17; American Fine Arts, 511 East 6th Street, through May 17.]

One of the most beguiling and questionable contemporary aesthetic procedures involves the transformation of the exchange value of the commodity object. The much-cited, primary example of this procedure is Duchamp's urinal, signed "R. Mutt," exhibited upside-down on a pedestal and titled *Fountain*. The Duchamp work has long been considered, by some, a nihilistic gesture against so-called high culture and its inscription throughout a network of institutions. Another view of the object recommends that we sensitize ourselves to the beauty of supposedly base, utilitarian objects. A third, and perhaps more complicated, problem raised by *Fountain* is the relatively slight degree of artistic involvement in the object's fabrication.

Works like *Fountain* spur indignation among those who conceptualize art-making in terms of physical labor. Perhaps what's most commonly ignored by the spectator and/or critic of art is the variousness of artistic labor. We call a piece of art a *work*, implicitly endorsing a scheme of value in which a product exemplifies quality, when its manufacture consumes either time or energy, or both. Even though the crude form of this expectation was dismissed in the latter part of the 19th century, Romantic notions of what constitutes art *work* continue to inform opinion, especially among those who would seem least likely to credit those notions.

Because the value of art is notoriously slippery, forms of work analogous to those prevailing elsewhere in the economy enjoy the most unequivocal reification even when the results are insipid. This is why Andrew Wyeth remains America's favorite artist. The trucker, the sanitation engineer, the Air Force pilot and the corporate lawyer can all behold a Wyeth and see that it took a great deal of time and effort to produce. Yet it is Wyeth, rather than Duchamp, who should inspire the Protestant query: *Yes, but is it art?* If we consider art in terms of effect rather than labor, *Fountain* is to art what the microchip is to the abacus. Its efficiency can be compared to that of the Exocet missile or the atom bomb. The true application of relativity to labor consists in gaining the greatest effect with the least expenditure.

In this regard, the mysterious John Dogg, direct descendant of R. Mutt, has outstripped his contemporaries, the estimable Jeff Koons and the sometimes trite, sometimes sweetly inspired mega-consumer Haim Steinbach. Dogg's (disputed) bio claims he was born in Los Angeles in 1952, educated "in painting and philosophy" at the University of Minnesota, and, before exploding (or imploding) upon the art scene in New York, took part in such arcane events as "The Laundry Show" in Minneapolis, during the summer of 1983. Dogg is rumored to have "participated in a number of land art projects in Minnesota and Nevada, 1980–1982," though Dogg's present dealers deny each item of this résumé.

The identity of Dogg, whose splendid show of automobile tires in open-faced wooden boxes last year animated instant critical attention, remains heavily veiled. In his debut show, Dogg combined the breathtaking purity of the Judd box structure with the equally rigorous, but Goodyear-manufactured, structure of the rubber tire. By enclosing the latter within the former, Dogg resolved the tension between rarefied and mass culture in favor of the former without resorting to the baroque display techniques of a Steinbach or the physics-lab gimmicks of a Koons. Dogg's boxes exemplify the rigorous classical forms, the circle and the square, with truly ingenious economy. But just as interesting, perhaps, is Dogg's aloofness from an art world rabid with the quest for celebrity, his refusal to grant interviews or be photographed, his insistence on the primary importance of his art rather than his personality. Compare Dogg's reticence with the vulgar media-posturings of an Ashley Bickerton or the Barnum-like Pataphysical stance of a Peter Halley: one can only conclude that Dogg's personality, even though it is nonexistent, has greater appeal than theirs. Dogg's art speaks for itself, emphatically, while Dogg remains tactfully hidden behind it.

In his quietly subversive way, Dogg has done it again this month, at adjacent galleries whose owners are fiercely protective of the Howard Hughes-like virtuoso's privacy. This is one two-gallery show where the work evenly commands both spaces, with neither clutter nor excessive sparsity. At American Fine Arts, a series of tire drums ranges along the walls, broken into sets and discrete pieces. At 303 Gallery, similarly fashioned works interact rather differently, for example in *Ulysses*, where two tire drums or covers face each other from opposite walls, one engraved with the word *DOGG*, the other with the word *GGOD*.

Variations within a standard, circular volume operate in Dogg's work rather the way audio loops function in the work of the brilliant English composer Gavin Bryars. While the basic form, in most cases, is a stainless steel casting with thin rubber gaskets that locks at the base, the convex facing has been coated or covered differently, sometimes with greenish-gray primer, as in *Twin CR-10s*; *Pony* has mottled cowhide, while *John Not Johnny* sparkles with blue-green metal flake behind the black-enamel scripted word *John*. (*John*, of course, is both the artist's first name and a slang word for toilet, or urinal.) The base lock in one piece has been secured with an actual padlock; in another the lock hole is ornamented with engraved Dogg tags.

An untitled work encloses the object in black vinyl, giving it a hermetic presence/absence evocative of the artist himself. While Dogg's fondness for simple, grippable automobile tires as ideal forms—objects the viewer can really sink his or her teeth into—affords seemingly infinite elaboration, Dogg's forays into blown-up scale are equally inventive. *Paris, Texas*, at American Fine Arts, features an enormous tractor tire in a white porcelain tub, fixed to the floor on a steel chassis with floor locks. The allusion to water sports and drainage is especially resonant when one considers that tractor tires are always filled with water rather than air; the enamel inscription on the tub, *Europe, Europe*, refers to the classical past and its ironic distance from today's civilization. The fissures and scars (and an internal patch) of the tractor tire reminds us of the mortality of all objects, including rubber ones, and hence of our own mortality as well. At 303 Gallery, *Sure Grip Loader* contains another used tractor tire, this one resting flat inside one of Dogg's signature wooden boxes, but only visible (except for the part sticking out at one end) through a hefty sheet of bulletproof Plexiglas.

While it might be claimed that Dogg has merely reinvented the wheel, it should also be noted that he has done so cannily, with much less brouhaha and hoopla than those who have, over the past two seasons, reinvented the pet rock as an upscale collectable. Dogg, at least, has located a metaphorically charged commodity object which relates to the basic functional premises of our society rather than its spectacularly disposable, ever-replenished dross. Dogg's gestural audacity is complemented by a visual intelligence and sculptural savvy unmatched by his peers (if, in fact, he was born in 1952). Indeed, there seems no real comparison. Dogg brings to mind the words of Gogol's biographer, in Landolfi's story "Gogol's Wife": "As a great man once said, 'I too have to pee, but for quite other reasons.'"

May 26, 1987

UNTITLED *(ARE WE HAVING FUN YET?)*

The following conversation took place in Los Angeles and New York, over the telephone: immediately after the opening of her (partly retrospective, partly new) show at Mary Boone Gallery, Barbara Kruger had—to put it in entertainment vernacular— split for the coast for some peace and quiet. The first 10 minutes were spent discussing our respective weathers and rejecting questions like "Who's the 'I'?" Although I've avoided the annoying practice of indicating laughter where it occurred, the reader should hear the interview punctuated by uproarious laugher at both ends of the telephone.

Gary Indiana: *Where does a work start for you: does it start with a phrase, does it start with an image?*

Barbara Kruger: I have the sort of deminarrative of phrases and linkages and paragraphs going on in my head all the time, just the way most people do, and I'm always on the lookout for pictures I think can either skew or connect with those phrases, and, together, make an effective visual displacement, or an arresting question. Since I worked for so many years as a picture editor, the whole process of procuring, shall we say, images—searching, finding, cropping, and changing—is one which I'm used to. It's almost involuntary, like the hiccups or something. And when I find these pictures, I think of what statements could work with them.

What in a particular image recommends to you that it take a particular form, for example, that it should be a lenticular screen, or a very large piece?

A lot of decisions have to do with the capabilities of the found image itself. How it's screened, what the resolution of the reproduction is. If I'm going to make a large-scale image, aside from the quality of the screen, the generative effectiveness of the image itself comes into question. The lenticular pictures are always on a smaller scale because the capability of the process is only about 20 x 30 inches, so that's what determines that.

The new ones—like the crumpled aluminum foil in the fist that says, "You get away with murder"—are those photographs of commercial, airbrushed images, drawn images?

I think one of them is photographic, and the others probably started out photographic and were re-rendered in the style of a militaristic sort of…*zeal.* That's what I used the picture for. It begged for allegiance. And it seems that a lot of pictures don't do that, this is a particular genre coming from a particular period of time that did. I also like those three new pictures because the quality of the color is not the most conventional image of perfection. It is a kind of perfected aesthetic, but it's a little off, and that's what interested me.

It's from the '50s?

The '40s and '50s.

That's when most of the pictures you've used are from, that's the period of most of the pictures?

No, not really; it ranges from the '20s to the '70s. A lot of the more recent pictures become older when they're converted to black and white.

They were originally in color?

Yes.

There's a lot of hands.

Lots of hands, lots of water—[changes voice] "because I like the way it looks." But there is a sort of aesthetic tumult that arises; the hands, again, I could say there's a formal explanation, and that's that I gravitate toward pictures that have a foregrounded, expository quality to them. In other words, where there's a strong figure-ground thing, or large elements that grab the eye.

There's a kind of sign language going on.

In some of them, yes. And in some of them obviously, in the series of prints I did a couple years ago, it is literally sign language.

Did you see the news tonight?

Yeah, I just watched it. I read the paper this morning, it was saying the same thing, one Republican member of the committee said—and they're saying this on the eve of the Iran-Contragate hearings—"There's nothing the Republicans can do to make this situation any better, and unfortunately, nothing the Democrats can do to make it worse." Which means we can get our entertainment through the rascals and finicky escapades of electoral politics for a few months. Whether in fact there'll be a systemic critique or whether it will once again be sort of credited toward a few "rotten apples"—it's pretty clear which it'll be. The point is, the news is the news. Even though it's about the delivery of information, it's also about the most conventional novelistic form of fiction.

We're both involved in breaking down the usual narrative construction of reality and leaching information from the outside world into this special hermetic place that's supposed to be art—I guess the stupid form of the next question would be, "Are you trying to break out of the art system"?

I've always said that I grew up looking at movies and television, photography and advertising, and because of that, I believe that pictures, and words, have the ability to tell us who we want to be, what we will look like, who we are and who we won't be. And that's what made me want to work visually at trying to displace the usual outcomes of those wishes and predictions, and you can do that in a number of different arenas. The art world was more accessible to me because it was a cottage industry, where you weren't dependent on an intimate client relationship the way you are in film production and in building buildings. I can't say I'm just working in the art subculture. The pictures reproduce well, and, hopefully, far and wide. And certainly the billboard projects over the past two years have allowed the work to go out into other places without my proper name on them, in situations where they define themselves as images outside of the art world.

There was an interesting review in the Times *book review section yesterday, of this woman's book that talked about cannibalism as a process that seldom arose because of food shortages but almost exclusively because of the need of one group to define itself in terms of who the core group was, who the enemies were, who had power, who was powerless, et cetera. Cannibalism was all about self-definition.*

But they had to eat each other, to prove that?

Evidently.

Oh! You mean, "You are what you eat!"

In some cases, the consumption of a dead relative might indicate you are what you eat, but eating of a tribal enemy enhanced the virility of the tribe.

So does that mean they only ate men?

I don't think so. There's something really cannibalistic about images.

I think that cannibalism is something that happens when the body doesn't count any more. It seems to me that when so much is displaced onto objects, when the commodity is so preponderant in the broadcast of its promised pleasures, that the body becomes totally superfluous. In that way we're cannibalized by the images and products around us; they use us rather than us using them—as if they *had* a use, because then they have more of a body than we do.

At the same time, we have a culture of physical perfection where everybody's at a gym, or doing aerobics—it's kind of '70s in a way, but it's still going on.

Maybe people think that if they jump up and down enough they'll shake their cancers out of them. Now that it's in the water, it's in the food chain, the ozone layer looks like a piece of Swiss cheese: shake it up, baby.

So how many places have you done billboards?

In Scotland and Ireland I did 80 billboards, 10 billboards in Berkeley, and about 50 in Las Vegas, some of which are still up now, and more coming. And the billboard projects became more accessible to me as I defined myself as a personage within the art system. You know. As the proper name looms bigger and bigger and bigger, doing picture projects outside the art world becomes more possible.

In terms of popular culture, media culture, what do you see right now outside the art world emitting interesting images?

Not much. In Hollywood it's really sad, the number of films being made has declined radically, and so many movies are making their sales back in cassette rentals and foreign sales because box office is dead, except in the demographic region between age 6 and 13. It becomes difficult to get any ideas—not only ideas that are supposed to be *intelligent*, but anything that doesn't repeat that stereotype where the body is already removed, so what you're left with is the skeleton of 12,000 deluded lunches and power breakfasts, those are the films we see. It's very depressing.

And magazine culture?

I guess having worked at magazines for such a long time takes the magic out, shall we say. When you see how magazines are put together, when you understand the real desperation that dances around the notion of the deadline, you can never read a magazine after you've experienced that.

After working at the Voice *I can never look at a piece of newsprint in an innocent way again. I really lost my virginity.*

A list of the magazines I read would only tell you how much time I spend in airplanes and dentist's offices. But of course, one of my fantasies is if someone got the *Post* from Murdoch, who probably doesn't really want it anyway, and did something interesting. But it would take a great expenditure of capital, and no one's really up for doing that. But it's cheaper than buying a network.

We could talk about laughing.

I think laughter and parody and irony have specific functions, most of which could be recuperated by the conventions they're cast within, but there are moments that escape those conventions. This could be called the difference between a comedian and a humorist. I'm not interested in humorists. I would rather laugh than smirk or knowingly acquiesce; comedy is important in my own work; and in general, in having a critical relationship to culture. Now, sometimes it can be used in the most reactionary ways. But it can also be displacing, very progressive; it can also make for pleasure and change.

June 2, 1987

UNTITLED (*CINDY SHERMAN CONFIDENTIAL*)

Cindy Sherman's new work at Metro Pictures (150 Greene Street, through May 30) is one of a handful of recent shows that people have had a lot to say about. It's interesting that the handful features so many women artists: Sarah Charlesworth, Gretchen Bender, Annette Lemieux, Barbara Kruger, Fariba Hajamadi. Cindy Sherman's most recent pictures depict gross violations of the body, in landscapes of baroque rot.

The interview takes place in Cindy Sherman's loft in Tribeca. Halfway through the interview we are joined by Sherman's husband, the video artist Michel Auder.

Gary Indiana: *Let's say you get the idea that you're going to begin doing pictures, as in this show, in which you're not especially featured. Is this triggered by a particular encounter with an image or an idea?*

Cindy Sherman: Over a period of time, doing what I've been doing, I finally wanted to shed a lot of baggage: of using myself, of being theatrical and portrait-like. I tried to completely break off from those things, I'd gotten so fed up with it. I didn't do any work for the last year and a half, in between those two shows. I tried things, but nothing clicked until I started playing with these landscapes.

Where do you get body parts?

I got some at Jamie Canvas; some I got at this place called Gordon's, that I've used before. And I looked in funny little gift shops, I got those ants in a gift shop.

The new pieces are all strange horror scenarios.

Yes. I didn't want to make pretty pictures. But I wanted to combine a sort of humor with it. I see them as fun, even though they're kind of gross and disgusting—in the way that it's fun for me to watch horror movies, because you know they're fake.

It's boring to ask questions about influences, but I did wonder if you'd had in mind specific images, as in the film stills.

It could still be a film influence, because it seems there've been a lot of films with horrible, real low-down camera angles, practically on the floor, looking around at these close-ups of decay. Like David Lynch's movie, and there's a new one out I want to see called *River's Edge*, it sounds like the same thing. They keep going back to this decayed body—it was described as getting more and more beautiful as it decays.

The photo for that poster is an extremely low-angle one.

With just a field of leaves, and then this little figure in one corner.

I think they were influenced by you, in that poster. You're in these pictures, aren't you?

Some of them.

I can see how you'd do a setting where you're in the picture, where everything's already laid out, but in these, sometimes you've got junk all over yourself.

No, actually I tried not to be in them as much as possible. So I used a dummy's head, too. It might read as if that's me with stuff piled over my head, but it's the dummy. And then, in some, it's just a reflection, because I didn't want to get all made-up, and in costume. So it's only the eyes you see. I didn't have to do any makeup because it's out of focus anyway. And I used Michel in one of them.

Really?

The one downstairs with the beard and broken glass in the background. That's him.

I'm sure everybody thinks it's you.

Well, I want to use other people like that, throw in other people. And people will just assume they're all me anyway. Once they realize there are other people mixed in, they won't be so intrigued by picking out the one that's me.

There were all these articles, "Who is the real Cindy Sherman?" "Who does Cindy Sherman think she is?"

So stupid.

Well, now you can just make photographs.

Yes, actually. We were in the country yesterday, and I was taking little pictures of the ground, thinking, "Well, maybe I'll just become a real landscape photographer, I won't even have to set it up."

(We phone up Michel Auder at his studio across the street. A few minutes later, he's there.)

I was having a little trouble here, so I thought I'd get you in on this. We're talking about these new pictures.

Michel Auder: I always saw them on little slides. When I came back from North Carolina to her show and saw them blown up, I was amazed. What's great about them is that they look beautiful from far away, and then, when you get into the detail, there's completely an opposite feeling. So there are two strong feelings coming from one image.

CS: Michel, when you were in that picture—I mean, I've used you before, but not in ones that were shown—was it boring? You just kind of lay there, and I made you up and everything.

MA: I guess the best way to be in your pictures is to be like a prop. There's nothing much to do. The best way to collaborate is to become like rubber, and wait until it happens. I never know what she's doing, but the show made so much sense to me.

CS: I used his daughter's sister a couple of times, too. In fact, for that same image he's in. But she's got her own personality altogether, and she's five-years-old, so it's hard for her to be like a doll. She kept saying, "Oh, the lights, the lights! They're too bright, I can't, please…"

A born actress. I think I assumed if you could see an actual person, that was the only one in the image, that the rest was just…

CS: Body parts, yes. It's just implied: there's an ass in one part, a face in another. In the one with the bloody underpants, there's a mannequin head with a wig, and then there's the body on top of it, so it looks like there's two people.

MA: I have to look at them again. For me it was like: "This looks disgusting, what's this, fish blood, and throw up, and asses, and bad skin, and scum from pollution…"

That's an interesting effect in that picture, that kind of bloody permafrost and broken glass.

CS: Special effects. (Pause) So what else?

MA: I think it's probably some part of…what everybody has in their minds, that kind of disgusting stuff, it comes out in the photographs, if she kept it in she would probably be even weirder.

CS: Even weirder?

MA: No, I'm glad it's out there, it's like x-ing it out. I mean, I have to sleep with that person—I was joking during the show, I would tell people, "When she was working, I woke up, I went to the bathroom and was walking all over the scum and stuff, it's all over the studio, all this stuff rotting away!"

I also kept picturing those pictures on certain people's walls.

CS: Yes, certain collectors.

Right over the dining-room table.

MA: One of those 80-year-old collectors who don't see very well, they buy five of them because they look so beautiful, know what I mean? Then the kids, when they bring them home, say, "Oh, Nanny, what did you buy, for God's sake!"

But obviously, to make an image like that expresses…a great disgust.

CS: I'm pretty disgusted, I guess, with the art world in general. The boy artists, the boy painters, the collectors, the crawl, and climb, and stabbing each other to the top sort of competition. I don't know why that work would come out from those feelings, but I think I wanted to make something that I couldn't imagine anybody buying. "I dare you to like *this*."

Of course, they're all sold.

MA: It's the magic of the artist.

CS: The ass with the pimples is the slow mover of the bunch, for some reason. I don't know why.

June 16, 1987

TRANSCENDENTAL MEDITATION

[**Contemporary Japanese Art in America (1): Arita, Nakagawa, Sugimoto.**
Japan Society Gallery, 333 East 47th Street, through June 28]

None of the three artists featured in "Contemporary Japanese Art in America" fulfills contemporary American wishes regarding aesthetic modernity or the imperatives of irony and disengagement that currently inform American art practice and reception. Yet all three have absorbed part of the mainstream ambience and refract it in different ways. At any given time, of course, there are thousands of artworks that fail to speak the dominant language of a particular culture, works that disobey the notions of center and periphery established in critical writing and exhibition trends. Although we have a pluralistic art culture, we also have a shifting hierarchy of importance, ideas about what art crowns a particular moment and tells us the latest news about ourselves.

Sometimes the news is visceral, sometimes intellectual, sometimes international, sometimes provincial. One interesting result of culture that is technologically transmitted is its loss of site-specific authenticity, its uprootedness, its free-ranging choice of sources and adaptivity. From this perspective, Arita, Nakagawa, and Sugimoto are interesting as hybrid artists whose works reflect the reciprocal effects of two cultures brought into contact by modernity. And for this reason, each in his way records the encounter of sensibility with otherness as well as the vagaries of a particular style or practice.

As an ensemble, these three artists have few deep connections. They were all born in Japan and have all lived in New York for a long time. Arita and Nakagawa are painters, and both practice an old-fashioned "fine art" stressing artisanal mastery, elaborate effort of the hand. Akira Arita's current work has evolved from earlier, exact renderings of objects into illusionistic abstractions: connected tubular shapes that appear to float before the canvas, chunks of unidentified architecture, bands and rings of matter set in muddily rendered perspectives. The surfaces of Arita's pictures hold drips and splotches and fissured episodes of paint that deface the solid image and give a corroded, peeling appearance overall.

As iconography, Arita's paintings are simultaneously sumptuous and vacant, offering imaginary objects as empty or near-empty signs. There is a diptych, for instance, called *OI*, in heavily worked browns, with a ring form and a diagonal tube "resting" against the canvas. The picture combines palpable symbolic objects with the plain abstraction of variegated color; although the technique has extremely retrograde associations, the painting itself has a very stolid presence, mainly because it is so "empty," so drained of meaningful content, so obtuse. Vis-à-vis contemporary art, Arita's kind of virtuosity is corny, a throwback to magic realism and academicism. But its lack of messages and pure concentration on form rescues it from ghastliness and even projects an agreeably theatrical sort of beauty. Arita uses lavish means to produce something as close to nothing as those means *can* produce; thus hobbled, his art oscillates between contradictory cultural impulses.

Naoto Nakagawa's paintings, by contrast, are stuffed with objects, painted with photographic accuracy, and cloyingly "composed." One must take into account the radical distance between traditional, allusive, flat Japanese painting and Western art to perceive the Pop dimension in Nakagawa's work, which in many cases resembles the most plangent and sentimental productions of Andrew Wyeth. The earliest picture in this show features a bicycle, a large withered clump of lawn, numerous rocks and a violin arranged on a tabletop in front of a double window, beyond which a snowy landscape stretches off interminably. A later work ranges the same or similar rocks on the same or similar tabletop, but against a black background, in company with a lawn mower, a set of pastels, a lightbulb, a TV set, a stuffed duck, and a telescope.

Nakagawa's more recent work is more vivid, not because it's less strainingly exact—if anything, it gets more obsessively slick and redundant in its method—but because its pictured objects begin to crowd each other (shells, dead fish, flowers, an African mask), the pictures looking increasingly like models of exacerbated claustrophobia. Things acquire a livid fleshiness, their tactility ranging from the slimy to the etiolated and prickly; traditional still-life items glower unpleasantly, like the glossy, menacing consumer products featured by Warhol and Rosenquist.

Like Arita, Nakagawa suggests an emotional sincerity that operates within recent Western art as a relative of kitsch. His technical gifts very probably exceed those of most contemporary American artists, but his vision remains grounded in prephotographic ideas of painting and picturing. The intensely personal feeling one gets from Nakagawa's work is more complicated than the pathos of a Wyeth, but only because Nakagawa is a more interesting person than Wyeth: more perverse, more queasily existential, more attuned to the sinister than to the "moving." And, again like Arita, Nakagawa seems aimed in the direction of a mineral blankness, an irreproachably phenomenological aesthetic—something akin to microphotography rendered by hand.

What is powerful in Arita's and Nakagawa's painting is an authoritative placidity. A similarly sedative effect emanates, with less protean fussiness, from the photographs of Hiroshi Sugimoto.

One series shows the interiors of various Pantages and Keith circuit movie palaces—from Massachusetts to Ohio—taken from the balconies, with the view-camera aperture open throughout an afternoon matinee, so the ornate and usually deserted interiors are lit by the condensed glow of thousands of film frames. These fantasy architectures, articulated around a serene, luminous blankness, are the true temples of modern spirituality; Sugimoto's photographs evoke the collapse of all images into the white light of death, apotheosis, possibly the atomic blast. The complimentary series, of sea/sky horizon lines, offers roiling and cross-hatching wave formations and cloud-bare skies as hyperrarified spectacles of nothingness, the views closest to eternity the world has to offer.

June 23, 1987

CLOWNOPHOBIA TODAY

Yowsa yowsa yowsa step right up ladies and gentlemen, read about the incredible AIDS disease, sur-rep-titiously sweeping the country today! Hear about the disgusting sex practices and sordid crimes that cause the deadly AIDS disease! Spread by a cabal of filthy homosesshuals and heeneeous dope fiends, the fatal killer AIDS virus threatens all human life on earth! Extra! Extra!

For several days now, W. C. Fields has been peddling newspapers in my dreams: I buy the *Times* before going to bed, absorb the stuff of tomorrow's conversations ahead of time, and wonder how much repression we will have to absorb before the apocalyptic imagination of America trains its prurient attention elsewhere. The situation shifts from day to day. When the *Times* refers to AIDS stigmatization that existed *until recently*, you have to laugh: this comes from a newspaper that tacked on "homosexual men and IV-drug users" as the primary victims of AIDS *until recently* to any AIDS story it ran; a newspaper that featured boxed stories on AIDS inside crackpot science items on "sissy boys," and anything else supposedly related to homosexuality, *until recently*; a newspaper—what a newspaper!—that has finally embraced the health crisis, piping its own voice through the ventriloquist's doll known as the HIV virus.

Last week the *Times* did a number on AIDS in the arts, tapping its usual roster of high-flown showbiz authorities on the subject—

all people on the *Times*' okay list of artists and performers. As a writer friend told me on the phone, I'd like to get my sense of compassion elsewhere. During a month's preparation for a story on *Art Against AIDS*—a story I found myself unable to write—I was told that the *Times* had demanded exclusive reproduction dibs on various artworks, and had also made its Sunday magazine coverage contingent on *whether or not it was first to appear*.

The *Times* is one of our symbolic markers. Its actual contents are heterogeneous, like those of any newspaper. Some of its AIDS stories have been informative, some have created incredible problems for people with AIDS—giving credence to the lie about the three "casually infected" health workers, for example. In terms of bias, what's most striking about the *Times* is not homophobia but a worship of conventional success and its symbols. The *Times* is perfectly capable of eulogizing Charles Ludlam—one of the greatest theater artists New York has ever seen—as someone who almost made it into the mainstream. ("Just *think*," an actress quipped, "Charles could have been as big as *Spalding Gray*!")

One of the reasons I'm blocked about dealing with AIDS, at least in a nonfiction context, is that so much concerning this very real, fatal malady has been displaced from the bodies suffering from it into the realm of the symbolic. Symbolism-poisoning is the true plague of American society. Signs have replaced the body: for society to respond to an epidemic, a movie star has to die. For the private sector to donate research money, another movie star has to ask for it. The President's attending a dinner party *makes the problem real to people*.

When the political manipulation of the HIV virus is stripped of its symbolic veils, it becomes obvious that persons with AIDS are of no concern to the government at all. The virus itself, which is not AIDS, has been claimed to be an implement of repression: it can be used to define and punish the Other, whether black or gay or simply foreign. The government envisions nothing for people with AIDS beyond incarceration, warehousing, or quarantine—Attorney General Meese, a public figure who might generously be described as a reeking tub of shit, thinks HIV infection should be a factor in parole eligibility for incarcerated persons. In effect, that people exposed to HIV belong in jail.

I think the point is moot. People with AIDS are already "in jail." Formalizing this arrangement with prison architecture is beyond the present capabilities of the system. With the economy heading for messy collapse by 1989 or 1990, a blood-monitoring bureaucracy serving to exclude infected immigrants and tag HIV-infected citizens must be viewed as another fascist pipe dream, cheaper than SDI but just as deluded. But what can you expect in a country run by clowns?

Here is the segue to art, our ostensible subject: among the many artworks in the *Art Against AIDS* benefit (which included 72 galleries, 615 artists), a work by Gretchen Bender, and another by Bruce Nauman, correspond to the mental weather in my own head. I'm sure there are others; here I reflect my own biases. Bender's *Untitled* is a 15-inch color television set with PEOPLE WITH AIDS in press type lined across the screen, the set running with the sound off (There are two of these, actually, one at Metro Pictures (150 Greene Street, through June), the other at Nature Morte). By a simple addition, Bender transforms the circus of inanity at the heart of every American home into a locus of AIDS consciousness, or unconsciousness, or brainwashing, or brain pollution—this piece is a stroke of brilliance with a Cheshire grin, collapsing the seemingly diverse representations of AIDS into a blunt symbolic overlay. Bender *projects the virus* into the electronic bloodstream, reconstitutes TV figures as physical bodies, infects inanity with anxiety and reveals a certain kind of *manufactured anxiety* as a hysterical spectacle.

Nauman's *Clown Torture*, at Leo Castelli Gallery (420 West Broadway, closed), consists of four videotapes, displayed in combinations on four monitors and two large wall projections. One tape, *Clown Taking a Shit*, is projected continuously, while the other tapes shunt from monitor to monitor, sometimes sideways or upside down. Actor Walter Stevens plays the clown, in thick greasepaint, orange hair, clown costume, and big clown feet. He opens a door and gets beaned with a bucket of water, reels around, comes through the door again, gets beaned again, reels, goes through the door again, et cetera; writhes on the floor, shouting, "No, no, no, no, no! Nooo! Nooo! No. No. No no no." He balances a goldfish bowl on a broomstick—presses it against the ceiling, really—gesturing and muttering at us interminably, until the fishbowl finally smashes to the floor. No. No. Noo! In close-up, the clown recites: "Pete and Repeat were sitting on a fence, Pete fell off, who's left?" Oh no: "Repeat?" A morphology of dismay races across the clown's face, he starts all over again; on the opposite wall, we see him ensconced on the toilet seat, picking his nose, flipping through a magazine, burping, gathering individual pieces of toilet paper, stuffing them into the magazine, while on the monitors he continues to scream, No! No! No!

Clown Torture is not specifically about AIDS. It is, rather, a purgative for media consumers, a synthesis of "information society" at its pinnacle of brutal stupidity, and that increasingly rare thing, a good laugh. And we need a good laugh, even right now.

June 30, 1987

'80S PEOPLE

["**Sculpture of the Eighties.**" Organized by Ileen Sheppard. The Queens Museum, New York City Building, Flushing Meadow Park, Flushing, through July 19.]

"Sculpture of the Eighties" at the Queens Museum features work by 10 artists, much of it quite large and difficult to accommodate in the kind of space this museum has. The installation is surprising because everything seems to fit without looking squeezed, and the variousness of the work has been dealt with subtly and respectfully. All 10 artists are women, but the museum has rather adventurously refrained from billing this as a "women's show." The casual museumgoer is free to encounter the art without following the thread of gender. While this is not an earthshaking exhibition strategy, it is an imaginative one, in striking contrast to the sclerotic exhibitions of the Met, MOMA, the Whitney, and the Guggenheim. Generally speaking, our borough museums tend even at their worst to offer more engaging fare than our uptown mausoleums, which are so ensorcelled by their own authority that when they choose to do something new, it is almost always something stupid.

One could read the Queens show through various filters, and certainly its strength and energy underline the large role of women sculptors in this decade. Again, though, it's interesting to put the issue of sexual difference aside, and also to see where it creeps into color perception. For example, the small and usually dormant chunk of my own mind that's still soaking in its New England small-town childhood continues to view large metal objects with moving parts, like Alice Aycock's *The Savage Sparkler*, as "masculine," while less imposing, emotionally expressive things like Pat Lasch's mixed media bursting hearts and toxic chocolates (*Poison Cookies for Past Lovers*) read as "feminine." This is nonsense, of course—but rampant nonsense, that Reaganite culture has instilled in the young and revived in the very old at heart. Another good reason to present a rangy show like this one.

The diverse paradigms of contemporary sculpture are well represented: the rationalized architectural caprices of Mary Miss and Jackie Ferrara; the organic, allegorically charged verticals of Ann Sperry and Barbara Zucker; Betye Saar's stylized ritual objects in rebuslike arrangements within a midnight-blue alcove; Judy Pfaff's audaciously balanced, toy-colored wall pieces. Not everything works: Mary Frank's *Standing Woman* and *Chimera*, in terra-cotta, are described in the catalogue as "very tactile and sensuous, yet ominous," but I find them very tacky and only slightly more ominous than Statue of Liberty figurines. Ursula von Rydingsvard's *Urzulka*—six crudely carved troughs, which resemble the carcasses of slaughtered livestock—and her blocky, cottage-roof-like *Ignatz Comes Home* have a certain forcefulness that one can detect in any large, partly chiseled piece of wood. *Urzulka* also has an evocative, ashen coloring. These works are not sufficiently dynamic to justify their bluntness.

Judy Pfaff's *Blue Vase With Nasturtiums*, an explosion of spheres and bubbles and wrought-iron chairs and summery striped tabletops, as well as *Post No Bills*, a grid of rectangular signs overlaid and obscured by plastic decals, look nervy and somewhat menacingly cheerful. Pfaff's work always requires an unusual amount of breathing room, and when it gets it, it's delightful and wickedly assertive. Its bright, overloaded balance counterpoints the nearby pieces of Pat Lasch—extremely delicate, frazzled, decaying symbols of bad love. Lasch's painted wooden cakes, candies, rotting hearts and deceased bird recast the Pre-Raphaelite vision from drowned Ophelia's point of view, with a smart core of malice buried in her grief, as if to remind us that no love is truly true unless it is really truly bad.

Betye Saar's objects, including crystal balls and sequined fetishes, have the faux-primitive fastidiousness and body-symbolic logic of voodoo paraphernalia—seductive, redolent of magic powers and ancient sexual wisdom, metaphorically just across the road from Lasch's inconsolable hearts. Differently extracted from religious sources are Barbara Zucker's *Decoys for the Spirit*, wooden poles on metal half-cone mounts terminating in free-form, painted interpretations of "angel wings" from the book of Exodus. Ann Sperry's *Cloud Pillar*, a helixlike column of acidic purpled metal, was likewise inspired by the book of Exodus; Sperry also has a tubular work illusionistically threaded through the walls of a separate room, something between a science-fiction snake and a lighting fixture from Art et Industrie.

If there is a clear binary division, it's between modestly scaled, arguably personal work and the crisp engineering aesthetic of Aycock, Ferrara, and Miss. These artists command more space; they articulate alternative visions of *building*, as in Miss's dreamlike extensions of a mirrored closet, Ferrara's spillways and arcades in precisely interlocked wooden geometries, and Aycock's double-chambered, rotating barrel, flanked on one side by diagonal banks of fluorescent lights resembling a double set of bedsprings. The drawings that accompany these pieces are especially fine.

In short, this is as substantial a survey of contemporary sculpture as any we might see this year in a local museum. A larger show, elsewhere, could expand the focus from midcareer artists, without violating the unadvertised, all-women trope, to include Louise Bourgeois, Nancy Dwyer, Meret Oppenheim, Daisy Youngblood, and Kate Millett (one of America's *best* sculptors), along with Lynda Benglis, Jackie Winsor, Rosemarie Trockel, and Valie Export. Among others.

July 28, 1987

AGITATIONS

[**Group Show.** 303 Gallery, 513 East 6th Street, through July 26.]

This is midsummer and *almost nothing* happens in or out of the art world, in New York, during summer. Many galleries simply fold their tents until autumn.

There is a significant show up now at 303 Gallery, which I'll get to, but first you should know the results of an informal poll taken this week among people whose opinions, like it or not, tend to reverberate.

Formica is kaput. Art objects crafted from Formica are no longer considered attractive or interesting. Indeed, they are no longer considered art objects.

Consumer-critique sculpture has gotten too big for its britches. What began as a stimulating and clever practice has become an absurd and probably meretricious excuse for the undertalented to go shopping on other people's money.

Bye, bye, Baudrillard. The first French intellectual to realize his 15 minutes were up before everyone else did has nevertheless failed to ingratiate himself in a lasting manner.

Ciao, knotty pine. The elegant look of natural wood, and the not-so-elegant look of imitation wood, may spice up that basement rec room but they do less than nothing for an art gallery, either in picture form or as ambient surface.

An artist is just an artist, but a good cigar is a smoke. What people would like, just now, is art that is *about* something. About people rather than objects. About life rather than television. People would like to see art that's as *reputable* as literature, reflecting the real complexity of our lives as we race toward extinction.

Neo-Expressionism will be just as dead this year as it was last year. But there may be a strong resurgence of glassware.

No more surrogates, for Christ's sake. So stop, already. You know who you are. No more dolls, no more teeny toys, no more simulacra. Everything must go.

Nobody wants to hear about heterosexual obsession. Watching it on TV is repulsive enough without seeing it embalmed in a gallery.

Now, here are some other observations. Writers like money as much as the next person, and the practice of hiring "name" writers to pen catalogue essays—that is to say, writers who are considered to be writers, rather than art critics—will spread throughout the art world in the coming season. This strategy has some built-in pitfalls, the first being that most big-time writers know nothing about contemporary art. The second pitfall is that no one reads catalogue essays. On second thought, perhaps these two problems cancel each other out.

The untitled show at 303 Gallery features several artists "to watch," as the saying goes, working in diverse media, and dealing with issues of politics and gender. The installation is thoughtfully fragmented with works by Fareed Armaly and Silvia Kolbowski dramatizing slippages between images and their ordained contexts; parts of Armaly's *It's a Whole New World* appear throughout the gallery, while Kolbowski's photographs appear outside their frames, which contain information (title, artist's name, etc.) normally placed outside an artwork on the gallery wall. Mark Dion's *Foreign Policy Spectrum (From Farthest Right to Center Right 1980–1988)* consists of a clothesline with message T-shirts ("Hey Moscow Up Yours!" "Kill 'Em All, Let God Sort 'Em Out"), a utility ladder with quotes from Henry Kissinger, Vernon Walters, and Jeane Kirkpatrick printed across the step edges, and a small basket of clothespins.

There are two strong pieces by Collier Schorr, with texts written on Lucite blocks projecting from the wall, and images of women behind the blocks. The texts articulate lesbian desire, and it's a welcome shock to see them. Schorr expands this writing in the show's catalogue: *This project is constructed from two of the most far-reaching ad campaigns. Guess jeans and Calvin Klein campaigns can be found in almost every magazine...I chose these images because I saw them as some kind of representation of homosexuality...Maybe...Calvin Klein and Bruce Weber would like all the world to be boys, but I open up* Women's Wear *and I see a dyke. No two ways about it. When you're rarely represented, you take it any way you find it.*

Both Schorr and Andrea Fraser, the latter represented by a six-image photo work called *Personal Apparel*, raise the subject of lesbian identity with work that criticizes the objectification of women's bodies. As Schorr further states: *The structure of this project illustrates this fork in the road, by allowing the viewer entrance into the realm of homosexual desire, only to be stranded in some unreal dream sequence constructed for the purpose of selling clothing.* Fraser's *Personal Apparel* is a body-vocabulary lesson in which the same body, in roughly the same posture through a succession of costumes, seems to invite very different kinds of attention, seems to promise various gratifications—but the essential toughness of Fraser's work rubs through all these images, exposing our reading of them as wish projections and claiming for the model/artist the fundamental secret of the human being.

Gregg Bordowitz's videotape *Testing the Limits* is a brief pilot for a longer work documenting the politics of AIDS, including interviews with PWAs and health educators along with footage from demonstrations and hearings. Within a conventionally rousing documentary format, Bordowitz amplifies the voices that most need to be heard, i.e., people with AIDS who refuse to be treated as society's garbage. This tape should be seen by every gay person in America because it's an incitement to rage and to organized political action.

This show makes necessary connections between *commodities* and *bodies*, instead of rehashing the rhetoric of commodification. The feeling of communally generous intelligence, directed at subjects such as sexual difference, personal autonomy, and political threat, makes this assortment of objects something much finer than a "group show"—its youthfulness works in its favor, and I would even call it noble if this word weren't clanking out of so many witnesses' mouths in Washington. Another prediction: the coming year will bring an even keener interest in *relevance*.

THREE MILE ISLAND

There is the port with its double promontory, ringed with private yachts. There is the stone landing-stage near the military school, where the giant cockroach hydrofoil and wedding-cake tour-liners dock in shifts, disgorging and swallowing hundreds of sun-dazed day-trippers who swarm through the shops, scarfing up silver jewelry and plaster Aphrodites and then settle under the café awnings to nibble braised crustaceans. Crustaceans were once a local product, but are now flown into Athens, frozen, from Japan. There are no cars on the island of Hydra, and no air-port. There is one truck that collects garbage and another that delivers water to the cisterns. Last year the garbagemen, drunk, drove their truck off a cliff into the Aegean.

There are donkeys to haul things, often incredible things. Crates twice the size of their bodies, strapped around their saddles. A half ton of cinder blocks. Thirty cases of Coca-Cola. The don-keys stand squinting at the edge of the port in the unblinking sunlight, which bleaches human hair and clothing within a half hour of exposure. Milling around them all day, perfectly mar-bleized human flesh, tanned to a crisp, entirely nude except for the merest spandex mask for the genitals.

There is a po-faced woman pharmacist who gives sound, laconic advice and quietly produces salves and pills from various white Formica drawers. The male pharmacist near the hospital, who slightly resembles Peter Lorre in *Mask of Dimitrios*, will sell you Valium and chloral hydrate without a prescription, but despises you for asking for it.

The port and its winding side alleys bulge with merchandise. Jewelry, scarves, souvenir bags, souvenir bathing suits, souvenir clasps, souvenir booklets. The young tourists, for whom the island is a place of casual mating, strut placidly between the harbor and the cluster of rock beaches at its nether end. Many wear T-shirts proclaiming, dubiously, NO PROBLEM, or, more credibly, BIG PROBLEM. As in Japan, one finds the English language inscribed on various artifacts in ways that suggest a rudimentary grasp of inflection and meaning. However, one less-than-ubiquitous T-shirt uses English unequivocally. DON'T TALK TO ME, it says in front, though on the back there reappears the fantastic claim, NO PROBLEM.

Food shops and banks close between one and five. The town is a natural stone amphitheater piled up along narrow cobbled paths, its grand houses the residue of merchants who ran the British blockade throughout the Napoleonic Wars and then promptly went bankrupt. Beyond the town, vertiginous tracts of scrabbly earth rise and dip, with small clusters of white housing tucked into curves in the landscape and monasteries perched on the tallest peaks. The land, parched in August, turns effulgent again in September. In August what grows are figs, almonds, lemons, and ice plant. Austerity and lushness alternate by seasons. It is a place of breathtaking beauty. You can see the spine of the Pelopónnisos across the water, turning to haze as the orange sun fades into pink mist and the sky slowly changes into a celestial observatory.

The clicking cicadas are almost deafening in the afternoon, and if their chirping suddenly goes dead it means weather. August offers very little weather. But when you get weather, you also get torrents of liquefied donkey shit pouring down the hill roads into the port. You get waterlogged awnings and mildewed café cushions. On days when you get winds, you also get headaches, bouts of neuralgia, strange behavior from the owner-less dogs.

The island features owls and tiny salamanders. At night you can't tell the bats from the sparrows. The Pirate Bar in the port blasts disco music from 10 p.m. until three in the morning—four on weekends. So does the Heaven Disco, on a hilltop at the port's far end, and the Cavos Disco, further down the sea walk between Hydra proper and Kamini. It is important to secure housing with acoustically buffered placement. It is important, in fact, to secure housing that offers psychological and physical protection from the port itself. You cannot walk through the port without encountering people you know. The American art colony. The European art colony. The demoralized expatriates, languishing on fixed incomes. The half-year people, who lead interesting lives elsewhere, off-season. The comely, smart young people in service jobs, who bear up amazingly well under the stress of the island's feral human flux.

Everyone knows who fucked whom the night before. Everyone knows which couples rowed until dawn. Everyone knows what feuds commenced or resumed during the night. However, no one gives precisely the same account of these happenings, and the narrative slippages that occur as stories pass from mouth to mouth become stories in themselves. Because the port could be justly rechristened Stolichnaya Harbor, even eyewitnesses of nocturnal bad behavior seldom recount it with total certainty. Everyone's memory sports a few bald spots. A person may avoid the port for days, mortified by some incident that no one remembers and which may not have happened.

Mornings, nearly all the interesting people appear at the Up & High, a terraced restaurant a few dozen steps above the port. Day tourists seldom find their way there. Regular patrons include the local estate agent, busy most mornings with his mobile telephone; a former bigwig in MI6; a retired journalist. Most of the American art colony turns up, along with some glamorous Italians, interrelated by birth or infatuation. An American art collector based in Paris, with his entourage. The Italians bevy around the famed woman painter whose sense of career injustice tends to flatten the atmosphere around her. The collector complains of faulty ventilation in an upstairs bathroom. The Italians quietly adore themselves and study fashion magazines.

Many regular inhabitants do not drink. Most do. When the Up & High closes at 2:30, everyone filters down to the café directly below, or books a boat to go swimming at the desolate tip of the island, or jumps in a water taxi for Kamini or, a bit further off, Palamidas. There the pebble beaches have fewer swimmers. The sea is a bright, clear ink the color of Windex, with darker patches that almost never turn out to be sharks. And there people find, at the outdoor tavernas, everyone with whom they have just had breakfast.

Certain guidebooks describe Hydra as a haven for artists and writers. Others call it "an artist colony." An outdated Fodor refers to it as "a natural center for artists." On Hydra, there are well-known artists escaping the social frenzy of the art world, as well as artists of a less determined, more romantic sort, who know nothing about the arty world but gravitate to Hydra because of the guidebooks. The artist population has sufficiently swollen to attract people in the art business (collectors, dealers, critics), amplifying the guidebooks' descriptions and making Hydra an obligatory stop for a particular kind of young tourist—the kind described in America as "Eurotrash," on Hydra as "the Boat People." Many come for a day or a week to pillage the shops and boogie through the discos in their NO PROBLEM T-shirts. They have as much sensitivity as pot holders, yet the presence of artists and "creative people" draws them to this island rather than another. The affluence of the Boat People, enterprisingly met by indigenous greed, has driven prices on Hydra through the ceiling. It has become the most expensive island in Greece, except for Mykonos, with disastrous consequences for pensioners and fixed-income residents, artist and otherwise.

There is no water on the island. All the water on Hydra arrives by ship. The actual land on Hydra, and hence all the cisterns, and therefore all the water of Hydra, is owned by the Greek Orthodox Bishop of Hydra. This old party issues from his highly polished mansion on lugubrious religious holidays to stroll darkly through the port, wearing an expression of addled saintliness and an extremely tacky black caftan—a cross between the Angel of Death and a vampire impersonating Santa Claus. Hydra is, by the way, a vampire island, having once been settled by Albanians. Natives claim the last vampire was expelled from the island in 1880. They claim. At any rate, water pressure is mercurial.

This is what happens to the cats of Hydra. Like Venice, Hydra swarms with stray cats. Black Burmese and silver tabbies, tigers and tortoiseshells, Peke-faced Persians and cameos. The cats have gouges in their cheeks and sides, molting fur, gouts of eczema, tails sheared off in brawls. They gravitate to the outdoor restaurants, despite the repeated kicks of waiters. The tourists feed them scraps, so the cats fatten and multiply. The food in Hydra's port restaurant is, without exception, wretched, and the tourists are happy to part with it. This benevolence is arbitrary and fleeting, naturally; no one actually adopts these animals. In September the tourists leave, the shops close, the half-year people depart for exotic climes. The cats kill each other over bits of food and when the food's all gone they starve to death.

These are some of the salient features of Hydra. Another salient feature of Hydra is this: Hydra is exactly the same size as Manhattan.

Small world, isn't it?

ENDGAME

[**Sherrie Levine.** Mary Boone Gallery, 417 West Broadway, through October 10]

The catalogue, wrapped in an especially abrasive shade of lipstick pink, is actually gray: a *creamy* gray, the color of Mary Boone Gallery legal-size envelopes and Mary Boone Gallery endpapers, a gray that bespeaks unutterable elegance and luxury as well as an underlying sense of proportion and seemliness. It is the gray of diplomacy, a superior kind of nouveau-riche gray that gloves and accessories for a certain type of funeral might come in, a gray that can hold its own against any splashier color, including the vibrant pink wrapper it comes in.

The artist's photograph is deep black and ethereal white. The facing page is black. The artist's eyes are invisible behind black sunglasses. On the following two pages, "Works in the Exhibition," all of them untitled, appear listed, in black, on paper somewhere between bronze and "salmon" in color. Next comes, on white pages, an essay by Donald Barthelme entitled, "On the Level of Desire." Between this and the biography section we find numerous reproductions of the work in situ: perched on an inlaid desk, propped on fireplace mantles and chairs, arranged in artfully crumbling interiors, and hung on the walls of the very space we have just entered.

Donald Barthelme's essay consists of bite-size sections separated by teeny black diamonds. At the top of page 9, floating all by its lonesome, is an incomplete sentence looking to turn into an aphorism: *Something wrong, something off, something not right.* Under the next diamond, Barthelme poses the unfortunate questions, *What is the correct wear for a hero of art?* Two sections later he asseverates, *One thinks immediately of Duchamp, then, perhaps, of Picabia, then of Rauschenberg.*

It might fairly be said of Sherrie Levine's current show at Mary Boone Gallery that one (whoever *one* might be) thinks rather less immediately of Duchamp or Picabia than one thinks, however reluctantly, that there is *something wrong, something off, something not right.* Just what is this something? Perhaps it's that one does think of Picabia, if not immediately then rather quickly, not in connection with the work on view, but with the gallery it's featured in. Specifically, one recalls that faraway season when, to bolster her marketing shove for David Salle, Mary Boone prefaced his show with one of late Picabia. And if Rauschenberg springs to mind, it can only be because that artist is represented by Leo Castelli, with whom Boone allied herself in order to promote Salle and Julian Schnabel.

Rather than recapitulate the reams of densely argued prose that have accrued around the work and thought of Sherrie Levine, I would have the reader consider to what extent Levine's work, in this show, functions as a side effect of its container. Almost unique among art dealers, Mary Boone has cultivated the kind of personal celebrity artists themselves might envy, test-driving automotive products and posing for tony national magazines. She has become synonymous with a special category of success, at once unassailable, inevitable, yet in an indefinable way chimerical—a success one could imagine happening in a different and slightly more dignified fashion, attended by less ambient noise and less enthralled collusion with those forces that produce big, empty spectacle and sudden, deserved fame indiscriminately.

It's easy to justify this collusion if you happen to be one of its beneficiaries, but for people outside the charmed loop of superhype and automatic sales there seems to be *something wrong, something off, something not right*, and that something is not necessarily envy. We all water our own lawns. But the Boone approach suggests the onset of an artistic culture that will exclusively consist of lawn-watering and back-patting and pretending we aren't neck-high in shit because we realize and say we're neck-high in shit.

According to Donald Barthelme, *Art is a commodity, art criticism is a commodity, the apple is a commodity, the air is a commodity....My emotions are a commodity, my desires the very locus of commodification....Perhaps it is time, Levine suggests, to stop worrying about art-as-commodity*. But look here, Donald, do you really think the people working this issue are *worried* about anything except how to remain successful commodities? And isn't it time we examined this conflation of emotions, desires, and events of the body with inanimate objects on sale in a store, with writing, and so on? Not so very far from the imploding hive of Manhattan's art world, there really do exist people who aren't obsessed with money as the supreme value, who don't confuse themselves with their possessions, who aren't so much worried as disgusted about the ease with which talent and cash combine to produce baubles for the oblivious rich to hang over the fireplace. (Of course they aren't all oblivious, and not everything is a bauble. But still.) *And this is my Sherrie Levine*, runs the litany, though where the object actually is and what particular person owns it may have nothing whatever to do with Sherrie Levine.

Of course, it's passé to *worry*, and the dialogue about commodification has been neatly folded into the object's discourse—or, when necessary, into the object's press release, as a kind of no-fault insurance policy that replaces the inner needs of the artist and the internal diction of the work with the requirements of the marketplace. What are essentially multiples become "unique objects," filling back orders from an ever-lengthening list of "important collectors." That many of these collectors are dreaded and even loathed by the artists themselves is a fiction which no one will be able to sustain much longer, since the two groups are becoming indistinguishable.

Levine's show is a sampler: 12 photographs "after Rodchenko," six varicolored chessboards, several backgammon-board-patterned paintings on lead, several check paintings, and six comparatively enormous plywood pieces, under glass, with gold-painted knots. Everything one could possibly write about these works has already been written. Of the plywood pieces I can only say that they remind me of fish that have grown to the size of a new tank, since the last batch had the modest scale of the other works in this show. Everything except the plywood works has its own intriguing physicality and optical draw, and a quality of paradoxical deadpan. The checkerboard pieces are particularly absorbing, since the colors appear to hover free of the surface, vibrating in space. Levine's allusions to board games can be considered allergic reactions to the art system itself, or as Barthelme indicates in his essay, may have *something to do with capitalism*. If you have never seen plywood before, prepare for a treat.

REALLY REAL

There's that magical moment in *Rosemary's Baby* when Mia Farrow wakes up to discover herself being raped by the Devil: "This is really happening!" But imagine a quieter epiphany of horror. You're a gay man who's trying to quit smoking. You're standing on the third floor of a very large building on 22nd Street. You look out the window at the buildings near the river. It's a clear day, you can see New Jersey. Not all that well, because you're wearing your glasses instead of your contact lenses and the prescription has been out of date for five years. Quite close to where you're standing, there's this immense billboard advertising Winston cigarettes. It says, REAL PEOPLE WANT REAL TASTE.

Pictured on the billboard are two real people. The foreground figure is a middle-aged male. He appears to be embracing a rectangular bale of hay. Behind him is a female. They are dressed in casual ranch-style clothing. From what you can make out, it looks like she just finished hauling one of these bales. Something in the male's upper-body language suggests that he might be planning to assault the female with this block of hay. Or perhaps he'll put it down and light a Winston. It's possible, too, that they've both got cigarettes in their mouths. If you had your lenses in, you could tell.

Even without contact lenses, you've interpreted this synecdoche of a narrative the way you're supposed to. Real people come in male/female units. And even when they are pictured on

Eleventh Avenue in Manhattan, they live in prairie environments, where tactile contact with hay is an everyday pleasure, comparable only to the joy of getting lung cancer. You enter the absolute imaginary through the advertisement of the real. Real people, real taste. Yet the only reality here is that of addiction and profit. You know this, but now you want a cigarette. The next thought is always about death.

Death is the only real subject, though the messages that intersect our public spaces project a hysterical discourse of optimism. In the absolute imaginary, everybody lives forever. However, not everybody qualifies as everybody. Those who don't are getting death on their plates every day, while others debate how best to protect *real people*. Perhaps the question has crossed your mind: Why didn't one of those AIDS patients in San Francisco spit in the pope's face? It could have been a terrific front-page photograph. But then, of course, more backlash, more frenzy on the right, more media pandering to "religious feelings."

The yawning chasm between what is really real and what's depicted as real seems large enough to fold America into the chasm whole. The contemplation of this chasm is our principal source of laughter. Our awareness of it gives us our only feeling of sentience. It is horrible and horribly funny. A kind of black hole in the center of human consciousness. In this current show at Metro Pictures (150 Greene Street, through October 24), **Ronald Jones** offers creepy intimations of *historical ironies*—the sort of ironies that slap you in the face whenever you leave your apartment or switch on the news. Jones has placed seven sleek-looking circular tables in the gallery. Each table has a differently designed surface...actually, the press release is perfectly adequate here: ...*based on the proposed designs of the peace conference table used during the 1969 Paris peace talks. Six of the designs were offered by the delegation representing South Vietnam and the United States and one design was suggested by the representatives of North Vietnam and the National Liberation Front of*

South Vietnam. Negotiations over the table designs prolonged the war for months.

The effect is quite sobering, and the bleak elegance of the installation conveys the appetite for abstraction endemic in the halls of power. One wall of the gallery is painted a soothing, almost homeopathic purple, while the others have been paved in a nauseating jaundice yellow. Well away from the tables, a blown-up black-and-white photo in a black frame shows a soldier, from what war I couldn't tell, on leave in Paris, embracing a statue. Jones has included a wall relief, also extracted from one of the table designs, and there is a red wooden square based on the floor pattern of North Carolina's death chamber, facing a wall clock.

The point that thousands of people died while the empowered quibbled over their seating arrangements can obviously be made about the AIDS crisis, too: until those illusory real people in the cigarette ads find their way into the demographics, mass death will have less significance than real taste for that great bunch of guys who control our lives.

Of related interest, or related atmosphere, is **Nancy Shaver**'s faintly overgenerous but entirely welcome show at Curt Marcus Gallery (578 Broadway, through October 10): superficially wistful, basically tough-minded assemblage works, many of them featuring picture frames and framed pictures as elements of partial interiors. Shaver's objects look extracted from some crumbling, memory-hounded rural home in a Truman Capote novel. Her work has many affinities with that of Annette Lemieux and Jennifer Bolande. Instead of saying this work is like that or bemoaning similarities, it's more interesting to consider why art that reflects feelings of loss and sadness and care for the emotions is being made by many artists now, within a rigorous formal practice. (I don't mean to imply that such work is lugubrious. It's just very affecting in places where many people no longer have places.)

Of further related interest: the DIA Art Foundation's new publication, ***Discussions In Contemporary Culture***, edited by

Hal Foster, containing edited texts and transcripts of the DIA-sponsored panels held in February and March of this year. Among the participants were Benjamin H. D. Buchloh, Rosalind Krauss, Dan Graham, Douglas Crimp, Barbara Kruger, Martha Rosler, Craig Owens, Virginia Domínguez, Krzysztof Wodiczko, and Aimee Rankin. The discussions deal with three overarching subjects: "The Cultural Public Sphere," "1967/1987: Genealogies of Art and Theory," and "The Politics of Representation." I also recommend the current issue of *Covert Action*, Number 28, particularly Robert Lederer's two articles, "Chemical-Biological Warfare" and "The Origin and Spread of AIDS."

Plus **Richard Serra** at Leo Castelli (142 Green Street, through October 17), **Blinky Palermo** at Sperone Westwater (142 Greene Street, through October 13), **Tyler Turkle** at Cable (611 Broadway, through October 17), and **Jean-Luc Vilmouth** at Barbara Toll (146 Greene Street, now closed).

October 20, 1987

STRANGE WEATHER

[**Betty Beaumont.** 55 Mercer Gallery, 55 Mercer Street, through October 17.]

Dear [name deleted],

You asked me to write you some news of New York, so I decided to go ahead, though I hope it won't change your mind about visiting next month. Everyone feels completely strung out and crazy, but this happens every year after vacations. [Name deleted] says it's because people come from vacation paradise back to hell, and it takes time to work up to total neuroticism from relative calm. Perhaps there are worse states of mind than the one that sets in after three weeks of seeing the same 30 people every night, and this is an expected occupational hazard for me. Even so, I'm exhausted. With the idea that a weekend out of here might ameliorate the shock of reentry, I had agreed to go with [names deleted] to their place in the country. But at the last minute I remembered I had to go to [name deleted]'s opening. This turned out providential because a freak snowstorm trapped [names deleted] in their cottage for two days. [Name deleted] said all he could hear were tree limbs snapping off. [Name deleted]'s phone line toppled and [name deleted] couldn't get her car out.

[Name deleted] feels this preternaturally early storm marks the beginning of the end, and it's hard not to agree with her. [Name deleted] also says that Styrofoam products contribute heavily to ozone depletion, so when these two review books from [publisher deleted] arrived packed in Styrofoam curls I thought I should register some sort of protest. Like all the books [name deleted] publishes, these two should've come with four legs to screw into the corners. It's incredible how certain forms of apprehension become stigmatized as retrograde or crazy: if you care about ecology, people think of Earth shoes and granola and tackiness, somehow. And despite all the evidence that the CIA has been overthrowing governments and "experimenting" with biological weapons for at least 30 years, just mentioning the CIA gets you labeled paranoid.

The art world is more static right now than it appears. It looks like a lot and there are plenty of interesting things, but what's mainly going on is the endless recycling of 30 proper names. [Name deleted] and [name deleted] both opened the season with what's now being called "power shows"—shows that have no compelling idea behind them except to establish the gallery's sustained economic viability by showing a few of the most expensive names. The power shows I've seen looked a little desperate.

[Name deleted] told the *Times* that he wasn't selling his gallery to [name deleted]. But [name deleted] is still very much on the scene, manipulating things. [Name deleted] is really a pernicious [expletive deleted] in my own view, but as [name deleted] said the other day, the way the art world is, if Andrew Crispo came back with a good show, all would be forgiven.

I saw a show you'd like, by Betty Beaumont at 55 Mercer, called *Toxic Imaging*. Hard to describe. It's in the back of the gallery, in two areas divided by a diagonal wall. The first thing you see is a yellow metal roundabout that rotates, with sets of metal brackets along the edge that frame these elegantly exposed black-and-white TV picture tubes, which face the center of the roundabout. You just see vertical roll and fuzz on the TVs. There's a pile of bunched-up, pale-yellow ticker tape in the center. On the diagonal wall there's a large message board with stock market quotations moving across it right to left, like the vulgar one in the Second Avenue Deli.

Then in the passage between the installation's front and back, two black oil barrels with maroon rims, the top surfaces covered by bound volumes of Xeroxed news clippings. These all relate to chemical poisoning, from dioxin spills and waste dumps to Bhopal and Chernobyl, collected over a 10-year period—more intensively collected, of course, in the past three years. Above this a metal photo-display grid, with pictures of factories pouring chemicals into the atmosphere. The pictures alternate night and daytime shouts, which makes a nice formal checkerboard. On either side of the grid Beaumont has two neatly spaced, square Auratone speakers mounted on the wall. Each one broadcasts a different TV network's disaster news coverage.

Behind the diagonal wall is a gorgeously designed greenhouse structure that curves to a peak on top. The floor consists of four wooden planks; inside there are four black oil barrels, three tape decks, a slide carousel and a projector that throws black-and-white images of moving water on the diagonal wall. The moving pictures reflect through the greenhouse and splatter out on part of the two walls behind it. Slides of boarded-up houses in the Love Canal area are projected against the rear wall, and also reflect through the glass so they appear on the side wall, less sharply. On either side of the greenhouse, on the floor, Beaumont uses television screens as light tables for two X-rays—both chest X-rays, if I remember correctly. The sound on the TVs is played low, while more sounds issue from two Poly-Planar speakers hanging from the ceiling: a narrative about Love Canal and toxic waste.

When you walk through it, the installation's audio jumbles up like a cacophony of ghosts, but if you stand close to the sound source you hear an intelligible verbal sequence. The predominant b-and-w imagery gives the gritty feeling of a Frederick Wiseman documentary, but the greenhouse structure opens the thing out into fantasy, the flicker of childhood memories and adult reveries. It provides moments of Syberbergian dreamtime along with the more prosaic commentary on environmental destruction.

As [name deleted] said, this season is about nostalgia and touching memories, which can be powerful but can more dependably be puerile. This show works for me, maybe because it indexes memories and associations that have become toxic in retrospect. It's hard to look at your childhoods without seeing the profligate spoilage of everything—which was, at the time, considered the luxury of American affluence. Of course you leave the Beaumont installation with the feeling there are too many things wrong with the world for anyone to fix it, and I personally am trying to finish this quick so I can catch *Gentlemen Prefer Blondes* and *How To Marry A Millionaire* at Theatre 80.

Most people seem to think that once [name deleted]'s show at [name deleted] has blown over we can all return to normal. [Name deleted] is said to be anticipating bad press. I'll ignore him, as usual, on the theory that if you don't have anything good to say, save it for the right occasion.

Love, G.

A TORTURE GARDEN

[**Robert Gober**. Paula Cooper Gallery, 155 Wooster Street, through October 28.]

If you happen to go all gaga over sculpture assembled from the contents of your local supermarket or souvenir items dipped in bronze, chances are you will find Robert Gober's recent works somewhat lacking in the aesthetic splendor you have learned to cherish in a box of Tide. A forthright collector admitted to "having problems" with Gober's art *because the artist made it himself.* Not so long ago, one of our gutsiest art consultants couldn't decide if she was or wasn't going to "make it happen for him." I think I'll just skip the patronizing and/or condescending blurbiage Gober has received from certain critics. The best way to view his work is to go view it.

To avoid setting up a binary opposition here, let's say that a sculptural practice that consists in pillaging Conran's and Forbidden Planet has its memorable moments, and as many inherent risks as the adventure of shopping itself. An arrangement of found objects can operate as metaphor, as semiological investigation, as cunning joke, as art. The $60,000 bronze of an inflatable fuck doll (actually, we're still waiting for this) may also tell us something important about ourselves and our values. Still, a case can be made for the handcrafted object, without relying on a jejune distinction between *cynicism* and *love.* (There are few artists of any kind who produce cynically, even if there are many who operate in near-total delusion.)

I'm personally inclined to place more importance on what's rare and hard-won than what's ubiquitous and factory-assembled, though the two things may yield comparable surface significance, like literature and journalism. Gober's work has gone through a much richer development than perpetual enlargement or serial statement of a single idea. It remains intimate and reflective of communal realities that are not exclusive to the middle class. While the consumer society belongs to "everybody" only in the most provisional sense (everyone sees the products, but not everyone consumes them), many of the structures Gober forms and deforms are truly basic.

There were sinks, early on, and a bed: objects found in jail cells and palaces. The funky distensions of the sink form suggested the hallucinatory claustrophobia of a slum apartment, or insomniac meditation on the bare physical facts of urban existence. The vacant tap holes spoke about a world where everything is out of order, dried-up, or blocked; but the monument-like stolidity of the object had a triumphant irony, indicating the persistence of imagination, and the bed was obviously there to dream in.

Gober's new work uncovers more disturbing possibilities in everyday objects, and in a stark way his show at Paula Cooper Gallery touches on everything from cradle to grave, from the gravity-tempting *Pitched Crib* and similarly twisted *Slanted Playpen* to *Two Partially Buried Sinks*, the latter an outdoor piece, temporarily planted in a carefully lawned box of topsoil. There is also an X-shaped crib and an X-shaped playpen, offering double triangular training jails for twins or schizophrenic children.

Gober's cribs and playpens embody the helpless condition of childhood and the invariably weird structures adults invent to shape it; their formal simplicity gives them an archetypal directness that any former child can read without a press release. For the large piece called *Plywood* resting against the left wall as you go in, some explanation may be necessary, since it is not, in fact, plywood, but laminated fir, assembled layer by layer to resemble plywood. (This may or may not be Gober's response to yet another postmodern collector who asked, *Why not just go out and buy a sink and show that?*)

Two sculpted urinals occupy part of the right wall, their placement making a visual segue from childhood torture garden to institutional gender-differentiation unit. And here the concept of the readymade, implicit in the choice of object, is decisively refuted as an option in Gober's work: these urinals have been touched, worked up, painted, if you will, *lovingly* by hand, in other words thought about as forms invented for males to piss in. The readymade urinal only talks about art, the art system, art values; Gober's urinals tell you about pissing, standing next to other people pissing, about cocks and having one or not having one in a disposal situation, and about being watched while you piss. Which is so much more basic than modern art, really.

There is a *Slip Covered Armchair*, a deceptively light-looking plaster-and-wood construction under fabric, pleated at the bottom, with painted flowers and birds scattered over it, less a relic of our parents' than our grandparents' time; the crusty, iron-hard feel of the thing through the slipcover suggests that nostalgia is a blanket for a past less pleasant than we remember. The most beautiful piece in the show is *Untitled (Dog Bed)*, in a corner by the front window, its cotton-flannel oval wrapped in off-white rattan: the bed for pooch is decorated with deer and hunters and slain deer with shotguns resting across their necks, a reminder that grownups are just as hypocritical and murderous toward animals as they are toward children.

Gober is very much "of the earth," artisanal, death-conscious, given to the more sweeping gestures of irony, in his sense of the irremediable somewhere between Samuel Beckett and Thomas Bernhard. *Two Partially Buried Sinks*, poking up from or subsiding into the sod (as you wish), echoes the "togetherness" of the urinals, and suggests an ideal happy ending for Beckett's *Happy Days*: put Willie in the mound there with Winnie and let them both sink. It reminded me, too, of the Cable Gallery show that Gober organized last year, in which his single bed stood next to an enormous cone-shaped pile of dirt by Meg Webster—the sleeper dreaming of death and regeneration, the furniture of living as the stuff of dreams.

November 3, 1987

MODERN SACRIFICE

[**Maura Sheehan:** "Mayarama." Bruno Facchetti Gallery, 476 Broadway, through November 4; Art Galaxy, 262 Mott Street, through November 14.]

One of Maura Sheehan's current exhibitions features three walls covered with plaster skull masks. The other is an environment in a darkened room containing trees, burnt material on the floor, and several disturbing black statues. This is not a formal interview, but a casually taped conversation over dinner, with help from critic and novelist Thomas McEvilley.

Maura Sheehan: One of the things I liked that I didn't anticipate is that the two exhibitions seem like the antithesis of each other, very unalike. Bruno Facchetti's was done first. I worked exclusively on the production of the skulls all summer. After that show opened, I was able to concentrate on Art Galaxy, where I wanted a more textural thing. The sense of "rama," or in the round, the circularity of the shows, I thought, was filled out by the fact that they were so different from each other.

For example, the floor in Bruno's is just the wood floor, there's nothing there. At Art Galaxy, I wanted a floor that gave a sense of driving through the Yucatán, through slash-and-burn agriculture. Slash-and-burn is the 500-year-old hangover from having the great books of the Mayans burned. There seemed some sort of analogy between the agriculture being completely singed, and incorporating those, so that you were sinking into it as you walked into Art Galaxy.

Gary Indiana: *The floor felt organic.*

MS: The Mayans burned the crops and the plants and the earth. And the books were made from pulp and all that jazz, from leaves, trees, and bark. It did lend itself to a sense of the organic, and yet it was the ultimate embodiment of culture, of literature and language, as opposed to earth and dirt and soot. The two things go interestingly together. With that floor, even through the books, you feel an organic thing. Also, there's a lot of sawdust underneath, it gives a cushion. And the books lend themselves to that kind of smooshiness as you walk on them.

Bishop de Landa burned all the Mayan codices, right?

MS: Yes, he was ousted then for having tortured so much, and he made these big bonfires he writes about. All the people gathered around, he made them reverse their iconography and change their attitudes; he thought he'd convinced them that these fires at night were a display of God, actually.

In the Facchetti show, that piece in the office area, the round reliefs that come together like gears, how are those related?

MS: The figure is this Yucatanian goddess. All her limbs have been severed, there's a kind of scalloped thing around her stumps. During the Christianization, she was set up as an example of a negative, demonic force. I made gears out of her, things that would fit into each other, to suggest the motion she's running in. It's a motion depicted in a lot of archaic Greek stuff, too, where the arms and legs are all stretched out. The figure is about a terrifically dynamic type of art, a time of experimentation and life-loving. She was held up by the Franciscans as a really badass person. I don't know, I could really identify with her—I think you could too, maybe.

Why not. Now, the Mayan civilization came to an end—

MS: In the 1500s with Cortés.

There's this strange historical coincidence, the Aztecs had certain prophecies that ensured that Cortés with his little band of people wouldn't be annihilated on arrival. The same thing happened with the Incas; there was this one historical moment, when Pizarro arrived, that it could be the fulfillment of prophecy. White people also brought all these diseases with them.

MS: There were something like 30 million people in Mexico in 1500, and by 1600 there were one million people left. It was an extraordinary example of genocide. Was it Cortés who arrived with a big shield and a cross?

Thomas McEvilley: It was Cortés. But you know, the thing about the prophecy and all, that they thought he was like their own former messiah returning—that was the Aztecs rather than the Mayas. Montezuma. I think what Maura's doing involves all that too. But—

MS: The arrival of Cortés wasn't accidental. He had his cronies who got really into the Mayans. They found out this was an important date. It was a prearranged situation, it wasn't a miracle. He was aware of walking in on them when they really needed him. They thought he was Quetzalcoatl, the big snake god. He arrived, he had all these troops behind him, he seemed like a snake to them.

But that wasn't true of the Incas at all. Nobody knew what was down there. Pizarro was just sure if he persisted there would be gold, he heard this and that from some tribes.

MS: They were all after the gold, of course. The humanity was just an awful thing to have to put up with, an inconvenience.

The skulls in the Facchetti show, the walls of skulls, is that from temple decoration?

MS: A piece of Mayan architecture, a platform found behind the ball court in Chichen Itza and also Mexico City, is a building specifically about sacrifice. The games were played (for religious purposes, not for sport), the winner would be sacrificed, and then a profile of the skull would be carved into the wall, it was a kind of tally sheet or scorecard reminding the gods of this sacrifice.

The entire exterior is covered with these profiles, primitively carved, all looking as if they've been done by formula, in strict proportion, but there's a certain stylistic differentiation in the way they're carved. On the top of these platforms, they had these big poles, at the end they'd have the actual skull of the person, like planters that the poles went into.

This type of architecture was a direct reference to human sacrifice. Something alien, and at the same time very familiar to me.

I saw pictures of a memorial the Vietnamese made in Kampuchea. They took skulls of people the Khmer Rouge had killed and arranged them in this atrocity museum, in a pyramid. They sent an expert, a curator, to Auschwitz, to consult with the people there about how to present this material authentically. You have statues downstairs in Facchetti and in the environment at Art Galaxy—

MS: They have stores in the Lower East Side devoted to Christian voodoo. They have rosary beads with savage little things on the tips of the cross. You pray to a stature of Mary, say, to put a spell on somebody. It's used in a practical way. They told me, for example, if you think someone is trying to kill you, you pray to this particular statue. Or if you have a fear that you're going to lose your job, or your neighbor is going to try to have you evicted and take over your apartment, there are practical things that these statues are aligned with.

You pay a little extra and they tell you which statues to get, and what herbs. Part of my process has been establishing a real working relationship with these stores.

The statues are painted black, and you've affixed these masks from other statues over the faces, with rubber bands or string.

MS: The black is a real flat black, there's something deadpan about the blackness. What I'm after is a burnt feeling. I burned some of these but the paint and plaster sort of melted.

TMcE: The fact that this stuff comes from Maura's neighborhood is an element of site specificity in the material.

MS: Avenue C is the modern Maya land. Right on the corner of Houston and B there's this liquor store that's unnamed. I've been talking to the woman about naming it Maya Land Liquors. She has agreed, if I will go up and paint it myself—the words MAYA LAND. Because it's a temple spot, practically, for the people in the neighborhood: they worship there.

TMcE: There's this poignant analogy between the displacement of Mayan culture by Christian barbarians, and the displacement of Puerto Rican culture that's going on right before our eyes in this neighborhood.

This has been an ongoing motif in my neighborhood, too. At first it was a multiracial area. Then, when Second Avenue started to get totally gentrified—it's not so heavily gentrified in terms of architecture, but instead of the indigenous population, there's this colonialist influx of affluent people, white people, upscale immigrants.

MS: When we got back from Mexico, though, it was like we were still there. I'd never been so comfortable coming back to New York. There's usually this hard-ass adjustment.

What about the masks that go over the faces on the statues?

MS: These are definitely non-Christian, pagan, a little on the savage side. There's the Gorgon mask—the figure with the tongue sticking out, that's Greek. Then there's a Mayan mask and an Olmec mask. The female, of course, is the Gorgon, there's a gender thing there.

The blindfolds on the faces, is that to prevent the Medusa effect?

MS: Well, also it was to get that mask on there without doing all these tricky things behind.

TMcE: You definitely explained it to me as the Medusa effect.

MS: True. I don't want anybody turning to stone in the gallery.

THE CRITIC'S ROLE

The critic's role has been widely debated in the past year. Only a few months ago, many theorists were wont to argue that artists themselves had usurped "the critical function." Art was being made that explored and exposed its own status as commodity, and the context in which the commodity functioned. Art looked at itself as art, too, and even positioned itself historically without any help from criticism. It was suggested by various writers and artists that critics should perhaps turn their attention to criticism itself, clean their own stables and figure out what to do next.

I bring this up only because a few weeks ago, after the stock market crash, certain dealers, collectors, and artists expressed the idea that now there would be less money floating around, and hence more prudence among buyers. One collector told *The New York Times* that, torn between throwing a dinner party or buying a drawing, he might just throw the dinner party. Along the Rialto, many were saying that *the critic* was about to become important once again, an essential, Mandarin consultant in the brokerage of reputations.

It seems to me very unfortunate that a quantum increase of power should befall critics at the same moment when they have been urged, by some of the art world's finest minds, to reinvent their practice and examine their souls. If you happen to skim the latest crop of art magazines, you will see that critics who just yesterday were known for churning out gallons of expedient prose every month are finally turning their attention inward. It would be a major loss to the world of belles lettres if this soul-searching were interrupted by the vagaries of the marketplace.

At least one novel critical strategy has occurred to me, and I will get to it presently, but first I want to mention, in the plodding "old criticism" mode, an exhibition called **"Art Against Apartheid,"** in the lobby of the General Assembly Building of the United Nations (through November 22). This is a traveling excerpt of an 85-work collection, the works donated by artists "from around the world," as the phrase goes, "to be installed in a museum in South Africa when a democratic government is elected there by universal suffrage."

This show is a fairly broad mixture of things. Some pictures deal explicitly with issues of race, with torture, with politics. Others are more allusive, and many are simply okay works by name artists. A statement issued at the opening asserts that "all express the artists' outrage about this inhumane and anachronistic system and their commitment to the dignity of man," which seems a rather large claim to make, say, for a plastic tea bag by Claes Oldenburg, a suite of photographs of white school-age children by Christian Boltanski, or a few dashing smears of black and white by Robert Motherwell.

The donation of these works merely signifies that the artists want to go on record as being "against apartheid," and on one hand it's wonderful that they have lent their cultural prestige to this project. On the other hand, gestures of this kind always remind me of a dowager writing a check to the ASPCA. Implicit is the idea that once blacks achieve a democratic government for themselves, they are just naturally going to want a museum full of pictures by artists who are mainly white and (in this show, anyway) entirely male, perhaps augmented by a special wing full of local handicrafts. That this might not be so, and that it might not take much imagination to detect a mellower sort of apartheid in Western artistic culture itself, is obvious to anyone who thinks about it for five minutes. But here, as so often happens, art is made to represent the transcendence of cultural particulars, or else "addresses" a political problem by reproducing some icon of generalized oppression—a hanging figure, for instance.

There is an inherent contradiction—though not a consciously malevolent one, quite the contrary—in deploying white cultural imperialism to combat a system of white supremacy. Although not all the artists are white and not all come from the First World, the importance of each proper name in this show has been determined by the same cultural establishment that has always reserved its top floor for white, male artists. An artist like Hans Haacke would be unthinkable in this show, since his work provides a systemic analysis of the cultural forces that produce apartheid with one hand and shows like this with the other. Again, it's beyond doubt that everyone involved *means well*, without for a second questioning their noblesse oblige in some future South African museum. In fairness to the artists themselves, it must be said that the nature of their practice—i.e., producing objects to fulfill or to "challenge" an overdetermined museum aesthetic—leaves them no role to play in the dynamic of culture besides that of privileged sympathizers for one cause or another.

Parenthetically, I find it interesting that the UN is sponsoring this show right now, when almost every country in the world—even ours—has more or less vigorously condemned apartheid and the present government of South Africa; interesting because the UN continues to pass genocidally lymphatic and half-assed motions worldwide against People With AIDS, the majority of whom are persons of color.

To return to our themes of the critic's role: when people in the art world say that critics have more importance in a shrinking art market, they simply mean that buyers will monitor the writing of critics more carefully for the frequency of proper names before making that risky investment. There are structures that exist to ensure that this, and nothing else, will be the critic's role. A concrete example: in the current issue of *ARTnews*, a number of critics, museum directors, and historians are tapped for their opinions about which artists are overrated, which underrated. "Their responses," says the introduction, "are highly provocative." I answered the first part of the question by mentioning some artists I like, and the second by saying that white heterosexual males are invariably given more attention than anyone else, since they own the world. This was, apparently, too provocative for *ARTnews*, which deleted the statement and just ran the shopping list. Well, there you have the critic's role. I've tried to come up with other methods the critic might employ to enlarge his or her horizons; being from the theater, I thought of a scenario like this:

The critic phones up a young artist, this good-looking 24-year-old white boy from Great Neck who's been sending him slides and little handwritten reminders that he has this show hanging somewhere, and tells the kid he wants to make a "studio visit." Then the critic has a friend phone the kid and tell him: "Listen, this critic is very eccentric, whatever he does, don't react, or let on that you think he's strange, just pretend everything's completely normal." Next, a stretch limousine, hired for the occasion, pulls up outside the artist's studio. A chauffeur steps out, goes around the car, opens the rear door…and out comes the critic, dressed as Bozo the Clown, with two pit bulls on leashes. He sweeps into the studio, sliding across the floor on his enormous shoes, pulled by the two growling, gnashing pit bulls, plants himself down on the nearest chair, crosses his legs and his arms malevolently, and demands to see the work. "Don't touch the dogs, they'll take your arm off." The artist, a nervous wreck, brings out one work after another while the clown puffs on an enormous cigar, his face a mask of deepening displeasure;

every few minutes, he pulls a raw steak from his costume and tosses it in front of the dogs. After an hour of terror the clown stands up, stamps his cigar out on the floor, and tells the artist: "Okay, I've seen enough…by the way, I'm an artist too, watch this." He blows up several balloons, ties the ends, and then twists them together into the shape of an elephant. "That's for you, kid…good-bye and good luck." And with a wink and a nod he slides through the studio and out the door.

November 24, 1987

FUNNY HA HA, FUNNY STRANGE

[**Meyer Vaisman.** Leo Castelli, 420 West Broadway, through November 28]

Before refreshing ourselves at the sacred fount of Art, let's give a thought to the cyclical, tail-eating nature of advertising and the rote responses it jerks out of us, the public. I'm thinking specifically of the new bus-shelter ads for *Werewolf* (a new TV series), and the spate of glossy magazine articles about, and excerpts from, Donald Trump's forthcoming book concerning the mystery and magic that is, according to him, Donald Trump.

First of all, we are unlikely to see any effective analysis of Trump's book in *Vanity Fair*, *New York*, or other such periodicals, for the simple reason that the editorial content of these publications *is* advertising, usually for one or another Celebrity Way of Being. You can be famous for allegedly murdering your spouse or discovering a cancer cure: either way, they'll put you on the cover. They will as readily publish the memoirs of a morally subnormal real estate doofus as an Amaretto di Mussolini eighth-of-a-page insert. The job of deconstruction at these rags often falls to the picture editor, and in the case of the Trump book we owe a debt of gratitude to the reflexive viciousness endemic in that profession. *Vanity Fair* takes the palm here, for a vertical sequence of snaps-and-quotes in which Trump looks like an especially virulent, shifty-eyed, loudmouthed accumulation of baby fat. Even if you were inclined to believe that rent control is a greater evil than the boorishness of developers, one look at the source of this wisdom would make you think twice about it.

For most New Yorkers, I think, the mental space occupied by Donald Trump closely corresponds to the visceral effect of the *Werewolf* ads. These are, as far as I know, the first public use of 3-D "synoptic photography," which would, and undoubtedly will, make a nifty art process when the price comes down. As ads, these pieces are not especially effective or scary. The werewolf is strictly from central casting, down to the tartar stains on his teeth, and the warning that HE ONLY COMES OUT AT NIGHT isn't likely to keep anyone home just to watch a mediocre television program. But the ads are 3-D enough to create a slight nausea, a fascination with the 3-D technique itself. *Werewolf* looks like the future of billboards.

Not long ago, when Ileana Sonnabend showed the works of Ashley Bickerton, Peter Halley, Jeff Koons, and Meyer Vaisman, hyperrealists of the media commenced grunting and sputtering about it as if it were the last possible straw, the final insult to Values, Standards, Culture, and everything we all supposedly believe in. There were accusations of venality and cynicism. The most damning thing of all, apparently, was that these artists were *barely out of art school.* Kay Larson's *New York* column forthrightly dubbed them "Masters of Hype." Calvin Tomkins, in *The New Yorker*, more circumspectly distinguished between artists he found unappetizingly cerebral and those who appealed to his notions of sincerity.

Personally, I found the whole business rather sordid. Not the art or the artists or the show—even though the gallery did presume a galvanized interest on the part of certain people whose attentions were elsewhere—but the phenomenon of critics creating the very situation they were pretending to deplore, seizing on one general-interest article about the artists as evidence that civilization had just been flushed down the tubes. The striking of this apocalyptic gong has a soothing effect on readers of *The New Yorker*, *Time*, and other staples of dental offices across the country. Indignation, it seems, is the most delicious sensation available to the sclerotic, since it recasts completely subjective impressions as universal absolutes.

An essay could certainly be written about the effect of *generational alienation* on criticism. To a lowering extent, people who do criticism as a lifetime career view artists their own age as exemplary, younger artists as parvenus and frauds. This probably has to do with the fact that older people are, generally speaking, closer to death than younger ones, a circumstance bound to produce resentment. The Sonnabend show elicited a particularly resentful response in many quarters because it was so unapologetically young. It would have been more sensible to resent it for being so unapologetically male, so much a *man's package*, so paradigmatic of an archaic bias in the blue-chip regions of the art world—but it could not be resented for that reason by the critics for *New York*, *The New Yorker*, *Time* and etcetera, since the defense of "standards," "values," and the trammeled glories of yesteryear goes hand in glove with the mythology of male "greatness" in the arts.

That said, I can honestly say that I had no opinion about the Sonnabend show. Because I didn't go to the Sonnabend show. But I do think Bickerton, Halley, Koons, and Vaisman are good artists. They are not always prudent or witting interviewees, and they share the probably erroneous notion most of us have that the media can somehow be outsmarted and made to do disruptive, intelligent things with essentially personal publicity. Meyer Vaisman's current show at Castelli is wonderfully entertaining, complicated, ambitious, funny—and, I hope, just as offensive to the people shocked by his toilet-seat piece in the Sonnabend show.

One of the felicities of Vaisman's work is its willingness to look like a parody of art—not just historically ensconced art, but immediately recent art. Another is its greasy sensuality, its flagrant and cheerful allusions to sex, scatology, and pornography. A Vaisman painting typically conveys an unrepressed curiosity about the basic things in life, whether money or a pulled tooth or a limp penis; in this sense, he is a liberating artist. His pictures reject "correctness" of any kind, they goose the viewer unmercifully just when s/he's determined to cop a straight face; there is a bit more evil tact at work than in David Salle's split-beaver/high-art conjunctions but the same hilarious hauteur involved in the regality of presentation. Vaisman's new pictures are monstrously big, but they certainly do command the wall.

These are modular pictures, some with regularly spaced oval canvases that extrude from a ground canvas, others with picture-frame shapes arranged in funky relief, most of the surfaces "textured" by enlarged canvas-weave screened over them, and iconography screened or painted over the texturing. They have a formal affinity with the splaying volumes of Lee Bontecou's sculpture, the same look of massed energy-blocks waiting to spring. The imagery slapped down on the various forms has the queasy, excessive look of something that really needs to be where it is even though it's ridiculous. For instance, in the piece called *Souvenir*, the drawing of a string of shrunken heads appears beside a silkscreen photo of pygmies, beside a white oval, next to a trophy-shaped painting of a mounted deer head (painted in the manner of Paladino), and another trophy head, of a smiling bear—this is the straight-faced whimsy of a smart, efficient comedian. *Portrait With Imaginary Siblings*, which contains *Punch*-style caricatures of Vaisman and close friend Lisa Phillips, Mae West, and someone I assume to be Curly of the Three Stooges, is the work of a comedian who also juggles.

Vaisman's imagery refers throughout to the notion of the souvenir: one piece features flat depictions of the relief portraits on various old coins, another displays an assortment of antique jugs, vessels, and candy boxes, mixed with pictures of fruit; two entirely abstract pieces consist of interlocking picture-frame forms, their recessed areas mainly blank, as if awaiting resonant old objects. But Vaisman's tone is one of tonic dissonance rather than nostalgia. One large oval contains a picture of weblike shattered glass, while other frames enclose, under glass, some dark, mucky substance you might get all over your legs in the course of a truly final orgy.

December 1, 1987

BLUE MOON

CARTAGENA, COLOMBIA—You can fly Avianca out of Newark or Miami into Barranquilla, change in Barranquilla for the local flight to Cartagena. Other flights take you first to Santa Marta and then to Bogotá, change in Bogotá, and fly directly back to the coast. This route offers the unnecessary risk of negotiating the Andes on Avianca, whose pilots enjoy entering the plateau of Bogotá sideways, but the view is spectacular: a vast, damp, muddy sky above an immense flatland of seething Antonioni green.

The way back to the Caribbean may take one hour or three hours or five hours: time turns syrupy in South American airports. The heat and light burn out synapses. The moorings of northern consciousness snap in the broiler of the day.

The Cartagena airport is in Boca Chica. Boca Chica features miles and miles of lagoonlike dirt roads and crumbling pavements, mud and sisal huts, free-ranging black pigs and scrawny chickens, clapboard shacks that sell Coca-Cola and beer. Between Boca Chica and the man-made sandpit of Boca Grande, the old walled city and its surrounding port offer the charms of decay, disintegrating gingerbread baroque, outdoor markets, the old bullring, the new bullring, the Palace of the Inquisition, the cathedral, the Jesuit church, $7 grams of cocaine, horse-drawn carriage rides between the Plaza de Bolívar and the carport at the Caribe in Boca Grande, tincture of watered coffee in medicine cups, and those endless stretches of deserted street found in all

South American cities, pockets of dead silence where nothing exists except architecture and garbage.

In winter months, rain bursts from the atomic-looking clouds each morning, followed by blazing sun, instant evaporation, gagging humidity. The scene repeats in the afternoon, and at night an electrical storm usually blows out all the power between Boca Chica and the tip of Boca Grande. On such nights the only visible thing in Boca Grande is the sign on top of the Hilton. There are, in fact, only two things which work reliably in Cartagena: the emergency generator at the Hilton and the submachine guns of the military police. The military police are, as a rule, boys between 16 and 22, achingly beautiful, perpetually horny, trigger-happy when drunk, and childlike in their hatred of Communism.

The port extends from the sea just beyond the fortress walls of the old town to the Paseo de los Mártires. Along this promenade, beggars display elephantiasis of the feet, the stumps of severed limbs, and radical facial wounds. The Paseo ends where the new convention center floats on the water, along a street full of arches and balconies, lit up like a film set, packed with cigarette stands, food carts, trinket vendors, and the colorful human swarm.

Cartagena poses certain hazards for the casual tourist. As in most Third World countries, sudden arbitrary loss of life is one of them. Persons who strike up instant friendship, who offer to show you the town, score coke for you, or service your body in unbelievably agreeable ways often have other plans, sometimes involving a handgun or a machete. It is best to stick to well-lighted, well-traveled areas.

The shore drive runs in one direction up to Boca Chica, the other into Boca Grande. Boca Grande has sparkling beaches that segue into sewage as you round the arm of the peninsula. Boca Grande has the Hilton and the Caribe and the Capilla del Mar, each with swimming pool, outdoor café, and security guards.

Boca Grande has shopping malls and myriad emerald emporiums, discos in the Miami style, cabana restaurants on the beach. On the beach there are hundreds of people selling sunglasses and slices of mango and Coca-Cola, trailed by beggars who surround any fresh arrival and return every five minutes until they are propitiated. This is, I think, exactly as it should be.

During Carnaval, the many beauty queens of Colombia assemble and are borne on gaudy floats through the streets of the old town, along the inland drive to Boca Grande, and on to the Hilton, where Miss Colombia is crowned. During Carnaval, security is noticeably slack at the Hilton, the Caribe, the Capilla del Mar. During Carnaval, various scores are settled by the so-called Medellín Cartel, because bursts of submachine-gun fire are indistinguishable from fireworks.

At night in Cartagena the moon and clouds are blue, really blue, as in "Blue Moon."

Private homes in Cartagena generally contain parrots, monkeys, boa constrictors, and sloths. The sloths hang from treetops in the courtyards. Sloths have no natural enemies, and so move in slow motion. Toucans, it is good to remember, are susceptible to heart attacks and shouldn't be surprised. Dogs and cats are seldom treated with kindness.

You can take a boat to the Rosario Islands. On the way, you can see Panama on your left, and on your right, the harbor islands, where fragments of European buildings slowly rot back into jungle. The boats to the Rosarios sit so low in the water that the trip is an experiment in terror, but on the main island there is a guest house with a good restaurant and thousands of parrots in the flame trees. You can consult the local voodoo priestess regarding problems of love and destiny, watch for scorpions on your bedroom ceiling, swim in water warmer than your own body, and forget all about America. Sort of.

December 15, 1987

THE LAST CIGARETTE

This has to be about the last cigarette as much as it's about Marianne Faithfull. And it has to be like a personal letter, because I've quit smoking and I can't write and letters aren't like writing. When you stop, the blood vessels in your brain expand and destroy your concentration and the sound of your own voice nauseates you.

I went to two of her six shows (November 30 and December 1) at the Bottom Line last week thinking for sure I could write about them because I'd listened to *Strange Weather* four thousand times. Before that *Broken English* a few million times, probably, after an incredibly twisted relationship with a fascinating junkie. And actually Marianne Faithfull was the first compelling reason I'd had to leave my apartment in an embarrassingly long time. I have avoided New York nightlife for years. Everything always looks to me like a stale parody of something else. Sexual opportunity is dead. So is romance. All anyone does any more is eat dinner, take meetings and die. Those who still dance have not heard the awful news. The only people who look as if they're enjoying themselves also look like the most deluded people in the room. Only fooling. Anyway, it is terrible to leave your house, if you are fortunate enough to have one. And the last cigarette is terrible, too.

Maybe it wouldn't be so terrible to go out once in a *very* great while. The Bottom Line was full of people, both nights, who I remembered fondly from the Mudd Club era. The thought crossed my mind that maybe they hadn't been out since the Mudd Club closed, but I'm sure they have. It's been what, six years? Even I have been out since then, actually.

Now, I'm just going to put this down here in any order as it occurs to me. It isn't that I want a cigarette. I can't concentrate without one. The last time I saw Marianne Faithfull play was at the Mudd Club, where she looked like she was waiting for an ambulance. Spectral as she was then, the evening was unforgettable, the kind of slash-your-wrists special Steve Mass contrived with such offhand genius. At the Bottom Line, though, she looked fabulous, coming on after a taped tango intro in a long leather coat and red gloves, her pale blond hair knotted in a French twist and flipped up in front, the naturally pensive features bemused, often smiling; under the coat she wore a full-length dress that hugged an ample, fortyish figure—and good for her for showing it off.

She was rattled in an amiable way, blew a couple of cues here and there, but her poise, as if welded to the microphone, evoked the silky, easygoing heftiness of Peggy Lee. She didn't move around that much on stage, mainly time-keeping gestures, and some minimal dramaturgy at the end of "The Ballad of Lucy Jordan," ditto at the end of "Guilt." She draped herself against the piano for "Love, Life and Money." She seemed happy as a clam and told the audience it was "one of those moments in life when everything is in the right place."

And it was like that. I felt it when people applauded the line from Tom Waits and Kathleen Brennan's "Strange Weather": "And I never buy umbrellas/For there's always one around." It's such a delicate, silly, throwaway line that whispers volumes about life and disappointment. There was much affection from audience to performer and back, a lot of obvious delight that Faithfull had resurrected and reinvented herself. (Most of my generation's legends didn't stick around much beyond 30.) At the last performance there was an influx of industry heavies, which I took to mean great word of mouth. (I found myself fitfully watching Ahmet Ertegun's hands, on the table beside mine, guessing when they'd spring into applause. And Mica Ertegun's wrap of little slaughtered animals, wishing I had a can of spray paint.)

When *Strange Weather* came out, a friend of mine taped 1964's "As Tears Go By" back-to-back with this year's version. The original is positively bouncy, its manner belying its meaning. The voice is girlish and miles from actual tears. The '80s voice is the voice of a woman who has crawled through hell. (I still think it's preferable to crawl through hell than to own it, though most of '80s culture doesn't read that way.) Her drug history turned up in the *Playbill* handed out at the Bottom Line and in last week's *Time*. It said somewhere that Faithfull is uncomfortable with the word *survivor*. I don't blame her. It's the kind of word they print the same morning you overdose. I was glad to know the singer had cleaned up, for her sake, but it's depressing that even at the end of Reagan's reign such life-negating moralistic copy about behavior that's nobody's business has to trail performers as well as politicians, that a person's complexity gets boiled down into paradigms of redemption and recovery. I have not quit smoking in order to become a more acceptable person.

Faithfull's voice, raggedly notched and erratic, sometimes starts flat or strikes a note like a bald tire hitting a patch of glare ice. But what's there all the time is this ripping knife of an alto, rueful and accusing and strangely vulnerable. What is in this voice? Only a few notes, perhaps, but a gallon of prussic acid, a season of tropical cloudbursts, the grittiest pale Northern skies, the emptiest gray hotel rooms. And endless, sleepless flights, thousands of cigarettes, Rémy Martin, sex that's the nostalgia of sex, and happiness that's just the memory of happiness. Hope that if you die before you wake you really won't be aware of it. And the most unexpected sweetness. *Strange Weather* isn't as aggressive as *Broken English*, the persona is mellower and slightly distanced from the material. It gives a fuller picture of Faithfull as a complex adult. If *Broken English* is about anger and lashing out and the phenomenology of guilt, *Strange Weather* is a little bit about growing older and finding less punishing ways to stay alive.

The last cigarette—oh, in *Confessions of Zeno*, he's forever lighting that last cigarette. Faithfull's band was a dream group: Garth Hudson on keyboards, Lew Soloff on trumpet, Allan Smallwood on synthesizer, J.T. Lewis drums, Bill Frisell guitar, Fernando Saunders on bass, and Mac Rebennack on guitar and piano. You could hear that they were perfect even if you don't know from bands, which happens to be the case with me. It was also the kind of band there's a little too much of, embellishing songs that were fine in the first place, overextending some numbers with solo after solo—everybody a diva for at least 15 minutes, and after a while a line from *Pride and Prejudice* came to mind: "Now Mary, you've delighted us quite enough for one evening." (Or, as an acquaintance put it, "She's just so incredible. Too much music, though.")

However, the audience was willing to take a few gratuitous arabesques in exchange for an epic version of "Sister Morphine" and brilliant renderings of "The Ballad of Lucy Jordan" and "Guilt." Two of the strongest songs, especially from an instrumental aspect, were from *A Child's Adventures*: "The Blue Millionaire," and for the pre-encore conclusion, "Times Square" with its evocation of accidental death, death by mischance in a sea of dazzling madness. I don't think "Times Square" was ever a hit, but Faithfull sang it like a signature tune and so it became one.

I suppose we were playing *Strange Weather* all summer into the fall and felt unusually compelled to go see Faithfull because this is not a singer whose interest rides or falls on your level of testosterone. *Broken English* was all about grown-up fuckovers and betrayals as well as sold-out-from-childhood lives and a stifling political system that drives people to suicide. *Strange Weather* is about losing out and not fitting in, wising up when it's too late, seeing through the filigree. The album is such a coherent statement about who the singer has been that a song like "Penthouse Serenade," with its promise of luxuried serenity and unworldliness, acquires a dark hilarity simply from the context.

Little of Faithfull's music is about *gender* per se, or hetero mating rituals in the pop spirit. Sexual wounding, yes. Broken dreams, definitely. It is much more about sexuality as a social construction than gender as a given condition, so there are fewer hims and hers than yous and mes. I didn't need winning over in the first place, but right after "Sister Morphine" Faithfull said, "It's an incredible example of addiction…that I'm losing my voice right now, and I can't stop smoking." And in fact she'd been lighting up every time a band member launched a solo, each first puff followed by an ominous though tiny cough. On my side I'd quit smoking two weeks previous and although I'd reached the point of being able to sit across from two chain-smoking television writers without losing control, the ability to write anything at all had dried up with the last cigarette. It was really with the utter inability to function, the onset of creative paralysis, that I began to understand with a bit more disinterested sympathy the addict friend whose memory is intertwined with the music of Marianne Faithfull. And of course when you do break down and give in to whatever addiction you have, it comes back to you just how intolerable reality can be and why people take drugs in the first place.

GUYS AND DOGS

Frank Majore's big new Cibachrome prints (Holly Solomon, 724 Fifth Avenue, through January 2) have titles like *Crimson Splendor*, *Chrysanthemum and Pearls*, *Reveries of a Bachelor*, and *Dreamsville*. These works have the dream juxtapositions of fuzzy urban streetscapes and sharp, shiny interior details found in TV commercials and magazine cosmetics ads. Majore's pictures always look as if they're selling something, even if it's only the aesthetics of the sales pitch. The product, then, is the photograph itself, a montage of perfections, a drizzle of luxurious tokens, oneiric life-furniture belonging, primarily, to that high-toned, club-hopping, smart-living stratum of 1930s Manhattan as it persists in 1980s magazine ad myth.

This is a world whose more or less offscreen inhabitants occupy gleaming penthouse apartments with seductive lighting and perfectly designed ashtrays, gaily fizzing champagne glasses, and negligently discarded jewelry. These swank objects bathe in sparkle-speckled sprays of directed light or squat regally in puddles of gel-thickened lavender or midnight blue. In some of these pictures, ravishingly made-up female faces are smudged across a corner of the print or seethe out from the surface in surreal, color-banded, come-hither masks of Attitude.

In the architecturally porous space of *Dreamsville*, a perfect square vase on a perfect blue-green, slender-stemmed end table has for background a spotted-windshield panorama of Times

Square, and above it, twinned, faces of Kim Novak in *Vertigo*, and over to the right, behind a satiny curtain, a supersaturated red-and-black still of Grace Kelly in *Rear Window*. Another picture sporting the corner of an ornate, gilt picture frame has a wraithlike BMW behind the frame, a telephone handset mirrored on a sleek oval table, and more indistinct but teeming color bubbles of nighttime New York. Oh, yes, and a curious deep blue halation containing another gauzy-looking ghost of Grace Kelly. This picture is called *Paris Is Calling*, which I believe is a line from Debbie Harry's song "French Kissin'."

We could explore *Crimson Splendor*, with its four luscious lipsticks protruding from swirl-patterned gold tubes, with wide, laser-red parabolas shooting from the right edge of the picture toward its center, and three women's faces ranged vertically toward the left edge. Or *Chrysanthemum and Pearls*, the flower in a rectangular black planter of the kind used on restaurant tables, its base ringed with a coiled double strand of pearls, the background a fake-looking sky graded from magenta to a mentholated blue. Pictorially, compositionally, and technically, Majore's photographs are gorgeous, more gorgeous than much of the best commercial photography. Yet the thing that in most instances makes them different from commercial—the smeary female visages projecting from an indeterminate spatial limbo—gives them the altogether silly "personal" quality of limp critique and 20-watt deconstruction. It's interesting that one of Majore's models is Ellen Carey, a model-turned-photographic artist who seems to believe that placing geometric grids over fashion photographs of herself constitutes some sort of revealing feminist statement. Actually, such pictures were used to sell dresses and makeup in the '60s, and Majore's photographs, despite their extremely likeable polish and theatricality, continue to cry out for the caption "WHAT KIND OF MAN READS PLAYBOY?"

If Majore's photographs suggest the fantasy images of the affluent, sophisticated young man on the make—the seduction staged on a $10,000 couch while the lights are dim, and the electric city splays out way down below—**Dike Blair**'s new paintings on glass (International With Monument, 111 East 7th Street, through January 3), which incorporate photographic elements, invoke another aspect of American male fantasy and its somewhat crasser staging in the bleary realm of alcohol. Most of Blair's new, extremely quirky-looking pieces feature large areas of black-painted glass, with ball-shaped image areas running up on one side, and on the other an eight ball stuck to the surface, a tiny printed message (the kind shown on the underside of those fortune-telling eight balls sold in novelty stores), and a spilled cocktail glass, a jagged pool of plastic "spill" around it in which part of a blacked-out photograph is revealed. These pieces are technically complicated and playful—in one, a painted bottle of Tanqueray and a painted pack of Marlboros are "reflected" by photographic reflections of a real bottle and a real pack. The ubiquitous drink spills contain plastic "ice cube" chunks. The vertical image circles, which are sometimes concentrically shaded to mimic the eight-ball motif, sometimes fuzzed at the circumference to resemble the cinematic iris-in shot, mainly feature hierarchical views of sky, sea, and sand or woods. One shows an atrium elevator in a vast hotel, one view looking down, another looking up, the center view a horizontal shot of the gaudily lighted glass elevator cage.

These pictures are a technical jump forward for Blair, who hasn't used photography to any appreciable extent before; they do proceed thematically from his earlier work, the preoccupation with atmospheres of sensual dystrophy, demoralization, laid-back, cocktail-lounge funkiness. With Majore's pictures they suggest a continuity of trampled macho that may extend throughout the world of white, heterosexual male artists with more or less enlightened impulses who try to address "romance" and socialization. Alcohol is the legal drug of seduction and sexual success is a fetish, if not a target, in work by Jeff Koons,

Frank Majore, Dike Blair, and, sometimes, Richard Prince. This is the provincial American aspect of their work, the up-from-lower-middle-class irony trained downwards at the artist's roots.

If it's a question of probing around for the psyche behind the photograph, or semiphotograph, I frankly find **William Wegman**'s pictures of Fay, his new dog, much more agreeable than the works discussed above (Pace/MacGill, 11 East 57th Street, through January 16). We have Fay bewigged and wrapped in a vermilion gown and tassel, next to the uniformed and blue-eyed Ed Ruscha in *Sworded*, or cryptically veiled in a snaggly fishnet in *Faynette*, or perched Sphinxlike on an ironing board (*Fay on Board*); Fay on roller skates, Fay in sneakers, Fay climbing from a box, Fay wigged and otherwise hairily augmented to resemble an Afghan hound. There are those who will dispute the notion that Wegman has found a new dog genius to carry on the work of the late, great Man Ray, and I am, I confess, not as taken by Wegman's Fay photographs as I am by the Man Ray ones. But Fay continues to improve as a performer, a thespian, a mistress of disguise. Fay has begun to display the whimsy, the panache, and above all the earnestness of Man Ray.

FAKING IT

There is no word in current art jargon quite so dreadful as *simulacrum* and its plural form, *-cra*. This was a perfectly nice word before artists and art critics began abusing it. It usually suggested a human or animal replica, typically a robot. Lawrence Durrell, I think, favored it as a common noun in *Tunc* and *Nunquam*. I'm quite sure that's where I picked it up, at any rate. No intelligent person could have wished this simple word to become a burning cause. The world would be a happier place if we had never heard about *simulationism*, for example, or learned to refer to any representation as a *simulacrum*. However, the horses are out of the barn. We can no longer refer to models or copies without a twinge of anxious doubt whether *simulacra* wouldn't sound more like it.

I suppose if we really wanted to roll cement around in our mouths we could say that *issues of simulation* are raised by various current shows. No, it's too awful. Forget it. In fact, at one of these shows I was advised that *simulation* was not the main issue. All right. You have on one hand **David Levinthal**'s pictures at 303 Gallery (513 East 6th Street, through January 17) and something called "**The Beauty of Circumstance**," a veritable Caesar salad of *simulation* organized by Ronald Jones, at Josh Baer Gallery (270 Lafayette Street, through December 30). That's three, and now four, *simulations* in one paragraph. You are getting sleepy. Your eyelids are becoming heavy. Don't you hate this word?

And yet, there does seem to have been a little paradigm shift taking place, whilst the art world's been afroth with topics like originality and appropriation and so on. Something has dropped out of the bottom, somewhere. It just doesn't matter anymore if something is real or not because everything is real. And, it almost goes without saying, nothing is real. Most of us can live with this, since we obviously have to. But we should choose our nothing carefully.

To some people it will seem extremely provoking that Ronald Jones has replicated certain pictures that he couldn't obtain for his show, that these copies unemphatically stand in for the originals, that viewers have mistaken the actual Judd shelves and Richter paintings for fakes and the fake Warhols and Rauschenberg's *Erased de Kooning Drawing* for the genuine articles. Most provoking of all, Jones really doesn't regard the substitutions as significant to his show's meaning. Well, yes and no. Museum shows always feature those blocky photomural replicas of things they couldn't get and nobody minds. However, the replicas here are rather creepy, most of them achieved through a complicated photo-transfer process. The surfaces look slick and oleaginous, like a tablecloth in a cheap restaurant.

I'm not all that riveted by the intended effects of "The Beauty of Circumstance," which uses an appealingly argued catalogue essay to make the show's fairly obvious groupings of artists (Annette Lemieux with Marcel Broodthaers, Peter Halley with Donald Judd, Nancy Dwyer with El Lissitzky, etc.) seem weightier than they are. "We seem to have lost our ability—even the desire—to distinguish," Jones writes, referring to the loss of historical sense, of the ability to contextualize. Yet this show is predicated on a collapse of distinctions, an indifference to history. After all, works of art are themselves historical artifacts. Picabia's *Portrait of Cézanne*, destroyed in World War II, can't be meaningfully reconstituted as a Steiff monkey attached to a canvas by Velcro snaps. And though it's logical to pair this pseudo-Picabia with an unpleasant gewgaw by the allegedly witty Martin Kippenberger, I do wish Jones had here thrown logic to the winds.

The main defect of this show is not its inclusion of fakes, but the presence of originals: the disjunction makes the whole thing look shabby, in a way that a completely bogus show probably wouldn't. If intended to stimulate meditation about connections between the works and the historical contexts in which they were produced, "The Beauty of Circumstances" is indefensibly coy, absurdly partisan in its choice of contemporaries. Jones knows how to make flattery look extremely rigorous. However, the replicant pictures short-circuit whatever legitimate conjunction might be drawn between, for instance, Picabia's painting of his mother, Warhol's painting of *his* mother, and two pictures of Cindy Sherman taken by her father. Or a Sherrie Levine copy of a drawing, a de Kooning drawing, and the famous Rauschenberg erasure.

The David Levinthal show isn't directly related to "The Beauty of Circumstance," except that Levinthal has also used, in three pieces, a sophisticated transfer process. The one used in Jones's show was first used for artwork by Alan Belcher; the top layer of a photograph is peeled off and mounted on canvas, then sealed with varnish. The result, technically, is a photograph. Levinthal's big pictures of toy cowboy and Indians are paintings, taken from photographs with a scanner and mechanically sprayed onto canvas. Levinthal's work deals in blatant fakery; more deliberately than "The Beauty of Circumstance," his fakes question the veracity and legitimacy of originals.

Most of the sepia-tone photographs here were done for an extraordinary book that appeared in 1977, *Hitler Moves East, A Graphic Chronicle, 1941–43*, which Levinthal and Garry Trudeau had used as their graduate thesis at Yale. The German advance into Russia, the tribulations of the winter, the defeat at Stalingrad are "captured" in these photographs, whose constituent elements are teeny model soldiers and tabletop dioramas. From the technical notes in the book: "A lake was formed by using topsoil and a large green garbage bag. Later it was filled in with more topsoil to portray the autumn sea of mud. The snowstorms were simulated by blowing flour across the miniature landscape with compressed air. On a separate table, a city and railroad yard were built, and then destroyed with a variety of ridiculously unstable homemade incendiary devices. Model airplanes attacking the city were held on guide wires and set on fire as they plummeted towards the ground.

"The sense of reality was augmented…by the narrow depth of field used in taking the pictures. Having only one small area in sharp focus permitted the models in the background and foreground to assume amorphous shapes that both obscured their identities as toys and contributed atmospherically to the compositions."

Many artists have since discovered the macro lens and the curious evocative capacity of micro models. Levinthal was the first to fully explore the possibilities and he is still the most interesting, if this show is anything to go by. The pictures from *Hitler Moves East* are remarkable for their deflation of photographic authenticity and the complex conventions of the "war photograph." One of Levinthal's dioramas also appears in this show.

January 19, 1988

1988: SOME THOUGHTS FROM 15 ARTISTS

Every so often *The New York Times* lets us know, in an especially fulsome way, what it thinks artistic culture is about. Its January 3, 1988, feature, "1988: Previews From 36 Artists," is particularly generous in this regard. Artists are like little self-contained countries, busy as beavers on projects that will "redefine our perception of the sensibilities we are just coming to know." The impression left by almost all the *Times*'s respondents is that of a self-absorption entirely disconnected from daily life. Unlike the rest of us, these Promethean figures pass their days in a bubbling broth of "conceptual ferment," constantly challenging us to marvel at the wonder that is them. As the *Times* so revealingly puts it, "They remain one step ahead of us." However, the gurgles of cheery careerism placed in all 36 mouths, either by their owners or, in some cases no doubt, by the *Times*'s editorial scissors, situate the artists firmly within their historical moment.

I confess that I am not even slightly interested in the work of 33 of the 36 artists the *Times* queried, except as unconsciously symptomatic of a larger illness. Still less am I interested in the details of their creative ferment. That said, the following is, emphatically, *not* intended as an alternative list of okay artists. It simply occurred to me to ask several people not only what they were doing in 1988, but what they were thinking about. I left the question open enough to allow people to talk about their work if they wanted to, or about anything else on their minds.

ROBERT GOBER
SCULPTOR

Every day as I walk down the street I think about AIDS. I see the busy preoccupied crowds, especially now at Christmas time moving into an election year, and I wonder why so few care. Then I buy the newspaper on the way to my studio, and I remember. Today Mayor Koch expressed his "rage" at the "unconscionable" raising of movie prices to seven dollars. He's angry, he's organized a boycott, it's news. This media-savvy mayor said nothing about AIDS for four years as the disease ravaged and claimed New York as its epicenter. That *The New York Times* should collude with these hypocrites in their silence is a crime. My anger is constantly arguing with my sorrow over this disgrace. Using that anger, that considerable energy to achieve something truly positive, is my agenda for '88.

NANCY CHUNN
PAINTER

The new year is a seamless continuation and is not a symbolic beginning or end of anything. We can't alleviate world problems that weigh heavily on individual lives simply by turning off our TVs, or our memories, or by marking the calendar. I'm just continuing my work on countries, even though it won't make these problems go away. At the moment, I'm painting Korea. It's not coming easy. I hope my work won't be construed as a selection from the Country-of-the-Month Club.

JEAN-PIERRE GORIN
FILMMAKER

1988—to do: make some film.
1. Work the edges of the screen, the edges of the subject, the edges of the story—make the detour the destination.

2. Forget the Big Idea—whatever that was.

3. Go older than yesterday's news. Don't talk about Reagan. Don't talk about Carter or Ford. Maybe do something on Johnson.

4. Style: put things together to see them together—not because they go. Then convince everybody they do go.

5. Make a film about crowds with a small cast. (Pronounce the Canetti name at PBS.)

6. Pretend not to know what is important. Get scale and priorities all mixed up.

7. Use information as drama. Sweat the details.

8. Juggle as many balls as possible but work dropping a few into the act.

9. Remember how to hold the country's attention with the story of a small child trapped down a deep hole. Resist the temptation to do so.

10. Keep maneuvering in tight spaces without falling through the cracks.

12. Get it done by the end of the year with Patrick Amos, writer…who knows all the above.

ROSS BLECKNER
PAINTER

I hope the late '80s will be remembered as a time when artists rose to the occasion of producing a discourse of generativity and hope that is so lacking in what is called "culture."

CHERYL CLARKE
POET

Being a working artist is what I'm doing in 1988—no different from all the preceding years since I decided to call myself a poet. I'm a working feminist and a working lesbian. Being black helps a lot, because that makes me no stranger to work. By working artist, lesbian, feminist, black, I don't mean getting up in the morning, meditating on my new book of poetry (though that's not a bad idea), enjoying midmorning tea and biscuits, then off to a writing room, then in the evening hanging out in Manhattan with friends of like interests, sweating it all out on a generous fellowship or a grant, in summer driving up the coast to Maine or my favorite artists' colony, or in winter flying off to St. Thomas. No, I'm a New Jersey state bureaucrat! I get up at 6 a.m., drive down the turnpike to Jersey City to a job every day. When that job's done, my real work begins—usually back in Manhattan or Brooklyn: two committee meetings a week for my work with New York Women Against Rape; editorial work for *Conditions* magazine, the oldest lesbian-feminist journal in the country—manuscripts, subscriptions, deadlines, last minute fund-raising to get the next issue on the streets; the ever-looming responsibility of promoting one's work—at one's readings, other writers' readings, at all the women's conferences, political events, and discos; the writing opportunities one must respond to in order to keep one's name out there between books. All in a day's work every day of the year. I'm working in 1988.

LAURIE HAWKINSON
ARCHITECT

Architecture is in an extremely tentative state. Architecture as integration and permanence is clearly in contradiction with our consuming society. Architecture is an expression of the hidden qualities and aspirations of society. The present "hyperreality," including falsification of time and history, is becoming our new criterion for authenticity. The subject of architecture needs to be redefined.

TAYLOR MEAD
POET AND ACTOR

For 1988, I'm writing a play called *Pay Your Bill*, and I've decided to become the world's greater composer-pianist this year, after being the world's greatest painter the year before, and the world's greatest poet the year before, and actor before that, and next year is tennis. Well, that's what happens when you give up sex. Also, even though I hit the lotto for $16 million this week, I intend to be just as shitty and petty as I ever was.

EILEEN MYLES
POET

Actually, I've been thinking it's time to stop living like I've got a gun to my head. I mean, what's the point? On January 2 I was so nuts I crashed into a killer chest of drawers in my apartment and nearly bled to death, calling my friends for help and getting their machines. I was obviously drunk when this workaholic thing began. I feel like I woke up and everyone was running down the street going yak yak yak yak about their 17 projects. I'd like to go slower in 1988.

DENNIS COOPER
WRITER

I'm thinking about how to fit back into New York after two and a half years in Amsterdam. I seem to be at an age where my friends and I are starting to either make it or not make it as artists, which is pretty exciting because all the hope involved with that coincides with a new determination to live. At the same time, I'm thinking how it's important not to be afraid to take extreme measures, because that's what it takes to accomplish great things politically, artwise, and in life.

CAROL SQUIERS
CRITIC

I see nothing good for 1988. Photographically speaking, if the '80s so far have been dominated by the work of women such as Barbara Kruger and Cindy Sherman, the waning years of this stunningly deranged decade may be reclaimed by the production of men. Yet, what are they trying to show us? If art gallery photography is any evidence, this new trend involves making pictures in which the image is obscured, hidden, out of focus, or simply absent, mounted on sometimes insignificantly sized projections which nonetheless aggressively protrude from the wall. In short, art photography is becoming more like a health club. Except that none of the art wears gold chains.

HANS HAACKE
ARTIST

I'm curious to see how the troubles of the Wall Street simulationists trickle down to the art world and affect its zeitgeist.

LYNNE TILLMAN
WRITER

AIDS, the Middle East, the presidential election—does it matter who's elected? How will aid to the contras be delivered this time? Will more money be spent to perfect a system for the complete erasure of computer memory from the hard disk than for AIDS research? Will every minority group in New York City fight every other one, leaving intact and untouched the power elite? With the Mafia in disarray, who owns the streets? More whimsically, does President Reagan know how sophisticated his comment about Errol Flynn was? Do Americans really believe that creatures from outer space will save us? Are people who are talking about greed serious? And, with Hollywood film and TV the only major American industries not ailing abroad, should we all learn to act, or have we already? Why aren't I happy?

WESLEY BROWN
WRITER

The escalating racial violence in this city and the large numbers of children I see daily who are abandoned to the streets are the cause of much anger and distress I brought with me into the new year. The disturbing facts of life in this city are not merely the subject matter for fiction or drama, but the context of whatever I attempt to do as a writer.

BARBARA KRUGER
ARTIST

Lately I've been thinking about the travesty of American electoral politics, about AIDS and the cruel inadequacies of health care, about how television news makes history, about how good it feels to walk down the street on a sunny day, about the pervasiveness of sexual oppression and how its guises vary from U.S. academia to the bureaucracies of global Catholicism to the dictates of the Afghani mujahideen, about the authoritarianism and short memory of the Israeli government, about movies, buildings, and how good it feels to hear the right song at the right time, about the racial hierarchies that constitute American cities, educational structures, and corporate systems, about Central America and how much better it would be to have a new daily newspaper in this town, about homelessness, about the screeching melodrama of families, and about how good it feels to share hot conversation and crazy laughter.

KEITH SONNIER
ARTIST

Making art is like extracting an exoskeleton from mixed bags that the culture has blown full of holes, and it's become more and more difficult to do. I'm questioning the cultural and societal changes in the role of the artist. I want to make work that will continue to expand the artistic arena, also address, hopefully direct, social change: I'm afraid if we don't address broader issues in art-making we'll be left with an empty bag.

January 26, 1988

QUICK! READ THIS!

1. *From an open letter to Douglas McGill and* The New York Times *from artist Paul Thek concerning Richard Serra's* Tilted Arc, *dated December 17, 1987:*

"NYC does not need 'culture commissars.' It needs NOT to have them, look what they have done to us. Those who are responsible for its original approval should all be removed from their positions. The people who rightly protest this 'work' are hardworking people, they really work, they work for a lifetime for less money than what Mr. Serra has bilked them for this one 'art object.'" Now, it becomes clear, his game plan is to exploit the situation even further so that he threatens to sue The People if they will not bow to his Will. To rob them even more of their public dollars. How very much better might all those dollars have been spent! Perhaps Mr. Serra spends too much time hiding in his luxury Soho loft, or on the beach at Amagansett, to know or to care about the legitimate and healthy needs of the workers of Federal Plaza, or about their right to a human environment. He has the gall to insult them with this monstrous absurdity and now threatens to rob them further!"

2. *From a list of rental films I watched between New Years' Day and January 10:*

Montenegro

M

Bill Liar
Caligula
Chained for Life
Triumph of the Will
Darling

3. *A brief review of "Arf Art," an exhibition at Trabia-MacAfee Gallery, 54 Greene Street, through January 31:*

This show has the longest list of participating artists I have ever seen. It was organized by William Secord, founding director of the Dog Museum of America. Not every work in this show is dazzling by itself, but if you can imagine how wonderful it would be, just for once, to walk into a crowded gallery opening—or any public place, really—and to find there, instead of a fat clutch of braying, backbiting, paranoiacal human beings, a comparable number of friendly, open-hearted dogs, this show is the nearest best thing. In fact, just being in a room full of dog pictures and dog sculptures brings out something benign and whimsical in even the most pretentious, humorless people. How appropriate, then, that such a room should appear in the art world, where pretension and humorlessness never seems to pass out of fashion.

The dog theme show was pioneered several seasons ago, by Massimo Audiello, with a group of works by "name" artists depicting ChiChi, Pat Hearn's loveable but nervous chihuahua. However, that show lacked the catholicity of this one and did not really reflect a love of dogs so much as an eagerness to compliment Pat Hearn's taste in dogs. One sensed that many artists in the ChiChi show had never really seen a dog. Moreover, the adulation of a single, purebred dog amounts to a Cult of Personality, whereas "Arf Art" celebrates the diversity of canine species and that ineffable, heart-winning quality we call Doggyness. One of my favorite pieces in this show is a painting by E. Smitt. Inscription: "Luba, the dog of Kazimir Malevich, dashes through a Suprematist Painting. Moscow, 1919."

4. *Fill in the blank:*

The young male lead in *Montenegro* has the most adorable, uncircumcised, user-friendly-looking _____ ever to appear in a commercial film.

5. *Jimmy De Sana, at Pat Hearn Gallery, 735 East 9th Street, through February 7:*

I always feel a bit strange visiting Pat Hearn Gallery, because of the location. The rubble-packed lots in the area, the general surrounding atmosphere of poverty and desuetude, vividly remind us that New York has washed its hands of the concept of social justice. Or as Alan Price once put it, "We all want justice but you got to have the money to buy it." Now, on nearby Avenue C, an elaborate open-shack structure serves as a soup kitchen for the homeless. So you can watch the dispossessed freezing to death on your way to the gallery.

Jimmy De Sana's recent Cibachrome photographs are attractive, cryptic, beautifully installed; I don't understand them, particularly the one that seems closest to saying something, a picture called *Gooseberries*. The word "deathlessness" is covered by three jagged rows of prosthetic eyeballs. A booklet accompanying the exhibition features numerous koanlike statements that relate, I imagine, to the photographs. For example: "A/simple/shoe/would fit/on/any/foot/if/the/simple/shoe/was any size." Not bad, actually.

6. *Billy Liar* is the story of a young man trapped in a horrible small English town. *M* tells the story of a compulsive child-murderer. *Caligula* is a porn fantasy starring Malcolm McDowell and Helen Mirren. *Chained for Life* features the Hilton Sisters, real-life Siamese twins who, in this film, have a dream sequence in which they separate. *Triumph of the Will* shows Hitler and other Nazi luminaries at a spectacular party rally in Nuremburg. *Darling* has Julie Christie as a glamorous fashion model sleeping her way to the top.

7. *"Media, Post Media":*

Another traumatic walking experience consists of perambulating through Soho on the weekend. A great variety of moneyed shoppers clog the streets, they and their airheaded offspring voluminously clad in senselessly murdered animals. I would like to see these people kept in pens, and when the demand requires it, they could be clubbed and skinned to provide warm covering for furless animals. The argument that "minks are raised on ranches" is entirely jejune: they get killed, don't they? Yes, people are brought up eating meat and can't always give it up. But only the very worthless are brought up wearing mink.

The Collins & Milazzo show at Scott Hanson Gallery (415 West Broadway, through February 9) features all women artists. I think it necessarily suggests the uniqueness and the built-in limitations of the Collins & Milazzo enterprise. As freelance curators, Collins & Milazzo have consistently devised imaginative group shows. As tastemakers, they have nothing to fear from curators who find their inspiration in the lyrics of popular songs and obscure poems. However, anyone engaged in the role of subcontractor, or surrogate gallery director, must ultimately either play to existing markets or create new ones, if only to ensure future curatorial opportunities. This show does both. The Collins & Milazzo imprimatur on a work doesn't guarantee that someone will buy it, but their shows have begun to attract the kind of collectors who will buy anything trendy, along with more serious people. There's nothing wrong with that, but for lack of an exhibition space of their own, Collins & Milazzo seem to have progressed from guest spots at good galleries to supplying unimaginative ones with instant relevance.

Personally, I don't see any reason why the same 15 to 30 more or less familiar artists need to circulate through every square foot of Manhattan gallery space on their way to glory, unless it's to provide Jerry Saltz, Christian Leigh, and a few other towering cultural philosophers with something to do with their nervous energy. Collins & Milazzo's shows have never seemed gratuitous or flatulently pedantic (at least not in the way that a recent show called "Lead"—as in lead pencil, lead paint, etc.—or a very ridiculous two-gallery exercise by Douglas Blau called "Fictions" did), though they've sometimes reflected certain earnest confusions that now seem dangerously close to affectations. The lack of eccentricity and risk-taking here is a bit of a letdown. Parenthetically, I'd also like to say that some female artists are just as egocentrically fucked-up as males, and there is one work here—you guess which one—that ought to be titled *Women Beware Women*. The show is well-installed, though not spectacularly so, and individual pieces—by Nancy Dwyer, Karen Sylvester, Jenny Holzer, Rosemarie Trockel, and Suzan Etkin—escape the aura of overfamiliarity that much of the work generates in this context.

BLOOD AND GUTS

1. I am going to use the same numbered sections as last week. Strange to say, this in itself breaks a stupid rule that's been implicit in the way this column has been done since I started.

2. This paragraph goes here in order to destroy any notion of continuity in what you're reading.

3. Fuck you.

4. If I want to tell you something, why drag everything irrelevant in because "art needs to be covered"? Cover art with a blanket and pour gasoline on it, then light a cigarette and throw the match away. You won't lose anything you can't live without.

5. There is no such thing as a normal conversation if the conversation feeds or starves somebody's career aspirations. What I'd really like to tell you about are shit-for-brains male artists who can only relate to me as the *Village Voice* critic although hustling me as a friend and then feel betrayed if I don't pay attention to them in print. These people suck. They imagine that everyone has the same conspiratorial mentality that they do and spend their every waking moment measuring their career success against other people's, as if anyone else's good fortune subtracted from their own. I would actually like to print a list of these jerks and their

girlfriends since the latter serve the function of gun molls in the art world, stirring up petty high school resentments between people and posing as *feminists*, thank you, of a very peculiar sort, the sort with tits and asses almost popping out of their clothing at specific functions where male artist power bonding happens to take place. *Les girls* like to write extremely divisive put-downs of successful women artists, supposedly on behalf of their neglected sisters, while actually getting off on pitting women against one another. This is how their boyfriends think they will take over the world.

6. These boyfriends are bad fucks, but I don't feel sorry for anybody involved.

7. "WEDDING BELLS RING FOR CHERYL. Cheryl Pierson was freed yesterday after 106 days in jail (*Post* flashback) and walked into the arms of boyfriend Robert Cuccio who presented her with a diamond engagement ring." They both look like trash.

8. There are people in New York so desperate to be anything at all that they will exploit other people's suffering as a matter of routine, and convince themselves they're being noble. This is certainly true of one decidedly straight male currently involved in putting together a panel on "the effect of AIDS on the arts" as if he cared about it except as an abstract *topic* he can stick his name on. Just what we need right now, a panel.

9. To paraphrase Kathy Acker, I like this structure because it's stupid. Language needs to be freed to do what it wants to and can't do when it's supposed to give you the satisfaction of thinking I care about jerking you off.

10. The *Times* Book Review doesn't like Acker because Palestine is located in her cunt.

11. The only artwork I want to mention here is one piece by Pier Paolo Calzolari in his show at Barbara Gladstone Gallery (through January 30, 99 Greene Street). *Untitled* (1970) is two pale blue neon lines and in the middle a couple of tapered white candles dripping onto the neon tubing. The nice thing about Arte Povera is that even though the people who made/make it are a bunch of macho Italian men who think it's innocently poetic to install live female nudes showing their cunts in galleries, most of what they put together as art doesn't reflect what they're like in person. I don't see why I should describe the rest of this show, since Kim Levin already did in the "Choices" last week, but it really is the most beautiful stuff you could want to look at.

12. If I made a record based on my experiences as an art critic I would call it *I Don't Care If You Never Forgive Me*, b/w *Fuck You If You Can't Take a Joke (Yourself)*.

13. Someone suggested that the purpose of Mike Bidlo is really to start a class war between old money dopes who own real Picassos and parvenus who own Bidlos, since buying either one is like pulling out your cock along with an enormous bankroll at a cocktail party and screaming, "LOOK HOW MUCH MONEY I'VE GOT!!!" Bidlo, introduced to an artist I know, immediately asked, "Well? Do you hate me?" as if all anyone else in the world could have on his mind was Mike Bidlo. I don't know why anyone would hate Bidlo, unless they wanted the same kinds of things he does—which nobody I know does.

14. Go see Jane Dickson's demolition derby paintings at Brooke Alexander Gallery (get info yourself). Dickson is recording charged pieces of American psyche, without theoretical pretensions or preening self-consciousness; she knows how to haunt a piece of canvas. Of these destructo-vehicles and cluster collisions

Dickson wrote, "I would like to claim they're about violence, but they're about futility." What a nice, intelligent thing to say!

15. Quiz Question: What Nobel prize-winning American novelist is a racist asshole? Answer: What Nobel prize-winning American novelist isn't a racist asshole?

16. Instead of the insipid symbol of body hatred and eternal masochism, Jesus Christ, Americans should adopt a new symbol of their religious palpitations: the grave. Since America is all about death to begin with, it makes sense that Americans should invest more thought in their ultimate disposal. When people die, they should have all the shit they have managed to accumulate through a lifetime of consumption piled up on top of their graves in the form of a giant pyramid: all the TV sets, all the cars, the stereos, the VCRs, the shoes, the designer dresses, the dishes, the chairs, the crystal, the paintings, the sculptures—and of course the bigger the pile, the bigger the shit you'll be remembered as. The whole thing could have clear plastic poured on top of it, preserving for space creatures who stumble upon our dead planet a notion of what we were and what we lived for.

SECRETS OF THE ROTHKO CHAPEL

HOUSTON

1. A woman named Priscilla raises pigs and the pigs keep getting addicted to the morning glories that grow on Priscilla's property. One pig has already been in detox and another pig definitely needs professional help. The first pig is something of a local hero, having saved a small child from drowning in the river. That pig has been a guest on Johnny Carson and the Letterman show. Priscilla's pigs are a credit to the community, even when they're on hallucinogens.

2. There's nothing much to do in Houston. On the TV in the hotel room, Jerry Falwell says he's asked the Lord for another three million dollars. Pat Robertson tells a small, enthusiastic audience that a Democratic congress is responsible for the soaring divorce rate. Mayor Koch explains to *60 Minutes* that New York isn't Russia.

3. The Menil Foundation is featuring, in one of its galleries, the urinal Duchamp attempted to exhibit in 1917, or rather, the first replica of the urinal, dated 1950. Only a fraction of the Menil Collection can be viewed at any given time. Some installations, I'm told, stay up an almost unconscionably long time. The Menil Foundation, though somewhat grudgingly open to the public,

seems basically intended as a research facility for art scholars. Like the Dia Foundation in its first incarnation, the Menil Foundation has some characteristics of an alternative religion, the self-sufficiency of a church. The gray houses in the area all belong to the foundation, and serve as a buffer between the actual museum building and the wider community.

4. In Richmond Hall, one of the foundation buildings, 83 paintings by Andy Warhol, the "Shadow" series, run continuously along four walls and across a fifth, detached wall, in colors ranging from thalo green to canary yellow. Sometimes the black is laid on in one place, sometimes in another, so there are two basic images, one suggesting a perspectival alley or corridor on the left side of the picture, the other a blunt, architectural spire. Acrylic paint was sloshed across a silkscreen with a mop. The paint sits flat on some pictures, while others are streaked with fat, arbitrary-looking strokes. The form of the shadow has a certain sinister vagueness. If you sit in the space long enough the canvases begin to look like the frames of a film. Something that takes place at night in the red-light district of a German city during the Weimar Republic.

5. Are the Warhols good, or are they bad? Is the Duchamp *Fountain* a big joke, or a landmark in art history? Well, a joke could be a landmark in history of any sort. And when people talk about art they usually end up saying what they think is good, bad, overrated, underrated, and so forth. Judgments of that kind are always vulnerable to the question "according to what?" History is always history according to somebody, a consensus of somebodies—the somebodies who have the power to say what's history.

6. History is the consensus of the empowered.

7. For every history there are histories without voices to speak them.

8. *Why we ask you not to touch...* (from a brochure, "The Menil Collection Guide"). *We hope your grandchildren—and their grandchildren—will someday visit our museum.*

9. The museum retrieves and suppresses histories as part of its normal functioning. Are the Warhols good or bad? Some people would say they're terrible. But again, according to what? The fact is that they look a certain way in this environment, it may even be that the room they're in is a great part of what they do.

10. *A painting is fragile and may be damaged forever by the gentlest touch. In fact, most damage is caused by innocent touches. Your touch may not seem like much, but a million visitors' touches will destroy a painting.* ("The Menil Collection Guide")

11. A man in Houston who drinks a lot of beer has covered his house and garage, as well as his trellises, with beer cans. They pour down from his rooftop like barrel tiles and shine like Christmas tinsel under moonlight. His lawn has a sign that says, "Live By Golden Rule." His lawn has a wheelbarrow full of packed dirt, with its own sign that says, "Culprit."

12. *Sculpture is not as sturdy as it looks. The tiny trace of moisture from your finger can, in time, strip the rich surface from bronze and rust the strongest steel. Fingernails and rings will, in time, gouge deep furrows in stone and wood. Handled carelessly, glass will crack and plaster will break.* ("The Menil Collection Guide")

13. The urinal says, This is a work of art because someone said so. How did the urinal acquire value as an *important* work of art? Through written history, obviously, and a consensus of opinion— through narrative, actually. Someone tells the story of Duchamp and the urinal, or the one about the man whose house was covered in beer cans, or Priscilla and her amazing pigs. Now why,

you could ask, does that particular story get told over and over again? Who tells it, and what's that person all about?

14. *Another legacy, by another major American artist...stands "miraculously" in front of the Chapel: the* Broken Obelisk *by Barnett Newman... "Miraculously"...because only this sculpture was of such significance and greatness that it could co-respond to the Rothko Chapel and create a dialectic and a liberating tension. Stepping out of the meditative and motherly space of the Chapel, one is met by the virile and exalting monument: an obelisk, its tip resting on the tip of a pyramid, surges toward the sky like a symbol of man's aspiration and endeavor, like a message rising toward the highest—up and up—till death interrupts it, only to allow it to expand differently into endless presence* (from a brochure, "The Rothko Chapel").

15. It's easier to say what something is if it's a joke: some jokes are anal, some are sexual, certain jokes tell you that the person telling them's an anti-Semite or a racist or deranged in some arcane way. In those cases the joke also demonstrates something else; it tells you why it's being told. The narratives of art are seldom as clearly one thing or another. The stories get told for all kinds of reasons. Museums make their pitch for notions of "posterity" that sound overdetermined: they are a relatively new kind of institution demanding permanence in a decidedly shifty world. What if the future decides that the present's aesthetic opinions were as silly as its political choices? (And what if the family turns out *not* to be the dominant form of social organization in that faraway time of hypothetical grandchildren's grandchildren?) In certain respects, private museums have a better chance than public ones to generate plausible, complicated stories. The Menil Collection's story of itself encompasses the creepy pretension of the Rothko Chapel, genuine social commitment, useful scholarship, impeccable taste, and the inevitable patches of obtuseness that accompany private wealth.

BLIND ITEM

"**Sexual Difference: Both Sides of the Camera,**" a show at New Langton Arts (1246 Folsom Street, through March 5), "guest curated by Abigail Solomon-Godeau." Here we have an exhibition in two sections, one called "Subject Position and the Erotics of Looking," the other titled "Critical Interventions." This show has previously appeared in Buffalo and will eventually come to New York.

The first section contains art photography of somewhat varied quality, by Francesca Woodman, Peter Hujar, Imogen Cunningham, and Baron von Gloeden. As a critical gloss on this section's title, Solomon-Godeau includes an "emblematic" work by Diane Neumaier, in 20 sections, its images culled from old photography magazines.

Woodman pictures herself, nude (among other things), holding things in front of her face or cropping her head out of the picture and holding cut-open melons in front of her breasts. (The melon picture, though it doesn't appear at this stop in this show's itinerary, comes in for lavish exegesis in the curator's essay.) Hujar pictures other people, nude, rather starkly; in one case a seated man contemplates his erection. Cunningham serves up her husband's attractive naked body in nature settings, and Baron von Gloeden offers us the jailbait of Taormina aping various classical poses in the buff.

These nude pictures are, each in its own way, "wrong," though apparently Woodman's are less wrong, say, than von Gloeden's or Cunningham's. Still, in the theoretical world of Solomon-Godeau, representations of nude bodies are not simply lacking in innocence but practically the same things as nude bodies. And therefore wrong. If they were not terribly wrong, we would not need terrible, correct artists like Diane Neumaier to show us exactly how and why they are wrong. Men have dominated photography the same way they dominate everything else, and even in these old technical manuals you can see it's always the man shown holding the camera, always the woman shown posing. "That those photographs most emphatically declaring their status as 'art' are frequently those in which the woman is nude, supine, fragmented, or otherwise 'worked over' (one especially grotesque example depicts a nude torso caged by lines incised in the negative with an X-Acto knife) is significant," Solomon-Godeau writes. Well, yes, except when it isn't significant—when, for example, the revelation of this scandalous situation occurs in settings where it is already obvious, i.e., an alternative art space.

The critical interventions on view are also a mixed lot. For Solomon-Godeau, apparently, it's a terrible strain to find excellent work correct enough to be good. So she's got some truly awful stuff mixed in with some good stuff, and her text blends them together to dreadful effect: "Broadly speaking, the work of Millner, Spence, Charlesworth, and Sherman…" Oh? Millner? Spence? And who, pray tell, are they?

A standard drawback of this kind of exhibition is the presumption that Millner and Spence, for example, because of their very correct ideas, are in the same league with Charlesworth and Sherman, when they patently are not, for reasons that have little to do with correctness. Spence, to zoom in here a bit, is a photographic artist whose "literal inscription of her self into the photographs," Solomon-Godeau tells us, "suggest [sic] that she as an individual is subject to the large historical forces, determinations, and sexual and social relations that her photographs attempt to symbolize." Lest my own description rob Spence's work of any subtlety, I quote Solomon-Godeau's: "...the two photographs captioned 'Victimization' use the genre of the police scene-of-the-crime photograph (Spence sprawled out nude under the wheels of a car next to a sign warning trespassers off private property) with a close-up photograph of Spence's hands doing laundry in a bowl...."

Millner, represented by collages of a painfully flat-footed obviousness, is contrasted in Solomon-Godeau's text with John Heartfield.

And then there are Connie Hatch and Richard Baim. Hatch's work is called *The De-Sublimation of Romance*. It consists of many, unremarkable snapshots of heterosexuals in groups, mainly at the beach, punctuated by three versions of a text that describes a spectator who is first male, then female, then plural. Baim's four photos are taken from a piece that normally uses music and multiple projections, called *Rise and Fall*. Solomon-Godeau's text claims that *Rise and Fall* investigates "the cultural construction of masculinity," which may be true but impossible to tell from the fragment offered here.

Louise Lawler has a wall. This one looks pretty and carries a message about the institutional context of cultural artifacts. It features four photographs containing "the female figure, a type rather than an individual...sculpted in an attitude of extreme abjection, seeming to cower beneath the stern and intimidating gaze of the portrait bust." I wouldn't be spreading any secrets by revealing that the portrait bust is male. Lawler asks the question: "Is it the location, the model, or the stereotype that is the institution?" To which the answer must surely be, "All three!"

Having admired both Lawler's art and Solomon-Godeau's writing on photography in the past, I find it troublesome and depressing to imagine this show's target viewers. I imagine them living in places like Montana, where the bare-boobs-and-googly-eyeball humor of an artist like Jo Spence might smack of urban wit. (And where the subtler, uncondescending artists in this show, like Richard Prince, Cindy Sherman, and Sarah Charlesworth, would probably be entirely out of range, like ultraviolet light. Nothing against Montana, but you know.) The overall effect is that of a dedicated leftist boor jabbing an elbow in your ribs and braying, "Get it??"

The installation itself has an inviting smart look despite the radical unevenness of the work's quality. However, as a retort to a recent conference called "Women in Photography: Making Connections," in which Solomon-Godeau ferreted out balefully "limiting and ultimately deceptive" essentialist and/or positivist positions vis-à-vis women in photography, "Sexual Difference: Both Sides of the Camera" simply presents its curator's own didactic agenda, pushed to abrasiveness by her conflation of first-rate work with sophomoric junk. Moreover, Solomon-Godeau's assumptions in dealing with homoerotic material like von Gloeden's as somehow normative within the history of photography are questionable. I find her discussion of von Gloeden's exploitations of Sicilian youths rather ponderous considering the cavalier way in which she herself has exploited—for instance—Peter Hujar, who would turn over in his grave if he knew how his work is used in this show.

NERVE METER REVISITED

[**Nancy Spero**. "War Paintings, 1966–1970," Josh Baer Gallery, 270 Lafayette Street, through March 5; and "The Artaud Series, 1969–1970," Barbara Gladstone Gallery, 99 Greene Street, through March 5.]

Nancy Spero's "War Paintings, 1966–1970" and "The Artaud Series, 1969–1970" are paintings on paper that have, if anything, gained in relevance and impact since their execution. Criticism about these works is plentiful, including a lot of parochially feminist and antifeminist writing; Spero is one of those artists whose bibliography will be useful to future sociologists of our era. The idealism in her work coaxes attitudes from all points of the critical spectrum. It affords art writers the chance to strike noble postures on behalf of Woman, or to decry the limitations of political art. My own interest in Spero's work is entirely selfish: I find it viscerally effective.

Spero has encouraged both a feminist and an anti-imperialist reading of her work, and, often enough, the content is sufficiently didactic to exclude most other kinds of appreciation. I consider some of her scrolls with goddess imagery and printed quotations from critical texts a kind of sincere political kitsch. Spero's scrolls are more involving than kitsch, but they have the overdetermined quality of a closed argument. They are typically praised for what they're not. Spero has been lauded, for instance, for making work on fragile paper when "men" were painting huge, explosive canvases, for creating open structures instead of tight formal pictorial arrangements—in other words, a binary argument gets wheeled out on behalf of whatever procedures Spero elects to follow, *against* something else defined as "male," and yes, the artist definitely colludes with people who read her work that way.

The basic problem I have with the text work isn't disagreement with what it says, but the fact that I would never read a word by Hélène Cixous, or some of Spero's other favored authors, *for pleasure*, though I would probably stick up for Hélène Cixous in a fight. So reading such an author in an artwork can only be a tiresome *duty*. And once you feel *dutiful* in front of a work of art, you aren't far from the repulsive set of emotions that well up as you enter the Metropolitan Museum, from that *odor of uplift* that is the veritable incense of patriarchy, though here it wafts on behalf of the Divine Vagina rather than the All-Conquering Prick.

I confess, an even more basic problem is that sincerity in art usually repels me, along with the self-righteous revolutionary anger of those who toil in capitalism's luxury industries. My idea of a pertinent cultural spectacle would be Julian Schnabel mud-wrestling with Andrea Dworkin. So I probably like the works in Spero's two current shows for the wrong reasons, or for reasons that lack sufficient specificity. It doesn't outrage me, for example, that war destroys the bodies of women in particular. The propaganda of the status quo is hysterically concerned to distinguish innocent from guilty victims. In reality, the state is an ongoing collaboration of men and women—the so-called *general population* of heterosexual men and women, who marry and reproduce with the sanction of the law. Granted, women get the raw end of this unholy pact, but they are an essential term in its equation.

The murder of everyone is the only logical outcome of the state system as miniaturized in the nuclear family, in the reproduction of state power in the relations between adults and children, in the industrial proliferation of prescriptive heterosexual imagery and narratives, which guarantee *the continuity of established patterns of domination* from one generation to the next. Until the actual diversity of human sexuality is not only acknowledged but welcomed into the structural arrangements of the body politic—legal, social, economic, and familial—nothing can truly change these patterns of domination. Sexual diversity must become part of the collective imagination, a part of culture, rather than a source of hysteria and punitive reaction.

Spero gives war a body as its site and injury/killing as its goal: not a means to an end, but the end in itself. For Spero, it's of supreme importance that the depicted body is female. Since her *War Paintings* were painted in response to the Vietnam War, in which civilians were deliberately slaughtered by American forces, this body's gender is appropriate. And it's appropriate in a more mythic or generalized sense, since women seldom start wars but always suffer because of them (though "conventional" warfare usually involves the sacrifice of teenage boys rather than the geriatric rulers of nations or women and children).

The scratchy, fast style of Spero's brush gives her war pictures the quality of something seen and quickly dashed down on paper, a court reporter's shorthand stroke. Her images of war picture the body ripped apart, exploded, penetrated, and mutilated by technical contraptions like helicopters and bombs that explicitly function like surrogate penises for the mechanized warrior. These pictures serve perfectly well as models for what is happening now in Central America; the connection between the "War Paintings" and "The Artaud Series" seems almost premonitory of the '80s relocation of "war" from the technological battlefield to the bloodlines of human bodies.

In the Vietnam period, among idealistic people at least, the alternative to making war was seen as making love. There was an effulgence of plein-air lovemaking in the '60s and a partial liberation of sexuality from the confines of legal marriage and reproduction. Artaud was an odd figure within the context of sexual liberation, for while he served as the avatar of various groups such as the Living Theater, what his writing exhibits to supreme pitch is revulsion with the body, an equation of sex with putridity and death, a loathing of sensuality that is palpably sensual in its expression: Spero has caught all this in the 43 pictures of "The Artaud Series," in twisted, tortured figures pasted down amid the language of total pain.

Anyone sensitive to the body will recognize in Spero's collaboration with Artaud the shudder of fear that's bonded itself to sexuality in the '80s—after a decade of repressive desublimation, the era of *the body without organs* living its own death as a commodity that *society sells to its products*. A body in which blood and sperm are the agents of death, a society where war is carried out invisibly through microbes and viruses and human surrogates. The squirmy sensations inspired by these cries from hell—"a horrible turd trembling expectantly in the void, on the verge of the still uncreated man, exploded," "the thick hemp in the neck of the priest about to be hung," "the human face in effect carries a kind of perpetual death with it"—are the same ones every gay man in America wakes up with every morning, even before ingesting the loathsome twaddle of A. M. Rosenthal in the *Times* and the other daily-refigured apparatus of our media-prepared biological Auschwitz. Spero's "Artaud Series" is an exact mirror of the moment.

SCIENCE HOLIDAY

[**Orshi Drozdik: "Adventure in Technos Dystopium."** Tom Cugliani Gallery, 508 Greenwich Street, through March 12.]

Orshi Drozdik's "Adventure in Technos Dystopium" has a loose family resemblance to other current work that alludes to, or uses, principles of mathematics and the physical sciences. A surprising amount of such work has recently appeared in galleries: Hanne Darboven's calendrically arranged photo works (which include, significantly, color photographs of magazine cartoons, most of them dealing with the theme of lechery) at Leo Castelli, Allan McCollum's excessively gimmicky ("no two are alike!") but visually effective table with 10,000 objects at John Weber, Kristin Jones, and Andrew Ginzel's ambitious colonization of City Hall Park with 66 sculptural elements (some kinetic, some static), called *Pananemone*.

Among recent shows featuring certain aspects of the science fair, one of the most impressive was a group show at 303 Gallery in early February. A thin circular incision in the wall, reminiscent of a Gordon Matta-Clark architectural cut, turned out to be a rapidly spinning disc, by Charles Ray; Nayland Blake showed a suite of handkerchiefs stained with various organic matter (blood, semen, coffee) and sculptures containing fluids, honey, and wax; Liz Larner's work included petri dishes in which laboratory agar nurtured cultures from fingerprints, orchids, pennies, and saliva, and a test tube filled with a mixture of cocaine and lead dust, recalling Arman's amphetamines in Plexiglas from 1970 and Penny Slinger's numerous drug artworks from the same period. (The 303 show also offered a cryptic, scan-line slatted painting on silk by that amazing visual poet, Richard Morrison, arguably the most venerated "unknown" artist of our period.)

A major source of pleasure in these works is that they don't look like art, entirely, or immediately. The viewer has some mental space in which to consider the object primarily as a thing: sometimes as a marvel of discoverable physical laws—for example, in the hallucinatory spatial mechanics of Jones and Ginzel—and sometimes as an intriguing model of inutility or melancholy dysfunction. When artists use scientific methods, we wrongly tend to consider this an expropriation, partly because science is so strongly associated with techniques of domination and control, with weapons, and with a steady proliferation of technological products, all powered by processes we are encouraged not to understand. Art achieves a subversion of conventional science by turning it to pleasurable and personal use, either by making things that work for purely aesthetic ends, or things that don't work.

Drozdik's "Dystopium" reclaims a discredited and therefore "useless" field of scientific inquiry as a poetic source, much as the Surrealists revived Charles Fourier's phalanstery as a hypothetical site of fascination. The source for three texts that appear on sandblasted glass panels is a 19th-century volume of *Popular Natural Philosophy*, elaborating then-current beliefs that magnetism and electricity were invisible fluids that might be collected in Leyden jars (also known as Kleist bottles, devised by a great-uncle of Heinrich von Kleist). A fourth glass panel, on display in the gallery office, adds an excerpt from Freudian theory to this suite of superannuated ideas.

Although the writing in these panels delineates certainties that are no longer considered true, the language has a romantic beauty valuable in itself, like Goethe's theory of color. Drozdik's show articulates the atmosphere of early scientific inquiry in a series of fantastic objects, many of them in glass cases. They suggest interrupted or arrested lab experiments, like objects in a medical museum, and bring to mind Garnett Puett's bee-colony sculptures; they also make the gallery into a sort of large vitrine. *Leyden Jar* is a Leyden jar (which stores static electricity), mounted on a small wooden base and partially wrapped in metal foil, stoppered with scumbled red wax; a bell-shaped *Aurora Jar*, similarly plugged, has a foil strip running on its surface in a helix. Another box contains a ball beaker full of yellow sulfur chunks clamped to a thin metal rod. *Popular Natural Philosophy* has the crumbling book serving as a base for a planting of wriggled lead rods. Directly in front of the gallery window, on a cast-iron table, a vitrine contains a curious frosted bulb full of water and an industrial-looking thermometer. The bulb is an early version of the fire extinguisher; in the last century clusters of such bulbs were suspended from ceilings and burst open when a certain temperature was reached. (The single bulb contains about enough water to extinguish a large charcoal briquette, but there you are.)

Two larger glass cases contain potentially sound-producing objects. *Vibration I* has a violin bow suspended on a diagonal hovering at one point just above a sand-covered copperplate; the sound of the bow, striking the plate, would scatter the sand. *Vibration II* is a large tuning fork, mounted on a dressed block of ancient-looking dark wood, with a hoop of steel string running through the tip of the fork's tines, its ends attached to opposite sides of the box. One side of this case has several round holes in a line along the glass. (What this one does or doesn't do, I don't know.)

Finally, two large combine works at roughly opposite ends of the gallery contrast dramatically, *The Black Mirror* being entirely black, *Designed Nature* mainly white. The former has an enormous photo of a child's half-dissected head and neck, preserved in a museum jar, looming murkily forward from a pitch-black background; this is mounted on a black wooden surface in a black frame, and on the floor in front of it are five square blocks of anthracite, their topmost surfaces polished to a reflective slickness. In *Designed Nature*, a steel shelf holds several flaming alcohol lamps on the wall above a double row of pail-shaped salt licks, the kind put out in the woods for deer, with the brand name embossed in the salt.

These works appear to be about nature and its transmutation into culture, salt representing the exploitation of the ocean, anthracite the mining of the earth. Drozdik's use of quirky materials is quite audacious and succeeds in drawing our attention from one layer of the work to another, from the object to the relations between, for example, the alcohol in the spirit lamps and the imaginary fluids of the Leyden jars. And of course what is strongly felt in these pieces is the pathos and charm of science before its conquest of nature, the pathos and charm of antique innocence that made industrialization possible. The pickled head in the photograph evokes the comparative simplicity of the 19th century's nightmares, its justified mistrust of technical progress reflected in myriad texts like Mary Shelley's *Frankenstein*. Beyond that, each object in this show is a meditation on the history of ideas about the physical world, and the fate of all things to end up as curiosities in an unknowable future. This first one-person show in New York is an exceptionally well-wrought and mature debut, full of fresh intelligence and sensibility.

March 22, 1988

SO BIG

["**Picturing 'Greatness.'**" The Museum of Modern Art, 11 West 53rd
Street, through March 29]

Barbara Kruger's selection of photographs of artists from the
Museum of Modern Art's permanent collection, "Picturing
'Greatness,'" is arranged around a central wall text that says, in
part, "As we tend to become who we are through a dense crush
of allowances and denials, inclusions and absences, we can
begin to see how approval is accorded through the language of
'greatness,' that heady brew concocted with a slice of visual
pleasure, a pinch of connoisseurship, a mention of myth and a
dollop of money."

Even this carefully modulated language, since it contains
actual, pointed ideas, seems wildly incongruous at MOMA. The
current MOMA season, which includes Rosemarie Trockel's
drawings and sculpture, Vito Acconci's sculpture, and a show of
political posters and books, as well as Kruger's show, has probably
led plenty of regular MOMA-goers to wonder, "Who died?"

However, I am confident that MOMA will continue, after its
teasing little flirtation with relevance, to resume its customary air
of a jaded taxidermist. After all, the "crush of allowances and
denials, inclusions and absences" Kruger writes of has long been
MOMA's bread and butter. It is hard to find any place outside a
government office where—"who we are and who we aren't" is

more brazenly hammered home than in Manhattan's museums. Victims of weird conflations of imperiousness with taste, intimidation with pleasure, consensus with value, and culture with class restrictions, our museums have been recuperating these late 19th and early 20th-century tropes with increasing desperation while many producers of art have shed them. What's seen at MOMA, the Whitney, the Guggenheim, and the bizarre Lila Acheson Wallace Wing of the Met are ventures in systemic, *mis*representation of contemporary art. Manhattan's museums primarily co-opt works of art to make them tell the story of the museum, confirm and reinforce the museum's pretensions and authority, and repel certain forms of curiosity.

These are not everyday skills. Our museums kill cultural inquiry and ignore ideological criticism with the majestic deftness of a teenage sociopath drowning a litter of kittens. In return, an hypothesized public, every bit as fictive as the perfect nuclear family targeted by detergent ads, is welcomed to the spectacle of man's, occasionally women's, highest spiritual achievements, framed and on pedestals. When something is *especially* great, significant, important, seminal, groundbreaking, magnificent, and/or unbelievable, the public may be gently but firmly guided from one masterpiece to the next by means of prerecorded headset tapes. Seldom do large historical forces producing the work of art count for more than informational garnish; the true heart of the work is located, instead, in hairsplitting details of technique, identification of the artist's contemporaries and accounts of his, occasionally her, personal life, exact *dating* of the work, arrangement of works in precise chronological sequence, descriptions of subject matter, choices of materials, anecdotal accounts of the artist's travels, and so forth. History exists, in this conservative scheme, in order to produce greatness; greatness is what deserves memory.

Let's acknowledge at the outset that everyone said to be great is great, in somebody's mind, and once you've acknowledged that, what then do you have, exactly? A quite typical current article in an art magazine begins with the excited question: What if artist X, subject of the article, turns out to be *truly* great? Well? Yes, what if he does, what then? (A truly great what, incidentally?) What then have we proved, unless it be that a sequence of greatness-spotters calls X "great." These people would be, one assumes, experts on greatness. Unlike scientists, they don't need to establish X's greatness by verifying certain experimental results. They deal in spirituality, not clinical data. Where does their concept of spirituality come from? From a sense of history? Whose writing of history? Whose criteria of appropriate emotions, appropriate responses to history? X is white, male, heterosexual, and some other things that *might* render him great to people like himself, traditionally the custodians of history and therefore the inventors of greatness as an end in itself: concentration camps or the Sistine Chapel, it's all great.

Photography is uniquely equipped to show us greatness as it's supposed to look on a human face, in a human body. In Kruger's selection of images, signs of nobility, intense concentration, aristocratic refinement, and sweaty masculinity are inscribed variously, with all the force of convention. Eccentric, even nutty behavior is rendered in terms of pictorial wonder and awe: Jackson Pollock splashing around in the studio, snapped from a vertiginous overhead angle; Picasso in triplicate—moving faster than the shutter!—drawing a squiggly, evanescent masterpiece with a flashlight. Then there's genius off-duty, brow furrowed in concentration or wearing an "ironic" look in the eyes; even when these guys aren't actually creating, they're thinking about it. There's Jackson Pollock again, this time brooding from the running board of a battered roadster, in an open shirt, denim jacket with unbuttoned cuffs, jeans, and paint-spattered penny loafers, one hand over the other, a cigarette poking up between fingers. Rodchenko: open shirt and cigarette, squinting intensity of the eyes. André Derain: open white shirt with the sleeves rolled up along the meaty arms, big oval palette in one hand, a cigarette pressed between tight lips.

Greatness is here in a wistful or melancholy mode, also; in Rozsa Klein's sensuous portrait of Giacometti, seated on a floor, his somber face staring at the camera while his forearms clutch his shins. He's dressed in soft casual clothes—sweater, wool pants—suggesting vulnerability. Nearby, in Nickolas Muray's pictures, the ancient Claude Monet is ensconced like a biblical patriarch on a slatted bench in Giverny. Here cross-legged, in a loose tweed suit and a shirt with delicately ruffled cuffs, with wrinkled hands and a ghostly white beard, glasses, a big straw hat; the photographer, half-kneeling at the Master's side, plays the adoring acolyte. There, in long shot, splendidly isolated on the bench, Monet sits before one of the lily ponds he made famous, his face dappled with shade, under a fecund arbor.

Greatness in action takes us into the wacky world of Pollock, as mentioned, but also lets us look over Ben Nicholson's shoulder as he completes a drawing, and to catch Matisse standing on a newspaper-covered studio floor, working on a drawing for the Vence Chapel with a brush, or maybe it's a pencil, attached to the end of a two-foot-long stick. Greatness in repose offers a contrast between Gertrude Vanderbilt Whitney—primly garbed in a largish smock with vast wing lapels, hat, T-strap shoes and striped stockings, aside her large, fig-leafed male statue—and Picasso, familiarly resting one hand on the hip of a fully nude, classical male marble, Picasso himself exposing a hairy geriatric chest in his unbuttoned shirt, the rest of him dressed in Bermuda shorts and sandals. Behind the artist, three of his own huge drawings are set in panels on the wall. His attitude in the museum space is a proprietary one, and appropriately so: the painter who said that "painting is something you do with your balls" understood that his own greatness consisted in getting other people with the same equipment to service his career, and those without it to service him.

Since these are memorable photographs and their arrangements are quietly if firmly ironic, some percentage of the casual viewers of this show have probably ignored Kruger's vivid text after glancing at it (even though it's in a commanding space in the center of the room) and looked at the pictures in the same ruminatively defensive way that many museumgoers look at everything. This is less the artist's failing than the result of the museum's conditioning the public to expect puerile, badly written, and complaisantly irrelevant texts whenever language appears on museum walls.

A CURIOUS PART OF THE PLANET

[**Meret Oppenheim**. Kent Gallery, 41 East 57th Street, through April 9.]

The paintings and objects by Meret Oppenheim currently being shown at Kent Gallery span a 50-year period. Thanks partly to art historians Dominique Bürgi and Bice Curiger, Oppenheim's work emerged from a long period of obscurity in the early 1980s; like Marcel Duchamp, Oppenheim was best known for several decades for a single piece of art. And like Duchamp, Oppenheim did not produce a vast body of work but an intensely rarefied one, integrated not only by visual resemblances between one piece and another but by a dramatically distinct and playful sensibility.

It seems that Oppenheim's long periods of creative silence were not voluntary. "Personal doubts and the refractory problems of being a woman held her up for seventeen years, until 1954," writes Jacqueline Burckhardt in *Parkett*'s 1985 special issue on Oppenheim. "These difficulties were compounded by financial straits." Many sculptural projects realized in the '70s and '80s existed on paper decades before; a blue glove with raised red veins and capillaries on its surface, produced in an edition of 150 in 1985, existed as a design that Oppenheim proposed to Elsa Schiaparelli in the mid-'30s. The singularity of Oppenheim's work is such that nothing seems dated, as works of a period date when they adhere too obviously to a school or movement. The impression given by her art is instead that of a self-defined set of problems and obsessions explored in different ways over time, often at odds with prevailing fashions. (In the '50s, for instance, her work fell into the cracks between orthodox postwar Surrealism and abstraction.)

The range of the work and its quirky self-assurance are striking. A simple charcoal drawing, *Rome Under the Earth* (1985), suggests two uninflected architectural slabs beneath a diagonal spray of dark strokes; the composition is almost stupidly blunt, but its chaotic-looking lines are deceptively precise, and the blank, shaded-around space of the buried objects gradually asserts the mysterious dimension of a broken monument. Concealment and layered planes are recurring preoccupations. In a pastel drawing called *Something Underneath a Haystack* (1969), pink-shaded red arrows point from several directions at a yellowish mound, inside which is a roughly oblong, boulderlike object. A painting titled *An Agreeable Moment on a Planet* (1981) is a variegated, bisected circle inside a rectangle, the top part mottled with wiggly black shapes on a midnight-blue "sky," while the lower, "earth" part contains several ellipse forms and two brick-red cylindrical ones, something like factory smokestacks, which echo the buried forms in *Rome Under the Earth*.

The presentation of a planet or a landscape as a kind of dissection-slide or ant-farm view that burrows under the surface creates one of Oppenheim's favorite effects of rendering the unconscious visible, a process she accomplishes in other pieces by splitting open the surface of a figure. In a sculpture called *Bon Appétit, Marcel* (1966), a white dessert plate rests on a chessboard of brown and light-beige squares; on the plate, between wood-handled knife and fork, a humanoid chess piece crafted from pastry dough has a surgical gash running down its middle, revealing a brie-like subcutaneous trench and a central bone suggesting the thorax of a large sparrow. The effect is subtle and insidious, owing to the uniform biscuit color of the figure and its innards. Another extraordinary piece, *Octavia* (1969), forms a female figure from a long double-handled saw, its teeth extended in bright painted stripes to the edge of the sculpture it's attached to, the right side of which copies the form of the saw. In the space between real and simulated saw, the figure's molded nose and tongue extrude from the painting surface in startling relief. The vertical sweep of this sculpture is funny because of the overall resemblance of the thing to a giant putty scraper, the base of which is a trompe l'oeil tree trunk. (Oppenheim has a terrific facility at mimicking natural surfaces with paint, as seen in the optically buzzing wood-grain background of *The Brownies Are Leaving the House* [1961] and in the painted mast of the sculpture called *Cloud on a Boat* [1963].)

It's remarkable how easily Oppenheim brings a whole world into view in a painting like *Genoveva Floating Over the Water* (1957), using only scattered gouts of white over modulated auburn and planting a solid black biomorph just off-center, and in the membranous monochrome veils of *Hazy Flower* (1974) and *Lily of the Sea* (1977). These pictures relate to the "anchored abstraction" of contemporary painters like David Diao and Ross Bleckner as well as the earlier referential abstraction of Yves Tanguy and late Max Ernst. Oppenheim's titles further anchor the works in a specific imagination, and are often drawn from the small but significant body of Oppenheim's poetry. Since her visual work and her poetry are strongly interactive elements of an extraordinary, creative mind, I think I'll finish this with Catherine Schelbert's translation of "My Favorite Dog," a poem Meret Oppenheim wrote in 1944:

> *I love my friend's*
> *Dog. He can say "yes" so*
> *Beautifully. He can say "yes"*
> *When you forget him. He condemns*
> *no one that compares himself to him.*

Wherever he goes, spring goes
too. When he weeps, nature
loses its feathers. But when he's
in a good mood, he skillfully pushes
your hand to his mouth to hear
its greatest secrets.
Like every brave man he has
two souls in each breast,
twenty-five in hands and feet.

April 12, 1988

WAVE THEORY

[**Susan Hiller**. Pat Hearn Gallery, 735 East 9th Street, through April 17.]

Susan Hiller was an anthropologist before she began making art. She wrote an essay explaining in detail her reasons for leaving anthropology. I haven't been able to get hold of it, but I'm told that Hiller was dissatisfied with the biased methods built into the profession. For example, on a dig in South America she came across fragments of pottery made by women. She was told these were insignificant. But remnants of similar artifacts made by men in Asia Minor and the Mediterranean were considered evidence of a high degree of civilization.

Hiller uses an anthropological curiosity in her artwork and often systematizes the presentation of her material in a scientific way. While the visual and linguistic investigations of traditional ethnography have inspired artists like Elaine Reichek and Lothar Baumgarten, Hiller's attention gravitates toward artifacts and psychological phenomena peculiar to developed societies: not the most obviously loaded cultural signifiers like magazines, TV, and big-ticket consumer items, but things like gravestones, photo-booth portraits, and postcards. In a current series, Hiller projects her own spontaneous calligraphy over samples of children's wallpaper. The theme of recovering eloquent ephemera from oblivion gives her work a melancholic tinge that's offset by her cool methodology. Her art is not mystical, but traps certain mystical elements.

The *Rough Sea* project is a collection of postcards manufactured over a 70-year period. Most, though not all, picture wave turbulence near various English coastal towns. One quite odd thing about the postcards is how the caption, "Rough Sea," appears over and over again; another is how the same kind of image performs as the sign of many places, virtually unchanged over almost a century. However, there are significant differences between the cards, differences that Hiller charts without assigning them overspecific meanings. "Just as the map of Britain, emptied of internal positions, can be seen as a series of coastal references existing as a thin skin between land and sea," Hiller has written, "so the piece as a whole balances on that edge: metaphoric and mythic meanings are *found* in the same act as they are *made*..."

The cards are numbers, and the locale, if given, identified. Next, the caption—usually "Rough Sea," but sometimes more particularly "A Rough Sea," "The Dog Wave," or "Rough Sea Off the Banjo Groin," and so on—and the legend or explanatory text on the back of the card are recorded. The final "linguistic trait" on Hiller's charts is the commentary, what people have written on those cards that passed through the mail. Naturally, this writing has the pathic quality of just slightly uncovering forgotten lives, amplifying a few notes of forgotten voice. "This I think is a moonlight effect. The wind is rising steadily and we shall soon have it just like it." "How would you like to stand here. You would get a splendid bathe. Plenty of water for the engine too." "The weather yesterday was somewhat like the view..." "We haven't had quite such a rough sea yet..."

Recovered, too, are the "unknown artists" who painted many of the cards, and doctored others with invented waves. Hiller classifies the visual traits of the collection: whether the original medium was photography or painting, the format horizontal, vertical, a composite, or a single image, monochrome or colored, the image embellished with a "frame" or extending to the margin of the card. If the image is signed, the signature is duly noted. Hiller further breaks down the types of pictures: sea and coast, sea and ship (the ships were always painted in), sea and pier, sea and buildings, sea and promenade. In this show, besides the charts and framed grid arrangements of postcards, Hiller includes several rephotographed, monochrome blowups.

Altogether, *Rough Sea* has the unnerving effect of a somewhat maniacal obsession (like any elaborate gathering of similar objects) and provokes questions about why this particular sign of "nature"—the crashing or foaming wave—had such ubiquity. What notion of the sublime made the idea "rough sea" so popular or necessary that in certain cases a fairly tranquil ocean would be captioned "rough sea"? It seems that it is still customary in English towns, among the middle classes, to visit the seaside during certain months, often when it's still chilly, to gaze at the sea. People flock to miserably bleak ocean villages, take in the view, and write postcards, less as a pleasure than a duty; the messages on many postcards simply confirm or dispute the resemblance of the postcard's picture to the actual view.

Hiller doesn't synthesize her findings into ethnographic truisms, though she does speculate about the cards and their senders; this restraint is partly what makes her collection art instead of anthropology. As an artist she's free to make her own inscription on the material—for example, by painting her own waves or projecting her automatic writing over the rather frightening samples of children's wallpaper she's currently working with—and to then consider her markings as exemplary of a kind of universal human presence. Although some of her projects clearly resemble Surrealist forays into automatism and spiritualism, Hiller seems to have a much more skeptical distance from the ethereal, despite her fascination with it.

Magic Lantern, a room installation, invites the viewer to sit in the dark and watch a slide presentation of overlapping color circles that fade into blackness, leaving dark, glowing afterimages on the wall. Meanwhile, a tape plays the artist's voice, alternately chanting and speaking an explanation of loud, crackling passages of static punctuated by bizarre noises resembling speech. These, we're told, are "dead voices" captured on tape by Konstantīns Raudive, a Latvian scientist. The voices speak German, English, Italian, and strange to say, Latvian. Raudive's theory seems to be that since sound waves never stop vibrating through space, the voices of the dead continue talking in some subregister of audibility. So he left a tape recorder going in an empty room and, incredible as it seems, picked up these queer little blips and grunts and bleeps. Once the interpretations are given, however, these noises do sound awfully convincingly like voices. Not just anybody's, either: one of them is Winston Churchill's. Even if it isn't (and we have no way of knowing), this is one of the funniest efforts of synesthesia anyone has come up with, and I think you should "see" it.

April 19, 1988

READ MY LIPS

> *We no longer have the sense of things being infinite or real or*
> *natural, and it is certainly not an artist's job to reinforce those*
> *cultural clichés, to let people imagine some immutable reality.*
> *Our job is to make what we thought of as natural become*
> *unnatural, so that ideas of the self are inscribed in language*
> *symbolically, not organically.*
>   —Ross Bleckner, interview in *Artscribe*, March/April 1988

Sandra Bernhard's show at the Orpheum Theater, *Without You
I'm Nothing*, begins by evoking an absence. "Sometimes I hear
the telephone ring/I answer it/but no one is there." A few lines
into the song, the identity of the singer shifts to that of the
person being sung to. This isn't the call-and-response of romantic
tunes but a bewilderingly uninflected switch of subject and
object. The earnestness of the song's message—you've ruined me,
but I'll survive—evaporates as Bernhard, "acting the song," glides
into a pose straight from a fitness-center ad. A recitative that
follows casts Bernhard as someone quite other than herself, one
of those unctuous and self-absorbed theater creatures who adores
show business and talks auditions, pics, and résumés with every
breath. She's doing a character, but the usual cues for separating
character from performer are left out.

    In routines that follow, Bernhard spins narratives about a life
that seems only intermittently her very own, blurring lines between

autobiography and fiction, while working through an assortment of pop numbers under the guise of "a woman of rock and roll." Woven through the show are vignettes in which she does impersonate other people—a hefty, embittered ex-manager ("Rappin' Irene"), a lounge singer "going out to you from the Mustang Motel," and, most powerfully, an ostensibly straight male, in 1978, having his first homoerotic experience in a gay disco. The latter narrative unfolds in the second person: "Your mind is screaming, 'I'm straight, I'm straight!' (Pause.) Somebody hands you a tambourine...."

Several presences distilled from American myths emerge, not so much distinct personalities as available, seductive archetypes. One is the latter-day, road-movie beatnik drifter as resuscitated by Sam Shepard and Wim Wenders, hitching her way from New Jersey to Kansas City. Another is a poet-rocker in the furious style of Patti Smith. There is also the "real" Sandra Bernhard, recounting an evening of ludicrous sensual enchantment at the hands of Stevie Nicks ("Tiffany lamps with antique scarves thrown over them, casting these medieval shadows around the room"); a postnuclear holocaust dream featuring Tina Turner and Madonna; and an adult "reach out and touch" episode involving Warren Beatty or someone like him, punctuated by choruses of "Ain't No Mountain High Enough," which builds to that magic moment when everything stops and someone says: "Have you got any rubbers? Mind putting one on? And while you're at it...make it two."

With an excellent band behind her—Mitch Kaplan on keyboards, Spyder Mittleman on saxophone and percussion, Ivan Julian's guitar and Denise Fraser on drums—Bernhard slips in and out of a polished musical format. She has a memorable voice that she pushes beyond its range at strategic moments, undermining naïve readings of any particular sequence. The lounge singer's amiable lesbian rendering of "Me & Mrs. Jones," for instance, shades into something less fictional, but then goes over the top as Bernhard's voice threatens to become an ambulance siren on the signature line. The Patti Smith number, baldly cribbed from

"Revenge," transforms Smith's rueful acidity into an ironic tantrum ("I look over my shoulder/you're getting older./Maybe it doesn't matter but/could you be a little fatter?") and a parody of choreographed rage. To complete the distancing effect, Bernhard copies Smith's theatrical trope of miming fellatio on the guitarist; the guitarist, Ivan Julian, used to play with Patti Smith.

Part of this show is a brilliant uninhibited attack on everything false and meretricious in American pop culture, from the career moves of rock stars embracing noble causes to the bogus return to the repressive "innocence" of the '50s, exemplified by "the Esprit philosophy" and Bruce Weber's coyly exploitative beefcake ad campaigns for Calvin Klein. Bernhard sums up the atmosphere of middle America in the age of the neo-malt shop: "Sit at the counter, order a Velveeta sandwich for eight dollars, pretend you're naïve and innocent, and then go out on the street and be the whore that you really are." *Without You I'm Nothing* is saturated in pop culture and is something of a monument to its fascinations—complicit and critical at the same time. But the critical part is the edgiest crossover from performance art to mainstream that anyone has attempted to date. Bernhard makes the boy wonders migrating from Soho to Hollywood look like hors d'oeuvres at a deluded power breakfast.

Bernhard's array of assumed identities is woven partly from real longings and wishes, partly from ubiquitous cultural models, and largely from advertising chimeras and consumer products. In one sequence, she projects herself into a Hallmark-perfect gentile family at Christmas, conjuring up the glazed ham with cloves, canned-fruit compote, her mother's burgundy velveteen dress, and a father who donates 10 percent of his annual income at midnight mass.

Another image of perfection, narrated over a Burt Bacharach medley, casts her as a secretary in romantic San Francisco, winning the boss after her first day on the job. The point of departure here is the infamous *Newsweek* article about the dismal marriage prospects of women over 35. Bernhard constructs an entire person from ad-copy prose and the advice columns of *Cosmopolitan*; here, as elsewhere, the little details are scathingly apt: Pier 1 split-bamboo curtains, chintz fold-out sofa, Rubbermaid daisies in the bathtub. Bernhard's Cosmo Girl, herself a montage of demographics, squeals her pleasure over not ending up a statistic.

One source for *Without You I'm Nothing* cited by Bernhard's co-writer and director, John Boskovich, was Dan Graham's essay, "Dean Martin/Entertainment as Theater." Graham analyzes Martin's woozy oscillations between sincerity and put-on and *The Dean Martin Show*'s habitual ruptures of the variety-show structure. *Without You* similarly punctures the conventions of one-person cabaret. It draws the audience close with the lure of confession; confession is folded over to expose the artifice. The Brechtian intent is clear from the staging: everything is revealed, the lights, cables, and projectors are naked, the performers claustrophobically foregrounded. When depth-making images project across the stretched tarps behind the stage, the images are blown-up details of the theater auditorium. The poster for the show, with one picture of Bernhard looking at another, identifies the true addressee of the title, which could read *Without Me I'm Nothing*.

Without You deals with the social construction of identity, the self mediated through and collaged from the realm of the symbolic. Bernhard's stage persona corresponds to the self-as-pastiche that serves as authorial presence in much contemporary art: the decentered "I" and mobile "You" of Barbara Kruger's photomontages (*You Are Not Yourself; You Thrive on Mistaken Identity*), the psychic wiretaps of subvocal speech in Jenny Holzer's posters and electronic signs, Cindy Sherman's photographic morphology of female stereotypes, the shredded first-person narratives of Kathy Acker. One could further cite the accumulation of authorial cues throughout Richard Prince's re-presentation of found images and jokes, and the "found autobiography" of Larry Johnson's picture-texts. *Without You I'm Nothing* belongs to this loose canon of works as much as it belongs to show business.

April 26, 1988

A PENNY FOR THE PEEPSHOW

["**Peepshow**." Windows on White, 55 White Street, through May 1]

The thing that instantly appealed to me when I got the press release for "Peepshow" was, of course, the title. It promised something private, possibly something lurid and sexy. So I walked down to White Street to peep in the window, which was blacked out except for these little holes. The first time I went, I walked up to the first little hole and stared in. How interesting, I thought. This person has built a miniature upholstery warehouse inside a tiny peepshow diorama. The next hole was entirely black. A subsequent hole offered a view of figured wood paneling. Then an empty space, just a box, with a slit at the far end, through which I could see another miniature upholstery warehouse.

It turned out that I had come on the wrong day, not being a careful reader of press releases, and was in fact viewing the innards of an actual upholstery warehouse where Windows on White is. This is not far from the Baby Doll Lounge, and I suddenly felt like some grimy masturbator waiting for the place to open. Already the whole thing seemed clever in that humiliating postmodern way, since dozens of truckers up and down the street were eating their lunch on loading platforms and staring at me while I squinted into the peepholes.

I usually hate art in windows. Don't you? On the other hand, it's a relief when galleries have the kind of space arrangement where you can see in from the street and spare yourself some nauseating indoor encounter with objects you don't want to know about. And that pretentious baffle wall that a lot of galleries feature, with the artist's name printed across it in huge letters, is cruder in its way than teaser photos in front of a porno movie house. The harder galleries try to look exclusive, the cheaper they become. After all, they're primarily stores for millionaires that pretend to "enlighten the public." As a member of the public, though, you like to feel you're being *invited* to see the art close-up if you want to, even if you don't want to. Whenever I got to the Fuller Building I notice the huge names being advertised across the street at Pace and think, *Oh, please, who on earth do you think you're intimidating.* I loved it when Leo Castelli had that Bruce Nauman neon piece outside the gallery windows all through the winter. You knew that Leo really wanted you to come in and look. Now it's gone. Maybe it will come back.

Anyway, the peepshows got installed the next day and a number of other people were staring in so it felt less awkward. Quickly, this is what's there: a room that looks like a disco in hell, with a low ceiling and rows of cork pylons standing on a street map of Paris, by Dean Motter. The room has curved, gold Mylar walls on right and left, and straight ahead a flat wall reflecting the room and the viewer's eye.

An interior by Dale Wilhelm with a silhouette of rooftops in the background, teen photographs planted in the windows of buildings, and an array of sculptural objects in the foreground. Stacks of silver bars, a black floor, a nighttime sky.

An immense-looking diorama by Daniel R. S. Trupiano of a curving river landscape, with scattered trees, brass promenades along the riverbank, streetlamps, carved horses, a bridge, a large house with dormer windows in the distance. In the immediate foreground is a verandah, or a porch, where a blue enamel table holds a miniature punch bowl.

By James Schmidt, a bathroom out of *Eraserhead*. Everything metallic and deeply depressive, from the toilet perched high on the wall to the shower stall, which is also a telephone booth. This is the most beautifully executed piece, full of winning details such as a roll of metal toilet paper unspooling from its holder almost to the floor. The phone receiver doubles as a shower head.

Augusta Talbot has installed, in a rectangular frame, a kind of bloated saint figure with galvanized hair and a large blue chair tucked under her arm. This figure is just floating there in front of your eyes, opaque and inevitable. I have no idea what it represents.

A cube room by James B. Cobb contains a revolving model of a room, a painting of the room, a Polaroid of the room, and so forth.

Finally, Michael Morris's peephole contains only a curved rectangular mirror in which you can see yourself and the industrial building behind you, across the street. The mirror is not bright enough to adjust your makeup but you get the idea.

May 17, 1988

THE AUCTIONS

The first thought that crossed my mind when I got to Sotheby's Monday night before last was, *I've got to get out of here.* I arrived early. I wanted to keep the lowest possible profile. I wore my Armani suit and a Gorbachev T-shirt and prepared to act *normal*, you know, like someone with money. And then I discovered—but of course!—that my ticket was for the *press section*. In case you didn't know, the press at such events is herded into standing rooms roped off to the left of the seats. Much of the working press is taller than I am. Once the bidding started, I couldn't see who was getting what.

Long before that, however, came the bizarre Warhol Crush: a suffocating onslaught of bared gleaming teeth, ostentatious jewelry, and surprisingly inferior couture. If everyone wants a piece of Andy so badly, perhaps they should fashion a new one from the snipped flesh of all these facelifts. In roughly 15 minutes, Sotheby's became a full-blown fire hazard of elderly women with no wrinkles and men with no lips. As Dorothy Parker said, if you want to know what God thinks about money, just look at the people he gives it to. But I think we have to qualify this in a country that has, at last count, one million millionaires: by the law of averages, some of them must be nice people.

Not everyone came to bid. I was relieved to see Steve Mass in the crowd. Steve Mass is still my personal guru and the final authority on scenes. He said he planned to watch the auction on closed-circuit TV in the "auxiliary gallery." This was a perfectly Andy idea and I tried to join him in there, but Sotheby's wouldn't let me go in, except to look around. There were three Japanese businessmen in front and a few bored-looking gigolos and dozens of empty seats. No Steve. I returned to the press section. Dealer Massimo Audiello said, "I can't believe you come for the auction of the year and you don't wear your drag clothes, baby."

I positioned myself next to the handsomest man I could find in the press section and dutifully filled in the gavel prices in my catalogue. You could, in fact, see the turntable with the art on it. The effect suggests an early-evening game show: "*Will she go for the $10,000, or what's behind the curtain?*" Everyone was wondering, naturally, if the Fine Art part of the Warhol estate would soar past its estimated prices as incredibly as the Warhol Collectibles had. It occurred to me that Andy had bought the farm in a hospital bed only a few hundred yards from this very spot, so every shred of the man was being disposed of within a tidy little area.

Well, not exactly. I've heard from at least a dozen Warhol associates and alleged intimates that Andy had zillions more knickknacks and pictures and goblets and clocks and silver and gewgaws stashed in warehouses. In other words, this estate auction represents the tip of a considerable iceberg. So how will they bill the next auction? The *New* Andy Warhol Estate? Will the yen stay inflated long enough for every minimagnate in Tokyo to own at least *one* complete set of Fiesta ware? A Cy Twombly? Do you, uh, care?

Any simple, unequivocal opinion about Andy Warhol is worth nothing. Marlene Dietrich said it best in *Touch of Evil*: "He was some kind of man. What does it matter what you say about people?" Of $300,000 for a small Hockney drawing of Warhol, or $550,000 for a particularly uneventful Lichtenstein, many people have had much to say in the past few days. For instance, that people are reacting to the stock market crash, snapping up the only objects they think *might* retain value in the absolutely inevitable collapse of the American economy. That the Japanese did all the top bidding, through various emissaries. But most people attribute the quirkier triumphs of the Warhol auction ($90,000 for a Basquiat, etc.) to a mixture of sentimentality, bravado, and panic.

What seems a watershed event is actually a vindication of something very American and, strange to say, extremely democratic: shopping. In the endless accounts of Warhol's buying mania, the most remarkable and consistently iterated observation is that Andy just bought and bought and bought things and chucked them away in a corner without ever bothering with them again. He bought junk and he bought things of high quality; this accumulation was in no sense a "collection," a careful assortment of treasured objects, but a sort of archaeological record of anything Andy saw that he was able to purchase. If you consider the methodology of his films and the omnivorous iconography of his paintings, the Warhol Auction comes to seem the logical last axiom of the Warhol Philosophy. He did say he wanted "Figment" engraved on his tombstone. Now everything he ever looked at becomes a figment of him.

In every American town there are men and women who work like slaves and take their hard-earned money to the shopping mall. They buy out-of-season clothes on sale, spare Christmas ornaments, appliances they never plug in, computers they never learn to use, anything their neighbors and anything they might have use for, one day. There are the brave working-class men and women who grew up during the Depression and lived through World War II and finally landed in the middle class after 1945. Their attics and basements tell the story of their lives: dreams and longings and wishes and hopes, and more than anything else, a grim determination never to slide back into poverty. You will always find a year's worth of canned goods crammed in their cupboards. The impulses that have ruled their lives are the same ones that account for the Warhol Collection. The success of the Warhol Auction marks the highest recognition of shopping as a way of life.

May 31, 1988

DOGLESSNESS

[**William Wegman.** Holly Solomon Gallery, 724 Fifth Avenue, through May 28]

William Wegman's new paintings are a complete surprise to people who always knew Wegman was an accomplished artist. His earlier paintings tended to look sketchy and almost gestural, and we valued them as records of a unique sensibility. They belonged less to the history of painting than to the history of Wegman's personality. This personality remains the most amiable and seductive personality in contemporary art. Wegman is one of the very few strong artists in our time who has nothing hateful or mean-spirited embedded in his work. His production hasn't been consistently "big" or invariably compelling, but the big things haven't served to bash other artists around and the fizzles haven't been failed acts of megalomania. This in itself is extraordinary.

The virtuosity of Wegman's latest work betrays one of the less emphasized secrets about Art. This is a time of art specialists, artists who do one kind of thing and keep doing one kind of thing until that one kind of thing becomes a desired commodity. Painters become experts at painting, sculptors at sculpting, and eventually arrive at a product that looks like they did it. The prices of an artist's work vary according to "how characteristic" a particular work is. Plenty of prized objects might be better works of art without the signature excrescence, the doodad, the broken plates or the overhanging shelf. But all except a few modern *art shoppers* collect *artists* rather than *art*. Wegman is a rare example of the contemporary artist who does what he feels like doing, whether or not it looks like something he already did. Artistic freedom has been widely redefined as making piles of money to spend on BMWs and co-ops and summer rentals in Montauk. That is, of course, more freedom than most people have. But you can sell guns or heroin and buy the same freedom. Artistic freedom consists in doing exactly what you want with your time, and being smart enough to know exactly what that is, even when the whole art world is kissing your ass for doing something else.

These pictures demonstrate that painting of a high order of sophistication and complexity is something an artist who hasn't previously concentrated on it can teach himself or herself how to do. The know-how isn't in the genes, or the gonads, but the brain, the hand, and the eye. I think Wegman fell under an enchantment while making these paintings, and, happily for us, got caught up in the felicitous challenge of painting them better and better. The pleasure involved in making these eccentric, luminous landscapes—which echo Turner and Joan Miró despite the presence of dinosaurs, irrigation spigots, passenger aircraft, and skyscrapers—transmits directly to the viewer. Wegman has found a way to fully exploit the seriousness of large-scale oil painting without arriving at *dead* seriousness.

May 31, 1988

WAS IT GOOD FOR LOU?

[*Friedrich Nietzsche: The Man in His Works.* By Lou Salomé. Black Swan Books, $22.50.]

Although Lou Salomé's study of Nietzsche has been long eclipsed by later investigations—among them Heidegger's four-volume *Nietzsche*, works by Gottfried Benn, Camus, Freud, Habermas, and Deleuze—*Friedrich Nietzsche: The Man in His Works* has the historical allure of having been written by Nietzsche's chosen disciple (though this status did not last long), the only woman besides his mother and his sister to play a significant role in his life.

The book appeared in 1894, a decade after their relationship ended, and whether Salomé has written a work of exegesis or of self-vindication depends largely on whose later opinion one reads. Walter Kaufmann, the exemplary Nietzsche translator whose own thoughts on the philosopher have a bewildering lack of resonance, equates Salomé's occasional blurring of facts and her philosophical gaffes with Elisabeth Förster-Nietzsche's quite systematic and deliberate misrepresentations. Kaufmann takes his lead in this matter from Rudolph Binion's *Frau Lou: Nietzsche's Wayward Disciple*, a 587-page character assassination that appeared in 1968. Binion and Kaufmann both know a great man when they see one, a talent which allows them to go blind in those areas of everyday life where even the great behave like assholes.

To the disinterested reader, *Nietzsche* seems a fairly conventional rendering of Nietzsche's philosophy, interesting mainly because it minted clichés rather than repeating them. Salomé combines heady admiration with cool distance from her subject, and though the book capitalizes on her brief and entirely mental intimacy with Nietzsche, it is hardly exploitative. Its main flaw is its relentless psychologizing of Nietzsche's writing, which Salomé breaks down into three main periods: the early metaphysical writings; the positivist period, in which Nietzsche moved away from his fidelity to Schopenhauer and engaged dialectically with the writings of Paul Rée (the third wheel in Nietzsche's longed-for ménage with Lou, which never came to pass); and the final "mystical" period, when Nietzsche glorified the notion of instinctual behavior and abandoned the concept of a fixed, discoverable "truth," celebrating instead the ideational lava available through intense feeling.

Salomé almost entirely ignores, or overlooks, Nietzsche's radical questioning of philosophical language, which set the stage for Wittgenstein's revolutionary deconstruction of philosophy's very frame; she confuses this keenly self-conscious linguistic probing with "self-expression" and finds tragic evidence of Nietzsche's confusion of his own subjectivity with the external world. Salomé trades on the then-burgeoning myth of Nietzsche as the "mad philosopher," driven to disintegration by the extremity of his thinking rather than by the organic disorders (chronic migraine, probably an early syphilitic symptom) he actually suffered from. However, Salomé's conclusions don't seem malicious; rather, they seem consistent with prevailing myths about mental and physical illness, in which temperament and character determined the state of one's health—myths that persist in many quarters today, even among people who should know better. In Salomé's book, Nietzsche's madness is the logical outcome of his radicalism, as if by thinking too hard he had blown his cerebral fuses.

Salomé's tendency to psychologize and hence miniaturize Nietzsche's concepts of eternal recurrence, the overman or Superman, and the "transvaluation of values" makes this book seem less original than it was when it appeared. Reading it today, one mainly detects a germinating interest in the scientific application of psychological theories, an interest Salomé later developed as a protégé of Sigmund Freud.

Salomé's book was the first serious work on Nietzsche ever written, and remained an important scholarly source for nearly 50 years. Simply by virtue of its dispassion and relative calm, it contrasted remarkably with the awesome falsifications and bombastic claims of the Nietzsche industry promoted by Elisabeth Förster-Nietzsche after her brother's mental collapse in 1889. Elisabeth understood almost nothing of his philosophy, and what she did understand scandalized her. However, after the debacle of her husband's failed Aryan colony in Paraguay, she recognized the spreading fame of her "mad philosopher" brother as her ticket to ride.

Elisabeth wrested control of his work from publishers and secured his copyrights from their mother. For decades after Nietzsche's death, she queened it over the Central European cognoscenti, extorting homage from Stefan George, Thomas Mann, Hugo von Hofmannsthal, and other luminaries. She even managed, incredibly, to get herself three Nobel nominations for a biography of her brother. It was Elisabeth whose ruthless editing of Nietzsche's writings rendered them useful to the Nazi movement, suppressing among other things his philosemitism and disdain for Christianity. In old age, Elisabeth persuaded her dear friend Adolf Hitler to revise the public domain status of Nietzsche's writing, ensuring her income for an extra 30 years.

Lou Salomé was an object of fanatical hatred for Elisabeth, whose machinations preempted Nietzsche's plan of setting up a study-household with Lou and Paul Rée, and effectively ended the relationship. In defense of Lou, it should also be said that, genius though he was, Nietzsche managed to avoid any mature relationship with anybody, preferring the slavish and finally diabolical devotion of people who didn't understand him at all.

June 28, 1988

VILE DAYS

[**Felix Gonzalez-Torres**. Rastovski Gallery, 560 Broadway, through June 22.]

This is my last art column for the *Voice*. Take it or leave it. I've had my fun and now it's time to do something else. If you didn't like this column, now you'll have to find something else to complain about. Frankly, most of the negative letters I've received here have come from incredibly stupid wiseass guys with dick problems, embittered failures of both sexes, and jerks with nothing better to do with their time than write letters to the editor. Writing a nasty letter to the editor is not an exceptional literary skill. It doesn't take much. Only obsessed imbeciles feel actively oppressed by things they read in newspapers. You don't have to buy the *Voice*. You certainly didn't have to read my column. If it annoys you so much, why drive yourself up the wall? Relax and take a pill.

In startling contrast, the supportive letters I've received have invariably come from bright, sensitive human beings who stole valuable moments from their busy schedules to write, and I thank each and every one of you. Here's a big kiss. Mmmm-whaaa. You people out there were my reason for sticking this out as long as I did. When times were dark and I began thinking there was no particularly good reason to keep on with the small but important job this paper had entrusted to me, I took a deep breath and told myself, "Wait just a minute, Indiana. (Not my real name.) It isn't just you. Think about all those…little people, out there in the darkness, scraping their pennies together all week to blow that hard-earned dollar on your magic words, your thrillingly turned phrases, and all the other special things you represent to the people of this great city." You know? I mean, where would New York City be, if, say Denis Hamill, or Jimmy Breslin, or one of those truly trailblazing, indispensable columnists started having existential doubts about the value of his or her own two cents? Imagine the darkness this city would be plunged into if Pete Hamill, for Chrissake, decided to throw in the towel and deprive you and me of those lightning shafts of perception that have added so much to our understanding of the world we live in.

Don't get me wrong. I'm not comparing myself with those guys with really big balls like Peter and Denis and Jimmy. And thank God none of them has ever experienced a minute of introspection or self-doubt. I was unbelievably shaken when I heard that Pete Hamill was leaving *The Village Voice*. I thought, "Oh my God, who next? Nat Hentoff? Andrew Sarris? Paul Berman? *Jack Newfield*? I mean, are we gonna lose it all here, or what?" And believe me, my relief when I learned that Peter had signed on at the *New York Post* at a generous salary—though really a mere fraction of what he's worth—was, you know, *palpable*.

Actually, I am going to write a different column in this paper starting in September. Right now I am leaving town. (Yes, the apartment is already taken.) It is already much too hot to think about anything. If you're spending your summer here I feel sorry for you. Anyway, good luck scrounging around for something to do. Of course, there is always the incredible New York International Arts Festival International or whatever it's called, maybe you can take in some *theater*. Go ahead. Get acquainted with Pina Bausch. Join the excitement. Another thing you could do is join Jerry and Mimi Rubin at Limelight for a "Hot Dance with DJ Tom Finn," according to a "VIP reduced admission card" distributed in large bales at cash-machine counters along lower Broadway. Imagine the fun you could have, partying with the same people you see on line at the cash machine. To say nothing of Jerry and Mimi Rubin. This may seem a far cry from those glory days when Andrew Crispo was a regular fixture at Limelight, but hope springs eternal: your dream date may still be waiting there.

You know the summer doldrums have arrived when local magazines run interviews with Henry Jaglom and Andrea Marcovicci. When exactly did Henry Jaglom slither into public view? Today, of course, he typifies a new genre of shameless talk-show gravedigger, Orson this and Orson that every other word, as if "Orson" indulging this pathetic creep with a few cameos in Jaglom's worthless movies meant that "Orson" thought Henry had loads of talent. Even if Orson was foolish enough to think so, you can be sure his head was turned by the circumstance of having Jaglom's lips pasted to Orson's tushy. If George Bush reminds every woman of her first husband, Henry Jaglom is the type of guy many lesbians remember as their last straw. He'll resort to any sort of cringing, groveling, manipulative pretense of "sensitivity" to get what he wants out of people, but he's all lard-brained male ego. As for Andrea, what about that romantic cabaret revival we've been hearing so much about? How adorable, and how appropriate for the AIDS era, that saucy, naughty nightclub sophistication. One can hardly pick up the phone these days without someone suggesting an *à deux* in some hotel lounge. Can one.

Felix Gonzalez-Torres's show at Rastovski is rather beautiful and unexpected—I mean I came upon it more or less by chance, and then remembered I'd seen some of his white-type-on-black-acetate "date pieces," of which there are several here. These works are rectangular with type running across the lower area. For instance:

Patty Hearts 1975 Jaws 1975 Vietnam 1975 Watergate 1973
Bruce Lee 1973 Munich 1972 Waterbeds 1971 Jackie 1968

These pieces are obviously simple as pie but intelligently collapse the real with the media real, the big with the trivial, the ominous with the obvious, into concise historical bitelets that make appealing but not didactically logical sense. One work, *For the Birds*, is a square wooden column supporting a plate of birdseed, the column inscribed with press type near the top:

> *Proud Viet-Nam Veteran*
> *Outlaw Biker*
> COORS BEER
> *Manhattan Project*

and on alternating sides,

> *Black Monday*
> *Genetically Altered*
> *Economy Experts*
> *Second Amendment*

Torres also has decorated part of a wall with rub-on transfer circles ranged in a virus pattern, their surface images merging crowd photographs with microphotographs of HIV. This is called *Double Fear*, meaning fear of infection and fear of mobs. "The crowd" is clearly a source of wary anxiety in Torres's work. Three jigsaw-puzzle images, in frames, show masses of people hemmed together (at a ball game, at a veteran's parade) in that poised-for-violence thickness so much a part of contemporary life. Three belts with engraved buckles hanging on one wall repeat the theme of mob rule. The buckles say *Supreme Court Georgia 1986* (the "sodomy ruling"), *Preventive Testing*, and *Pater Patriae*.

Although I have been accused in *Artforum*—by another homophile, depressingly enough—of being "obsessed with AIDS," I'd like to point out here than in the past few weeks of semiretirement from the art world, I've gone into galleries in the most unsystematic and disinterested way possible and discovered dozens of works that refer in some way or other to the present health emergency. Perhaps if you're on a career roll, organizing the Venice Biennale and knocking out catalogues for the Saatchi Collection, you can convince yourself that *art*, and maybe your own HIV-negative status, is enough to give you a happy life, and it's just too bad about the others. But somehow I think that attitude is not going to play too much longer, even in Peoria.

Afterword by Bruce Hainley

WHO TAUGHT HER EVERYTHING

SHE KNOWS

Thirty years since turning in his last column, Gary Indiana has remained point-blank and beautifully consistent about what he thinks of the art criticism he wrote for three years in the mid-1980s for the *Village Voice*. In *I Can Give You Anything But Love*, the work's "a bunch of yellowing newspaper columns I never republished and haven't cared about for a second since writing them a quarter century ago." Much closer to having washed his hands of the enterprise, when asked in 1994 to reflect upon his "art-writing career," he stated that he'd "avoided any prolonged retrospective glance," summing it up this way: "I have always had mixed feelings about these efforts, mainly because other people seem to like that work more than I do." Hell is other people.

* * *

The epigraph to Gary's memoir is from *Nausea*, but it's the notorious declaration near the end of *No Exit*—"*L'enfer, c'est les autres*"—that's my cue. I fall, as many do, into the category of other people. After years of dropping more than a few hairpins in front of cute young things who appeared literarily bent and/or gay (whatever that means anymore), dropping them in the hope he/she/they would feel compelled to do the thinking a solid and collect Gary's columns, yellowing or not, I got tired of waiting.

So, two summers ago, in a slough of despond due in no small part to what continues to go down in the U.S. of fucking A., I spent a week in the Charles E. Young Research Library at UCLA, making a digital file of all the columns I could find. The *Voice* microfilm reels, however ratty, contained resources, more than enough to lure me through the tediousness of the digital transfer process. Every night, I'd return from the library and start reading, and it was clear from the get-go that while other people can be hellish that doesn't mean they were misguided in craving a collection of Gary's art columns. The *Voice* unindexed, its archive never fully online, this work had been hiding like a sleeper cell, on silent red alert. My feelings were unmixed. I put the columns on a flash drive and gave it to Hedi El Kholti for his birthday.

* * *

Despite the fact that I've been addressing him as "Gary," I don't really know Gary Indiana. I've talked to him perhaps three or four times in two decades, the first time in the mid-1990s, sharing a taxi in New York, after we both took part in some odd radio show on art; he told me a louche tale about Lauren Hutton. I got out of the cab—cut to: twenty years later—and then participated in an event to celebrate Gary's writing at the deeply missed 356 Mission in Los Angeles. In paying homage, I was fairly certain that most would go for one of his skewerings of a bloated reputation, for a bit of perfectly American violence, or for a bristling sex scene. Instead, I showed two film clips (one of Peter Kern and the incomparable Ingrid Caven lip-synching, gorgeously, gloriously, with the Alps as a background, to an aria by Erich Wolfgang Korngold, a mesmerizing scene from Daniel Schmid's *La Paloma*, a film I first learned about from Gary's brilliant tribute to it; another of Candy Darling singing "Ramona," a set piece from Werner Schroeter's *Der Tod der Maria Malibran*), said a little something, and then read from his memoir a funny, moving section about his initial encounter with Schroeter at Harry's bar in Munich. However long he's traveled under the alias of *Indiana* ("the Crossroads of America") and however brutally accurate he's been in his studies of the country (his crime trilogy should be seen as an achievement of American political theory, with the words DEPRAVED INDIFFERENCE a fitting, Twitter-ready pledge of allegiance), I wanted to remind anyone whose mind it had slipped that Gary's aesthetic cohort—many of whose names and works shimmer in the columns—is Schroeter and his troupe, Schmid and Caven, Veruschka, Jean-Jacques Schuhl, rowdy Rainer Werner Fassbinder nearby. Not unlike lieder sung by Caven (or Marianne Faithfull), his words can break your heart.

* * *

Hedi talked to Gary, Gary agreed to let the art columns become a book, I started retyping the cloudy microfilm documents. At some point, I made a trip to the Special Collections of the Fales Library, where Gary's papers are housed, not only finding pieces I'd missed but also clearing up illegible patches of microfilmic slurry. Through my friend Maureen, I contacted R.C. Baker, still at the *Voice*, and received some final clarifications. All the essays collected, it was immediately, abundantly evident: in those three years, that brief, scuzzy moment, Gary re-envisioned what writing "about art" could be. He starts off by strutting the fictive as a way to get at something else entirely: we meet poor Gaston Porcile Vitrine, under the Janus-faced aegis of "art" and "money"; our columnist suggests that if we spy Gaston, or someone like him, "marooned at an otherwise deserted table in some overpriced restaurant, tormented by the gay voices and hyena laughter of his former peers," that we send him a *kir royale*. It's still good advice, the current situation even more overpriced, more porcine, Vitrines or much worse everywhere you look. The vivid dispatches continued, week by week, Gary never content with mere content, always testing form and voice: blind item, diatribe, letter, commonplace entry, cut-up, list, philosophical stroll, searing exposition. In the midst of Reaganism, the grim toll of AIDS, and the frequent jingoism of postmodern theory, he found a way to take up the stakes of Daniel Defoe's *A Journal of the Plague Year*, but his (nonfiction) report now occured in the moment of its making. Gary never shirks from sizing up the disgusting for what it is; like Baudelaire, he values spleen—but also delight, erotic and intellectual, serious. Joining his novelistic and theatrical gifts with an acute eye and a startling political acumen to assess culture, the unruly ecologies that give it context, he turned the art review into a chronicle of life under siege.

* * *

I didn't seek out this early work in some sense that I would find documents of Gary's prescience about environmental immiseration, a certain militarization, corporatization and/or *currencification* of almost every instant of daily existence—matters he was tracking right away (you will have noticed how soon in the proceedings he interrogates electronic surveillance, various computer automations, homelessness, Trump). Rather, my own curiosity about these storied columns was piqued by what I'd gleaned through hearsay about his engagement with some still key artists who were at crucial junctures of their careers, many of them women deploying the photographic in all of its guises. While I might run across bibliographic citations of essays by Gary on these artists, I would rarely see them quoted, never reprinted. Could it really be that many art historians of the period were just, I don't know, that lazy?

* * *

Renata Adler, in her famous/infamous review of Pauline Kael's *When the Lights Go Down*, opens her essay, and spends no small amount of time in it, thinking about the life and energy of a critic in relation to what he or she writes, and writes about. "Normally," Adler observes, "no art can support for long the play of a major intelligence, working flat out, on a quotidian basis." Gary wrote about the art scene no longer than its art could possibly support him, and then he stopped. He continued to write flat out, but in other genres: his first novel, *Horse Crazy*, appeared a year or so after his last column hit the newsstands. While jarring recognition of art and artists, some obscured in the barrage of the senses known as history, *Vile Days* also allows anyone who cares to observe how a major intelligence exercised his forms and voices from the start. About these "yellowing newspaper columns," which provide one of the most vital accounts of that New York moment ever accomplished, even Gary once admitted: "I like to think I brought a breath of scandal, suspense, and fresh air to a period and a place, that I punctured a few follies and got things better than right at least part of the time, and I especially like to think I bailed out at exactly the right moment—that leisurely half hour before the aircraft hit the ground."

* * *

N.B.: This book is both a little less and something more than the complete art columns Gary Indiana wrote for the *Village Voice*. After reviewing the manuscript for *Vile Days*, Gary asked that one of the columns be removed from the book. In sorting through all of the articles Gary did during his stint as senior art critic, March 1985 through June 1988, I found a few things he wrote that weren't strictly art columns but nevertheless threw, directly or obliquely, light on his thinking about culture: his ode to Marianne Faithfull and cigarettes; his obituary for Jackie Curtis; his reviews of *Art After Modernism* as well as books on men's fashion, Friedrich Nietzsche, among other things. Two art columns that were first republished in *Let It Bleed* have been reprinted here. His brilliant reading of Witold Gombrowicz, published in the *Voice Literary Supplement* as "Heart Like a Heel" in May 1987, has not been reprinted; in a revised form, it appears in *Utopia's Debris* as "Cunning, Exile, Contingency," a title that would suit, when the time comes, Gary's collected works.

Index

Goethe, Johann Wolfgang von, 182, 538
Goetz, Bernie, 84
Gogol, Nikolai, 340, 426
Goldstein, Jack, 59, 253, 313
Gombrich, E. H., 65
Gombrowicz, Witold, 216, 580
Gonzalez-Torres, Felix, 569, 571, 572
Gorey, Edward, 245
Gorin, Jean-Pierre, 313, 508
Gornik, April, 357
Goss, John, 377
Gould, Glenn, 306
Gourdji, Joseph, 232
Goya, Francisco, 420,
Graham, Dan, 186, 467, 556
Gratacós, Juanito Durán, 348
Grayson, Tracy, 357
Gray, Spalding, 445
Green, Vanalyne, 186
Greenberg, Clement, 205
Greenblat, Rodney Alan, 15
Greene, Robert, 416
Greenstreet, Sydney, 262
Greyson, John, 376, 378
Gris, Juan, 346
Gropius, Walter, 271
Grossman, Nancy, 64
Grosz, George, 113
Guercio, Gabriele, 304, 306
Guerrilla Girls, 417
Guevarra, Francisco Gonzalez, 349
Gussow, Alan, 141
Guston, Philip, 120

Haacke, Hans, 75–78, 120, 152, 227, 304, 306, 352, 367, 484, 512
Habermas, Jürgen, 101, 565
Hajamadi, Fariba, 434
Halley, Peter, 19, 65–66, 239, 253, 282, 305, 352, 425, 488, 489, 504

Hambleton, Richard, 15, 143
Hamill, Denis, 570
Hamill, Pete, 307, 570
Hansell, Freya, 357
Haring, Keith, 16, 121, 199
Harnett, William, 74
Harries, Mags, 82
Harrow, Gustave, 54
Harry, Debbie, 11, 500
Hatch, Connie, 530
Hausmann, Raoul, 113
Hawkinson, Laurie, 510
Hawkins, Robert, 243–245
Hayden, Sterling, 387
Hearn, Pat, 18, 516
Heartfield, John, 113, 530
Heidegger, Martin, 196, 565
Heiss, Alanna, 140
Heizer, Michael, 152, 155, 263, 312
Held, Al, 373
Hell, Richard, 11
Helm, Robert, 417
Helms, Jesse, 61
Helmsley, Harry, 84
Henderson, Skitch, 103
Henry VIII, 358
Hentoff, Nat, 570
Heramedia Group, 377
Herodotus, 184
Hiller, Susan, 549–551
Hilton sisters (Daisy and Violet), 517
Hitchcock, Alfred, 267, 407
Hitler, Adolf, 33, 58, 117, 176, 186, 231, 232, 505, 506, 517, 567
Hobsbawm, Eric, 184
Höch, Hannah, 113
Hockney, David, 40, 561
Hodgkin, Howard, 202
Hoffmann, E. T. A., 156
Hofmann, Hans, 42
Hofmannsthal, Hugo von, 567

Gary Indiana is a novelist, playwright, critic, essayist, filmmaker, and artist. Called one of "the most brilliant critics writing in America today" by the *London Review of Books*, and "one of the most important chroniclers of the modern psyche," by the *Guardian*, he published a memoir, *I Can Give You Anything But Love*, in 2015.

Bruce Hainley is the author of *Under the Sign of [sic]: Sturtevant's Volte-Face* and ~~*Art & Culture*~~, both published by Semiotext(e). The editor of *Commie Pinko Guy*, he wrote, with John Waters, *Art—A Sex Book*. He co-chairs the Graduate Art program at ArtCenter College of Design and is a contributing editor of *Artforum*.